INSTRUMENTS OF PEACEMAKING 1870–1914

This book focuses on Anglo-American disputes arising out of the civil war in the United States and British interests in the American continent: the Geneva Arbitration, the Anglo-Venezuela Arbitration and the Behring Sea Arbitration. It draws on those cases as model proceedings which laid the foundations and inspiration for a promotion of international law through the Hague Conferences and by the work of English and American jurists. It considers the encouragement these cases gave to the promotion of public international law and how that contributed to the resolution of inter-state disputes.

Instruments of Peacemaking 1870–1914

Michael Reynolds

•HART•
OXFORD • LONDON • NEW YORK • NEW DELHI • SYDNEY

HART PUBLISHING
Bloomsbury Publishing Plc
Kemp House, Chawley Park, Cumnor Hill, Oxford, OX2 9PH, UK
1385 Broadway, New York, NY 10018, USA
29 Earlsfort Terrace, Dublin 2, Ireland

HART PUBLISHING, the Hart/Stag logo, BLOOMSBURY and the Diana logo are trademarks of Bloomsbury Publishing Plc

First published in Great Britain 2021

A catalogue record for this book is available from the British Library.

Library of Congress Cataloging-in-Publication data

Names: Reynolds, Michael P. (Solicitor), author.

Title: Instruments of peacemaking 1870–1914 / Michael Reynolds.

Description: Oxford, UK ; New York, NY : Hart, 2021. | Includes bibliographical references and index.

Identifiers: LCCN 2021011490 (print) | LCCN 2021011491 (ebook) | ISBN 9781509938308 (hardback) | ISBN 9781509950096 (paperback) | ISBN 9781509938322 (pdf) | ISBN 9781509938315 (Epub)

Subjects: LCSH: Pacific settlement of international disputes—History. | Arbitration (International law)—History. | World politics—19th century. | World politics—1900–1918.

Classification: LCC KZ6010 .R49 2021 (print) | LCC KZ6010 (ebook) | DDC 341.6/6—dc23

LC record available at https://lccn.loc.gov/2021011490

LC ebook record available at https://lccn.loc.gov/2021011491

ISBN: HB: 978-1-50993-830-8
ePDF: 978-1-50993-832-2
ePub: 978-1-50993-831-5

Typeset by Compuscript Ltd, Shannon

Acknowledgements

THIS STUDY RELIES on various primary and secondary sources, with much original material found in the Bodleian Library at Oxford, the National Archives at Kew, the House of Lords archives, Chatham House Library and the Library of the London School of Economics and Political Science. The secondary works are mainly biographies and reminiscences of the statesmen and lawyers, as well as histories of the events concerned. A realistic approach to this research has been adopted, where one is mindful as to the limitations of archives and the opinions of biographers.

This project would not have been possible without the facilities granted to me as a Visiting Senior Research Fellow at the London School of Economics. I am especially grateful to Professor David Stevenson of the Department of International History for his comments upon the draft manuscript and encouragement in approaching this research.

To assist the reader, I have included some maps – two representing the territorial changes to Balkan state boundaries effected at the conclusion of the Balkan Wars reprinted here with permission from the publisher, and from George Kennan, *Other Balkan Wars: A 1913 Carnegie Endowment Inquiry in Retrospect* (Washington, DC, Carnegie Endowment for International Peace, 1993). My thanks and acknowledgement go to Mina Moshkeri, a cartographer who drew all other maps.

Finally, I must express my thanks to the team at Hart Publishing, to Kate Whetter, Rosemarie Mearns, Linda Staniford and especially Victoria Broom and also to those unnamed who reviewed some early drafts.

MPR
March 2021

Table of Contents

List of Maps

Table of Cases

English Cases

US Cases

French Cases

The Hague Court Reports

Table of Statutes

British Statutes

United States Acts of Congress

Table of Parliamentary and State Papers

Great Britain

Hansard Reports

Parliamentary Archives, House of Lords Research Office, London

United States

Congressional Record

Foreign Relations of the United States

Office of the Historian

Theodore Roosevelt Papers

Austria

France

Russia

Spain

Table of Treaties and Conventions

Introduction: A Utopian Dream?

On the 28th February 1871, Professor JR Seeley[1] gave a lecture in which he espoused the cause of international dispute resolution through interstate arbitration. His thesis was that if disputes between people could be settled through arbitration, then why not disputes between states? He presaged a similar idea by President Taft, later Chief Justice of the United States, who believed that reasoned judicial decisions given to states that respected the rule of law would reduce tension and lessen the risk of war. Such conclusion was prescient and underpinned the Treaty of Washington which established what Lord Bingham[2] called the greatest arbitration in history – the Geneva Arbitration which prevented two great English-speaking Common Law nations going to war. It was followed by further Anglo-American arbitration treaties settling pelagic sealing in the Behring Sea and a boundary dispute between Venezuela and British Guiana.

In Seeley's opinion the '… proper cure for popular indifference is a feasible and statesmanlike scheme of arbitration, such a scheme should take account of details and provide contrivances to meet practical difficulties'.[3]

His conclusions were:

1. That such a system could not be operated within the framework of the Congress system. What he wanted was something akin to a law court. He felt in the Congress system the Great Powers as parties were judges in their own cause. Ambassadors were not judges: they represented the interests of their own country.
2. That such a system should be a federal system. Law courts were national courts, but what he had in mind was an international court inferring that it was the offspring of an international state. In order therefore for such an entity to exist, Europe would have to form itself into a Federation.
3. This would require an organisation akin to that of the United States of America 'with a complete apparatus of powers, legislative, executive and judicial and raised above all dependence upon state governments'. This would require, in his opinion, a strong federal bond disentangled from the state governments.

[1] Reprinted from a lecture given at the University of Oxford entitled 'The Possible Means of Preventing War in Europe' in W Evans Derby, *International Tribunals* (Forgotten Books, 2015) Reprint.

[2] Lord Bingham, 'The Alabama Claims Arbitration' (2005) 54 *ICLQ* 1, 8.

[3] Evans Derby (n 1).

4. That only the federal government should have the authority to raise troops and be responsible for defence, not the states.
5. That 'all federations are mockeries that are mere understandings between governments'.[4]

Seeley's views would be difficult to accept amongst Eurosceptics in Britain today, but Seeley, like many of those statesman and diplomats we shall discuss here who tried to prevent war in Europe was certainly not alone in considering that European wars could be prevented by the idea of a United States of Europe.[5]

> There has been found hitherto but one substitute for war. It has succeeded over and over again; it succeeds regularly in the long run wherever it can be introduced. This is, to take the disputed question out of the hands of the disputants, to refer it to a third party, whose intelligence, impartiality and diligence have been secured, and to impose his decision upon the parties with overwhelming force. The last step in the process, the power of enforcing the decisions by the federal union only, is just as essential as the earlier ones, and if you omit it you may just as well omit them too.[6]

Seeley's suggestion that force was an essential element to enforcing arbitration awards is something history tends to reject. He had perhaps an idealistic view of what arbitration between sovereign states could achieve, although as we shall see, his dream was realised in the Geneva Arbitration and the case of the Confederate cruisers, but unachievable where a sovereign state's national interests and honour conflicted with international law norms. Such an instance occurred in July 1914.

Perhaps only through an analysis of the history of those times and the statesmen who wrestled with complex national and international competing interests can we learn how state actors and others might better handle the affairs of nations. As part of that process this would entail a highly developed scheme of international dispute/conflict resolution processes in order to maintain economic and global harmony and amity between peoples and nations. For as Thucydides wrote so many centuries ago:

> I shall be content if those shall pronounce my History useful who desire to give a view of events as they did really happen, and as they are very likely, in accordance with human nature, to repeat themselves at some future time- if not exactly the same, yet very similar.[7]

[4] *Ibid.*

[5] Sir Winston Churchill suggested such a body in a speech at Geneva on 19 September 1946 as did his colleagues, Duff Cooper MP and Harold Nicolson MP.

[6] Evans Derby (n 1) 95.

[7] Thucydides, *The Peloponnesian War* (JM Dent, EP Dutton, 1910).

1

Approaches to International Dispute Resolution

THIS STUDY LOOKS at the processes of international dispute resolution in several case studies between 1870 and 1914, namely: the Geneva Arbitration; the Behring Sea Arbitration; the Venezuelan Arbitration; the Dogger Bank Enquiry; the Balkan Crisis 1912–1913 and the July 1914 crisis. It is fundamentally intended to be a study of the means by which disputes between states were resolved amicably without resort to force whether by means of diplomacy or dispute resolution usually arbitration or a commission of enquiry. Much of this came about as a result of the Geneva Arbitration and the growing interest of international jurists which inspired the Hague Conferences and the two conventions which aimed to civilise warfare and promote arbitration. Hence, the title, Instruments of Peacemaking. The processes employed necessarily involve the approaches taken by statesmen, lawyers, arbitrators, commissioners and the parties to the disputes and the means by which they tried to avoid war which in those times was a remedy of last resort.

The aims of this book are to identify the techniques used to resolve particular disputes whether by diplomacy, mediation, arbitration, enquiry or conference. In pursuing that aim the role of lawyers and statesmen are examined and the contribution they made to the resolution. In looking at these matters three general hypotheses are considered in the case studies in the context of a progressively jurisprudential approach to disputes between states:

- First, that international crises and disputes in this period could only be resolved through a particular form of dispute process acceptable to the parties and capable of resolving the conflict of national interests whether through arbitration, mediation, round table conference, bilateral negotiations and enquiry where there was a common interest to do so.
- Second, that this was only possible where the norms of international law were recognised principally through Treaties and there existed a will to resolve through peaceful means respecting international law norms.
- Third, that if there was no common interest, respect for international law or disregard for international moral opinion, but a decided will to dominate the conflict was likely to end in war.

In order to consider these hypotheses and approaches to the crises, the following questions have been researched to come to a view from the primary and secondary sources identified:

1. What type of international crisis in this period could be resolved through a particular form of dispute process acceptable to the parties?
2. What type of issues and arguments were raised in these cases?
3. How did the lawyers and diplomats resolve or attempt to resolve these conflicts?
4. Was there any alternative to war to resolve conflicts of national interests?
5. In selected cases why did the method chosen succeed?
6. What part, if any, did respect for international law play in these cases?

In examining these hypotheses and questions through a variety of distinct cases, any assessment must encompass a range of disciplines: foreign policy, international relations, international law and diplomacy.

In terms of what type of international crisis in this period could be resolved through a particular form of dispute process acceptable to the parties, the study considers three arbitrations involving Britain and the United States. In many respects these were model examples of their time and laid the foundations for a system of interstate arbitration. In discussing these cases we shall examine the merits of the arguments advanced by the states against each other and the resulting determination in the form of the arbitral award. We shall observe how international lawyers and diplomats worked to resolve those disputes and how the method of resolution was determined in most cases by negotiation of an arbitration treaty and rules setting the scope of the tribunal's jurisdiction. Importantly we shall see how wars were avoided between Britain and the United States through statesmanship and diplomacy and the facilitation by the legal teams. In the case of the Venezuela arbitration, some of its success must be attributed to the relationship between arbitrators and counsel resulting in closer ties between the English and American Bars. Definition of the issues and clarity of the questions to be answered by the tribunal were instrumental in a fair determination. Setting out the questions in terms of rules as in the Geneva Arbitration were especially helpful. Questions of international law were indeed at the forefront of these cases; they contributed to international law and importantly created precedent for future tribunals, most notably in incentivising the Hague Conferences.

I. RESOLVING DISPUTES BETWEEN STATES: INFLUENCES ON POLICY MAKING

In resolving such disputes, attention needs to be paid to the tensions that arise between states just as strains and disputes may arise between individuals. Indeed, such was the notion of many international lawyers who felt they could resolve state disputes as they resolved disputes between individuals or corporations. In some respects, the national interest is what the government of the day determines, but it is also determined by public opinion led by the press and media. A good example would be July 1914.

In their study of international relations, Jackson and Sørensen[1] considered the contributions of Thucydides, Aristotle, Machiavelli, Hobbes and Morgenthau[2] regarding a situation where there was a high risk of war between states. Thucydides considered such conflicts inevitable.[3] Aristotle considered man's animal tendencies, while Thucydides considered that states had to adapt to a world of unequal powers. In his view, foreign policy required caution, prudence and regard to the consequences of any action that was contemplated. There was always an ever-present danger as well as opportunity.[4] In his *History of the Peloponnesian War* he wrote that it was essential for each state to recognise its actual position. In the opinion of Jackson and Sørensen, international relations is a matter of 'anarchy of separate states' that have no real choice but to operate power politics where security and survival are the primary rules and war the final arbiter.[5] If that is the norm then what is the role of international law and arbitration? The law and its disputes processes have a very hard task indeed but if peace is to be sustained then such law must be observed and enforced, hence the internationalist view. Contrary to that view is the Machiavellian approach. It is said that Machiavelli saw international relations through the eyes of a lion or a fox (power and deception). As Jackson and Sørensen opine in *Introduction to International Relations Theories and Approaches*, Machiavelli saw national freedom as the supreme political value-independence. Rulers should be lions and foxes. This lies at the heart of the realist theory of international relations which is opposed to the internationalist and liberal concept. A good example, which we shall assess in the context of the July 1914 crisis, is the liberal internationalist approach of Sir Edward Grey and the realist, but more Machiavellian approach, of Herr Von Bethmann-Hollweg and Count Berchtold.

In this study we see the conflation of foreign policy, national interest, international law and the rule of law. This is not so much governed by any particular theory but often determined simply by events, action and counter action. We may look at Aristotle's animal concept, or Hobbes in *Leviathan* who considered that the state of nature was a state of war. Hobbes required a sovereign with absolute power to protect the people of that state. His idea of power could only exist within the domestic state. He believed that the international state of nature was war or potential war and as such he did not countenance any

[1] R Jackson and G Sørensen, *Introduction to International Relations Theories and Approaches*, 5th edn (Oxford University Press, 2013) 65–76.

[2] Whilst Morgenthau post-dates 1914, his views are worth mentioning and have relevance to how we consider resolution of international disputes.

[3] Jackson and Sørensen (n 1) 67.

[4] *Ibid* 68.

[5] *Ibid* 69.

world government or a global state. Alternatively, we could consider the works of Hans J Morgenthau who distinguished private and public morality and said that Woodrow Wilson was wrong to equate private and public ethics and that states could not be held liable in the same way as individuals.[6] In Morgenthau's view – the realist's view – you have to take people as they are and not how they or you might wish them to be. In this study the facts speak for themselves as found by the tribunals as well as the policies which led to the dispute and resolved the dispute.

II. THE NINETEENTH CENTURY APPROACH

This study must be considered in the context of attempts to prevent war by means of precepts based on Christianity, hospitality, justice, charity and peace to the conduct of international and internal affairs. Attempts from 1815 onwards resulted in a process known to history as the Concert of Europe. This Concert was given legal effect between states by the Treaties of Paris and Vienna. Here the Great Powers attempted to abolish the old European States System or Community of Nations for a new type of society or confederacy under the control or dictatorship of a committee of the Great Powers.[7]

At the Congress of Aix-la-Chappelle in 1818, the Great Powers declared their 'unalterable determination never to swerve from the strictest observance of the principles of the law of nations even in their relations with one another or with other states'.[8] Unfortunately the alliance between the states fragmented when Britain and France refused to sign the Troppau Protocol in 1820 which excluded states that had undergone revolution and change. Britain withdrew altogether from the concert system at the Verona Congress in 1822. It is perhaps a sad postscript to the efforts made by Britain that in the words of Harold Nicolson:

> … how Great Britain, having intervened as a god machine, in the *lusis* of the tragedy, thereafter, and by slow gradations, resumed her natural isolationism; and how, having by her intervention, tautened and solidified the Coalition, she caused it by her increasing abstentions to disintegrate.[9]

It is within the context of that concert system where the powers resolved their disputes by way of discussions between leading statesman that the peace of Europe was preserved with a few exceptions in the nineteenth century. Those exceptions were: the Crimean War culminating in the Treaty of Paris of 1856, the Danish War culminating in the Treaty of Vienna of 1864, the Austro-Prussian War culminating in the Peace of Prague in 1866, and the Franco-Prussian War

[6] HJ Morgenthau, *Scientific Man versus Power Politics* (Il Phoenix Books, 1965) 180.

[7] AS Hershey, 'History of International Law Since the Peace of Westphalia' (1912) 6 *American Journal of International Law* 30, 47.

[8] *Ibid* 48.

[9] H Nicolson, *The Congress of Vienna* (Methuen, 1961) 34.

culminating in the Treaty of Frankfurt in 1871. The Treaty or Declaration of Paris in 1856 not only ended the Crimean War, but also contributed to the development of maritime international law in terms of abolishing privateering and the law relating to neutral goods, contraband and blockade. Indeed, one may see in the outcome of the proceedings of the Congress of Paris the beginnings of internationalism. The Declaration of Paris 1856 was followed by the Geneva Convention of 1864 ameliorating the conditions of the wounded in war. In 1868, the Declaration of St Petersburg went further outlawing the use of projectiles of less than 400 grammes in weight. In 1871, the Conference of London[10] proclaimed:

> ... that it is an essential principle of the Law of Nations that no Power can liberate itself from the engagement of a treaty, or modify the stipulations thereof, unless with consent of the contracting Powers by means of an amicable agreement.

In 1874, the Brussels Conference published a code of warfare based on the American 'Instructions' which eventually became a model for The Hague Code of 1899. This was an initiative of the Russian Tsar Alexander II requesting that the representatives of 15 European countries consider the laws and customs of war.[11]

At this time, it appears, as Paul Kennedy opines, that Britain may have adopted an international relations policy post 1880 of appeasement, not in the sense of Chamberlain appeasing dictators, but a

> policy of settling international (or for that matter domestic) quarrels by admitting and satisfying grievances through rational negotiation and compromise, thereby avoiding the resort to an armed conflict which would be expensive, bloody and possibly very dangerous.[12]

According to Kennedy, taking a Cobdenite view of the world as a harmonious community, the instruments of policy could be exercised through international arbitration conciliation and compromise which had moral justification save in cases of self-defence.[13] For Britain this was a time of realisation of the limits and burdens of an imperial and isolationist policy which could no longer be sustained on the basis of a relatively declining industrial economy.[14] Hence the British interest was served by support for such an approach.

Another important influence on policy towards the end of the nineteenth century and early twentieth century was liberalism. Although Sir Edward Grey, the British Foreign Secretary, was a member of the Liberal Party he was regarded as an imperialist by association with those of his party who wanted to maintain

[10] It seems by this time the descriptions Congress and Conference were interchangeable.

[11] Both the Brussels Declaration and the Manual of the Laws and Customs of War were adopted at Oxford in 1880 and formed the basis of the two Hague Conventions on land warfare and the Regulations annexed to them, adopted in 1899 and 1907. *International Committee of the Red Cross.*

[12] P Kennedy, *Strategy and Diplomacy (1870–1945)* (George Allen and Unwin, 1983) 16.

[13] *Ibid* 16.

[14] *Ibid*17.

Britain's overseas possessions.[15] A Liberal Imperialist was perhaps not a liberal democrat in the Wilsonian sense, but it appears from this study that Grey and his leader Herbert Asquith believed that liberal democracies such as France and Britain were instrumental in keeping the peace of Europe by holding the balance of Power. As Sir Eyre Crowe wrote in 1907:

> History shows that the danger threatening the independence of this or that nation has generally arisen, at least in part, after the momentary predominance of a neighbouring state and once militarily powerful, economically efficient, and ambitious to extend its frontiers or spread its influence, the danger being directly proportionate to the degree of its power and efficiency, and to the spontaneity or 'inevitableness' of its ambitions. The only check on the abuse of political predominance derived from such a position has always consisted in the opposition of an equally formidable rival, or of a combination of several countries forming leagues of defence. The equilibrium established by such a grouping of forces is technically known as the balance of power, and it has become almost an historical truism to identify England's secular policy with the maintenance of this balance by throwing her weight now in this scale and now in that, but ever on the side opposed to the political dictatorship of the strongest single state or group at a given time.[16]

Grey became Foreign Secretary at a time when that balance of power was changing. Britain had not had alliances in the previous century save in the Napoleonic Wars and the Crimean War. After the Franco-Prussian War and the rise of the *Kaiserreich* (the name given to Germany under Kaiser Wilhelm II, 'the Kaiser's state') with Germany's construction of a modern navy to rival Britain's Grand Fleet, the policy changed from one of isolationism to one of alliances; first with Japan, then France and Russia. As the armaments race and scares about possible German invasion grew,[17] so did the interest in international law and the pleas for increased interdependence as suggested by Norman Angell in his book *The Great Illusion* published in 1910.[18] He argued that there was a danger of predominance by the most powerful state and that if a state did not prepare to defend itself it would be defeated. His controversial claim highlighted the probability of a collision between Imperial Germany and the British Empire as Germany wanted to ensure the best conditions of its people through territorial expansion and industrial power translated into military force through its army and new navy.[19] At the same time however he accepted that military power was economically futile and that no state's moral or social possessions could be conquered.[20]

[15] K Robbins, *Sir Edward Grey* (Cassell, 1971) 31.

[16] Foreign Office Papers 371/257. *Memorandum by Sir Eyre Crowe* 1 January 1907.

[17] Such concerns were exaggerated by the publication of W Le Queux's *Spies of the Kaiser* (Okitoks Press, 2017) in May 1909. Although this book was a work of the author's imagination but also of his alarm at government complacency, it nevertheless inspired a more serious approach to intelligence gathering and the formation of what became MI5.

[18] N Angell, *The Great Illusion* (GP Pitman's Sons, 2010).

[19] N Angell, *The Great Illusion* (Jungle Land Publishing, 2015) 1.

[20] *Ibid* 2.

He expounds natural law theory and realism in his arguments for and against war and accepts that it is justified in certain cases. He appears to make the first attempt at a discourse on international relations before the subject was recognised as a study in itself after 1919.[21] He argued that although Britain might possess a large Empire, its value was never worth what imperialists imagined and it was a liability.[22] His ideas of interdependence amongst nation states were then a forlorn hope, but they were revived by President Wilson in his idealistic Thirteen Points and found greater acknowledgement in the Kellogg-Briand Pact of 1928. Interesting to note that the efforts of those lawyers and diplomats described in this study were not in vain and that this Pact outlawed war as a means of international dispute resolution. Sadly, Wilson's grand design of a League of Nations was doomed when the United States Senate failed to ratify US membership. This was a repetition of the opposition led by Henry Cabot Lodge against the Anglo-American Arbitration Treaty in 1911.

Whilst Wilson and many international jurists may have dreamed of these ideals of 'Utopian liberalism', realists argued in the sole interest of the sovereign nation state. In such cases the national interest is paramount. Such states are jealous of their power and jurisdiction and reluctant to surrender any part of their sovereignty. From this stems isolationist policies as seen in Britain before 1902 and during the 1920s and 1930s. As predicted by Angell, this led to another world war. In all this it is hard to apply the dreams of Locke for a rule of law or *Rechtstaat*, or foresee a time when Bentham's respect for international law by liberal states would maintain the peace, or Kant's declaration that republics would maintain perpetual peace – a dream crushed by the French Revolutionary Wars.

III. APPROACH TO ARBITRATION

In the times of the crises discussed here, foreign affairs were not so much inhibited by domestic policy or public opinion save when matters became a matter of national pride and honour as in the years before 1914 and the German scare. The press, however, became an increasing factor in directing public opinion on foreign policy at certain times, for example during the Dogger Bank Enquiry and in late July 1914. From 1815 British foreign policy was aimed at preserving stability in Europe and maintaining British imperial ambitions by means of naval supremacy without continental commitments. It had three basic tenets: the balance of power, the hegemony of Europe and the aim of preventing one power domination on the continent. This policy was enabled by reason of the accommodation between states which resulted from the Napoleonic wars and the Treaty of Vienna in 1815 following Napoleon's defeat by the allied armies

[21] *Ibid*13–18.
[22] *Ibid* 36–37.

at Waterloo. This system, as mentioned earlier, was known as the Concert of Europe and enabled statesmen to discuss international differences and seek agreement without resort to force. This provided a panoply for diplomacy as well as enabling preservation of the status quo. This system, also known as the Congress System, had flexibility in that meetings at various diplomatic levels could be convened as the situation demanded through Heads of State, Foreign Ministers and Ambassadors. This system in effect lasted until July 1914 by way of the Congress System and ambassadorial conferences. Thus, situations as this study describes varied considerably and for each we can apply instrumental analysis in determining the best approach to resolution and at what level a resolution can be achieved whether at an international, national or at a personal level between statesmen and ambassadors. Each state had its own interest and requirements which dictated outcomes. If the realist view is taken, a dominant military Power can dictate terms to the weaker Power, which is what Austria-Hungary attempted with Serbia in 1914. If the Powers are evenly matched, as say between Britain and the United States in 1870, then they could reconcile their differences through negotiation and an agreed disputes process. In a sense they took the internationalist view of resolving their dispute by means of international arbitration. Once Britain and the United States showed the way, other states were encouraged to follow their example.

Such encouragement was given expression in the Convention of 1907 for the Pacific Settlement of International Disputes between States where diplomacy had failed. Such a process applied where parties were not always bound by an international convention but permitted ad hoc agreements to be made after the dispute arose *forum prorogatum*. Article 39 of that Convention provided that the Convention applied to questions already existing or to other questions that might arise in the future between states regarding any dispute or particular disputes. The process set up under the 1907 Convention enabled parties to the Convention to have recourse to arbitration for international differences submitted to the Permanent Court of Arbitration which was established by the First Hague Peace Conference in 1899.

Statecraft was seen by Morgenthau as comprising a number of elements, focusing on: the decision maker, a traditional method; comparative view of foreign policy; the political aspect is rooted in human nature self-concerned, self-regarding, and self-interested which could not be reduced to morals; self-interest changes and international relations is not governed by private morality; that the leader is responsible to the people for security and welfare; that realists are opposed to one country asserting its will upon another; and finally that statecraft involves awareness of human limitations and human imperfections and as Jackson and Sørensen conclude, 'That pessimistic knowledge of human beings as they are and not as they might wish them to be is a difficult truth that lies at the heart of international politics'.[23] What Morgenthau asserts may be

[23] Jackson and Sørensen (n 1) 75.

true in certain cases, but Britain's intervention in August 1914 could hardly be called self-interested.

As against these approaches, the legal interest is involved where international law is respected as Charles Russell, Lord Russell of Killowen, recalling the words of Sir James Stephens, said: 'Strictly speaking, international law is an inexact expression, and it is apt to mislead if its inexactness is not kept in mind. Law implies a lawgiver and a tribunal enforcing it and coercing its transgressors.'[24]

In that address Russell went on to distinguish the Austinian view of law as a command and the law as emanating from custom and practice. Law, he said, was developed by 'usage and popular faith' and then by legislation. It was not necessarily ordained by what he called 'the arbitrary will of the lawgiver'.[25] In terms of international law, his definition was that international law was 'the sum of the rules or usages which civilised states have agreed shall be binding upon them in their dealings with one another'.[26]

Like all arbitration, the essence of Russell's observation was consent of the parties. In the case of sovereign states, the great difficulty with attempting to resolve disputes between states lies in the legal status of the sovereign state. As Lord Birkenhead once wrote: 'A nation cannot indefinitely surrender the treaty making power to another, and at the same time keep alive its claim to be a sovereign international state.'[27] Thus, it may be argued that a sovereign state governs itself and does not accept any superior authority. On that basis it could not accept the *diktat* of an international tribunal as that may be regarded as a surrender of sovereignty. On the other hand, submission to an international inquiry or tribunal is better than war. A lesson of the Geneva Arbitration is that only when the states, like the parties to a domestic arbitration, have a common interest in arbitrating will states surrender their sovereignty to it, ie where the national interest coincides with the common interest.

In order to understand this more fully before embarking on a discourse on interstate arbitration, we need to appreciate the jurisprudential and theoretical understanding of the times this study covers. If we take John Westlake's approach to international arbitration in an article in the *International Journal of Ethics* in October 1896, he opined rightly that: 'Over independent states there could be no power to enforce submission to arbitration or performance of an award.'[28] Westlake was mindful of the illusory Grand Design of Henry IV of France and the idea of a federation of European Christendom where Westlake describes how people felt a closer affiliation with co-religionists than with their fellow countrymen. In 1896, perhaps like the western world in 2016, he described people as being deeply attached to 'the independent national existence which they feel to

[24] Lord Russell of Killowen, 'Address before the American Bar Association at Saratoga 20 August 1896' (1896) 2 *Virginia Law Register* 399.

[25] *Ibid.*

[26] *Ibid* 399–400.

[27] FE Smith, *International Law* (Georgen Morang Co Ltd, 1903).

[28] J Westlake, 'International Arbitration' (1896) 7 *International Journal of Ethics* 2.

be their own existence'.[29] Westlake added that although arbitration had logical imperfection in enforcement, the fact was that in most cases the award was recognised and implemented ensuring a peaceful outcome. In this context international arbitration was ancillary to international government by federation. Westlake also recognised the limits of international arbitration, citing Ferdinand Dreyfus: 'There are controversies to which there can be no obligation to apply it. When the independence or the integrity of a nation is at stake, all the treaties in the world could not force that nation to accept it.'[30]

Westlake considered arbitrations involving Switzerland, Spain, Belgium, the Americas, the African republics, Portugal and the Netherlands and recognised limitations when awards did not accord with the principles of justice or were seen as a threat to states' independence. The way to avoid such threat was to express the limitations in a treaty, eg the Treaty of Washington.[31] A clear limitation was the nature of the dispute. Political questions were in Westlake's view not capable of being subject to arbitration. Disputes had to be legal in nature which meant that both state parties to the dispute had to accept the governing law/rules of the process. Westlake explained the legal difference between the parties which provided the ground for international action.[32]

Westlake opined that states could arbitrate political disputes and gave the example of Russia repudiating the Black Sea Clauses of the Treaty of Paris 1856. Russia took advantage of French indisposition following her defeat in the Franco-Prussian War to re-establish her arsenal at Sebastopol. Neither France nor Britain felt able to act alone and acquiesced in the disavowal. In that case Westlake acknowledged that it was a matter for statesmen. On the other hand, one might argue that a breach of a treaty is like a breach of contract for the aggrieved party to contest, but in this case several states were involved and neither Britain nor France were inclined to insist on observance.

Treaties according to Westlake were to be regarded as matters standing – *rebus sic stantibus*, ie the Treaty is only binding so long as there is no substantial change.

He contended that arbitration was a process determining the legal right or wrong, but that did not mean it could be used for all international differences.[33] Some could be referred to arbitration if the parties agreed, but others would be matters for statesmen. It was his opinion that the arbitrator was both a judge and, if need be, a legislator and

> to combine the offices of arbitrator and mediator, with the addition that when in the latter character he proposes a solution not as what is legally just but as what is best,

[29] *Ibid* 3.

[30] F Dreyfus, *L'Arbitrage International* (Paris, 1892) 355.

[31] Signed on 8 May 1871 to resolve issues arising from the American Civil War between Great Britain and the USA.

[32] Westlake (n 28) 9. Examples being the Costa Rica Packet Arbitration regarding compensation awarded in respect of the seizure of a packet vessel by the Dutch, the Behring Sea Arbitration and the Geneva Arbitration.

[33] *Ibid* 12.

> his proposal shall have what the advice of a mediator has not, the same force as the award of an arbitrator, binding the parties and creating a new right between them.[34]

Westlake argued that in some cases arbitrators should have more flexibility in such cases and be able to adapt the treaty to the changed circumstances. To implement the best solution, creating new rights between the parties should be the function. He concluded that not all matters were capable of being resolved by arbitration, eg where the parties do not act in good faith as in the Geneva arbitration *pro hac vice*.[35] Westlake also considered mediation as an amicable means by which …'even without passing sentence on the justice of their respective claims, is an important proceeding, known by the technical name of mediation, or, in its less formal shape, by that of good offices.'[36] On this he suggested that it was the means by which statesman gave advice on serious matters between two disputant state parties. It was the moral weight that was of great importance which mattered to society and the influence of international opinion. This appears more appropriate where there are political issues and where the good offices of a friendly power might be employed before any recourse to arms as in the Treaty of Paris.[37] Turkey applied this when Russia declared war in 1877. This also applied where the dispute could not be entirely resolved by arbitration or where there is no legal title to possession or prescription as in the Anglo-Venezuela Arbitration.

[34] *Ibid* 13.
[35] *Ibid* 12.
[36] *Ibid* 6.
[37] Mediation between the Sublime Porte (an expression often used for the Government of the Ottoman Empire) and another state.

2

The Geneva Arbitration

I. THE ANGLO-AMERICAN RELATIONSHIP 1782–1861

THERE WAS AN uneasy relationship between the hegemon of this era, Britain, and its former colonies, which became the United States of America. The surrender of General Cornwallis at Yorktown in the autumn of 1781 had not ceased military hostilities. Controversy reigned over the seizure of American sailors and the continued occupation of forts in the northern states. An accommodation was reached in 1794 with the signing of the Jay Treaty and the enhancement of diplomatic relations.[1] In 1812, following their victory at the Battle of Bladensburg, the British army reached the newly renamed Federal City – Washington – and promptly set fire to the Capitol and the Executive Mansion causing President Madison and his wife Dolley to flee.

Following the War of Separation between England and America, peace was concluded in 1783 with the independence of the United States recognised by Britain. In 1794 Congress passed the Neutrality Act during the Napoleonic Wars to the benefit of Britain. Whilst the Jay Treaty succeeded in settling claims between England and America, hostilities recurred when British ships impressed American sailors into the British navy.[2] In 1842, Britain and the United States settled the boundary between Maine and Canada and in 1846 the 49th parallel was adopted as the border between the United States and Canada. In 1850, the United States recognised Britain's interests in Central America in the Clayton-Bulwer Treaty, but in 1861 relations became strained when 13 southern states seceded from the Union. Secession was followed by civil war with both sides seeking armaments and munitions from Britain.

These conflicts were followed in 1861 by a serious deterioration in diplomatic relations exacerbated during the Civil War by the construction and escape of a number of vessels purchased by Confederate agents in England. This became so serious that the American Minister in London, Charles Francis Adams, warned

[1] Jay's Treaty, *Leading American Treaties* 45.1922 at http://heinonline.org. This Treaty also included agreement as to the definition of contraband of war, privateering and a common approach to piracy which would be punished.

[2] *The Case of the United States, Tribunal of Arbitration under the Provisions of the Treaty between the United States of America and Her Majesty the Queen of Britain concluded at Washington, May 8 1871* (Richard Bentley and Son, 1872) (hereinafter '*The Case of the United States*') 32.

Earl Russell, the Foreign Secretary, that such activities would lead to war. The Federal Government claimed that Britain had violated its international law obligations as a neutral power by supporting the Confederate rebel states. The risk of war was high but avoided until the British and Federal Government agreed to resolve the American claims through arbitration. An international arbitral tribunal was constituted which convened at Geneva and completed its Award on 14 September 1872. It found Britain liable for breaches of such duties in relation to the cruisers *CSS Alabama* and *CSS Florida*, their tenders and the refitting and provision of the *CSS Shenandoah* in Australia. The American counterclaims for indirect losses and damages were dismissed. Whilst Britain was found liable in relation to those naval vessels, the United States' secret service and its diplomats were able to interdict five ironclads, 14 other cruisers and several gunboats and torpedo boats. It must also be said that Britain not only gave benefit to the Confederate States but much more to the Federal Government.[3]

President Lincoln was elected on 6 November 1860 with an anti-slavery policy which would prohibit slavery being adopted by any Territory of the United States, ie those areas of the United States that were not already admitted as a state of the Union. For many southern states this was unacceptable. Led by South Carolina, 13 states seceded from the Union and formed a confederacy. This constituted the 'cotton belt': cotton in those days was regarded as 'King'; highly marketable and valuable and regarded as the mainstay of the southern economy. The mills of Lancashire and thousands of British workers relied on cotton for work and sustenance. Without cotton the workers would be idle.

On 9th April 1861 the United States Minister in London, Mr Dallas, acquainted Lord Russell[4] with Lincoln's Inaugural address and expressed the desire that the two countries would continue their friendly relationship.[5] Russell promised to discuss the matter with the new Minister, Charles Francis Adams.[6] Ten days after the meeting Lincoln called up the militia and ordered a blockade of all southern ports. The problem was that the plan (known as the Anaconda Plan) would be ineffective as the United States navy had insufficient naval forces at that time to patrol the entire southern coastline.

Gradually this became an increasing problem for Britain's textile industry once the Federal navy tightened its grip on the South. Workers in England were out of work and starving. The facts were related in a report by Dr John Watts, a member of the Central Relief Committee in 1866.[7] He relates the story of how the cotton workers of Lancashire were relieved of their distress during the Civil

[3] Hansard, HC Deb (series 3) 27 March 1863, vol 170, cols 33–72. During the period 1 May 1861 to 31 December 1862, Britain supplied the Union forces with: 41,500 muskets, 341,000 rifles, 2,650 gun flints, 49,982,000 percussion caps and 2,250 swords. Between 1 January 1863 and 17 March 1863 Britain supplied Union forces with 23,870 gun barrels, 30,802 rifles and 3,105,800 percussion caps.

[4] British Foreign Secretary.

[5] *The Case of the United States* (n 2) 43.

[6] Adams was one of the arbitrators appointed to serve on the Geneva Arbitration.

[7] J Watts, *The Facts of the Cotton Famine* (Simpkin Marshall & Co, 1866).

War. In 1862 those in distress rose from 1,000–10,000 in January 1862 to 57,000 by December that year. Fortunately, these numbers declined in 1863 and 1864 to 25,000 and then to 17,000 respectively. The price of bread remained stable and disease was only prevented by the charity of many, from the Queen herself to a brigade of shoeblacks.[8] Watts was of the view that the Confederates banked on using 'King Cotton' as a weapon to persuade the British to support their cause. But their gamble did not pay off because it caused widespread suffering to an estimated 500,000 people. Money was raised across the country with a large donation and food supply donated by a merchant in New York.[9] According to Watts, unlike the Southerners the Federal donation was no inducement for support: the Union just wished to avoid foreign intervention. Donations came from all parts of Britain and Ireland, with Belfast contributing £4,378 and Dublin £25,000.[10] Cotton prices inflated as the blockade tightened and cost £12,989,000 more in 1862 than in 1861.[11] As between 1861 and 1863, cotton prices increased 141 per cent.[12] Bankruptcies followed in the wake of price inflation and erratic fluctuations in the cotton market. In Manchester, for example, they rose from 175 in 1861 to 387 in 1864.[13] News of Federal victories resulted in a fall in prices on the expectancy that the war would soon end, but as it went on losses rose so that Watts estimated that the Lancashire manufacturing industry lost £15,000,000 per annum or more during the war.[14] The effect of the blockade fell mostly on the cotton spinners and manufacturers, but not on the banks and agents which exacted commission for holding stock and for sales. They charged five per cent on advances and for guaranteeing the spinners' debts.[15] Thus, the spinners and manufacturers bore the brunt of the blockade and the losses.

Public opinion in Britain was divided. The old Mother Country had some sympathy for both sides; the English landowning classes and the Tories tended to sympathise with the upper classes of southern society, whilst English workers in the cotton mills and Liberals could readily sympathise with the North against the evils of slavery in the South, even though many mill workers starved as result of the Union blockade on cotton exports from the South. It must be said, however, that Mr Gladstone caused much embarrassment in the summer of 1863 when he referred to the Confederacy as having formed a nation state; he admired its self-determination.[16] Disraeli favoured the North contrary to his

[8] *Ibid* 230.
[9] *Ibid* 235.
[10] *Ibid* 246.
[11] *Ibid* 358
[12] *Ibid* 359
[13] *Ibid* 360.
[14] *Ibid* 371. This loss of £60,000,000 overall was not considered as part of any claim by Britain in the Geneva Arbitration. It was partly mitigated by Federal aid to tens of thousands in the north of England.
[15] *Ibid* 361.
[16] A Wood and G Gooch, *The Cambridge History of British Foreign Policy, 1783–1919: Volume 3* (Cambridge University Press, 1923) 56.

party's leanings. But gradually public opinion changed, as it does when it is better informed, and the revulsion against slavery, which drove the South's economy, began to sway public opinion more in favour of the North.

II. HOW THE CLAIMS AROSE

After Southern Confederate forces had fired on the Federal fortress at Fort Sumter in Charleston harbour, South Carolina, marking the outbreak of the American Civil War, the British Government declared neutrality. On the 1st June 1861, the British Government forbade any Federal or Confederate ship from carrying any prize to any British port and on the 31st January 1862, it excluded ships of war from the Bahamas. No ship of war was to stay more than 24 hours in any British imperial port.[17] The British Government recognised the Federal Government's 3000-mile-long blockade around the Confederate States.

On 16th May 1862 Thomas Dudley, the United States consul in Liverpool, reported the launch of *Hull No 290* to Washington. A month later the ship had its trial and Dudley went to London to report his suspicions to Charles Francis Adams, the newly appointed United States Minister to the Court of St James. Adams reported the matter to Lord John Russell so that the British Government could take legal action under its municipal law, namely the Foreign Enlistment Act 1819 (59 Geo III c 69).[18] The action taken by the British Government was subsequently called into question at the Geneva Tribunal. The question that faced them at Geneva was whether they acted with 'due diligence'.

On the 5th July 1862 Dudley made a further report giving a full description of the ship's design and construction to the Liverpool customs officers, and the involvement of Captain JD Bullock of the Confederate States Navy.[19] Dudley had to comply with legal formalities which required admissible evidence in the form of sworn depositions. The Customs Office were delayed by lack of clear advice from London and when it came it was too late for the ship, known then as *No 290*, which sailed on 28 July 1862, thus frustrating the execution of any warrant for its arrest. In the meantime, Adams had obtained a legal opinion from Mr Collier KC, who advised that this was a fundamental breach of the Foreign Enlistment Act 1819. The Law Officer's Opinion was delivered to Lord Russell late, after some delay caused through the sudden illness of the Queen's

[17] This became a problem for *USS Tuscorora* which was ordered by Adams to intercept the *CSS Alabama* if she should return to Liverpool after her surreptitious departure. She was ordered to leave Belfast having overstayed her time there.

[18] Section 7 of the Act and the provisions of the Treaty of Paris 1856.

[19] JD Bullock, *The Secret Service of the Confederate States in Europe* Vol 1 (GP Putnam's and Sons, 1884) 4. Bullock admitted that he was an agent of the Confederate Government responsible for managing and directing their general naval operations in Europe, and chief representative of the Navy Department of the Confederate States of America during the whole period of the civil war. He was the officer responsible for the dispatch and equipping of the cruisers *Florida, Alabama* and *Shenandoah*.

Proctor. When off the Azores, *No 290* was commissioned into the Confederate States navy as the *CSS Alabama*.[20]

A. Ineffectiveness of the Foreign Enlistment Act 1819

The Federal Government considered and later alleged at the arbitration that the insurgent rebel Confederate States Government had set up military departments in England.[21] These were financed through the agency of Fraser Trenholm & Co in Liverpool, a commercial house based in Charleston, South Carolina.

After the firing on Fort Sumter, the Confederate Government sent agents to Europe to obtain financial and other assistance. The South lacked a modern industrial base with few foundries and munitions works. It had a naval base at Norfolk Virginia, but this was destroyed by Union forces. Captain Bullock, a former naval officer in the US navy, was commissioned in the Confederate navy and was instructed by his government to procure six steam-driven screw propeller cruisers through the agency of Fraser Trenholm & Company in Liverpool. A scheme was devised whereby they would order the ships without attracting any suspicion. An English merchant captain would acquire the vessel and sail it to a place where it could be armed for hostilities against the United States. Arming it outside British waters would avoid supposed criminal liability under the Foreign Enlistment Act 1819. Numerous vessels were ordered in this way.[22] Not all the vessels engaged in hostilities. The principal offenders were the *Florida*, the *Alabama* and the *Shenandoah*.

During the Civil War President Lincoln suggested the idea of arbitration but this was ignored by the British.[23] In 1870 Lord Tenterden accepted in principle the idea of an arbitration treaty to settle the *Alabama* claims. An arbitration treaty had been proposed by the Federal Government and accepted by Lord Clarendon

[20] The order for detention was issued on the 29th July but the ship sailed the day before.

[21] 'The Geneva Arbitration and its Results' (1872–73) 7 *American Law Review* 193, 194.

[22] The *Florida* and the *Alabama* were both built by Lairds, while the *Alexandra* was built by William C Miller, Liverpool, plus two turreted iron clad rams. The *Georgia* was built by William Denny and Sons in Scotland.

Six twin screw torpedo boats were to be built in London and six larger steel torpedo boats in Liverpool. A large ironclad frigate was also to be built in Glasgow, 270 feet long by James and George Thompson together with a steam auxiliary cruiser named *Pampero*. A second-class screw sloop was purchased and named the *Rappahannock*. She was detained in Calais. Another ship, the *Hawk*, was purchased by the Virginia Volunteer Navy Company from Henderson and Colborne of Renfrew Scotland. A steam clipper named the *Sea King* built on the Clyde was commissioned the *Shenandoah*. Four steam clipper corvettes and two further iron clad rams were built by French builders Jollett & Babin of Nantes. Of the French construction only one, the *CSS Stonewall*, was sold to the Confederacy but never saw action. See KJ Foster, 'The Diplomats Who Sank a Fleet: The Confederacy's Undelivered European Fleet and the Union Consular Service' (2001) 33 *Prologue (Washington)* No 3.

[23] C Murray, *Salus populi suprema lex: The Development of National Security Jurisprudence Prior to the First World War* (Durham University, 2006), available at Durham E-Theses Online: http://etheses.dur.ac.uk/2700/.

but this was initially rejected by the United States Senate.[24] Lord Tenterden then suggested to the cabinet that the United States and Britain appoint High Commissioners to consider questions relating to Canadian fisheries and allied subjects, these to include the *Alabama* claims. According to Gooch, the British Government used a backchannel, Sir John Rose, a Canadian lawyer who lived in England and had substantial business interests in the United States to agree matters with the US Secretary of State, Hamilton Fish. The agreement was made through an exchange of Notes. The first of these dated 26 January 1871 by the British, proposed a High Joint Commission on Canadian Fisheries and similar questions. On 30 January 1871 Fish requested that the *Alabama* claims be included. Britain agreed and on 3 February 1871 US acceptance was officially notified.[25] It was due partly to the efforts of John Rose, a Canadian lawyer, who had gained the confidence of the United States and Britain that the negotiation succeeded.

III. THE DIPLOMATIC NEGOTIATIONS REGARDING THE TREATY OF WASHINGTON AND THE TRIBUNAL'S TERMS OF REFERENCE, THE ARGUMENTS OF THE PARTIES

Under the Declaration of Paris 1856 certain principles of Maritime International Law were agreed by all the powers represented at the Congress of Paris at the conclusion of the Crimean War. These leading principles were:

1. That privateering was abolished.
2. That a neutral flag covered the enemy's goods with the exception of contraband of war.
3. That neutral goods, with the exception of contraband of war, were not liable to capture under the enemy's flag.
4. That blockades, in order to be binding, must be effective, ie maintained by force sufficient to prevent access to the coast of an enemy.

The Declaration was to prove a critical instrument in the downfall of the Confederate navy by denying them European and Latin American ports. The Confederacy relied on privateers who were given authority by the Confederate Government by Letters of Marque to harass federal shipping and run the blockade.[26] The Federal Government may well have regretted that President Pierce's administration did not accede to the Declaration of Paris which would

[24] AW Ward and GP Gooch (eds), *The Cambridge History of British Foreign Policy* (Cambridge University Press, 2012) 65. The story is told in A Cook, *The Alabama Claims* (Cornell University Press, 1975).

[25] *Ibid* 65–66.

[26] J Lemnitzer, *Power Law and the End of Privateering* (Palgrave Macmillan, 2014) 115.

have clarified the legal position and outlawed Davis' privateers.[27] On the other hand, when Lincoln decided not to accede to the Declaration it acted as a warning to Britain that if she interfered on the side of the South her navy might face Union privateers. For the British Government the position was difficult having accorded belligerent status to the South. Was it not bound to ignore the Letters of Marque as illegal instruments and treat the privateers as pirates? Lord Russell was asked about this in the House of Commons[28] and stated that Britain would send a naval force to protect British ships and interests but would not wish to intervene unless these were attacked.

A. The Treaty of Washington and Terms of Reference for the Tribunal

It was said that this Treaty constituted 'one of the most notable and interesting of all the great diplomatic acts of the age'.[29] This was achieved in no small measure to the approach taken by Queen Victoria and President Grant in their appointment of competent commissioners who negotiated and settled the terms of the Treaty. This was despite previous attempts to negotiate a resolution of the American claims and British counterclaims which at one point included British owned property destroyed by the Union army in the South and the captured British ships that attempted to break the blockade.[30] William Evarts, the United States Attorney General, estimated that the British claims amounted to $100 million and United States' losses at $8 million. The British shipping claims were excluded because such claims were within the jurisdiction of the United States' Prize Courts and were not within the scope of the arbitration reference (the Rules) agreed in the Treaty of Washington.

The Commissioners were well chosen for their expertise; five from each side. On the British side, Earl De Grey and Ripon,[31] Sir Stafford Northcote, Sir Edward Thornton,[32] Sir John MacDonald,[33] and Professor Montague Bernard.[34] On the American side were Hamilton Fish, Robert Schenk, Samuel Nelson, Ebenezer Rockwood Hoar and George H Williams drawn from the legislative and judicial branches of the Federal Government. The secretary was Lord Tenterden. He expressed regret on behalf of the Government that the *Alabama* and other vessels had escaped from British ports. This expression of regret went some

[27] The effects of this are analysed in *ibid* 116–53.

[28] Hansard, HC Deb (series 3) 2 May 1861, vol 162, cols 1378–79.

[29] C Cushing, *The Treaty of Washington: Its Negotiation, Execution and the Discussions relating thereto* (Harper & Brothers Publishers, 1873).

[30] A Cook, *The Alabama Claims* (Cornell University Press, 1975) 62. Cook tells the story of the negotiations for the Treaty of Washington and the difficulties faced in the initial discussions and the negotiations for the Treaty.

[31] President of the Queen's Council.

[32] British Minister in Washington.

[33] Prime Minister of Canada.

[34] Chichele Professor of International Law and Diplomacy in the University of Oxford.

way to assuage the animosity and grievance felt in the United States especially amongst the American merchants who had lost valuable cargoes and the American merchant marine.

Although this sentiment was accepted by Hamilton Fish,[35] the Federal Government required referral to a competent tribunal subject to the following principles/Rules:

1. That a great maritime power should have exercised active diligence in preventing occurrence.
2. That power should have detained such vessel(s) when they came into or returned to other British ports.
3. That such ships should have been arrested.
4. That failure to observe the rules of international law resulted in liability for damages caused by such vessels.

The Commission's deliberations were completed on the 8th May 1871.[36]

The British Cabinet was divided on this question. Forster and Roundell Palmer agreed; Lowe, Goschen and Cardwell opposed any amendment to the Foreign Enlistment Act 1870, Gladstone, Kimberley and Halifax were doubtful but agreed. Hartingdon was doubtful.[37] In the end these four principles were accepted as a basis for the arbitration. The policy of Lord Russell and Gladstone's early praise for Jefferson Davis having built a nation was misplaced especially after the tide of war turned and Union military forces began the invasion of the Confederate States leading to the inevitable surrender of General Lee's army at Appomattox on 9 April 1865 and subsequently of all Confederate naval and military forces. Following Lee's surrender President Grant had available an experienced military force capable of taking Canada in the event of a new war with Britain. At the same time, British foreign policy was influenced by the change in the balance of power in Europe caused by Germany's defeat of Austria-Hungary and then France. It was therefore in Britain's interest to seek a diplomatic resolution of the American claims through the careful skill of its commissioners in Washington.

B. Negotiations in Washington

Neither the British nor American Government wanted another Anglo-American war, but at the same time President Grant wanted reparations for the illegal activities of the pirate cruisers. To the United States it appeared that the British Government in permitting the construction and escape of these warships had acted contrary to international law. Grant held discussions with Britain's

[35] US Secretary of State 1869–77.
[36] Cushing (n 29) 13.
[37] Ward and Gooch (n 24) 67.

emissary Sir Edward Thornton[38] in January 1871 which led to the appointment of the Commission. Concluding their discussions, the Commissioners issued a protocol to the thirty-sixth conference. The Commissioners set out a summary of their work and concluded that the United States had suffered 'a great wrong and that great injuries and losses were inflicted upon the commerce and their national interests by the course of conduct of Britain during the recent rebellion in the United States'.[39]

The United States alleged that due to the fitting out, arming, equipping and augmenting of the Confederate naval forces by Britain and her colonies, there had been extensive direct economic losses and destruction of and damage to a large number of merchant vessels and their cargoes. Indirectly this had resulted in a transfer of much of the American commercial marine to the British flag.[40] The United States also claimed financial losses in relation to insurance costs, and damages for loss of and damage to private property. In addition, there were indirect claims for general damages for the resultant prolongation of the rebellion, interest on damages and a right of indemnification. It also sought an expression of regret. In mitigation the British Commissioners denied any breach of international law and denied liability for alleged loss and damage. The British Government had gone to some trouble to acquire the Anglo-Chinese fleet to prevent it being sold to the Confederate insurgents. Nevertheless, the British agreed to arbitrate, but the United States insisted that Britain agree the terms of reference first. Further discussions ensued,[41] and Britain confirmed that although it could not accept the rules proposed as a statement of international law as at the date the claims arose, it was prepared to agree them for the purposes of strengthening the friendly relations between the two countries. To that end Britain agreed the rules.[42] These were incorporated in the Treaty. It was suggested on the American side that the terms of reference[43] did not go further than the rules of the British Foreign Enlistment Act 1819. This was contested by Sir Alexander Cockburn, the British arbitrator in the subsequent proceedings. Following these negotiations, the Treaty of Washington was signed on 8 May 1871 and ratified by the Senate on 22 May 1871.[44] Whilst Sir Henry Maine suggested that the rules agreed were detrimental to Britain's interests in presenting a greater

[38] British Minister in Washington.

[39] *The Case of the United States* (n 2) 10. It will be noted that the Commissioners acknowledged that the Confederate States had been in rebellion against the Federal Government. This questions the efficacy of the Queen's Proclamation recognising the South as a belligerent. In that context it was in hindsight seen as a mistake. If Adams had been heard before the British Government issued the Proclamation as he argued he might have put a different light on the matter but on the facts it seems unlikely.

[40] *The Case of the United States* (n 2) 10.

[41] These discussions regarding the terms of reference to arbitration as provided in the rules were held on 10,13 and 14 March 1871.

[42] *The Case of the United States* (n 2) 15.

[43] The Rules of Guidance for the Tribunal of Reference. *The Case of the United States* (n 2) 15–16.

[44] Probably due to Earl de Grey's diplomacy. See Wood and Gooch (n 16) 67.

obligation on a neutral state than international law then required, it was, on the other hand, important for any reference made to arbitration to be precise and concise. It was Vattel who observed, 'the arbitration articles should precisely specify the subject in dispute, the respective and opposite pretensions of the parties, the demands of the one and the objections of the other'.[45]

C. The Treaty

The Preamble to the Treaty described its purpose as providing for: 'an amicable settlement of all causes of differences between the two countries'. The key provisions of the Treaty which set the terms of reference for the arbitration and the arbitrators' jurisdiction and powers were Articles I to XVII.

Articles I to X referred exclusively to the claims arising out of the construction of the Confederate cruisers.[46] Articles XII to XVII related to claims by citizens of each state of the Union in respect of claims for damages of injury to property caused by the hostile acts of the Confederate cruisers.

Article I referred to the 'acts committed by several vessels which have given rise to the claims generally known as the *Alabama* claims'. It also contained an expression of regret for the escape of the vessels. The matters that could not be agreed were referred to a Tribunal of Arbitration of five arbitrators each to be appointed by the Queen, the President of the United States, the King of Italy, the President of the Swiss Confederation and the Emperor of Brazil. In the event of anyone ceasing to act or refusing then a replacement by the King of Sweden and Norway would appoint a replacement. Geneva was the seat of the arbitration and each party could appoint an agent.[47] The Treaty provided that the parties should submit their respective cases and relevant documents with evidence within six months of the Treaty's ratification.[48] The parties could then submit respective counter-cases (defence and reply) within four months of the service of the respective cases.[49] Within two months of that each party's agent was to submit Points of Argument referring to the evidence upon which his party relied.[50] The Award of the Tribunal was referred to in the Treaty as 'the Decision'. It was to be delivered by the arbitrators within three months of the close of the parties' arguments.[51] There was no provision in the Treaty for counsel, but the Tribunal could require elucidation of the argument by counsel if so required with a right of reply by the opposing party. This process was to the disadvantage of the British side because it had no notice of the particulars of the claims in making its case.

[45] *Droit des Gens I.ii* c.xvii. s 329.
[46] *Alabama, Florida, Shenandoah* and *Georgia*.
[47] Art I Treaty of Washington 1871 signed 8 May 1871, ratifications exchanged 17 June 1871.
[48] Art III *ibid*.
[49] Art IV *ibid*.
[50] Art V *ibid*.
[51] Art VII *ibid*.

D. Rules

The Treaty specified three rules of the law of neutrality which had been agreed in Washington by the Commissioners. These would be applied as the applicable governing law as to duties required of a neutral Power. The aim of such rules was to prevent departure of armed vessels, the use of its ports, and the prevention of the violation of such rules in national ports and territorial waters. Rule 1 was covered by the Foreign Enlistment Act 1819, Rules 2 and 3 extended to territory not limited to ports and waters.

The Treaty provided:

> First, to use due diligence to prevent the fitting out, arming or equipping, within its jurisdiction, of any vessel which it has reasonable ground to believe is intended to cruise or to carry on war against a Power with which it is at peace, and also to use like diligence to prevent the departure from its jurisdiction of any vessel intended cruise or carry on war as above, such vessel having been specially adapted, in whole or in part, within such jurisdiction, to warlike use.
>
> Secondly, not to permit or suffer either belligerent to make use of its ports or waters as the place of Naval operations against the other, for the purpose of the renewal or augmentation of military supplies or arms, or the recruitment of men.
>
> Thirdly, to exercise due diligence in its own ports and waters, and, has to all persons within its jurisdiction, to prevent any violation of the foregoing obligations and duties.[52]

By accepting these rules governing the contentious issues in the case the British Government conceded what it had denied since the sailing of the *Alabama*. Whilst that was criticised at the time it was however statesmanlike and acknowledged a respect for and an advancement of international law. The Treaty also provided for assessors to be appointed if the arbitrators could not award a gross figure in respect of the *Alabama* claims. Importantly by way of procedure and case management the other advantage the American negotiators gained was that each rule was applied to the case of each vessel in the context of Britain's obligations and duties under international law. More than that, the particular wording of the rules was determinative of the resultant *opinio juris* of the Tribunal.

These rules required the neutral power to act impartially, neither engaging nor abetting any belligerent power engaged in the Civil War. In this case, the position of Britain was contradictory in that Britain had declared neutrality, but then recognised both sides as belligerents. Under the Common Law as practiced in the United States and under the United States Constitution clearly the Southern States were in rebellion. The President of the United States, Lincoln, had the duty to preserve, protect and defend the United States in accordance with his Oath of Office. Britain aided both sides with weapons of war as did France, which like Britain, did not recognise the Confederacy.[53]

[52] Art VI *ibid* and see *The Case of the United States* (n 2) 22.

[53] France gave loans as well as the provision of a cruiser, the *CSS Stonewall*. The French Government stopped the sale, but it eventually found its way into Confederate service in 1864. Union forces

These rules covered the main claims, but there were some indirect claims made by the Federal Government in respect of profits and losses sustained by American merchants resulting from the loss of cargoes or destruction of their merchant ships.[54] Altogether the Treaty dealt with the five key areas of serious controversy between these two Great Powers, the chief of these being that the British Government had recognised the southern Confederate States as belligerents, although Britain had declared its neutrality. Britain gave both equal status even though the Federal Government maintained that it was the legitimate government of all the United States including the southern states. The problem for Britain was that the Queen's Proclamation gave licence to British subjects to trade with the Confederate States despite the imposition of a Union blockade.[55] The United States would argue that this enabled the British to provide the Confederate States with warships, safe harbours, crews and provisions, financial assistance and other war materials. In their view this was tantamount to hostile acts of war.

Articles XXVIII to XXXIV related to the question of fishing rights off the coasts of the British North American colonies and the Eastern Seacoast shores of the United States North of the 39th parallel of North latitude, the navigation of the St Lawrence and Yukon Rivers, the use of canals on the border and free access to Lake Michigan. These matters had been outstanding since the English colonies in America had declared their independence from Britain but were included as part of the reference to arbitration. In this sense the Geneva Arbitration ended the differences between the Mother Country and its former colonies, opening the way for a closer relationship which developed between them towards the close of the nineteenth century.

E. Neutrality Laws

Before considering the American case, it is important to set out the applicable law.

Britain as a neutral country had certain international legal obligations, but the Government's manner of interpreting them was to cause serious contention with the United States. It appears that the British Government considered the building of vessels by private companies for the Confederacy a matter of private commerce regardless of the consequences should the vessels subsequently become cruisers for a belligerent.

avoided any engagement and the vessel was subsequently sold in Cuba to the Spanish authorities which surrendered it to the United States.

[54] Such indirect claims were rejected by the Tribunal as being outside their jurisdiction and terms of reference.

[55] It was argued that a blockade was not lawful unless effective per Lord John Russell. Hansard, HC Deb (series 3) 6 May 1861, vol162, cols 1564–67.

The rights and obligations of Britain were set out in the Foreign Enlistment Act 1819. Section 7 provided:

> That if any person, within any part of the United Kingdom, or in any part of His Majesty's dominions beyond the seas, shall, without the leave and license of His Majesty for that purpose first had and obtained as aforesaid, equip, furnish, fit-out or arm, or procure to be equipped, furnished, fitted-out, or armed, or shall knowingly aid, assist, or be concerned in the equipping, furnishing, fitting-out, or arming of any Ship or Vessel with intent or in order that such Ship or Vessel shall be employed in the service of any Foreign Prince, State, or Potentate, or of any Foreign Colony, Province, or part of any Province or People, … as a Transport or Store-ship, or with intent to cruise or commit hostilities against any Prince, State, or Potentate, … with whom His Majesty shall not then be at war, … every such person so offending shall be deemed guilty of a misdemeanor …

and those of states in the Treaty of Paris 1856, Articles 1–4:

> The Plenipotentiaries who signed the Treaty of Paris of March assembled in conference,
>
> Considering: That maritime law in time of war has long been the subject of deplorable disputes;
>
> That the uncertainty of the law and of the duties in such a matter gives rise to differences of opinion between neutrals and belligerents which may occasion serious difficulties, and even conflicts; that it is consequently advantageous to establish a uniform doctrine on so important a point;
>
> That the Plenipotentiaries assembled in Congress at Paris cannot better respond to the intentions by which their Governments are animated than by seeking to introduce into international relations fixed principles in this respect.
>
> The above-mentioned Plenipotentiaries, being duly authorized, resolved to concert among themselves as to the means of attaining this object; and having come to an agreement, have adopted the following solemn declaration:
>
> 1. Privateering is and remains abolished;
> 2. The neutral flag covers enemy's goods, with the exception of contraband of war;
> 3. Neutral goods, with the exception of contraband of war, are not liable to capture under enemy's flag;
> 4. Blockades, in order to be binding, must be effective-that is to say, maintained by a force sufficient really to prevent access to the coast of the enemy.
>
> The Governments of the undersigned Plenipotentiaries engage to bring the present declaration to the knowledge of the States which have not taken part in the Congress of Paris, and to invite them to accede.
>
> Convinced that the maxims which they now proclaim cannot but be received with gratitude by the whole world, the undersigned Plenipotentiaries doubt not that the efforts of their Governments to obtain the general adoption thereof will be crowned with full success.

> The present Declaration is not and shall not be binding, except between those Powers who have acceded, or shall accede, to it.[56]

The British Government was of the view that it was the neutral sovereign, not a neutral sovereign's subjects, who had the obligation to observe neutrality under the rule of international law because the nation's subjects were not at war. The point was strongly argued in Sir A Cockburn's dissenting award. This changed in 1918.

The legal questions for the British Government were: 1. Was the *Alabama*, the ship itself, a contraband item? The answer was yes, because it gave assistance to a belligerent. 2. Did British nationals have a right to intervene? The Foreign Enlistment Act 1819 and the Queen's Proclamation of 13 May 1861 clearly made it a criminal offence for any British subject to take any part in this foreign war. This would apply to Laird shipbuilders in Liverpool and the others. The point was that contraband would be confiscated by the belligerent power if it gave assistance to the enemy. The law of blockade stemmed from the law of siege. Professor Gooch says what was important to understand is a history of the policy and of the doctrine which it was their duty to apply in the case before them.[57] Unfortunately, what this episode did was to damage the image of the mother country's attitude during the Civil War. As Gooch stated:

> It was unfortunate, at such a time, that British statesmanship should not have perceived the line that lay between the duty of neutral governments not to intervene in war and the right of neutral nationals, at their own risk so to intervene, and they should have confused the notions of the ship as a contraband article and of a ship as an illegal expedition. The line of distinction was clear enough, had British statesman known the history of the policy and of the doctrine which it was their duty to apply in the case before them.[58]

Gooch's view is supported by the position taken by Sir A Cockburn in his award, even though he disagreed with the other claims.

IV. THE CLAIMS

There were two classes of claims presented by the United States in this arbitration. The first were those which applied to those cruisers and other vessels originally purchased, constructed and fitted out, or adapted to warlike use in Britain. They committed a hostile act by the very fact of sailing from Britain. The second were those which were adapted to warlike use and commenced their hostilities in the Confederate service outside Britain.[59]

[56] M Nijhoff, *Conventions and Declarations between the Powers Concerning War, Arbitration and Neutrality* (Springer, 1915).

[57] Ward and Gooch (n 24) 63.

[58] *Ibid.*

[59] There were other ships such as the *Bahama* which facilitated the fitting out of the *Florida* with munitions when she met her at Nassau. Another British ship the *Agrippina* assisted by the *Bahama* completed the equipping and crewing of the *Alabama*. 'The Geneva Arbitration and its Results' (n 21)193, 197, 201.

A. First Class Claims

These included damage and loss caused by the *Florida (Oreto)*,[60] the *Alabama*, the *Georgia*, the *Pampero* and the *Laird Rams.*

B. Second Class Claims

These included damage and loss caused by the *Sumpter*, the *Nashville*, the *Retribution*, the *Tallahasse*, the *Chickamauga* and the *Shenandoah (Sea King).*

C. Damages Claims

The Federal Government claimed damages and reparations directly caused by the hostile activities of the Confederate cruisers built, crewed, fitted out, provisioned and manned in England, and in her colonies, actions equivalent to acts of war. These were known as the direct claims. The United States also claimed damages for national injuries, later referred to in the proceedings as indirect or constructive losses. These national losses were claims by private individuals whose property had been seized, damaged or destroyed by the Confederate cruisers. Mr Cushing, the Counsel for the United States, argued that these indirect claims were 'claims on the part of the United States' but these did not constitute legitimate claims under international law and were consequently excluded from the Tribunal's jurisdiction.[61] The United States also made the claim that England was the virtual Navy Department of the Confederacy with a branch office in Richmond, Virginia.[62] It was alleged that England was the main arsenal of the Confederacy; and that it protracted the Civil War. This caused consternation in London since the claim was rejected by the Commissioners in Washington during the Treaty negotiations[63] and in any event (as Mr Forster told the House of Commons in 1863) vast supplies of munitions were supplied continually to the Union armies.

V. CONSTITUTION OF THE TRIBUNAL AND THE PROCEEDINGS

The Tribunal constituted under, Article I of the Treaty of Washington was composed of five arbitrators: Mr Charles Francis Adams for the United States;

[60] She was arrested in Nassau under the Foreign Enlistment Act 1819, but the warrant was discharged. The counsel for the owners also acted for Confederate agents in Nassau.

[61] See Cushing (n 29) 70 as to the Decision of the Arbitrators Respecting National Losses; Opinion of Count Sclopis.

[62] 'The Geneva Arbitration and Its Results' (n 21) 194.

[63] The British feared that the Government would have to pay similar reparations as the French paid Prussia after the Franco-Prussian War. France was forced to pay Prussia five billion gold francs (£200m) to be paid within five years and suffer the loss of Alsace-Lorraine.

Sir Alexander Cockburn for Britain; Count Frederic Sclopis; Mr Jacob Staempfli; and Baron d'Itajuba. The agents appointed were Lord Tenterden for Britain and JC Bancroft Davis for the United States.

Counsel for the United States were: Caleb Cushing; William Maxwell Ewarts; and Morrison Remick Waite. Counsel for Britain were Roundell Palmer QCMP and Professor Montague Bernard.

The Tribunal held its first case conference on the 15th December 1871. The parties agreed that Count Sclopis should preside. The Tribunal appointed Mr Alexander Farrot as its secretary. Mr Bancroft Davis filed the United States case and Lord Tenterden filed the British case. The British case was not a defence or response to the United States case because it was drafted without sight of the United States case. Counter cases were filed on the 15 April 1872.[64] The meeting was then adjourned to a further case conference set for the 15 June 1872. The British team seemed totally unprepared for the case of the United States. They exhibited what Caleb Cushing described as 'an explosion of clamour' of the ill-informed British press. Communications between members of the Tribunal were in French but the cases were printed in French and English.

The Tribunal had 32 sessions and its award was published on the 14 September 1872. In the end the arbitrators found against Britain in respect of damages caused by the *Alabama*, *Florida* and *Shenandoah*. The *Georgia* was subsequently excluded. 'Due diligence' was found as being in proportion to the risks to which either belligerent was exposed from failure to fulfil its obligations of neutrality.[65]

VI. THE CASE OF THE UNITED STATES

The view of the Federal Government was that Britain and her colonies had been 'the arsenal, the navy yard and the Treasury of the Confederates'.[66] The Federal Government charged that Britain, by its 'provocative recognition of the belligerence of the Confederacy' and by its direct aid or support given to the ships in British ports, had prolonged the Civil War.[67] Britain had, in effect, committed an act/acts of war on the United States, entitling the United States to declare war on Britain.[68] Despite all the written warnings given to Lord John Russell, the British Foreign Secretary, by the United States Minister in London, Charles Francis Adams, the cruisers were able to escape.

In the arbitration, counsel for the United States charged that the British Government had from the start of the rebellion adopted 'a studied unfriendliness or fixed predisposition adverse to the United States which furnished a constant

[64] The case for the United States comprised 5,442 documents in eight volumes; the British case 2,823 pages in three volumes.

[65] At the First Hague Conference in 1907 the words 'due diligence' were substituted by 'To employ the means at its disposal'.

[66] Cushing (n 29) 15.

[67] *Ibid* 16.

[68] *Ibid*.

motive for the several acts of omission or commission, hereinafter complained of, as inconsistent with its duty of the neutral'.[69]

A. The Confederate States of America: 'Belligerents'

This impression arose partly through an incomplete communication of Lincoln's Proclamation of the blockade and also through Britain's recognition of the Confederate States as a belligerent two days after meeting Confederate agents in London.[70] There was further embarrassment when the complete text of Lincoln's Proclamation was received in London on 11 May 1861. This was 10 days after Britain conferred belligerent status on the rebel states, and eight days after Russell had referred the matter to the Law Officers of the Crown for a legal opinion. It was also five days after the Government had announced its decision to the House of Commons.[71] In other words, the American complaint had some foundation in that the Government had acted before a formal receipt or confirmation of Lincoln's Proclamation, and before it had requested or received legal advice.

It was a settled rule of international law that for a blockade to be lawful and binding it must be effective.[72] At first the Union blockade was not completely effective and there were disparities, but any neutral ship could be warned off or seized.[73] During these days it seemed as if the British Government was unaware of the facts or its policy, although on the 6 May Lord Russell confirmed the advice of the Attorney and Solicitor General and the Queen's Advocate that according to the principles of the Law of Nations 'the Southern Confederacy of America … must be treated as a belligerent'.[74]

On 1 June 1861 the Government referred to hostilities in America as 'imminent' but according to the Queen's Proclamation of the 13 May hostilities

[69] *The Case of the United States* (n 2) 29.

[70] On the 6th May 1861, Lord John Russell declared the Confederacy a belligerent.

[71] As to the blockade *Earl Russell to Lord Lyons* 15 February 1862 to the effect that: 'The adequacy of the force to maintain a blockade being always and necessarily, a matter of fact and evidence, and one as to which different opinions may be entertained, a neutral state ought to exercise the greatest caution with reference to the disregard of a de facto and notified blockade; and ought not to disregard it, except when it entertains a conviction, which is shared by neutral is generally having it an interest in the matter, that the power of blockade is abused by a State either unable to institute or maintain it, or unwilling from some motive or other, to do so'; M Bernard, *A Historical Account of the Neutrality of Britain During the American Civil War* (Longmans, Green Reader and Dyer, 1870) 245.

[72] The use of the words 'lawful blockade' created further anxiety on the part of the United States because the meaning leaned towards the strict French interpretation of a blockade. The practicality was that the Federal navy could not police the southern coasts in 1861 and it was a matter of opinion in each case whether the blockade was effective, eg, it might close New Orleans, but it might not close Savannah. Lemnitzer (n 26) 120.

[73] Bernard (n 71) 245–46 and see Lemnitzer (n 26) 139–43.

[74] Hansard, HC Deb (series 3) 6 May 1861, vol 162, cols 1564–67.

had already commenced. Both Houses of Parliament debated the war on the 29 April and 10 May respectively. In the Commons, Mr Gladstone, Chancellor of the Exchequer, seemed little concerned about privateers hovering around British coasts, but in the House of Lords the Lord Chancellor, Lord Campbell, opined that if any English subject joined the belligerent forces in America then that person would be liable under the Foreign Enlistment Act and subject to punishment by the English courts. He would have no right to protection by the British Government. However, he would not be regarded as a pirate because he was acting under a commission from a belligerent state carrying on *justum bellum*. In Campbell's opinion if such a person were executed for piracy that would be murder.

At the hearing Counsel for the United States submitted that Campbell's opinion had the effect of granting immunity to British subjects taking part in such hostilities. But counsel also quoted Lord Lyndhurst (a former Lord Chancellor) who was of a contrary opinion to the effect that if British subjects combined and conspired together to excite a revolt against a friendly state and took part in hostilities, they would be liable to suffer punishment under English law. Such an offence was also an offence against the Law of Nations and as such part of the law of England.[75] It must be pointed out that this was clearly the expressed intention of the British Government as expressed in debate in the House of Lords on the 10 May. Earl Granville had confirmed that the Government would not be prepared to save the offender from the consequences of any prosecution under the laws of the United States and this was made plain in the Proclamation.[76] Lord Brougham, in the same debate, took the view that any interference in a foreign war by fitting out, manning and going on board ships to take part in the war was a crime. His remarks were prescient for what was to happen.

As to the Letters of Marque that Jefferson Davis had granted to privateers, as the Confederacy had no navy, the question arose as to whether these sailors were pirates. Lincoln wanted to prosecute them for piracy, but under threat of retaliation by the Confederate Government to hang a Union soldier for every privateer executed. Lincoln relented and no privateers were hanged.[77] Was the British Government justified in conferring belligerent status on the Confederacy? The United States did not think so and declared that:

> … such an act depends upon the occasion and the circumstances, and it is an act, the sovereign act of war, which the variety of the public more practice requires should be deliberate, reasonable, and just in reference to the surrounding facts.[78]

[75] *The Case of the United States* (n 2) 60–61. See also Sir George Cornwall Lewis Bart, *On Foreign Jurisdiction and the Extradition of Criminals* (JW Parker and Son, 1859) 56.

[76] Hansard, HL Deb (series 3) 10 May 1861, vol162, cols 1829–34. Question by Earl of Derby, Lord Granville's reply and Lord Brougham's observations.

[77] *The Case of the United States* (n 2) 61. See also Lemnitzer (n 26) 130.

[78] *The Case of the United States* (n 2) 64 *Mr Fish to Mr Motley*, 25 September 1869.

B. Deterioration in Relations between the United States and Britain

It was inevitable that other issues would arise not just in relation to the rights of privateers and the recognition of the South as a belligerent. Although relations between the Mother Country and the United States had been strained since 1776, Americans retained connection with England not just through a similar Common Law, religious affiliation and the English language, but it was suggested that the United States relied on England and Ireland for its merchant marine – far more in the South than in the North.[79]

Belligerency appears to have been assumed by the British Government five days before the receipt of Lincoln's Proclamation.[80] Lord Russell's instructions to Lord Lyons, the British ambassador at Washington, to inform the Federal Government that the British Government could not accept a renunciation of privateering by the United States coupled with a condition that they should enforce it on the Confederate States.[81] The Federal Government considered the communication of Lord Russell's despatch regarding this statement to Her Majesty's Consuls in New Orleans and Charleston for communication to Mr Jefferson Davis at Montgomery as an abuse of diplomatic privilege and inconsistent with the duties of a neutral state so serious in fact it might be regarded as a reason for war.[82] Later Lord Lyons was to make similar objection to the closure of the southern ports to foreign trade.[83] It was suggested that the policy of the British Government seemed to conflict with their concurrence to the Protocol agreed at the Congress of Paris at the conclusion of the Crimean War; namely the abolition of privateering and the legal necessity for a blockade to be efficient.[84] At that time Britain had asked the United States whether they would agree but the United States would not agree to abolition of privateering unless there was agreement over the exemption of private property from capture on the High Seas.[85]

The pre-emptive action of Britain in recognising the states in rebellion as belligerents before the arrival of the American Minister in London could explain the state of affairs to Lord Russell. Russell's despatch to Lord Lyons for communication via consular officials to Mr Davis clearly soured relations between the two countries. What made matters worse were the secret discussions entered into between Britain and the insurgents through a Confederate agent seeking

[79] Hansard, HL Deb (series 3) 28 May 1861, vol 163, cols 188–90. Mr T Duncombe's information appears exaggerated, but there were a significant number so employed as to cause concern.

[80] *The Case of the United States* (n 2) 65. The Queen's Proclamation was published on 13 May 1861.

[81] *Ibid* 67.

[82] *Ibid* 68.

[83] Lord Lyons to Lord J Russell. Washington, 12 August 1861. *New York Times Archives*.

[84] 24th Protocol, 16 April 1856 Congress of Paris. At the suggestion of Count Walewski, the Congress adopted the four principles: 1. Privateering is and remains abolished; 2. The neutral flag protects the enemy's goods, except contraband of war; 3. Neutral goods, except contraband of war, are not subject to seizure under the enemy's flag; 4. Blockades, to be binding must be effective, ie maintained by force sufficient to render approach to the enemy's coast really dangerous.

[85] *The Case of the United States* (n 2) 70.

clarification as to the secessionist treatment of neutrals. Britain had much to lose in the blockade of the South and therefore it was reasonable to obtain such explanation. This might have been seen as deceitful by the Federal Government and increased the lack of trust. Lord Russell's objective in securing the rights of neutrals was met by the Confederate Congress in that the insurgents accepted the second and third rules of the Declaration of Paris that blockades to be binding must be efficient and that they maintained the right of privateering. To the consternation of the Federal Government, the British Government did not insist that the seceding states accept the first Article of the Declaration. Mr Bunch, the British Consul, at Charleston said that '... it could not be expected that they should do so of their own accord, particularly as it is the arm upon which they must rely for the injury of the extended commerce of the enemy'.[86]

To accept such a position would appear to confirm a duplicitous policy. Britain had signed the Declaration of Paris abolishing privateering and here she was allowing a de facto state in rebellion to act illegally. The Federal Government had not signed the Declaration of Paris and this was regretted after President Lincoln had declared the blockade. Sewell, the American Secretary of State, opened negotiations with Britain, but Russell rejected the American proposal. According to Sir Henry Maine,[87] the United States agreed to adopt Article 1 to abolish privateering if all private property at sea was excepted from capture. The effect of this agreement with the secessionist states was that Britain could trade with the South with goods save contraband of war. The question that Maine asked was what was contraband? Was it raw materials, sails, cordage, something in the course of manufacture? Would iron or brass or provisions be contraband? Weapons and munitions were certainly within the definition, but there was some uncertainty as to other goods.[88] Talks between Adams and Russell reached an impasse so that Adams reported to his government that:

> Her Majesty's Government thus placed themselves in the position of a party which proposes what it has no authority to perform, and which negotiates upon a basis on which it has already deprived itself of the power to conclude.[89]

If the United States did not agree Article 1, then the rebel states were enabled through the means of privateering to acquire a navy. It appears that Russell may have been instructed by the Cabinet not to agree such provision with the United States as it inclined towards the secessionists.[90] The inclinations of the British Cabinet were revealed further when Russell spoke of the calamity of the 'subjugation of the South' which would be 'especially calamitous to the negro race'.[91] He also hoped that hostilities could be resolved otherwise the economy would be

[86] *The Case of the United States* (n 2) 76.
[87] Sir Henry Maine, *International Law* (John Murray,1888) 62–63.
[88] *Ibid* 64. Maine gives the example of Britain's refusal to send coal to the French fleet in 1870.
[89] *The Case of the United States* (n 2) 80.
[90] *Ibid* 81.
[91] Lord Russell, Speech at Newcastle. Reported in *The Times*, 16 October 1861.

destroyed and expressed the fervent hope that: 'Her Majesty's Government has felt that it was its duty to use every possible means to avoid taking any part in the lamentable contest now raging in the American States.'[92] Despite this unfortunately for Anglo-American relations, Mr Gladstone went too far in saying that Jefferson Davis and other leaders had made an army, navy and a nation. He thought there would be a separation.[93] Compounding the impression of bias by the British Government and Parliament was a speech by Mr Laird, a Tory MP,[94] who had a direct fiduciary interest in the war; his yards built the *Alabama* and the *Laird Rams*.[95] He accused the Federal Government of 'reducing liberty to an utter absurdity'.[96] Two years later Mr John Bright MP (a proponent of free trade and an anti-slavery exponent who sympathised with the North in the Civil War) accused Mr Laird of being a felon who had abused his position as a magistrate and a deputy lieutenant as well as an MP in admiring ' the greatest example which men have ever seen of the greatest crime which men have ever committed' and building a cruiser for such perpetrators in breach of international law and contrary to the Queen's Proclamation.[97] Other political statements from Gladstone, Palmerston and Russell were brought to support the argument that Britain had exercised insincere neutrality towards the United States; statements by Mr Gladstone as to whether the emancipation of the negro could be accomplished by force on 30 June 1863 and Russell on 9 June 1864 lamenting that thousands were being killed for 'acting on those very principles of independence which in 1776 were asserted by the whole of America against this country'. Thus, the leaders in Parliament: Palmerston, Gladstone and Russell all appeared to sympathise with the South as did a majority of the press, but public opinion was divided and some like John Bright, a Liberal, supported the Federal Government.

After the war there were some reflections and admissions from Lord Westbury, the Lord Chancellor. He told the House of Lords in 1866 that the 'animus with which the neutral Powers acted was the only true criterion'. Mr Seward's chief charge against Britain was that Britain had precipitately issued the Queen's Proclamation recognising the Confederate States as a belligerent Power. This he charged was proof of Britain's 'insincerity and want of impartial attention'.[98]

C. The Duties of a Neutral Power

A record of how Britain carried out her duties as a neutral power are contained in the American case and in Professor Montague Bernard's historical account

[92] Hansard, HC Deb 2 May 1861, vol 162, col 1378–79.
[93] Mr Gladstone, Speech at Newcastle on 7 October 1862. Reported in *The Times*, 9 October 1862.
[94] Hansard, HC Deb (series 3) 27 March 1863, Vol 170, col 68–72.
[95] These were state of the art warships which may well have seriously threatened the federal forces.
[96] *The Times* (28 March 1863).
[97] *The Case of the United States* (n 2) 92–93.
[98] *Ibid* 102.

of how Britain exercised that role during the war of secession.[99] Britain was constrained by its national law, principally the Foreign Enlistment Act of 1819. But the US Counsel argued that such duties in international law went beyond national law. George Canning, speaking on 10 June 1819, had extolled the virtues of the US neutrality laws prohibiting any US citizen to engage in the armies of any belligerent Power. As to the Foreign Enlistment Act 1819, US counsel charged that British subjects were recruited to serve in the Confederate navy and armies; that the British Government had a duty to seize any vessels built in Britain for service in the Confederacy; that it was criminal to equip, furnish, fit out, or arm any vessel intended for such service or assist the Confederates in its war against the United States. This included adding guns or equipment for use in war. The Federal Government encouraged the British Government to adopt the form of their Foreign Enlistment Act 1819. In January 1867 a commission was appointed to consider this. They recommended that the scope of the Act should be extended to cover the dispatch or cause to be dispatched any ship for the purposes of waging war against any state with which Britain was at peace. It was also suggested that no ship of a belligerent state should be equipped, fitted out or despatched contrary to such enactment or should be able to access British ports.[100] The Report was published in 1868 but not enacted until after the Franco-Prussian War in the form of the Foreign Enlistment Act 1870.

In one of the first cases to come before the courts under the Act, Sir Roger Phillimore, who had been one of the Commissioners, held that the Act was intended to bring the law of England into line with the Law of Nations.[101] In effect this followed the course adopted by the United States. The argument facing the British Government in the arbitration was also based on the view of Lord Mansfield who said that in the case of *Brevot v Barbot* Lord Talbot declared that 'the law of nations, in its full extent, was part of the law of England'. This was also the opinion of Lord Hardwick and Lord Chief Justice Holt.[102]

Two principles of the Foreign Enlistment Act 1819 appear to be conceded by the Proclamation of 13 May 1861, first that it is the duty of a neutral to observe neutrality as to both belligerents during hostilities, and second to observe impartiality of conduct towards both belligerents.[103] The United States argued that these duties were not dependent municipal law. Subjects of a neutral sovereign would therefore be liable under the national law for violations or contraventions of the Law of Nations.

[99] Bernard (n 71).

[100] Including British dominions and territories.

[101] Reported in *The Times* (18 January 1871).

[102] *Brevot v Barbot* 1 Black Com 43, 354; 1 Woodsons Lecture 31 and see *Papers Relating to the Foreign Relations of the United States Transmitted to Congress with the Annual Message of the President* 2 December 1872, Part II, Vol I, 53, available at https://history.state.gov/historicaldocuments/frus1872p2v1/pg_53.

[103] *The Case of the United States* (n 2) 123–25.

The British Government issued clear instructions for the supplying or harbouring of belligerent ships. Any ship was to depart within 24 hours except if repairs were required to make it seaworthy. Supplies were only allowed as of necessity. Ships could not be supplied with more coal than necessary to take her to the home port. Such ships could only be supplied with two supplies of coal. Not more than two supplies were permitted from ports of the same neutral within less than three months of each supply.

The three legal principles adopted by Britain and the United States after the War of Independence and the Crimean War amounted to:

1. That the belligerent may call upon the neutral to enforce its municipal proclamations as well as the municipal law.
2. That it is the duty of the neutral to prevent by all means any violation.
3. That when there is such a failure the neutral must pay compensation for the injury resulting.[104]

The rules required the neutral to exercise 'due diligence'. Under the laws of the United States this did not detract in any way from the duty that was imposed by the Law of Nations. In relation to the United States' claims the definitions of 'negligence' and 'diligence' were those of English Common Law and Roman Law. An absence of 'diligence' implied 'blameable fault' from a derivative of the Roman *Culpa*. 'Due diligence' was derived from the Roman '*exacta diligentia*' as applied in the *jus civilis*.[105]

The extent of diligence was a matter of fact determined by the circumstances of the case, the extent of the injury/damage, and the ability of the party having the duty to exercise diligence required by the exigencies of the case.[106] Today it would be argued that it is a matter of what is reasonably foreseeable and not too remote, the injury being within the scope or proximity of what may happen according to the nature of the risk. In this case however there was good authority for the counsel of the United States to use. John Ayliffe was quoted[107] as to want of proper care and Lord Cairns, later Lord Chancellor of England, put stress upon the words 'due diligence'. He was supported by another subsequent Lord Chancellor, Sir Roundell Palmer, later Lord Selbourne, who opined that this requirement under the Treaty of Washington imposed upon Britain a duty to use 'all means legitimately in its power' in relation to its duties as a neutral.[108]

So far as the application of this duty was concerned the United States argued that the British Government was obliged to prevent any construction of vessels for use by the insurgents and if constructed to detain them. In the case of the *Rappahannock* which sailed from the Thames, it was intercepted by a French

[104] Arts VI and VII Treaty of Washington 1871. See also *The Case of the United States* (n 2) 135–36.
[105] *The Case of the United States* (n 2) 151.
[106] *Ibid* 152.
[107] J Ayliffe, *New Pandects of Roman Civil Law* (Thomas Osborne, 1734).
[108] Sir Roundel Palmer, *Speech in the House of Commons 4 August 1871* (Macmillan & Co, 1871).

warship and detained. In the case of the *Alabama* she escaped through delay in the execution of preventative measures although the United States' Minister was assured that she would be stopped at Queenstown or Nassau.[109] Failure to stop her was a breach of Rule 1 of the Treaty of Washington. Under Rule 2 of the Treaty belligerent vessels could not use neutral ports as bases for operations, eg Nassau. Only humanitarian supplies could be provided. In terms of precedent Britain was out of step with what had been provided to Spain in 1819, Portugal in 1827 and to Britain by the United States in 1793 in relation to her war with France.[110] The respective cases of the United States and Britain were supported by eminent legal opinion. In the case of the former by President Woolsey, President of Yale[111] and in the latter case by Professor Montague Bernard, the Chichele Professor of Law and Diplomacy at Oxford but in counsel's submission the respective cases could not be regarded.[112] Other opinion in support of the United States was provided by the jurists Hautefeuile and Rolin-Jacquemyns, in addition to the opinion of Lord Westbury given in the House of Lords on 7 March 1868. This opinion was damaging to the British case because Lord Westbury was clear that any construction of warships for one belligerent with a view to war operations knowingly permitted by the neutral powers was a breach of neutrality.[113]

In summary it is clear that the case for the United States was supported by some weighty legal authority whether under civil, common or international law rooted in the pandects of ancient Rome.

In many respects Britain condemned itself in its statements by its leaders and their admissions. On 7 October 1862, Mr Gladstone had affirmed that Jefferson Davis had an army and appeared to be making a navy. However Lord Russell, Principal Secretary of State for Foreign Affairs, went further saying:

> … But it so happens that in this conflict the Confederate States have no ports except those of the Mersey and the Clyde, from which they fit out ships to cruise against the Federals; and having no ports to which to bring their prizes, they are obliged to burn them on the High Seas.[114]

Furthermore, the admission in Article 1 Treaty of Washington that the rebel vessels had escaped and caused despoliation made it clear that Britain had responsibility for the consequences. Lord Cairns was right in his opinion that the expression of regret was an unguarded statement in that it referred to an 'escape'. An escape may be prevented and in this case the construction works were complained of by the American Minister Charles Adams, but no effective

[109] *The Case of the United States* (n 2) 166.
[110] *Ibid* 169.
[111] Author of *Introduction to the Study of International Law* (1860) (University of Michigan Library, 2006).
[112] Bernard (n 71); *The Case of the United States* (n 2) 169–70.
[113] Hansard, HL Deb (series 3) 7 March 1868, vol 191, cols 347.
[114] Speech of Earl Russell on 26 of April 1864.

immediate steps were taken to prevent the *Alabama's* escape. This enabled the American lawyers to present a damaging chronology of mishaps to the Tribunal that enabled Confederate agents to ensure completion and procure the vessel's escape with a British crew. Evidence was led as to the construction and escape of several cruisers and other vessels from the Mersey, the Clyde and the Thames to British ports at Nassau, Bermuda and Melbourne. It was alleged that Nassau was a Confederate naval base, Liverpool a branch of the Confederate Treasury and Navy Department. The Confederate agents in Liverpool were Fraser, Trenholm & Co with its head office John Fraser & Co at Charleston, Virginia.[115] It is interesting to note that between 1 October 1861 and 31 March 1862, 12 vessels entering the harbour flew the British flag and 65 that of the Confederacy.[116] Jefferson Davis took the view that if he sustained his war at sea against the Federal navy then Britain would recognise the Confederacy.[117]

Britain was more deeply involved than just building warships. It was alleged that British ships like the *Gladiator* were used to ferry contraband into the Confederacy albeit commanded by a Confederate officer. This ship transhipped her cargo to the *Kate* at Nassau after eluding a Federal warship. It was alleged that the British authorities in Nassau changed the rules in favour of the *Gladiator*, so she escaped from the Federal navy[118] transferring her cargo to another ship sailing under the Union Jack. Counsel for the Claimants alleged that Nassau was the supply base of the Confederacy because the British Government failed to exercise due diligence in the matter.[119] As a result, the Foreign Office issued instructions that:

1. No warship or privateer to enter the Bahamas unless given special permission by the Lieutenant Governor and only then to get necessary supplies for immediate use and then to put to sea as soon as possible;
2. No such ship was to use British ports or waters for any warlike purpose;
3. If such ship entered a port it was required to embark within 24 hours unless there was stress of weather taking necessary supplies for immediate use. It was not to remain in port more than 24 hours after completion necessary repairs.
4. Subsequently limited to necessities for subsistence of the crew and to take enough coal to reach the nearest home port.[120]

But the fact was that several British ships were plying between the Bahamas and the Confederacy. These were the *Gladiator*, *Economist* and the *Southwick*. The breaches of neutrality were not simply confined to the activities of the rebel cruisers. The Confederate Government had an agent in London, Major Caleb Huse, who lived in Notting Hill and purchased 157,000 rifles and other war munitions.

[115] Bernard (n 71) 289.
[116] *Ibid*.
[117] *The Case of the United States* (n 2) 218.
[118] *Ibid* 227.
[119] *Ibid* 233.
[120] *Ibid*.

These were shipped to the Confederacy via Nassau; the insurgents having paid $9,000,000 for the supplies.[121]

When the *Alabama* left the Mersey, she was flying the Union Jack. Off Anglesey she took on 20–30 men and then sailed to the Azores still under the British flag, but at the Azores she hoisted the Confederate flag.[122] In his correspondence with Mr Adams Lord Russell admitted that: 'it is undoubtedly true that the Alabama was partly fitted out in a British port'.[123] But not only did the Confederates procure the construction of two cruisers *Alabama* and *Florida* but Jefferson Davis, the President of the Confederacy, planned for six more iron clad vessels at a cost of $3,500,000 to be built in Liverpool.[124] Additionally, the colonial authorities in Trinidad permitted the *Sumter* to remain for five days supplied with coal and 'necessary outfits'.[125] Despite this, and the allegations as to the procurement of further vessels, Lord Russell informed Mr Adams that the Confederate agents had not broken the criminal law and Adams was lacking proof for any action to be taken by the Government.[126] The Lord Chancellor rejected a proposal by the Federal Government for any change[127] to the Foreign Enlistment Act 1819 to include provision for 'the construction in British ports of ships destined for the use of belligerents'. Belatedly, Lord Russell admitted to Mr Adams that 'the cases of the *Alabama* and the *Oreto (Florida)* were a scandal and in some degree a reproach to our laws'.[128]

The failure by the Government to stop or impound the cruisers or to interrupt the activities of the Confederate agents in England constituted in the opinion of the American Counsel, Mr Caleb Cushing, a violation of Britain's obligations to the United States as a neutral.[129] He gave the further example of the *Alexandra.* This ship was seized by the Customs authorities in Liverpool on 5 April 1863, after the Law Officers advised its seizure the day before. The ship was built of teak. She appeared to be designed as a gunboat because her bulwarks were low and enabled pivot guns to operate. In the trial the Chief Baron of the Court of Exchequer left the question to the jury:

> Was there any intention that, in the Port of Liverpool, or in any other port, she should be either equipped, furnished, fitted out, or armed, with the intention of taking part in any contest? If you think the object was to equip, furnish, fit out, or arm that vessel at Liverpool, then that is a sufficient matter. But if you think that the object really was to build a ship in obedience to an order and in compliance with a contract, leaving to those who bought it to make what use they thought fit of it, then it appears to me that the Foreign Enlistment Act has not in any degree been broken.[130]

[121] *Ibid* 237–40.
[122] *Ibid* 244.
[123] *Ibid.*
[124] *Ibid* 246.
[125] *Ibid* 247.
[126] *Ibid* 249–50.
[127] *Ibid* 251–52.
[128] *Ibid* 253–254.
[129] *Ibid* 256.
[130] *Attorney General v Sillem and Others* 2 H & C 431.

The jury decided that there was no breach of the statute and despite a further appeal the ship was released. It sailed to Nassau where it was again impounded by the British authorities with further proceedings in the Vice Admiralty Court which resulted in a further release. But because of this intervention by the British authorities, she remained in Nassau until the end of the war. The Federal Government proceeded to claim her in the Admiralty Court and its claim was upheld.[131]

Another contentious issue was that of the *Laird Rams*. These were vessels built of teak and covered with four-inch-thick armour plate. Each vessel was to have two turrets. They were very formidable weapons, probably in advance of United States' designs at that time. They had a stem made of wrought iron, about eight inches thick, projecting about five feet under the waterline, intended for purposes of penetrating and destroying other vessels. At first Lord Russell said that he could not interfere with the construction, but on 5 September 1863 Charles Adams protested to Russell saying: 'It would be superfluous in me to point out to your Lordship that this is war'.[132] A response was received on the 8 September to the effect that instructions were issued to prevent two of these vessels' departure.

Just before this the *Alabama* sailed into Table Bay, South Africa, having seized the *Tuscaloosa*. Having detained the ship, the British authorities in Cape Town decided after consultation with London that the *Tuscaloosa* should be returned to Captain Semmes of the *Alabama*.

Apart from these episodes Cushing exposed a catalogue of evidence as to the export of cotton from the Confederacy to England where the cotton was traded for munitions. In the build-up to the battle of Gettysburg in Pennsylvania, Confederate agents placed heavy orders for weapons such as 150,000 bayonets ordered on 6 May 1863, and 20,000 rifle bayonets wanted 'as soon as possible'.[133] At Gettysburg the Confederate Army of Virginia under the command of General Robert E Lee was defeated and this was seen as a turning point in the policy of Britain towards the South to the end of the war.[134] Encouraged by this victory Adams was able to press Lord Russell to end what he termed 'toleration of the outrages abuses of the belligerent privileges that have been granted to the insurgents'.[135] Relations had deteriorated to the extent that Adams warned Russell that if British subjects violated the Union blockade of the South then they would be treated as enemies and if captured be regarded as prisoners of war. Blockade runners would be treated as prisoners of war. Lord Russell refused to accept this. His view was that British subjects were not inhibited from trading with either belligerent subject only to the capture of their vessels and to 'no other penalty'. This view was supported by the Lord Chancellor,

[131] Bernard (n 71) 353–55.

[132] *The Case of the United States* (n 2).

[133] *Ibid* 277.

[134] There is some question about this. The historian Frank J Merli in his book edited by David M Fahey, F Merli, *The Alabama, British Neutrality and the American Civil War* (Indiana University Press, 2004) 20, opines that the turning point for Britain was the Battle of Antietam in September 1862 when Lee's incursion into Maryland was defeated.

[135] *The Case of the United States* (n 2) 283.

Lord Westbury and by the High Court of Admiralty.[136] As late in the war as July 1864, the Confederacy was placing further orders for 14 steamers to carry 1,000 bales of cotton each; four to be delivered in August 1864, eight in December 1864 and two in April 1865.

VII. THE CASE OF BRITAIN

As illustrated from the submissions by British and American Counsel, views differed as to the duties of a neutral state regarding the degree of prevention to be exercised against its citizens who were aiding a belligerent power. Having considered the case presented by the American Counsel, we now look at the case presented by Sir Roundell Palmer and Professor Montague Bernard.

The first point made by the British Government was that the United States had not submitted a particularised and complete statement of its claims, nor given the grounds on which they were founded. The claims made by the United States alleged that Britain had failed to fulfil its international duties as a neutral in relation to the vessels, and to have fitted out, armed or equipped the vessels as specially adapted for warlike use in Britain against the United States.[137] Roundell Palmer submitted that there was no failure by Britain discharging any of its international obligations such that Britain would have to make any reparations to the United States by acts committed by its Government or by any persons out of British jurisdiction.[138] The problem was however that Britain had accepted the rules of arbitration laid down by the Treaty of Washington. Whilst this was a significant concession in terms of an advancement of international law norms, it posed difficulties for the British case to the extent that these were not rules current at the time the offences were alleged to have occurred.[139] In other words, Britain was judged by rules unknown at the time of the incidents.

Palmer agreed the following general propositions of law so far as the British case was concerned: that it was the duty of a neutral government in all matters relating to the war to act impartially towards the belligerent powers; that such a duty was not affected by the political relationship that had existed between the belligerents before that war; that in matters of maritime law a neutral was bound to recognise commissions issued by each belligerent and captures made by each; and where a belligerent did not constitute a sovereign state, it was recognised as a state de facto. As such commissions issued by such belligerent were recognised in wartime as if they had been issued by a sovereign government.

[136] 11 Jurist NS, 400. Law Reports, Admiralty and Ecclesiastical Courts, Browning edn. Vol 1, 1.

[137] *Case Presented on the Part of the Government of Her Britannic Majesty to the Tribunal of Arbitration Constituted Under Article One of the Treaty Concluded at Washington 8 May 1871 Between Her Britannic Majesty and the United States of America* (Richard Bentley and Son, 1872) (hereinafter '*The British Case*') 207–208.

[138] *Ibid* 210.

[139] A key point made in the opinion of Sir Alexander Cockburn.

Britain was an unhappy bystander in this civil war between English speaking peoples and had natural sympathy for a country once its colony. What made it more difficult was its trading relationship with the southern states where 'Cotton was King'. The mills of northern England depended on it. But events destroyed this trade. Fort Sumter surrendered to the Confederates on 13 April 1861, and on 15 April 1861 President Lincoln issued a proclamation calling up 75,000 militia men. On 17 April 1861 Jefferson Davis, President-elect of the Confederate States, published a proclamation inviting applications for Letters of Marque and reprisals against ships and property of the United States and its citizens.[140] Responding to this on 19 April 1861 President Lincoln proposed to blockade Confederate ports. Mr Seward, the United States Secretary of State, assured Britain that the blockade would be conducted according to the recognised rules of public law and with as much liberality towards a neutral, as any blockade ever was by a belligerent.[141] Whilst armed vessels of neutral states would have a right to enter and depart from the interdicted ports, merchant vessels in port at the time of the blockade would be allowed a reasonable time for departure but that was all. This would thereafter prevent mercantile trade between England and the Confederate States following the imposition of a blockade. A considerable number of neutral ships and cargoes were captured for breaches or alleged breaches of the blockade; some at or near the mouth of blockaded ports, others on the High Seas. Such vessels and cargoes were condemned by the United States' courts as prizes and these cases were upheld on appeal to the United States Supreme Court.[142] The losses were estimated by Caleb Cushing, US Attorney General, at $100 million.[143]

A key issue here was whether the President's Proclamation of a blockade was lawful. He had no power to declare war on a state of the Union. A state of civil war was never publicly proclaimed, *eo nomine*, against insurgents, its actual existence was a matter of fact which the Court was bound to notice and to know. As Justice Grier opined, the true test of its existence, as found in the writings of the sages of the Common Law, may be thus summarily stated:

> When the regular course of justice is interrupted by revolt, rebellion, or insurrection, so that the Courts of Justice cannot be kept open, civil war exists and hostilities may be prosecuted on the same footing as if those opposing the Government were foreign enemies invading the land.

He quoted Lord Stowell who observed,

> It is not the less a war on that account, for war may exist without a declaration on either side. It is so laid down by the best writers on the law of nations. A declaration of war by one country only, is not a mere challenge to be accepted or refused at pleasure by the other.[144]

[140] *The British Case* (n 137) 212.
[141] *Ibid.*
[142] *Ibid* 213.
[143] Such claims were outside the scope of the Terms of Reference and Rules agreed under the Treaty of Washington 1871.
[144] 1 Dodson, 247.

In the *Prize Cases*,[145] Justice Grier concluded that the President had a right *jure belli* to institute a blockade of the ports in possession of the states in rebellion which neutrals were bound to respect. In the same case Mr Justice Nelson dissenting held that no state of insurrection existed until the Congress passed legislation on the 13 July 1861. Further, it is arguable that as between 13 April 1861 when Fort Sumter surrendered and 13 July 1861, the proclamation of blockade was not lawful because the President of the United States had no power to declare such blockade either as a matter of international law (Law of Nations) or under Federal law until the Congress had passed the Act. Furthermore, it is arguable that he had no power to declare war on any state in the Union. Although he issued a proclamation for the raising of the militia in early 1861 it is also questionable whether, until the Act of 13 July 1861 was passed, there was no lawful authority for this (at least that was the dissenting view of Mr Justice Nelson in the Supreme Court) in that the Civil War did not indeed exist between the United States and the Confederate States until the Act of Congress was passed on 13 July 1861. The President did not possess the power under the Constitution to declare war or recognise any belligerent rights because that right belonged to the Congress. He had no power to declare the blockade either under international law or under Federal law without congressional approval. If that were the case then the legality of any interdiction of British merchant shipping in a southern Confederate port, which was seized by the Federal forces and confiscated by a Prize Court of United States prior to 13 July 1861, would be questionable. It could be argued that the value of such ships and cargoes ought to have been fairly deducted from any award made by the Tribunal. The Prize Courts were municipal (national) courts which determined property rights in captured goods and vessels at sea. In this case the courts determined the rights of the US Federal Navy to intercept and capture vessels breaching the President's Proclamation of the 15th April 1861 establishing a blockade of the southern Confederate ports.

Of all the countries in the world, Britain by reason of her geographical position, and its extensive trade with the United States in manufacturing and its deployment of military assets and its commercial marine which was dispersed throughout the world, was the Power most immediately and profoundly affected by the Civil War. The Government was thus forced into a position where it had to issue a Proclamation. This Queen's Proclamation required all subjects to observe strict neutrality and to abstain from violating or contravening English law and statute as well as international law. It strictly prevented any British subjects from taking part in any military activity whether by land or sea in the service of or aiding a belligerent state. It specifically prohibited the equipping, furnishing, fitting out for war, arming of any ship or vessel with intent or in order that such ship or vessel would be employed in the service of a belligerent. It also empowered customs and naval officers to make seizures where appropriate. In effect it incorporated the prohibitions of the Foreign Enlistment Act 1819.

[145] *Prize Cases* 67 US (2BI) 635 (1863).

It strictly commanded that no persons whatsoever should commit any act or matter contrary to the statute and warned all subjects that they would forfeit any protection of the state if they became involved in such activities.[146] This proclamation was issued three days after President Lincoln's Proclamation had been officially communicated to Lord Russell.[147] On 1 June 1861 the British Government ordered that any warships of either belligerent including privateers were interdicted and therefore prohibited from carrying prizes into any British port including British colonies or possessions abroad.[148] Both Napoleon III and the Queen of Spain issued similar proclamations.[149] Once Britain had closed its ports to privateers, the Federal Government saw little point in acceding to the Declaration of Paris.[150]

A. Charges in Relation to the *Florida*

Regarding the *Florida*, the British case in summary was that she was built in Liverpool and was built for speed; she was not designed as a ship of war and was unarmed, carrying no guns or ammunition or warlike stores of any kind before she left Liverpool. There was nothing to suggest that she was intended as a warship to cruise against the United States. Charles Francis Adams, the American Minister in London, had suggested that the firm of Fraser Trenholm & Co were instrumental in its purchase. Unfortunately for Adams there was little evidence to sustain any case for seizure. The ship sailed from Liverpool with an English captain. When the vessel arrived in Nassau the ship was placed under surveillance and was eventually seized by order of the governor. She was released and then sailed for the Confederate States. There she was commissioned as a warship and began her hostilities. On the British case there was no breach of national or international law.[151]

B. Charges in Relation to the *Alabama*

So far as the *Alabama* was concerned the British case was that the vessel was built in England and received her armament from England. Supplies were provided for her in England and many of her crew were British subjects. The Law Officers advised at the time that no proceedings could be taken against the

[146] *The British Case* (n 137) 216, 217.
[147] *Ibid* 218.
[148] *Ibid*. Hansard, HC Deb (series 3) 3 June 1861, vol 163, col 471.
[149] *The British Case* (n 137) 218, 219.
[150] Lemnitzer (n 26) 123. He opines that the Proclamation was essential to prevent any misunderstanding or mistake that might lead inadvertently to hostilities and because of the British declaration as to the closure of its ports to privateers there was no need for the United States to accede to the Declaration of Paris 1856.
[151] *The British Case* (n 137) 306, 307.

Alabama save that any natural born British subjects were undoubtedly offenders against the Foreign Enlistment Act. Once outside British territorial waters and jurisdiction no action could be taken against them. The ship was not a piratical craft because it was a vessel armed and commissioned as a public ship of war by the Confederate States and commanded by a Confederate naval officer acting under their authority.[152] The British defence such as it was suggested that the building and delivery of this vessel was a transaction in the ordinary course of the builder's business. The builders John Laird of Birkenhead may have known for what purpose she was intended. The design of the vessel suggested that it was intended for war and not for commerce. Attention was drawn to the vessel on 24 June 1862 by Mr Adams. Evidence was submitted by Thomas Dudley, the United States consul at Liverpool, to the Collector of Customs at that port. Admissible or material evidence tending to prove the existence of an unlawful intention was first obtained by customs officers on 21 July 1862. The evidence was quite insufficient and consisted of one witness statement.[153] Further testimony was obtained on the 23rd and 25th July. The customs officials delayed in taking action due to the need as they saw it of consulting official legal advisers. In the ordinary course of events the Queen's Advocate would have advised, but he was seriously ill at the time and was indisposed. However, on 29 July 1862 the Law Officers[154] gave their opinion that there was sufficient evidence to justify seizure of the *Alabama*. This reached the customs officers too late.[155] Orders for arresting the vessel after her escape from Liverpool were sent by the Government to various places. The *Alabama* sailed and then received her armament 1,000 miles away in the Azores. The guns and ammunition however were procured and exported from England. The *Alabama* was commissioned by the Confederate States and commanded by its officers.[156] Most of the crew were British subjects. The *Alabama* visited several colonies of Britain during the war.[157]

No admission was made in respect of any liability for damages due from Britain to the United States as a breach of any international duty. This was the weakest of all the cases and the failure to arrest the ship was admitted by Sir Alexander Cockburn.[158]

[152] Opinion of the Law Officers, Roundell Palmer and RP Collier. *The British Case* (n 137) 351.

[153] According to Professor Merli, the description given by Thomas Dudley was that the vessel was intended for war use against the United States and that she was the best in her class. Merli (n 134) 48.

[154] The Solicitor General and Attorney General.

[155] This delay was the subject of contention at the time as in the proceedings. Merli in his study absolved Lord Russell of this delay, see Merli (n 134) 49–56. However, the Arbitrators considered otherwise, indeed as we see Sir A Cockburn could not excuse the lack of vigilance.

[156] This was outside British jurisdiction. The United States navy sent a warship the *Tuscarora* to the Irish Sea and it docked at Belfast. Unfortunately, it missed the *Alabama* which sailed onto the Azores where it picked up its guns and crew. See Francis M Carroll, 'Belfast and the American Civil War' (2011) 19(3) *Irish Studies Review* 245–60.

[157] *The British Case* (n 137) 352, 353.

[158] Opinion of Sir Alexander Cockburn.

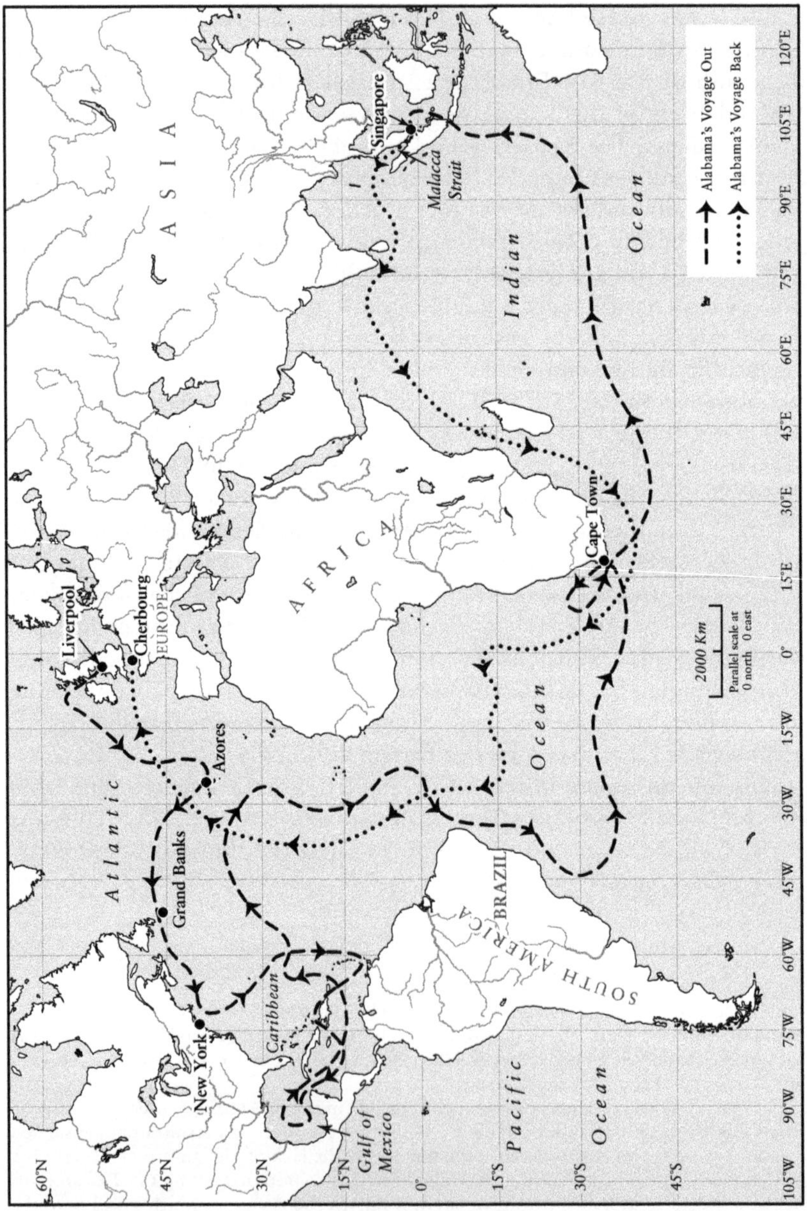

Figure 2.1 Map illustrating the voyage of the CSS *Alabama*

Credit: Mina Moshkeri

C. The *Georgia*

The *Georgia* was a vessel built at Dumbarton in Scotland (it was registered as the *Japan*) and sailed from the port of Greenock. This ship was not fitted out, armed or equipped for war or adapted for warlike use when she sailed. She was constructed as a ship of commerce. After being at sea for nine months, the ship was dismantled and remained in the harbour at Cherbourg and then at Bordeaux. The ship was armed and equipped for war in French territorial waters where she took on board her commander and officers. Her armament was brought from Newhaven in a British steamer. Whilst Charles Adams had received some the information about the *Japan* in London, he did not have sufficient evidence to support proceedings. It appears that some British seamen were recruited, and the ship was then commissioned as the *Georgia* in the Confederate States navy. She was received in the British port colony of the Cape of Good Hope in that capacity. But after having been disarmed, dismantled and sold in a British port she was intercepted by a United States' cruiser. Britain denied any failure of international duty with regard to this vessel.[159]

D. The *Shenandoah*

This steamship was built for commercial purposes for the China trade. It was not fitted out or armed or equipped for war in any manner or degree, nor specially adapted for warlike use in England and appeared to be just an ordinary merchant steamer. The ship sailed from London in October 1864 and was then known as the *Sea King*. There was nothing to indicate any suspicion at the time of sailing that this ship was intended as a cruiser for the Confederates.[160] During the voyage from London she was sold to the Government of the Confederate States. The master, officers and crew had been increased to a compliment of between 70 and 80 men except for officers who numbered about 20. They all embarked as passengers on a ship called the *Laurel* which sailed from Liverpool on 18 October 1864. The *Laurel* also carried armament and munitions for the *Shenandoah*. The *Shenandoah* then proceeded to attack various vessels and captured a number before she arrived at a British colony. On receipt of information from the British consul in Tenerife, the master of the ship, Corbett, was indicted and tried under the Foreign Enlistment Act, but was acquitted by the jury for lack of evidence.[161] The *Shenandoah* was able to make repairs and obtain supplies of coal at Melbourne. A watch was kept on the ship and persons who had boarded it for the purpose of joining her crew were prosecuted and brought to trial.

[159] *The British Case* (n 137) 371–73.
[160] *Ibid* 403, 404.
[161] *Ibid* 405.

Roundell Palmer submitted that no one had been enlisted in the service of the Confederate States whilst the ship had been in Melbourne and that it had in no way violated the neutrality of the port. It was later discovered that people had secretly boarded the ship during the night before she sailed from Australia. The vessel continued to attack United States' vessels after General Lee had surrendered the Confederate Army of Virginia and after all other insurrectionist forces had surrendered.[162] On its arrival back in Liverpool the vessel was seized by the British authorities and was handed over to the Government of the United States as Charles Adams had requested. Britain denied any breach of international duty for which reparations were due.[163]

By way of defence, Roundell Palmer pleaded that neither the *Georgia* nor the *Shenandoah* were ever in any manner or degree fitted out, armed or equipped for war or adapted to warlike use in Britain. They were fitted out as merchant ships. The British Government received no warning of the identity or use to which the ships were to be put to until after they had departed from Britain.[164]

As far as the *Alabama* and *Florida* were concerned, although they were suitable for war they were not armed when they left Britain. They had no armament whatever and did not receive any until they were far outside British territorial waters. As soon as the *Florida* entered the Bahamas, a British colony, she was seized under the authority of the Governor at Nassau, but had to be released for want of proof.[165] In considering this question the Tribunal had to bear in mind that the British Government had to act at all times upon the sufficiency of information and evidence and that Britain had been engaged for a long time in constructing ships for foreign governments in all parts of the world, as well as the equipment and sale of ships of war. There was great difficulty in trying to obtain evidence to prove the actual purpose for which a ship of such character would be constructed. This proved especially difficult in the case of the iron clad rams known as the *Laird Rams* being constructed at Liverpool. Such commercial transactions were legitimate on the face of it. Subsequent transfer of ownership and the embarkation of Confederate crew and officers outside the jurisdiction was beyond means of prevention and made enforcement difficult.[166] In these cases where all the vessels escaped from British ports it was noted that no serious attempts were made by the United States' navy to intercept the ships save in the case of the *Alabama* which was later sunk off Cherbourg. Whilst these particular vessels had escaped, others such as the *Alexandra*, the two iron clads: the *Canton* or *Pampero*, were seized and prevented from taking part in the war.[167]

[162] In its time it destroyed 40 ships and took 1,000 prisoners.
[163] *The British Case* (n 137) 406.
[164] *Ibid* 407.
[165] *Ibid.*
[166] *Ibid* 408.
[167] *Ibid* 409.

In concluding his submissions, Sir Roundell Palmer stated that his client was at an unavoidable disadvantage of having to meet a case which had not yet been presented. They expressed their deep displeasure and regret that such vessels had been procured in British ports. Their procurement had been obtained by means of an artifice and concealment which defeated the vigilance of the customs officials although they were not armed when they left British ports. The charge of injurious negligence on the part of a sovereign government in the exercise of or any other powers of sovereignty had to be sustained on strong and solid grounds. Every sovereign government claimed the right to be independent of external scrutiny or interference in the exercise of these powers. The general assumption was that they were exercised with good faith and reasonable care was taken so that laws were fairly and properly administered. This ought to have subsisted until it was displaced by proof to the contrary. An administrative act founded on error or an erroneous judgment of the court, might, under some circumstances, found a claim for compensation by a person or government injured by the act or judgment. But a charge of negligence brought against a government cannot be supported on such grounds.[168] To make such a claim for compensation for a breach of international duty would be to exact international perfection of administration which few governments or none can attain. Counsel questioned whether a nation is to be held responsible for a delay or omission which had been occasioned by mere accident and not by the want of reasonable foresight or care. In this case it was also necessary to prove that there had been a failure to use means of prevention of an act which the Government was bound to endeavour to prevent, such care as governments ordinarily employ in their domestic concerns, and may reasonably be expected to exert in matters of international interest and obligation.[169] Losses of which such negligence is the direct and proximate cause are commonly not easy to separate from those springing from other causes.[170] It would not be consistent with any reasonable view of international obligations that a belligerent state alleging itself to be aggrieved by some imputed negligence of a neutral government, should on that account, claim indemnity from the neutral for losses in the course of warlike operations which it has not actively and diligently exerted itself to prevent or arrest. In the final analysis, Britain was prepared to accept the award, whether favourable or unfavourable to her, provided it was just. Britain claimed only that it would be founded on 'a true and equitable interpretation of the law of nations for and on principles which Britain itself and all other powers maybe satisfied whether as neutral or belligerent, to acknowledge and abide by in time to come'.[171]

[168] *Ibid* 412.
[169] *Ibid*.
[170] *Ibid* 413.
[171] *Ibid* 413.

VIII. FINAL AWARD OF THE ARBITRATORS

A. The Opinions of Frederick Sclopis

i. Due Diligence

The Tribunal had asked the British counsel to address three particular questions related to 'due diligence', Confederate ships entering British ports and the question as to supplies of coal. Frederick Sclopis' observations on due diligence were that the meaning of due diligence imposed on the neutral that measure of care, and no other, which was required by the ordinary principles of international jurisprudence, and the absence of which constituted negligence. The United States had sought to increase the measure of responsibility they maintained towards belligerents who had a right to require the neutral to enforce its municipal laws and the proclamations of the executive.[172] Sclopis said that at its highest due diligence incumbent on a neutral would require that it should act with regard to the belligerent as it would act in similar circumstances in its own interest.[173] He regarded Article VI as having preference, being founded on general equity, over the municipal law, in this case Article VI of the Treaty would supersede the obligations imposed on Britain by its Foreign Enlistment Act 1819.[174] Sclopis applied the two conditions of the neutrality laid down by Dr L Gessner[175] to take absolutely no part in the war, and to abstain from all that might give an advantage to one of the belligerent parties, and second, not to permit on the neutral territory any proximate hostile act of one party against the other.[176] Sclopis' view was that the neutral should take the initiative where there was a special danger for the belligerent who had no direct means of protecting himself in the circumstances.[177] He reasoned that the greater the actual danger to the belligerent on the territory of the neutral, the more the latter is bound to watch over his neutrality and to prevent it being violated to the profit of either of the belligerents.

ii. British Unfriendliness

Sclopis said that the British Government was fully informed that the Confederates had established 'a branch of their means of attack and defence against United States in England'.[178] Commissioners representing the Confederate

[172] Opinions of Count Sclopis, *Papers Relating to the Treaty of Washington, Opinions of the Arbitrators* Vol IV – Geneva Arbitration (Government Printing Office, 1872) 55–58.
[173] *Ibid* 58.
[174] *Ibid* 59.
[175] *Ibid* 60, referring to L Gessner, *The Law of Neutrality at Sea* (Berlin, 1865) 22.
[176] Gessner, *ibid* 22.
[177] Opinions of Count Sclopis (n 172) 60.
[178] *Ibid* 62.

Government or 'government of Richmond' as Counsel preferred, had a residence in London and put themselves in communication with the British Government. Lord Russell had received Confederate representatives in an unofficial way. In Parliament itself opinions were openly expressed in favour of the Confederates. Against that were the voices of Mr Cobden and Mr Bright which were raised in favour of the United States. Opinion in Britain was so divided that these movements of public opinion formed an atmosphere of agitation which ought to have kept the British Government on its guard.[179] It also seemed to Sclopis that when a vessel had been built and fitted out for war there were strong reasons for believing that it had been purchased for the service of a belligerent and that it would suddenly go to sea. It could be further supposed that at a short distance from territorial waters it would be armed as a warship. Sclopis inclined to the view that this was precisely that which Sir Roundell Palmer as Attorney General had referred to in his speech in May 1864 'to act upon suspicion, or moral belief going beyond suspicion'.[180] 'Such evasions by fragments', he said, 'this complication of different forms of action with one identical object, should not mislead the mind of the judge'.[181]

Sclopis rejected the idea that the generality and breadth of the rule under the Treaty of Washington could be limited by municipal law.[182] In other words he was holding Britain to what was agreed in the Treaty as overriding the interpretation of the duties of a neutral as Roundell Palmer submitted under the Foreign Enlistment Act and international law at the time of the incidents. According to Sclopis, there was a certain amount of feebleness in certain branches of the public services which resulted in great danger to the United States. The British Government, although subject to waves of public opinion, had to exercise diligence equal to the gravity of the danger.[183] Indeed the Law Officers in their opinion dated 12 December 1863 regarding the *Georgia* had advised that the facts resulting from the depositions received 'furnish additional grounds to those already existing for strong remonstrance to the Confederate government on account of the systematic violation of British neutrality by their agents in British Territory'.[184]

The key argument that Count Sclopis put forward was that a ship that was built in such circumstances had violated the sovereignty of the neutral state because she was built with the object of privateering on behalf of one of the belligerents. He referred to the statement of the Attorney General[185] that certain ships or classes of ships could be excluded from British ports if they had violated neutrality, but this power was simply discretionary and had to be exercised with

[179] *Ibid* 63.
[180] *Ibid* 64. Speech of Sir Roundell Palmer, 13 May 1864, House of Commons.
[181] Opinions of Count Sclopis (n 172) 64–65.
[182] *Ibid* 66.
[183] *Ibid* 68.
[184] *Ibid*.
[185] Sir Roundell Palmer, House of Commons, 13 May 1864 in reply to questions by Mr Baring.

regard to the circumstances of a case.[186] Sclopis took the view that where such a ship had escaped but re-entered the territorial waters of the neutral, this compromised the neutral's sovereignty towards the other belligerent. This gave the neutral a right to seize the vessel.

iii. Supplies of Coal

It was common ground between the United States and Britain that there was no violation of international law in furnishing arms to a belligerent.[187] But, what about the supply of coal? If there was an excessive supply of coal used as *res hostilis* then there is an infringement of the second rule of Article IV of the Treaty. Scoplis considered that this was not just enough fuel to sail to a southern port, but fuel to enable it to attack other United States' ships.

iv. The Alabama

Count Sclopis took the view that Mr Adams had warned Lord Russell that the *Alabama* was about to undertake a projected expedition and should be stopped.[188] The Government ascertained that the ship was being built as a warship and it should be watched. But the customs officers took no action. The American consul in Liverpool obtained counsel's opinion from RP Collier QC, MP, who did not hesitate to conclude that the vessel in question could be seized by the principal officer of customs. He advised the consul to apply to the Foreign Secretary for seizure. Five affidavits were produced providing conclusive evidence of the character and destination of the vessel. Mr Collier thought that if the Act was not enforced against the *Alabama* then it would be 'little better than a dead letter'. The Under Secretary of State took no immediate steps and orders were belatedly received on 28 July.[189] That same day the Law Officers gave their opinion confirming Mr Collier's view. Orders were issued on 29 of July accordingly. Before the order could be enforced the *Alabama* escaped. Count Sclopis dismissed the British submission that preserving British neutrality was very complicated and over arduous. In his view the customs officers should have been more attentive, more alert and less prejudiced in favour of a cause which had become popular at Liverpool and other British shipbuilding centres. The customs should have taken prompt action. Britain did not need to wait for information from the belligerent; it should have protected its own neutrality.[190]

[186] Opinions of Count Sclopis (n 172) 72.

[187] Lord Chancellor, House of Lords, 12 June 1871, and Opinions of Count Sclopis (n 172) 74.

[188] Opinions of Count Sclopis (n 172) 75.

[189] Merli (n 134). Merli questions this and took the view that there was no untoward delay.

[190] Opinions of Count Sclopis (n 172) 77. It appears that Customs had good reason to suspect contravention of the Foreign Enlistment Act 1819 and yet did nothing to prevent what the crew suspected that she was a privateer commissioned by Jefferson Davis. Hansard, HC (series 3) 27 March 1863, vol 170, cols 33–40.

However, the *Alabama* took time to sail to the Azores where it rendezvoused with two British ships the *Agrippina* and the *Bahama* which supplied her with guns stores and munitions. Count Sclopis quoted the words of Sir Robert Peel:

> Was it then to be contended that no expedition was a military expedition except the troops had their arms on board the same vessels with them? If they were on board one vessel and their arms in another, did that make any difference? Was such pretence to be tolerated by common sense?[191]

Not only was there deception with regard to her deployment and destination, but on various occasions she replaced the Confederate Stars and Bars with the Union Jack in order to deceive vessels which she was about to attack.[192] After she destroyed the Federal steamer *Hatteras* she was replenished and well received in Jamaica by the British navy.[193] She then went to the Cape of Good Hope and captured a prize; the *Tuscaloosa*. This vessel was seized, but then released on the orders of the British Government as the *Tuscaloosa* was deemed to be a warship.

So far as the *Alabama* was concerned, Count Sclopis decided that the neutrality of Britain was gravely compromised, and consequently Britain was responsible for the acts of this vessel as well as those of the tender *Tuscaloosa*.[194]

v. The Shenandoah *or the* Sea King

The *Shenandoah* or the *Sea King*, as it was known during construction, was built on the Clyde. This was sold to Richard Wright whose son in law was the senior partner in the firm of Fraser Trenholm & Co which acted as shipping agents for the Confederate Government.[195] Despite protestations from Mr Adams and evidence from two sailors on board the vessel, she was allowed to sail; two days later she rendezvoused with a privateer named the *Laurel* in the bay of Madeira and took arms and ammunition on board. Of the 80 British crew members, 23 remained on board. The damning evidence that Count Sclopis found here was the fact that most of the officers on the *Shenandoah* were British subjects.[196] The warship then sailed to Melbourne destroying several Federal merchant navy vessels and their cargoes on a 90 day voyage.[197] In Melbourne she re-equipped effecting repairs and no proceedings were taken against her. Despite the Confederate captain's assurance that no sailors were recruited, a number were clandestinely taken on board the night before she sailed.[198] The *Shenandoah*

[191] Sir Robert Peel, House of Commons, 28 April 1830.
[192] Opinions of Count Sclopis (n 172) 78
[193] There were three British warships in Jamaica at the time. Opinions of Count Sclopis (n 172) 79.
[194] Opinions of Count Sclopis (n 172) 81.
[195] *Ibid* 81.
[196] *Ibid* 82.
[197] *Ibid.*
[198] Ibid 84. Although the Melbourne police kept watch many were able to board the ship due to the terrain in Hobson's Bay and Port Philip.

left Melbourne with 400 tons of coal, 300 tons of which was shipped from Liverpool. It would appear that 60 to 70 sailors joined this ship at Melbourne.[199] The conclusion that Sclopis drew was that Britain was liable within Article VI of the Treaty.

vi. The Florida

This was registered as a British vessel crewed almost entirely by English sailors. When this ship arrived at Nassau, a British naval officer Captain Hickley of *HMS Greyhound* requested the Governor to seize the ship. Although the ship had been arrested and the matter tried, this did not provide a defence to the allegations under Article VI of the Treaty.[200] The Vice Admiralty Court had opined that 'all the circumstances of the case taken together seem sufficient to justify strong suspicion that an attempt was being made to infringe that neutrality so wisely determined upon by Her Majesty's government'.[201]

Whilst the judgment enabled the release of the ship it did not bar the United States from making any claim against Britain *res inter alios acta*.[202] Sclopis found that the Confederate captain had obviously violated the sovereignty and neutral rights of Britain, but also found that taking all the resources which the Florida had obtained at Nassau, Bermuda and Barbados was equivalent to providing a base of naval operations which enabled her to make prize of 14 Federal vessels. He also found that responsibility extended to the cases of the *Clarence*, *Tacony* and *Archer* which acted as tenders to the *Florida*.

B. The Opinions of Viscount D' Italjuba

The question that Viscount D' Italjuba addressed was whether the fact that the vessel held a commission and was built in violation of the laws of a neutral state should be treated in its ports in the same manner as any other warship belonging to a belligerent state and built according to law. The last part of that question 'built according to law' was the key point. If that vessel was built for the Confederacy and its purpose was disguised by fraud without the knowledge of the British Government, it ought to have been seized and detained as it was clearly in violation of British sovereignty and neutrality (it was also in breach of the Foreign Enlistment Act and the Queen's Proclamation). In such case no commission of the Confederacy would provide a defence.[203]

[199] Melbourne Police Evidence, *The British Case* (n 137) 564. Opinions of Count Sclopis (n 172) 87.
[200] Opinions of Count Sclopis (n 172) 92.
[201] *Ibid* 92.
[202] A thing done between others – since the Federal Government were not a party to the proceedings in the Admiralty Court they were free to make their case.
[203] Opinions of Viscount D' Italjuba, *Papers Relating to the Treaty of Washington, Opinions of the Arbitrators* Vol IV – Geneva Arbitration (Government Printing Office, 1872) 96–98.

Having decided this point of law the Tribunal then proceeded through Viscount D' Italjuba to give its own judgment on the specific cases.

i. The Florida

The Tribunal issued the following judgment:

- That the British Government had failed to use due diligence in the exercise of its duties as a neutral.
- Her taking on supplies enlisting a crew and her seizure but subsequent departure was negligent on the part of the British colonial authorities.
- That despite the *Florida* being a confederate cruiser, the vessel was admitted to the ports of British Colonies.
- Britain had therefore failed to fulfil its duties prescribed in the rules laid down in Article VI of the Treaty of Washington and was consequently responsible for acts imputed to the cruiser as well as those in respect of her tenders.[204]

ii. The Alabama

The Tribunal issued the following judgment:

- That the British Government had failed to use due diligence for the fulfilment of its duties as a neutral notwithstanding the repeated warnings and representations of the diplomatic and consular authorities of the United States whilst the *Alabama* was in the course of its construction and such measures as were taken were so late they could not be executed.
- That insufficient measures were taken to arrest the vessel after its escape from Liverpool.
- That despite the infractions of neutrality of Britain this vessel was admitted to its ports.
- That Britain was consequently responsible for the acts of the *Alabama* and her tender the *Tuscaloosa*.[205]

iii. The Shenandoah

The Tribunal issued the following judgment:

- That Britain was not negligent in respect of the *Shenandoah* in terms of her duties as a neutral.

[204] *Ibid* 99.
[205] *Ibid* 100.

- That Britain was not negligent in respect of certain irregularities which occurred at Melbourne due to the deception by the cruiser's commander and the exceptional difficulties of surveillance due to the topography of the area.
- That Britain did not fail in her duties prescribed under Article VI of the Treaty of Washington.[206]

C. The Opinions of Mr Jacques Staempli

Mr Staempli reiterated the guiding principles of the Treaty and the three rules. He then considered aspects of those rules in the context of the international law. He opined that a belligerent had the right to require neutrals to observe their obligations. Due diligence, in his view, meant that the neutral had to be vigilant and take the initiative with the object of discovering and preventing any violation of its own neutrality.[207] The vessel built in Britain could then be detained if it returned to Britain unless it had been sold on. Mr Staempli gave a detailed analysis of the claims relating to the cruisers.[208] In short, he agreed with his colleagues rejecting the objections raised in the British case regarding the *Alabama* finding negligence in not seizing the vessel and in arming and equipping it.[209] As to the *Shenandoah* he found, unlike his colleagues Sir A Cockburn and Count Sclopis, that Britain was liable for the destruction of Federal shipping by the *Shenandoah*.

D. The Opinions of Mr Charles Francis Adams

Mr Adams was formerly the American Minister in London. He was however appointed as the American arbitrator. No objection was taken that he by reason of his former office, had a conflict of interest. This was overlooked as that was entirely obvious to all at the time; it was a matter of public knowledge and with his experience he was undoubtedly qualified for the task. However, as an arbitrator one might question his independence and impartiality, but that could also have been said for Sir Alexander Cockburn.

Adams' first point was as to the meaning of 'due diligence'. The British argued for limitations on the scope of the duty required to prevent breaches of its municipal law.[210] He opined that 'due diligence' was to work with a will. 'Due' he defined through the works of lexicographers from the Latin verb, '*debere*'

[206] *Ibid* 101–103.

[207] Opinions of Mr Jacques Staempli, *Papers Relating to the Treaty of Washington, Opinions of the Arbitrators* Vol IV – Geneva Arbitration (Government Printing Office, 1872) 104, 105.

[208] *Ibid* 108–41.

[209] *Ibid* 123–25.

[210] Opinions of Charles Francis Adams, *Papers Relating to the Treaty of Washington, Opinions of the Arbitrators* Vol IV – Geneva Arbitration (Government Printing Office, 1872) 142–43.

a compound of '*de*' and 'habere' meaning '*quasi de alio habere*', meaning 'to have' or 'from another'. '*Debere*' in Latin means 'to owe', and in French '*devoir*' means debt, duty obligation. In English, Richardson and Webster agreed it was something that was owed and could be demanded or as Adams suggested 'due diligence' was 'earnest labour owed to some other party which that party may claim as its right'.[211] Adams argued that the test as to due diligence was measured by the neutral putting itself in the position of the injured belligerent. One may wonder how Britain would have reacted if the United States had supplied the Fenians with a few warships. A number of ex-soldiers of Irish Union Regiments facilitated the so-called Riel rebellion[212] in 1871 so that this matter may well have been in the minds of the British Government at the time of the arbitration.[213]

On the question of commissions Adams accepted that any vessel recognised as belonging to a sovereign or belligerent power had a right to claim reception in a neutral port under the privilege of extra territoriality. But he distinguished that in the case of the cruisers in question. They had their origins in a systematic and fraudulent abuse of the authority of a neutral power.[214] The outfitting and equipping of the *Alabama*, *Florida*, *Georgia* and *Shenandoah* were in defiance of the Foreign Enlistment Act 1819 and the Queen's Proclamation. Britain therefore had a right to exclude all these vessels from its ports.[215] Adams went so far as to suggest that this was 'quasi-treason' under the law of England even though the officers were not British subjects.[216] Britain's approach was not impartial.

As to the supplying of coal both Federal and Confederate ships were supplied by Britain. The question was whether the supply was simply for enabling the ship to steam home or whether a regular supply constituted a base of operations. This had to be determined according to the evidence in respect of each vessel.

As to the *Florida* there had been a record of

> the most continuous, persistent, wilful and flagrant falsehood and perjury carried on in the British possessions by individuals associated in the American insurgent cause and the British affiliation from the date of the sailing of the *Oreto* in the beginning, to that of the return of the *Shenandoah* to Liverpool, at the close, that has as yet been brought to light in this history.[217]

[211] *Ibid* 143.

[212] The story of this Fenian uprising is told in H Le Caron, *Twenty Five Years in the Secret Service* (William Heineman, 1892). However, the reader must exercise caution with Le Caron's story. Le Caron was a witness at the Special Commission in 1888 and was not seen as a credible witness after being cross examined by Sir Charles Russell QCMP.

[213] Part of the boundary between the United States and Canada was a question to be settled under the Treaty of Washington.

[214] Opinions of Charles Francis Adams (n 210) 146.

[215] *Ibid* 147.

[216] It may be that Adams would have included the Confederate agents in England.

[217] Opinions of Charles Francis Adams (n 210) 151–52.

Adams listed the warnings given to Lord Russell and the apparent lack of vigilance by certain customs officers, one of whom 'probably knew of the fraud'.[218] Adams submitted that the duty of the neutral in these circumstances was to prevent treasonable conspiracy and to expect friendly powers to render such movements and combinations abortive. He concluded that the British Government failed to exercise due diligence to prevent fitting out within its jurisdiction when it had reasonable grounds to believe that this ship was intended to be used to attack the United States' commerce. He suggested that the insurgents and certain British subjects combined to overturn the Federal Government. There was strong evidence in point from Commander McKellop of the British navy as to equipping the *Florida* as an armed cruiser in Nassau. Whilst the Governor General at Nassau instructed McKellop to take preventative measures against the *Florida*, his Attorney General advised that no order could be made.[219] McKellop resigned, but his successor Captain Hickley took the same view that the *Florida* was a warship.[220] Although Hickley had posted an officer on the ship he was told there was no case for seizure. But then the Governor changed his mind and ordered its arrest. When the case came before the local admiralty court, the judge found evidence to justify seizure but nevertheless ordered its release.[221] Adams concluded these facts demonstrated a clear breach of Rule 2 of the Treaty.[222] Following that episode the *Florida* was enabled to cruise for many months on British coal and Britain was liable for breach of each of the three rules of the Treaty in respect of these violations.[223]

As to the *Alabama* Adams protested about the construction of the '290' but the Law Officers advised Lord Russell that: '... the building and equipment of the steamer is a manifest violation of the Foreign Enlistment Act and steps ought to be taken to put that Act in force and to prevent the vessel from going to sea'.[224] But as there was no evidence of a destination she was allowed to proceed. This was despite the US consul in Liverpool giving information to the Collector of Customs. What clearly laid the responsibility upon the British authorities, especially the customs, was the opinion of Mr Collier who concluded that '... he who allows the vessel to leave Liverpool, he will incur a heavy responsibility of which the board of customs, under whose directions he appears to be acting must take their share'.[225] Adams placed responsibility on the customs officers as Mr Collier had advised. So far as the duty of prevention was concerned it appeared that the Collector of Customs 'had chose to look any way for it rather than the right way'.[226]

218 *Ibid* 154–55.
219 *Ibid* 159–62.
220 *Ibid* 162.
221 *Ibid* 163.
222 *Ibid* 166.
223 *Ibid* 171.
224 *Ibid* 172.
225 *Ibid* 175
226 *Ibid* 177.

When the *Alabama* arrived in the Caribbean she destroyed the *US Hatteras* and then put in to Jamaica for repairs. Despite its violation of the sovereignty of Britain and breach of the Queen's Proclamation, it was received without question.[227] Adams contended that the vessel was constructed, equipped and supplied by Britain; that it was crewed by British seamen; that it was provisioned and fuelled by Britain and escaped by reason of absence of due diligence and connivance by HM customs officers.

In relation to the *Tuscaloosa*, Adams said he would find liability if the claim was valid. In relation to the *Florida* he concluded there was no neglect or failure of duty by the British Government.

In respect of the *Shenandoah*, the insurgents, having realised with the arrest and seizure of the *Laird Rams* that speed was of the essence, sought to purchase fast vessels that could be quickly acquired. The *Shenandoah* was purchased in London by a Mr Wright who was a British subject disguising its true purpose. It proceeded to rendezvous with the *Laurel* from Liverpool to obtain its guns and ammunition. The owner was arrested and sent back to England for trial. The *Shenandoah* was allowed to provision in Tenerife. She then proceeded to Melbourne in Australia as explained in the Opinion of Count Sclopis. Adams charged that the replenishment and support given in Australia was in contravention of English law and Britain's pledge of neutrality. He then gave a detailed narrative of the events subsequent to this.

On the basis of the evidence Adams concluded that Britain had failed in her obligations under Rule 2 of the Treaty allowing the *Shenandoah* access to the colony and for its subsequent actions causing damage to the United States. Adams opined that none of the other Confederate vessels which sought shelter and assistance in British ports amounted to breaches of the Treaty rules.

IX. SIR ALEXANDER COCKBURN'S DISSENTING AWARD

Sir Alexander Cockburn, Lord Chief Justice of England, was the arbitrator selected by the British Government to the Geneva arbitration. He presented a number of arguments in his opinion following the submissions of the British Counsel, Sir Roundell Palmer. The British Government submitted that the terms of reference of the Tribunal did not reflect the true state of both the municipal and international laws of neutrality as interpreted by Britain during the American Civil War. For the purposes of the arbitration and for fostering friendly relationships between the two great nations the British Government had accepted the terms of reference as the law applicable to the matters referred.[228]

[227] *Ibid* 179.

[228] Opinions of Sir Alexander Cockburn, *Papers Relating to the Treaty of Washington, Opinions of the Arbitrators* Vol IV – Geneva Arbitration (Government Printing Office, 1872) 230–31.

During the negotiations for the Treaty of Washington the British negotiators wanted to put the facts to the Tribunal to decide *lex fori* but the United States insisted on principles governing the arbitration to be negotiated and agreed before referring the dispute to the Tribunal.[229] The British Government conceded those rules in order to improve the relationship with the United States. Cockburn submitted that the problem was the rules were rather general and imprecise, in particular the key words 'due diligence'. Negligence was not defined and in those days before the advent of a sensible definition[230] the words were open to interpretation. In 1872 every country generally accepted that 'due diligence' meant whether by reference to a contractual obligation or due care to avoid harm to the person or property of others – *ne alienum laedat*.[231] The Treaty was an admission by Britain as to the equipment of the ships which Cockburn submitted was not in accord with its neutrality obligations under international law. The degree of diligence required was to be determined by principles of international law or whatever the nature of the obligation.[232] Cockburn accepted that any breach of international law was regarded as part of English Common Law which would result in an offence against the law of England. The key problem for the Tribunal was to interpret the extent to which a neutral owed one belligerent a duty to prevent its subjects aiding another belligerent. But if the neutral exercised proper due diligence to prevent the law being broken, why then should the neutral be liable?[233] The question was whether a neutral could prohibit its subjects from undertaking commercial business with a belligerent. The key point as Cockburn stated was the distinction between assistance to a belligerent *animo adjuvendi* to overcome its enemy and *animo commerciandi* – in the way of a trade or commerce.[234] A neutral state could not simply supply one belligerent against another, but a subject of that state could. A neutral state could trade with a belligerent, although the other belligerent could intercept to forfeit any contraband of war. The restraints imposed upon a neutral were in Cockburn's view 'manifestly in derogation of the common right of peaceful trade which all maritime nations enjoyed in time of peace'.[235] Thus, the US navy could bar a neutral ship from trading with the Confederates. If British ships transported Confederate goods those goods were subject to seizure; the British flag was no protection. Similarly, a neutral was prohibited from having its goods carried in a belligerent ship because they will be subject to seizure by another belligerent.[236] Although neutrals had a right to trade with belligerents, they were

[229] *Ibid* 231.

[230] This came about when Lord Atkin famously defined negligence by reference to a duty to one's neighbour in the leading case of *Donoghue v Stevenson* [1932] 1 AC 562.

[231] Opinions of Sir Alexander Cockburn (n 228) 233.

[232] There was a problem here for the British case in that the Swiss arbitrator, Mr Staempfli, a former President of the Swiss Confederation, opined that international law did not exist.

[233] Opinions of Sir Alexander Cockburn (n 228).

[234] *Ibid*.

[235] *Ibid* 237.

[236] The Declaration of Paris 1856.

subject to search and seizure of contraband of war.[237] In Cockburn's submission this did not mean that British subjects trading contraband in defiance of the Federal blockade constituted a violation of neutrality. The Government was not a party to the trade.[238] Cockburn quoted Hautefeuille who opined that coal and unarmed ships were not contraband of war.[239] Hautefeuille could not be relied upon however because he did not consider anything to be contraband except what was capable of being immediately supplied for the purposes of destructive warfare. But Cockburn conceded that an armed and manned ship was an efficient instrument of warfare. He also conceded that coal which provided the motive power of the vessel was in the same category as masts and sails, ie contraband.[240] It was the view of one jurist Lampredi that goods did not become contraband of war until they had left the neutral territory.[241] Cockburn submitted that it was not so much the sale of munitions to belligerents within the territory of the neutral that gave rise to the problem, but rather the actual conveyance of the weapons or soldiers in assisting a belligerent.[242] However, Cockburn was at pains to point out that the views of jurists, no matter how eminent, were not decisive.[243] International law was not settled by jurists but by the common consent of nations as matters of common practice. In fact, such a position was taken by Thomas Jefferson in 1793 regarding the French purchase of munitions and weapons in America during the Napoleonic wars. Jefferson could not suppress the private arms trade of American citizens. They were free to export and were not to be interfered with by the Collector of Customs.[244] During the Crimean War the United States supplied munitions to France and Britain and also transported troops, provisions and munitions to the Crimea, as well as bringing home their sick and wounded.[245] Britain supplied £2,000,000 worth of arms and munitions to the Federal Government during the Civil War.

If Cockburn was to succeed in this case, he had to demonstrate that what the British Government did was not a breach of the laws of neutrality. In support of this he argued that there was no difference between the sale of a ship and the sale of other articles for warlike use prior to 1861 because no one distinguished between ships which could receive arms and those which were armed.

[237] Supplying articles of contraband of war by way of trade (or what he called passive trade) was inconsistent with the duties of a neutral. Hautefeuille. Opinions of Sir Alexander Cockburn (n 228) 244.

[238] Opinions of Sir Alexander Cockburn (n 228) 239.

[239] *Ibid* 240.

[240] The weight of juridical authority supported this view – Opinion of Martens, Tetens, Galiani, Hübner, Piantanida, Rutherford, Lord Stowell, Chancellor Kent, Heffter, Ortolan and Sir Robert Phillimore.

[241] Opinions of Sir Alexander Cockburn (n 228) 241.

[242] In the cases of the *Alabama* and the *Florida*, it was the construction and escape of warships with weapons and crew taken from a neutral country and the ships then being armed at sea.

[243] He referred to the 'lucumbrations of learned professors or speculative jurists' who cannot make law.

[244] Opinions of Sir Alexander Cockburn (n 228) 245.

[245] *Ibid* 246.

It was the equipping and arming that was a violation of neutrality once hostilities had begun.[246] A distinction was to be drawn between a ship that was contraband merchandise sent to a belligerent for sale, and another ship fitted out and immediately ready to cruise against the commerce of any nation with whom the neutral was at peace. In the latter case the neutral had a duty to prevent such expedition. In the former case, it was for the belligerent to prevent that ship from being used.[247] If the *Alabama* was made to order as a warship it was the view of M Ortolan that it was a breach of neutrality.[248] Also if she was sent out on a military enterprise it would be a breach of neutrality as organising aggression against a friendly state.[249] Cockburn emphasised this point by submitting that the sending of a hostile expedition was plainly a violation of neutrality under international law and one which the neutral government would be under a duty to prevent.[250] Importantly he also admitted that sending out a ship without its crew or armament which were transported by a different vessel and put on board at some place outside the jurisdiction of the neutral made no difference. The ship, armament and crew, although sent out separately, were part of the same enterprise or undertaking. Taken together they constituted a hostile expedition.[251]

Cockburn further submitted that the Tribunal could not judge the case on the basis of what the law should be, but on what it was as stated in the Treaty. In support he referred to the *Santissima Trinidad*. The case concerned a ship that was built and armed in Baltimore and instead of heading northwest it went to Buenos Aires and was sold to the Argentine Government which was then at war with Spain. It came back to the United States and took on board a crew and operated against Spain. This was held to be a commercial venture.[252] Justice Story held:

> The question as to the original illegal armaments and outfit of the *Independencia* may be dismissed in a few words. It is apparent, that though equipped as a vessel of war, she was sent to Buenos Aryres on a commercial venture, contraband, indeed, but in no shape violating our laws or our national neutrality. If captured by a Spanish ship

[246] *Ibid* 247. A key point mentioned by the Solicitor-General in the debate on the 27 March 1863 was that it was not illegal under international law nor English law to send an armed vessel or munitions for sale in a foreign port because it was deemed at that time a commercial venture. He also pointed out that in America the collectors were not empowered to detain a vessel even if armed unless the owners intended hostilities against a state with whom the United States was then at peace. Hansard, HC Deb (series 3) 27 March 1863, vol 170, col 49.

[247] Opinions of Sir Alexander Cockburn (n 228) 249.

[248] From a design point of view the evidence appears to be that the *Alabama* was designed as a warship in terms of its compartmentalisation below decks for storage of ammunition, crew and coal storage, as well as its twin-screw propellers which could be raised. More suspiciously its funnel could be lowered so as to disguise its true intentions.

[249] Opinion of Bluntschli quote by Sir Alexander Cockburn. Opinions of Sir Alexander Cockburn (n 228) 250.

[250] Opinions of Sir Alexander Cockburn (n 228) 254.

[251] *Ibid* 254–55.

[252] *Ibid* 251.

> of war during the voyage, she would have been justly condemned as a good prize for being engaged in a traffic prohibited by the law of nations. But there is nothing in our laws, or in the law of nations, that forbids our citizens from sending armed vessels, as well as munitions of war, to foreign ports for sale. It is a commercial adventure which no nation is bound to prohibit, and which only exposes the person engaged in it to the penalty of confiscation. Supposing, therefore, the voyage to have been for commercial purposes, and the sale at Buenos Aryres to have been a bona fide sale, (and there is nothing in the evidence before us to contradict it) there is no pretence to say that the original outfit on the voyage was illegal, or that a capture made after the sale was, for that cause alone, invalid.[253]

The judgment of Justice Story may have been in the mind of Charles Adams when acting as the American Minister in London. He wrote to Earl Russell on 6 April 1863 stating:

> The sale and transfer by a neutral of arms, of munitions of war, and *even of vessels of war*, to a belligerent country, not subject to blockade at the time, as a purely commercial transaction, is decided by these authority is not to be unlawful. They go not a step further; and precisely to that extent I have myself taken no exception to the doctrine.[254]

In the course of further submissions, Cockburn submitted that it would have been against considerations of humanity if the English Colonists in America fighting for their independence from Britain had been unable to acquire warships.[255] Where a small nation was fighting a great nation it would be against the laws of humanity to deprive them of a means of self-defence which they were unable to provide for themselves.[256]

Cockburn was at pains to explain that in the Queen's Proclamation British subjects were warned that any person offending against the laws of neutrality in assisting or giving aid to one or other of the belligerents would be liable to penal consequences. That was a consequence of the Foreign Enlistment Act 1819. Such persons would also forfeit any right to protection of the state in the event of arrest or seizure by a belligerent; that was a matter of international law.[257] Cockburn's central point was that Britain had complied with her international and municipal law obligations. But he then had to deal with a key accusation by the United States that Britain had failed to prevent the escape of, and the damage caused by, the cruisers. Furthermore by its failure it had not exercised proper due diligence in or about its obligations under municipal and international law.[258]

[253] Cited in *ibid* 251–52.
[254] *Ibid* 253.
[255] *Ibid* 254.
[256] Such an argument might well be raised to justify President Roosevelt's supply of munitions and armaments to Britain during World War II.
[257] Opinions of Sir Alexander Cockburn (n 228) 259.
[258] *Ibid* 260. The unfortunate circumstance here was that the customs in Liverpool despite repeated warnings failed to take action that they were authorised to take and should have acted sooner. In the United States the customs could rely on the courts which sat regularly to deal with such cases. Hansard, HC Deb (series 3) 27 March 1863, vol 170, col 55.

Thus Cockburn argued that it was not a matter of *ex facto jus oritur* in that the matter could be decided on the facts of the individual case, but a need to apply the general principles of jurisprudence to guide the arbitrators in judging how far the obligations of Britain had or had not been satisfied.[259] So the question at issue was what standard of due diligence should have been observed by the Government of Britain to ensure the obedience of its subjects in matters of neutrality. The interpretation of the American Counsel and Attorney General, Caleb Cushing, was too wide and vague. A more concise definition was required to be consistent with that degree of diligence and attention which can be exercised by men of ordinary capacity.[260] But perhaps a more persuasive authority was that of Justice Story who opined that it may not be possible to lay down a very exact rule applicable at all times and in all circumstances but it: 'may be said to be common or ordinary diligence in the sense of the law which men of common prudence generally exercise about their own affairs in the age and country in which they live'.[261]

English law took the same approach as Justice Story in so far as the true test of negligence was whether: 'there had been, with reference to a particular subject matter, a reasonable degree of diligence and care for which a man of ordinary prudence and capacity might be expected to exercise in the same circumstances'.[262] Cockburn observed that the degree of diligence required related to the state of municipal law, the means possessed by it to prevent infractions, and to the diligence to be used accordingly. A neutral government had to ensure that the prohibitive element of the law would prohibit acts contravening neutrality, but that it would also mete out adequate punishment. As regards to the preventative element of the law, a government should be armed with power to prevent such infractions when it knows or has reasonable ground to believe that such an infraction is about to take place. Cockburn was at pains to explain that proof had to be required to prosecute and punish the offender following investigation. In this case Cockburn was of the view that the Government could not be held liable for a 'mere error of judgment'. Suspicious circumstances were insufficient. But if the Government seized the vessel and proper proceedings were undertaken it could not be held responsible if that vessel was then permitted to leave the jurisdiction.[263] The judiciary was independent of the executive and the Government could not interfere. The question then arose whether that Government used all the means to prevent offences and acted honestly and diligently for the benefit of those who were entitled to its protection.[264] Where the

[259] Opinions of Sir Alexander Cockburn (n 228) 261.

[260] *Ibid* 263, citing the Opinion of Stubenrauch and others. See *Stubenrauch, Comm. Zum allg.öst. B. Gesetzbuch* 1294–97.

[261] Opinions of Sir Alexander Cockburn (n 228) 264 and J Story and E Bennett, *Commentaries on the Law of Bailments*, 7th edn (Little, Brown and company, 1863).

[262] Opinions of Sir Alexander Cockburn (n 228) 264.

[263] This happened in the case of the *Tuscaloosa*.

[264] Opinions of Sir Alexander Cockburn (n 228) 266–67.

Government acted in good faith desiring honestly to fulfil its obligations it would be difficult to find it liable for errors of judgement unless such was of so patent a character as to amount to *crassa negligenta*; gross negligence.[265]

Cockburn presented this part of his arbitral Opinion in the context of a comprehensive and well-reasoned interpretation of the key principles of the law. Whilst in principle his opinions were sound, in law the problem was in the context of good faith and honesty as the evidence of abuse in terms of the frequency with which rebel cruisers were supplied, crewed, fuelled, repaired and harboured in British ports appear to contravene his concluded opinions.

X. THE FOREIGN ENLISTMENT ACT 1819

The United States had charged that the English statute was inadequate in terms of enforcement, but when Cockburn compared it to the United States Foreign Enlistment Act 1818 the language was identical save that the English statute was more stringent. The English Act was stricter because, whereas the United States Act provided for fitting out and arming which was conjunctive in terms of interpretation; the English Act was disjunctive. In both cases the Acts were specifically designed to prevent the neutral state from being used for fitting out privateers and hostile expeditions.[266] Cockburn argued that the powers were there in the English Act in the cases of the *CSS Alabama* and the *CSS Florida* but the evidence was not. In terms of official procedures, Cockburn acknowledged the affective use of District Attorneys in the United States who could investigate and produce evidence in reporting matters to the Federal Government. In 1870, a new English Act was passed which reversed the burden of proof against the owner and made it an offence to build such vessels without any question of intention being required.

Lincoln's Proclamation of the blockade was communicated to Lord Russell by Mr Dallas on 11 May 1861. Only after such confirmation was the Queen's Proclamation published on the 14th of May 1861 declaring that both parties in the Civil War were belligerents. Cockburn explained that when Lincoln referred to a war between the states Britain had no alternative under international law other than to declare both sides belligerents.[267] In his view the Treaty of Washington required Britain to use due diligence to prevent the equipping of ships as a matter of neutral obligation and not as a matter of municipal law. In determining whether Britain acted accordingly the Tribunal had to look at the relative position of the parties at the time of the offence. It was to be judged by those obligations in force at the time.[268] In his analysis of liability for the

[265] *Ibid* 267.
[266] *Ibid* 270–71.
[267] *Ibid* 324.
[268] *Ibid* 367.

escape of the *Alabama*, Cockburn considered the Opinion of the Law Officers who gave their view in the absence of the Queen's Advocate who was ill at the time. The reference to the Law Officers and the delay that was incurred through the Queen's Advocate's illness was explicable, but not the need for the reference. The Law Officers' Opinions supported an earlier Opinion by Mr Collier of the Temple given on 23 July 1862 but the officers went further to advise that on the witnesses' dispositions it was clear that the vessel known as No 290 *CSS Alabama* was intended for warlike use. It was constructed as a vessel of war, there were gun sockets, there was a magazine and there were placements for shot and canister rows on the decks.[269] Counsel concluded:

> We, therefore, recommend that without loss of time that the vessel be seized by the proper authorities after which an opportunity will be afforded to those interested previous to condemnation to alter the facts, if it may be, and to show an innocent destination of the ship.[270]

Cockburn entirely agreed with the Opinion of Sir Robert Collier that the duty fell to the collector of customs at Liverpool as on the 22nd July 1862 the customs officials could have detained the vessel.[271] He did not need to refer to counsel for a legal opinion. It was an error of judgment and it was also plain and unmistakable. Cockburn considered that there was an absence of due diligence which ought to have been exercised. In effect he concluded that the Government had a 'common liability'. The *CSS Alabama* had only sailed 50 miles from Liverpool to a point off the Welsh Coast and remained there until the 31st of July.[272] During that time she could have been seized and arrested.[273] Cockburn considered on the evidence that the *CSS Alabama* was equipped by being prepared to receive her armament in England, crewed, armed and prepared for immediate warfare – all this he regarded as part of one hostile expedition issuing from a British port. He concluded: 'the liability of Britain, in respect of want of due diligence, is established by the facts'.

When deciding the question of interest payable on the US claims, Cockburn argued that such an imposition was extraordinary because in an ordinary case Britain would have been able to seek an indemnity from the Confederate States of America if it had won the war. As it was the Confederate States were reunited

[269] *Ibid* 457.

[270] *Ibid* 458.

[271] The customs surveyors at Liverpool were Edward Morgan and Samuel Price Edwards and it was the junior of the two, Edwards, who inspected the *Alabama* on the 28th June but reported that he had seen nothing that might require a 'special report'. This is quite surprising when one reads the Opinion of Mr Collier QC who clearly concluded there was sufficient evidence to detain the ship from the factual evidence submitted to him by Mr Dudley the American consul. See Merli (n 134) 56, 65–68.

[272] The Law Officers' Opinion was available on the 30th July. Adams ordered USS *Tuscarora* to the Irish Sea in early July. HMS *Ajax* was in Belfast at this time. Either of these warships might have intercepted the *Alabama*. See Carroll (n 156) 245–60.

[273] Opinions of Sir Alexander Cockburn (n 228) 460.

with the northern states and as such were in fact the Claimant in the arbitration. Since the Confederate States ceased to exist Britain had no recourse against the Confederacy. However, Cockburn argued that it was the Confederate States that had caused the damage to the United States' shipping and its citizens' property, not the British Government. But the fact was that the ships were built, crewed, armed, fuelled, repaired and harboured in Britain and its colonies which questioned the charge that this was all caused by the Confederacy.

Cockburn's Opinion was in fact a dissenting opinion and in it he dismissed all the indirect or consequential claims of the United States. He found some liability in respect of the *CSS Alabama*, but none in respect of the *CSS Florida* or the *CSS Shenandoah* and no claim for interest. His conduct at the end of the arbitration was subject to some criticism, but it must be said that the arguments he raised, as explained above, were well put and opened an interesting debate as to a neutral state's obligations in time of war.

A. Comment

It is useful to look at the conflicting legal analysis during the American Civil War as described by FE Smith KC, as he then was (later Lord Birkenhead, Lord Chancellor of England), writing in 1903. He considered the vexed question of belligerents using neutral ports. He referred to Canning who in 1823 adhered to the American view as to the illegality of fitting out and arming French ships in American ports to attack British ships during the Napoleonic wars. In 1793 it was accepted by President George Washington and Secretary, Thomas Jefferson, that such fitting out was contrary to the laws of neutrality and Washington's Government immediately issued orders prohibiting the fitting out and arming of such ships. Canning said that this was 'incompatible with the sovereignty of the United States and tended to interrupt the peace and good understanding which subsisted between that country and Britain'.[274] It was also the opinion of Thomas Jefferson that the right of raising troops was a sovereign right and that

> … no foreign power or person can levy men within its territory without its consent … If the United States have a right to refuse the permission to arm vessels and raise men within their ports and territories, they are bound by the laws of neutrality to exercise that right, and to prohibit such armaments and enlistments.[275]

What Smith identified in the *Alabama* case was the problem of whether a neutral power could supply arms and military equipment to belligerents.[276] The better

[274] FE Smith, *International Law* (Georgean Morang & Co Ltd, 1903) 134.

[275] *Ibid* 135. *Thomas Jefferson to American Ambassador in Paris*. American State Papers I, 116. It is extraordinary that Smith himself, a close associate of Sir Edward Carson KC, supported the raising of the Ulster Volunteers, a private army, to oppose the Home Rule legislation in England in 1912. This was quite contrary to the principle he espoused regarding national sovereignty.

[276] Smith (n 274) 135.

view was that sales were inconsistent with the duties of a neutral. But those individuals independent of the Government who trade in arms to belligerents were subject to a different test and standard. Such people do not compromise their Government's neutrality, but as Smith opines where this occurs the belligerent who does not receive those arms is entitled to repress that arms traffic. Such arms traffickers who supplied the Confederacy therefore did so at their peril. But was the Government under any duty to restrain them? Smith quoted Justice Storey as saying 'in the law of nations that forbids our citizens from sending armed vessels as well as munitions of war to foreign ports for sale. It is a commercial adventure which no nation is bound to prohibit'.[277] More pointedly the question in the *Alabama* was whether it set out on an expedition or was the vessel an object of contraband? The problem was that the Foreign Enlistment Act 1819 prohibited the equipping of the vessel for war, in other words the vessel would be incapable of attack or defence. So, if such vessel sailed, the Government was under no duty to prevent it. Baron Bramwell, as Smith points out, contemplated precisely the circumstances that arose in the *Alabama* case and ruled that in such case the 'spirit of international law may be violated, and the letter and spirit of municipal law evaded'.

In the *Alabama* case the Commissioners of Customs followed Bramwell's guidance that if the ship had no means of attack or defence she was regarded as not as within the Foreign Enlistment Act 1819 as she was not so equipped. Also, the authorities were unaware at the time of the sailing of the *Agrippina* and the *Bahama* which equipped the cruiser off the Azores.

XI. RESULTS OF THE ARBITRATION AND EFFECT

In considering the Award of the Tribunal as with all arbitrations this case resolved the case on the particular terms of the referral contained in the Treaty of Washington. It resolved the dispute by way of an award of damages regarding the hostile action committed by the *Alabama*, *Florida* and other vessels provided to the insurgent states.

As to the extent of that provision these include the two named above, together with the *Gladiator*, *Economist*, *Southwark*, *Hercules*, *Kate*, *Georgia*, *Alexandra*, *Tuscaloosa* and the *Shenandoah (Sea King)*.[278] So far as international and English law was concerned at the time there was no prohibition against a private concern exporting arms from a neutral to a belligerent country. FE Smith regarded it as a legitimate branch of commerce subjecting the goods to seizure as contraband which did not involve the government. But he also opined that the Government had a duty to prevent its subjects from handing over a commissioned

[277] *The Santissima Trinidad* 7 Wheaton 346; Smith (n 274) 136.

[278] In the proceedings 29 vessels were mentioned but not all were built in Britain.

armed vessel to a belligerent within neutral territory.[279] The fact that these ships were crewed by English sailors and provisioned with armaments and supplies gave these transactions the aspect of a warlike expeditionary force.

A. US Claims Tribunals

The damages award of $15,500,000 was paid in gold by Britain. It was subsequently subject to claims by United States' citizens in respect of their claims regarding vessels and property destroyed or damaged by the Confederate cruisers. The United States Congress passed an Act to appoint five suitable persons who should constitute a court to be known as the Court of Commissioners of *Alabama* claims.[280] Three judges constituted a quorum. The concurrence of all three judges was required to make a judgment or decide any question. The Court sat in Washington for a term of one year, subject to an extension of six months. All claims were required to be submitted within six months of the Court convening. The rules of the Court closely followed the rules of procedure and practice of the Circuit Courts of the United States. Interestingly, the Court's jurisdiction was confined to direct claims resulting from damage caused by the cruisers *Alabama*, *Florida* and *Shenandoah*. The Federal Government was not admitting any claims for the alleged indirect losses which were originally suggested in negotiations between the United States and Britain. Only those owing allegiance to the United States during the Civil War were qualified to claim.[281] Claimants could claim interest at four per cent per annum, not six per cent as awarded by the Geneva Tribunal to the Federal Government. The just and reasonable expenses of counsel were allowed. These tribunals adopted the time rule of the Supreme Court of United States for oral argument of counsel.

XII. DIPLOMATIC REFLECTIONS ON THE AMERICAN CIVIL WAR

In terms of dispute resolution, the attempt in the United States to resolve the differences between North and South in February 1861 under the chairmanship of President Tyler was a failure.[282] Irreconcilable differences simply emphasised the political division. When the war came the South pinned its hope on 'King Cotton' and the effect it would have in Europe, particularly Britain, whose upper class they thought would support their cause. But the British Government which included Prime Minster Palmerston, and Lord Russell his Foreign

[279] Smith (n 274) 138.

[280] J Bassett Moore, *History and Digest of the Arbitrations to Which the United States has been a Party. International Arbitrations* (Forgotten Books, 2018) Ch K, 4639.

[281] A total of 1,382 claims were presented by way of petition to the Court. Bassett Moore (n 280) Ch K, 4644.

[282] This is told in Mark Tooley, *The Peace That Almost Was* (Nelson Books, 2015).

Secretary, although appearing to Adams to give licence to the South, were waiting to see how events unfolded. It was a policy of 'wait and see'. But the South did not help itself as Professor Merli suggested. Its diplomacy was 'inept, naïve and ill timed' especially in the autumn of 1862 when Britain nearly intervened. Antietam was decisive in Russell's evaluation.[283] Merli opines that if the South's agent Captain James D Bulloch had succeeded in securing the escape of the two *Laird Rams* with large calibre rifled shell guns and a ram they could well have broken the Union blockade and the war might well have gone in favour of the South.[284] Although Adams was critical of the Queen's Proclamation, Merli's view was that it prevented some accident that might have led to another Anglo-American war.[285] Cotton was no longer King and because of the glut of 1861, the cotton famine was not as bad as might have been. The economic effect on Britain was not so severe. Gladstone, then Chancellor of the Exchequer, managed to produce a £3.75 million surplus in 1862–1863. Whilst the North sent Charles Francis Adams to London, the South sent William L Yancy and James M Mason, neither of whom distinguished themselves or their compatriots. The Confederate Secretary of State who was English, Judah P Benjamin,[286] was also unable to befriend the British Government.[287] The result of the secret dealings of Confederate agents to flout the Foreign Enlistment Act and abuse British neutrality was that the British Government became increasingly wary of southern attempts to procure vessels and impounded the *Rams* buying them for the Royal Navy. Above all, however sympathetic certain parts of the British population might be to North or South, Britain had no interest in getting involved. In his work Professor Merli sought to exonerate the ministry of Palmerston and Russell as to the charges relating to *The Alabama's* escape. That is not the object of this exercise as that would be to undermine both the findings of the Arbitral Tribunal and those opinions of Mr Collier and Sir A Cockburn. The Tribunal's Award stands as it was even if historians quarrel about the events. The fact remains that the *Alabama* was built in Britain, crewed with British sailors under the command of Confederate officers in an act of rebellion against the lawful constitutional government of the United States with whom Britain was at peace and in respect of the insurrection was neutral. Belligerent status did not permit the sending of a maritime expedition or naval units to fight for the South. What this episode in Anglo-American relations showed was that whereas Britain had been 'sovereign of the seas' master of maritime law and the laws of war, neutrality and blockade as she was not instrumental in this war, she was unable to set the laws directly. This was taken over by the Federal Government and after the arbitration America and Britain developed further interest in this area.[288]

[283] Merli (n 134) ix.
[284] *Ibid* 25.
[285] *Ibid* 7.
[286] Lawyer and author of *Benjamin on Sale of Goods* published after the war in England in 1868.
[287] Merli (n 134) 12–13.
[288] *Ibid* 44.

XIII. LESSONS OF THE GENEVA ARBITRATION

The major lesson of this arbitration was that it prevented a war between a great Power and an emerging Power and settled outstanding grievances between these states. This was undoubtedly facilitated by a common language and a common law. Its effect gradually was to forge a new relationship and essential trust which led to closer ties and common foreign policy objectives in certain areas. In later years, the US shadowed UK foreign policy to an extent; while there had been a *Pax Britannia* when Britain ruled the waves with her unrivalled naval power, the United States developed a *Pax Americana* after 1945. We shall see with Presidents Teddy Roosevelt and Howard Taft, two statesmen who believed firmly in international law, and that arbitration could resolve conflicts between sovereign states with competing interests.

From an international perspective, there is no doubt that the Geneva Arbitration led to an expectation amongst jurists and some statesmen that international arbitration was a useful mechanism that would resolve disputes between nation states and thus avoid war. This heralded anticipation that the new century would be peaceful and may have inspired the work of The Hague Peace Conferences of 1899 and 1907. Also, there was renewed interest in the process evident from the publication of five volumes of the *History and Digest of Tribunals* published in 1904. The great work of John Bassett Moore listed 228 instances of arbitral disputes between 1791 and 1901. Moore's work indicates that the Geneva Arbitration gave impetus to the process of settling disputes between states in that he recorded 91 cases prior to 1872 and 137 between 1872 and 1901.[289] Contrary to expectations during this period up to the First World War, Europe became an armed camp and despite a movement for arms limitation, as well as a certain accommodation of German imperial ambitions by Britain and France, war between the two European camps; the Triple Alliance and the Triple Entente, became inevitable. Although diplomacy was unable to avoid the catastrophe of 1914 it did manage two important achievements. The first was The Hague Peace Conference of May 1899.

The Russians proposed a plan of inclusive and limited compulsory arbitration, but this was rejected and an Anglo-American proposal for a 'Permanent Court of Arbitration'[290] was adopted despite German objections. This scheme was to be applied 'in questions of judicial character, and especially regarding interpretation of treaties.[291] In addition a code of arbitral proceedings was adopted. Questions as to the rights and duties of neutrals were left to the Second Hague Conference in June 1907 delayed by the intervening Russo-Japanese War, a Russian Revolution

[289] A Hershey, 'History of International law since the Peace of Westphalia' (1912) 6 *American Journal of International Law* 30–69.

[290] This was a panel or list of arbitrators.

[291] Art 16 First Hague Convention.

and the Third Pan-American Conference. However, at the conference a Convention of 97 articles was agreed on the Pacific Settlement of International Disputes, a convention as to the status of enemy merchant ships upon the outbreak of hostilities, the adaption of the Geneva Convention of 1906 to maritime warfare, the rights of capture in maritime warfare and regulations regarding the disposition of crews of enemy merchant ships captured by a belligerent-14 articles and a convention of 33 articles respecting the rights and duties of neutral powers in naval warfare. It is arguable that this would not have been achieved but for the Geneva Arbitration. Despite this the conference failed to agree a scheme of obligatory arbitration and, as we shall see in chapter five, this was opposed by Germany and Austria-Hungary. However, there was some support for a United States' proposal for exclusive limited compulsory arbitration.[292] Further to this in 1909 the leading naval powers met in London and agreed a declaration which produced a code of rules and discussed a possible Judicial Arbitral Court. The conference underlined the issues argued at the Geneva Arbitration, finally agreeing a universal application of a code of rules regulating the rights of neutrals and belligerents with respect to neutral commerce. The rules covered the matters of blockade, contraband, continuous voyage, hostile aid or neutral service.[293] This was timely considering what was about to happen five years later.

From a national perspective however, FE Smith was undoubtedly correct when he identified the issue as being whether a neutral nation was bound to use due diligence to prevent the equipping and outfitting in its territorial waters of a vessel intended for the military or naval service of a belligerent. The sixth article of the Treaty of Washington imposed such a duty on a neutral and this in effect withdrew from the Arbitration the deliberation of the only question of international law which could be determined on the facts. This unsound direction of the law fortunately was not followed in any succeeding international arbitration.[294]

But perhaps the legacy of the Geneva Arbitration was Gladstone's remarks in a debate in the House of Commons on 6 February 1873, when he said:

> The serious question is, whether arbitration is not a comparative blessing when being resorted to without the slightest sacrifice of honour, it becomes the means by which worse, far worse, results can be avoided? And by those far worse results I do not only refer to the contingency of war, much less the mere cost of war; but refer to the planting of habitual and perpetual discord between countries that every consideration of interest and duty ought to lead into closest alliance. For the avoidance of mischief such as this-even without speaking of the avoidance of bloodshed-arbitration, whatever inconvenience it may entail, is, in my opinion, to be hailed as a great blessing.[295]

[292] A total of 35 states supported the proposal and nine voted against with three abstentions.

[293] *The Declaration of London, A Collection of Official Papers and Documents Relating to the International Naval Conference held in London December 1908–February 1909* (Oxford University Press, 1919).

[294] FA Smith and NW Sibley, *International Law as Interpreted During the Russo-Japanese War* (T Fisher Unwin, 1905) 261.

[295] Hansard, HC Deb (series 3) 6 February 1873, vol 214, col 104.

3

Forms of Dispute Resolution as Instruments of Prevention: Part I

In this chapter we consider two further cases involving Britain and the United States: the Behring Sea and the Anglo-Venezuelan Arbitration.

The significance of the two arbitrations is the common approach adopted by Britain and the United States in seeking resolution of international disputes through arbitration facilitated by diplomacy despite national interests. The success of these arbitrations building on the experience of the Geneva Arbitration led to a closer relationship between the two English-speaking countries culminating in negotiations for an arbitration treaty. This then led to the United States promoting the idea with other states. Such case studies exhibit the interaction of diplomacy and international law as well as the collaboration of diplomats, arbitrators and lawyers in effective interstate dispute resolution between sovereign states.

I. THE BEHRING SEA ARBITRATION

The Behring Sea Arbitration arose out a dispute between Britain and the United States of America regarding the culling of fur-seals in the Behring Sea. In simple terms the United States claimed that the fur-seals were the property of the United States and it had a right to protect the fur-seals not only on the Pribilof Islands but on the High Seas outside the three-mile territorial limit. The fur-seals bred on the Pribilof Islands located to the north of an archipelago of islands part of the state of Alaska which was ceded to the United States by Russia in 1867. The United States claimed jurisdiction in the waters of the Behring Sea for the preservation of the fur-seals in or habitually resorting to the sea. Its municipal law placed restrictions and prohibitions on the taking of fur-seals in or habitually residing in the Behring Sea outlawing the practice of pelagic sealing. This was the indiscriminate capturing, wounding and killing of defenceless fur-seals on a large, industrialised scale.

A. Pelagic Sealing and Culling on the Pribilof Islands

This practice can be illustrated by Counsel for the United States, Mr Phelps,[1] who referred to one experienced witness stating that all the fur-seals killed on such trips were old and mature fur-seals, and at least 75 per cent of them were female. They were mainly shot on the ice or killed with bats. When shot on open or floating ice many of them escaped into the water and died from bleeding. Of every seal shot and captured it was alleged that three escaped wounded and two died in the water. It was also said that the effective way of killing a seal was to shoot it in the head. If shot in any other part, it could escape and not be caught but die at sea. The United States maintained that this form of industrialised killing was the reason why the seal population was so endangered.

On the other hand, Sir Charles Russell, the British Attorney General, described the practices adopted by the company operating on the Pribilof Islands. He referred to the ways in which the fur-seals were forced to move overland to the killing grounds, and quoted the American expert Elliott:

> … over rough, sharp rocks, rolling clinker stones, deep loose sand, mossy tussocks, and other equally severe impedimenta, they in their fright [This is the domestic animal] exert themselves most violently, crowd in confused sweltering heaps one upon the other, so that many are often ' smothered' to death; and in this manner of most extraordinary effort to be urged along over stretches of unbroken miles, they are obliged to use muscles and nerves that nature never intended them to use, and which are not fitted for the action … and then suffered to escape from the clubbed pods on the killing-grounds; they are alternately heated to the point of suffocation, gasping, panting, allowed to cool down at intervals, then abruptly started up on the road for afresh renewal of this heating as they lunge, shamble, and creep along. When they arrive on the killing-grounds, after four or five hours of this distressing effort on their part, they are then suddenly cooled off for the last time prior to the final ordeal of clubbing; then when driven up into the last surround or pod, if the fur-seals are spared from cause of being unfit to take, too big or too little, bitten, etc., they are permitted to go oft' from the killing ground back to the sea, outwardly unhurt, most of them; but I am now satisfied that they sustain in a vast majority of cases internal injuries of greater or less degree, that remain to work physical disability or death thereafter to nearly every seal thus released, and certain destruction of its virility and courage necessary …[2]

B. Immediate Cause of Dispute

Following the introduction of legislation by the United States to prevent pelagic sealing in the Behring Sea and the threat to the seal industry, in August 1866

[1] *Proceedings of the Tribunal of Arbitration Convened at Paris Under the Treaty of Washington*, 20th February 1892 Vol 12 (Government Printing Office, 1895): *Fur Seal Arbitration Oral Arguments of Counsel on Case and Counter-Case* (hereinafter '*Oral Argument of the United States*'), Hon E J Phelps, 99.

[2] *Proceedings of the Tribunal of Arbitration Convened at Paris Under the Treaty of Washington*, 20th February 1892 Vols 13 and 14 (Government Printing Office, 1895): *Oral Argument of Great Britain, Behring Sea Arbitration* (hereinafter '*Oral Argument of Great Britain*'), Sir Charles Russell, 203–204.

three British schooners which were engaged in pelagic sealing[3] 60 miles beyond any American territory were seized by United States revenue cutters and taken to Unalaska. The ships were impounded, and the crew were tried in the US District Court of Sitka and sentenced to a term of imprisonment. In response, the British Government protested at the seizures on 21 October 1886 following which the vessels and crew were released in February 1887. According to Russell, the crew were set adrift hundreds of miles from their homes.[4] The first vessel arrested was an American vessel.

Further seizures of British vessels were made in 1887 and 1889. Three years later, the Treaty of Washington was agreed following protracted diplomatic negotiations.

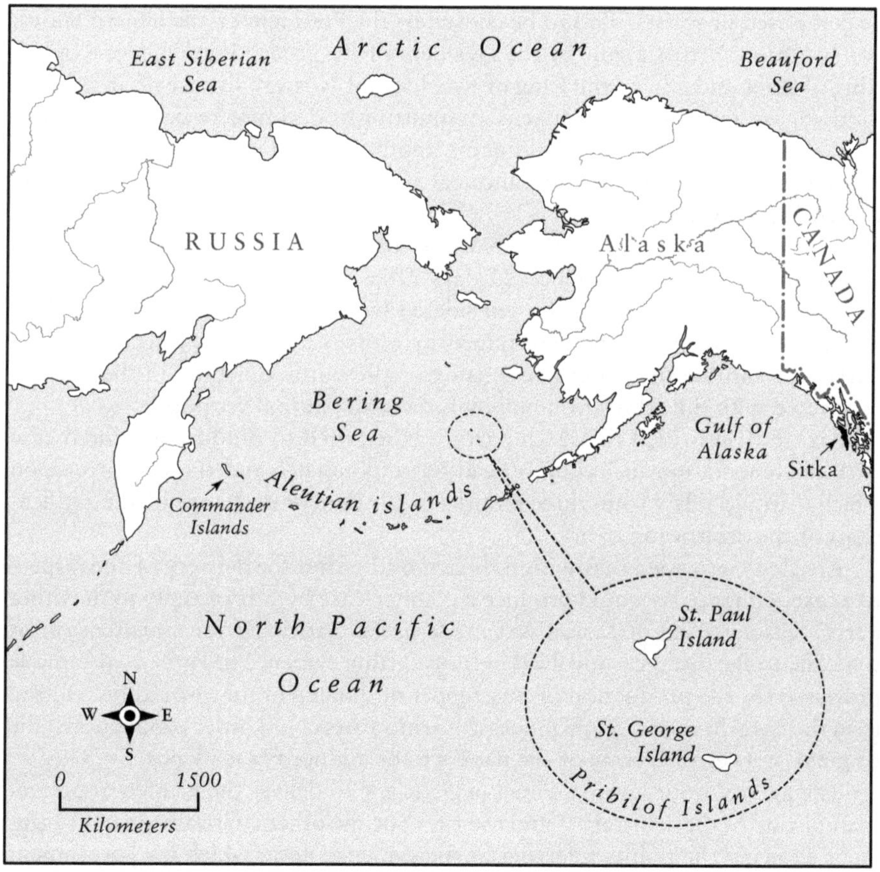

Figure 3.1 Map illustrating the Behring Sea
Credit: Mina Moshkeri

[3] This was the indiscriminate capturing, wounding and killing of defenceless fur-seals on a large scale. Carter and Coudert charged that up to 75%-95% were female fur-seals.
[4] *Oral Argument of Great Britain* (n 2) 2.

C. Treaty of Washington 1892

A treaty of arbitration was signed on 22nd April 1892 by the American Secretary of State, James G Blaine, and the British ambassador to Washington, Sir Julian Pauncefote. Its purpose was to resolve the various claims that had arisen over the rights of British and Canadian fishermen to catch fur-seals in the region and to formulate regulations for the protection of the fur-seals.[5] This set out the questions for referral and outlined the Constitution and powers of the Arbitral Tribunal.

Under Article I, the Treaty referred to jurisdictional claims of the United States in the Behring Sea and the preservation of fur-seals. The Tribunal was to be composed of jurists. Two to be chosen by the President of the United States, two by Queen Victoria, one by the President of the French Republic, one by the King of Italy, and one by the King of Sweden and Norway. In case of an arbitrator dying, suffering some incapacity, or omitting or declining or ceasing to act as such, these Heads of State would name another person to act in such capacity. If such person declined the appointment it would be made as Britain and the United States agreed.

Article II provided that the venue of the arbitration would be in Paris and hearings would commence 20 days after delivery of the party's respective counter-cases. All questions considered by the tribunal including the final decision (Award) would be determined by a majority of the arbitrators. Each party was entitled to appoint an agent to represent it generally in the matters connected with the arbitration mainly for administration purposes.

Article III provided that each party was required to produce a printed case with documentation including official correspondence and the evidence upon which it would rely within three months of the date of exchange of the ratifications of the arbitration treaty.

Article IV provided that within three months after the delivery of the respective cases either party could produce a counter-case by way of reply to the other party's case. Special provision was made under Article IV for an extension of time due to the distances involved in transmitting evidence to Paris. It also made provision for the production of any report or document that would be referred to in the case. In such circumstances the arbitrators could order productions; the original or a certified copy of the papers to be adduced as evidence.

The agents' duties were defined in Article V to deliver the printed argument in duplicate to the arbitrators and the agent of the other party, the printed argument showing the points referring to the evidence upon which his government relied; this could be supported by oral argument of counsel. The arbitrators were given power to require elucidation by way of a written or printed statement or oral argument of counsel with liberty to the other party to reply.

[5] This was the seventh such agreement between the United States and its former Mother Country.

It will be remembered that in the Geneva Arbitration, Britain and the United States agreed certain rules of application governing the submissions. In this arbitration the parties agreed the questions that the Tribunal had to answer. These were set out in Article VI as:

1. What exclusive jurisdiction in the sea now known as the Behring Sea, and what exclusive rights in the seal fisheries therein, did Russia assert and exercise prior and up to the time of the cession of Alaska to the United States?
2. How far were these claims and jurisdiction as to the seal fisheries recognised and conceded by Great Britain?
3. Was the body of water known as the Behring's Sea included in the phrase 'Pacific Ocean', as used in the Treaty of 1825 between Great Britain and Russia; and what rights, if any, in the Behring's Sea were held and exclusively exercised by Russia after said treaty?
4. Did not all the rights of Russia as to jurisdiction, and as to the seal fisheries in Behring's Sea east of the water boundary, in the treaty between the United States and Russia of 30 March 1867, pass unimpaired to the United States under that treaty?
5. Has the United States any rights, and if so, what right of protection or property in the fur-fur-seals frequenting the islands of the United States in Behring's Sea when such fur-seals are found outside the ordinary three-mile limit?[6]

Article VII sought the co-operation of Britain in the regulation of the protection and preservation of the fur-seals in the Behring Sea, but of greater significance was the request that the arbitrators should determine:

> … what concurrent regulations outside the jurisdictional limits of the respective Governments are necessary and over what waters such regulations should extend, and to aid them in that determination the report of a joint commission to be appointed by the respective Governments shall be laid before them, with such other evidence as either Government may submit.

Under this provision the parties agreed to co-operate in securing the acceptance of other Powers to the regulations.

In effect, despite the differences of opinion between Britain and the United States over the issue, the Treaty is evidence of a much deeper and closer relationship than had existed at the time of the Geneva Arbitration. However, without that reconciliation of the former Mother Country and its offspring, this understanding between Britain and her former colony would have been difficult. It also perhaps marks a turning point in Anglo-American relations where Britain appreciated that the people of the United States and Britain not only spoke a

[6] These questions are taken verbatim from the Treaty, the only slight modification being the reference to Behring's and not Behring as written in the Treaty in Article V. Behring's was the spelling used in the questions. There is not thought to be any particular significance in this.

common language, respected the same Common Law, but also had the same Anglo-Saxon and European inheritance.

Article VIII provided that where the parties were unable to agree about a question of liability, eg the British ship owners claims for unlawful seizure, these could be referred to the Tribunal or subject to further negotiation. This would not impede the determination of the central issue.

Article IX provided for the parties' appointment of commissioners to investigate and report to the Tribunal with joint or several reports on matters of fact, together with their recommendations. This procedure was not unusual in those times especially in the context of English procedural law and the Rules of the Supreme Court with power to refer a matter to an Official Referee who would report back to the High Court judge and whose report would be part of the High Court judge's judgment.[7]

Under Article X, each side was responsible for its own Commissioners' costs.

Article XI provided that the Tribunal make its decision three months after the close of the argument. The decision was what arbitrators would term an Award. Here it was agreed that it should be in writing and signed by the arbitrators who agreed to it. The decision was to be delivered to the agent of the United States and to the British agent.

Under Article XII, each government would pay its own agent and remunerate its counsel and the arbitrators appointed by it. Each government would be responsible for the costs of submitting its case to the Tribunal. All other expenses would be paid in equal shares by the governments.

Article XIII provided for the keeping of proper records by the Tribunal.

Article XIV provided that the parties would engage after the Award was published. This presumably was to ensure that the Award was factually correct and answered all the questions referred to the Tribunal.

Article XV provided for the ratification of the arbitration treaty within six months by the President of the United States, by and with the advice of the Senate, and the Queen; in effect, by Her Government exercising the prerogative power.

This was a basic framework for the Tribunal, but no provision was made for the calling of witnesses and all evidence would be produced in documentary form with witnesses having been deposed beforehand.

D. Constitution of the Tribunal

The Tribunal was composed of John M Harlan, a Justice of the United States Supreme Court and Senator John T Morgan, appointed by the President

[7] MP Reynolds, 'Caseflow Management: A Rudimentary Official Referee Process 1870–1970' (PhD Thesis, London School of Economics, 2008).

of the United States, Lord Hannen, Lord Chief Justice of England and Sir John Thomson, appointed by the British Government, Baron de Courcel, the Marquis Visconti-Venosta and Mr Gregers Winther Wulfsberg Gram, appointed respectively by the President of the French Republic, the King of Italy, and the King of Norway and Sweden. Counsel for the United States were The Hon Edward J Phelps, Hon James C Carter and Mr Frederick R Coudert. Counsel for Britain were Sir Charles Russell QC MP, Sir Richard Webster QC MP and Mr Christopher Robinson QC.

E. Claims of the United States

The United States claimed exclusive rights in and over the Behring Sea and in the fur-seals in that sea, purporting to give it the right to exclude ships of all other nations engaged in pelagic sealing and enabling it to search, seize and condemn such ships. This amounted to a territorial claim of exclusive possession of the seas or a *mare clausum* contrary to any concept of freedom of the seas and the right of free passage outside territorial waters. The second claim the United States made related to establishing rules of protection and preservation of the fur-seals in the Behring Sea. The United States claimed such rights were inherited from Russia when the United States purchased Alaska and the Russian American territories in 1867. It may be thought the United States looked upon fur-seals as they did a herd of cattle on the plains; that they were capable of ownership and regarded them as property. Such extraordinary claims were supported by an application of certain principles of common and civil law, to the practice of Nations, the laws of natural history, and the common interests of mankind.[8] The claim of property in the fur-seals rested on an argument that the United States had a right to the fur-seals as 'products of the soil'.[9]

More particularly, the claims of the United States may be summarised as:

1. The United States' claim of dominion and the right to legislate against foreigners, in the Behring Sea.
2. A right of property in wild animals which resort to their territory, derive no sustenance therefrom, and during the greater part of the year live many hundreds of miles away in the ocean.
3. A right to protect the United States' right of property in the fur-seals by search, seizure and prosecution under its municipal law.
4. Alternatively, to the claim of property a right to protect the fur-seals in the ocean and apply the above sanctions.
5. Rules framed in the interest of the United States excluding other nations from sealing.

[8] *Oral Argument of Great Britain* (n 2) 3–4.
[9] *Ibid* 7.

The case of the United States was confusing if not contradictory, and also based on a false premise.[10] The United States claimed its rights over the Behring Sea under the Treaty of Cession 1867, its possession of the Alaskan territories and by virtue of its claim to dominion over them. It claimed jurisdiction over the eastern part of the Behring Sea as its territorial waters and additionally jurisdiction to protect the fur-seals as well as a property in the fur-seals arising from their breeding and temporary residence on the Pribilof Islands as well as a right to follow and protect them. Further, it claimed a right to protect the fur-seals apart from any property right. The last three claims were outside the Tribunal's jurisdiction.

F. British Counter-Claim

Britain denied the existence of any such dominion and jurisdiction by the United States in the Behring Sea, but accepted and recognised the need for regulation to protect and preserve the fur-seals. As to the Russian rights, Britain rejected such argument because Russia had never exercised such exclusive sealing rights. As to the argument of property rights in fur-seals swimming in the High Seas, Britain contended that they were incapable of ownership and the application of law was simply an unprecedented pretension. In terms of the seizure of British vessels the British argument was that the United States could not simply base its justification for seizure on the possession of Alaska, and upon the Treaty of Cession with Russia.[11] The rights of the United States depended on what was ceded and what title was transferred. In law, the principle *nemo dat quod non habet* applied so that if the title was imperfect the United States would not acquire such rights if Russia had never had them in the first place. The relevant treaties of 1824, 1825 and 1867 demonstrated that Russia never made such claims and if she made a claim of a different nature regarding the seas it was immediately abandoned. If the case of the United States was based on its municipal law this would be ineffective against foreigners under international law and therefore ultra vires. Thus, the courts of the United States would have no jurisdiction and the legislation of the Congress was ineffective. Statutes passed by Congress in 1868 and 1889, as well as the President's Proclamation of 1889, warned foreigners entering the Behring Sea that their vessels may be liable to seizure. Sir Charles Russell was to argue that they were not justified by the Treaty of Cession of 1867, or by the Tsar's Ukase, or by the Treaties of 1824 and 1825 let alone United States' legislation and its municipal law.

[10] Counsel for the United States discovered that there had been a mistranslation of the Russia Treaty of Cession which appeared in the appendix to their case. The falsification was discovered after the cases had been exchanged and after the British authorities had discovered the fraud. Foreign Office (FO) 97/544 (Preliminary Draft).

[11] *Oral Argument of Great Britain* (n 2) 3–5.

As to property in the fur-seals, they were not classified as 'products of the soil' but wild animals. The fur-seals were *ferae naturae*, they were frightened of man. No property existed in them save when in possession, but when they left land any exclusive right of possession was lost. Catching fur-seals on the High Seas was a matter of rival trading. Thus, there could be no claim against British fishermen for taking fur-seals in the Behring Sea because they were exercising their lawful right of fishing on the High Seas. The United States could only claim property or possession when the fur-seals were on its land, not when they were swimming in the High Seas.

So far as international law was concerned, the Opinion of Lord Mansfield in *Triquet v Bath* was pertinent:[12]

> I remember, in a case before Lord Talbot, of *Buvot v. Barbuit*,[13] (at a motion to discharge the defendant (who was in execution for not performing a decree) 'because he was agent of commerce, commissioned by the King of Prussia, and received here as such;' the matter was very elaborately argued at the bar, and a solemn deliberate opinion given by the Court. ... Lord Talbot declared a clear opinion, 'That the law of nations, in its full extent, was part of the law of England.' ...' That the law of nations was to be collected from the practice of different nations and the authority of writers.' Accordingly, he argued and determined from such instances, and the authority of Grotius, Barbeyrac, Binkershoek, Wiquefort, there being no English writer of eminence upon the subject. I was counsel in this case; and have a full note of it. I remember, too, Lord Hardwicke's declaring his opinion to the same effect; and denying that Lord Chief Justice Holt ever had any doubt as to the law of nations being part of the law of England upon the occasion of the arrest of the Russian Ambassador.

G. *Mare Clausum*

The United States' argument as to exclusivity of its dominion over the 'waters of Alaska' was contrary to the earlier British and American positions taken in their negotiations with Russia in 1824 and 1825 upholding freedom of the seas. It was also far away from any notion of *res extra commercium* or *res communis*. As to the Russian position pre-1867, the Ukase of 1799[14] was purely territorial and it did not claim the Behring Sea as *mare clausam*, it was open to free navigation. Even the Ukase of 1821 purporting to extend Russia's maritime limits to 100 Italian miles to protect Russian commerce was abandoned after protests from Britain and the United States.[15] To support its case the United States submitted

[12] *Triquet v Bath* (1764) 3 Burr 1478; 97 ER 936.

[13] *Buvot v Barbuit* (1736) 3 Burr 1478, 1481.

[14] This was a decree of Tsar Paul I issued on 8 July 1799 as to the southern border of Russian America granting certain trading and settlement rights to Americans with some reservations to Russian fur traders.

[15] *Oral Argument of Great Britain* (n 2) 42.

that the definition of the Pacific Ocean included the Behring Sea under Article I of the United States Treaty of 1824.[16] The Treaties between Britain and Russia (Article VII) and the United States and Russia (Article IV) provided for a reciprocal right to frequent the sea for ten years.[17] Britain argued that the United States Congress had no power to legislate *mare clausum*[18] and that the right of protection of the fur-seals was totally devoid of legal certainty. The claim as to a right *ratione sole* did not import a right off the land and in any event pelagic sealing was not a form of piracy.[19] From a practical point of view this would necessitate inspection of vessels on the High Seas which did not exist save in cases of piracy. The attempt to demonstrate justification for such a gross extension of territorial jurisdiction by reference to certain foreign states was defeated by reference to the acceptance of the three-mile limit.[20] No other country claimed such a right of interference on the High Seas. The principle: *extra territorium jus dicenti impure non paretur* applied – no person is subject to the laws of a country in which he is not. The territory meant the land extending to the low watermark. The sea was regarded as *inter fauces terrae* although there were exceptions.[21] What the United States sought was to prohibit sealing to preserve the seal herds.[22] In his oral argument Sir Charles Russell was to submit that even if there was a property right it did not follow that there was a right of protection.[23]

H. Prelude to Arbitration

On 23 February 1893, the Tribunal met with Sir Charles Russell, Sir Richard Webster, Mr Tupper, the British Agent and the Acting Agent for the United States. The United States would be represented by Mr James Carter,[24] Mr Frederick Coudert[25] and Mr Phelps. Mr Christopher Robinson QC assisted Russell and Webster. It was adjourned to 23 March when the printed argument would be presented. Mr Tupper was instructed to attend upon counsel at that hearing which might cover questions as to confidentiality and secrecy of the submissions of the respective states' cases, counter-cases and arguments. Lord Rosebery[26] had instructed him to let the Tribunal decide such matters, although he thought the discussions with the Tribunal would be secret. Tupper was to report to

[16] *Ibid* 66, 72 and 75.
[17] *Ibid* 49.
[18] *Ibid* 34.
[19] *Ibid* 35.
[20] *Ibid* 38–51.
[21] *Ibid* 50–53.
[22] *Oral Argument of the United States* (n 1) 121.
[23] *Oral Argument of Great Britain* (n 2) 111–13.
[24] New York lawyer, educated at Harvard College and Harvard Law School and Founder of the firm Carter, Ladyard and Milburn.
[25] New York lawyer, educated at Colombia University, New York Firm Coudert Brothers.
[26] Foreign Secretary, 1892–1894.

Rosebery on each meeting of the arbitrators.[27] When Tupper had arrived in Paris, Baron de Courcel suggested an adjournment to the 6 April, with the arguments submitted on the 30 April to avoid Holy Week.[28] In the event, counsel for the United States did not agree to extend the adjournment but agreed to publication of the cases and argument.[29] The proceedings of the Tribunal were to be kept secret pending consideration when the full Tribunal met.[30] Tupper subsequently confirmed the names of those who would be assisting in the case apart from counsel to include Dr Dawson, an expert who had investigated the condition of the fur-seals.[31] Contrary to what had been agreed at the first meeting, the United States subsequently objected to what its Acting Agent had agreed as to publication of the cases. Rosebery accepted this and agreed that it be left to the meeting on the 23 March when a full meeting of the Tribunal would rule on the matter.[32] It was subsequently agreed by the United States Government that the cases should be published provided there was no objection from the Tribunal.[33] When the Tribunal met on the 23 March it decided that all proceedings should be in public.[34]

In the event, the hearing started on the 4 April.[35] Not only was there some misunderstanding about the earlier question of publication of the cases and the proceedings being public, but when the hearings commenced the United States' Agent took exception to the British submission of a copy of a Supplementary Report of the British Commissioners and also to a transcript being made of the hearings.[36] In a report entitled 'British Tricks at Paris', *The New York Tribune* complained that Sir Charles Russell, the British Attorney General, ignored the provisions of the Treaty of Washington in submitting the Supplementary Report to the Tribunal.[37] Under the Treaty this should have been a joint report as provided by Article VII by the respective governments, and under Article VIII, if the parties were unable to agree about questions of liability then these should be referred to the Tribunal. What was submitted according to the United States Agent should have been put in the British case and counter-case. It was regarded as a violation of the Treaty.[38] In addition, Mr James Carter wanted certain parts

[27] Foreign Office (FO) Papers 414/289 No 1 *The Earl of Rosebery to Mr Tupper* (17 February 1893).

[28] FO 414/289 No 2 *Mr Tupper to The Earl of Rosebery* (22 February 1893).

[29] FO 414/289 No 7 *Mr Tupper to The Earl of Rosebery* (23 February 1893).

[30] FO 414/289 No 12 *Mr Tupper to The Earl of Rosebery* (24 February 1893).

[31] FO 414/289 No 16 *Mr Tupper to The Earl of Rosebery* (3 March 1893). It was thought better not to include Sir G Baden-Powell who had also been involved because that might not appear impartial to the British Case.

[32] FO 414/289 No 20 *The Earl of Rosebery to Mr Lincoln* (15 March 1893).

[33] FO 414/289 No 31 *Sir J Pauncefote to The Earl of Rosebery* (21 March 1893).

[34] FO 414/289 No 33 *Mr Tupper to The Earl of Rosebery* (23 March 1893).

[35] FO 414/289 *Minute of Meeting* (4 April 1893).

[36] FO 414/289 No 58 *Mr Tupper to The Earl of Rosebery* (11 April 1893); Enclosure No 1 *Mr Foster to Mr Tupper* (10 April 1893); Enclosure No 2 *Mr Tupper to Mr Foster* (11 April 1893) and *Mr Tupper to The Earl of Rosebery* (12 April 1893).

[37] FO 414/289 Enclosure in No 70. This was submitted to the Tribunal earlier on 25 March 1893.

[38] *Oral Argument of Great Britain* (n 2) 119–20.

of the British counter-case dismissed. On 4 April Sir Charles Russell had applied for disclosure of a report on the fur-seals by Henry W Elliott produced under an Act of Congress of 1890. Mr Phelps objected, but then waived his objection. Elliott was regarded by the British as the leading American expert responsible for official reports in 1873, 1875, 1881 and 1884. On the 12 April (the seventh day of the hearing), the Tribunal refused to admit the Supplementary Report at that stage but suggested it might be introduced later when the British oral argument was made. The appendices attached to it were reserved for further consideration. Mr Phelps' application to strike out parts of the British counter-case was also postponed. It seems that the Tribunal was anxious not to spend time on interlocutory applications but to proceed with the case. The President also told counsel to treat the matters of right and regulation separately.[39]

I. The United States' Argument

Carter commenced the argument by submitting that there was no *onus probandi* on the United States and introduced it by relating the origins of the Russian expeditions in the eighteenth century and the development of a sustainable fur-seal industry. When the United States acquired Alaska by its cession in 1867, it inherited the fur-seal trade that Russia had built up and followed Russia's approach by placing the industry in private ownership subject to restrictions on catches in Alaskan waters where transgressors were liable to seizure and confiscation.[40] The United States profited by leasing the breeding islands to corporations that paid tax and $60,000 rent per annum, as well as duty to be paid on every seal caught. Carter submitted this trade benefitted the whole of mankind. The pecuniary advantage to the United States was obvious, but it also benefited England since the seal skins were processed in London employing thousands of workers which was more than were employed on the Pribilof Islands.[41] After 1883 they ventured into the Behring Sea and pelagic sealing was made a criminal offence. It was not until 1886 that its extent became a threat to the United States' interests and US authorities began to intercept and arrest the intruders, British and American. This drew protests from the British Government in September 1886.[42] The United States' argument was that it, as the successor in title to the former Russian territory, acquired all Russia's former rights of possession, sovereignty and dominion including the seas (*mers formées*) and second, under the Ukase of 1821, a prohibition against any foreign vessel coming within 100 Italian miles of any part of its domain.[43]

[39] FO 414/289 *Minute of Meeting* (12 April 1893).
[40] *Oral Argument of the United States* (n 1) 8.
[41] *Ibid* 9.
[42] *Ibid* 10–11.
[43] *Ibid*11.

Mr James Carter addressed the diplomatic exchanges that took place between Mr Bayard, the American Secretary of State, and Lord Salisbury, the British Foreign Secretary. These exchanges were diplomatic and friendly as were the further discussions between Lord Salisbury and Mr Phelps, the American Minister in London. Indeed, the parties were agreed on the need to protect the seal population by regulation. The key time for this was 15 April to 1 November between 160° longitude west and 170° longitude east in the Behring Sea.[44] Britain also agreed to assist with any preventative measures. The Canadian Government objected to this and Salisbury then suggested a shorter close period.[45] This was not the first time Britain and the United States had differences over fishing rights involving Canada.[46] No convention was agreed and in 1888 President Cleveland and Secretary Bayard were replaced by Republicans Harrison and Blaine who took a stricter approach to Britain by reintroducing the prohibition on pelagic sealing. Harrison maintained that if pelagic sealing continued the seal population would face 'total extermination'.[47]

Further negotiations took place between Pauncefote and Blaine, the former suggesting a mixed tribunal of experts with some provisional regulations introduced without prejudice to the findings of the experts.[48] These proposals were unacceptable since the British proposal excluded pelagic sealing during the months of May to June and in October to December leaving the more popular season from July to August open to the threat. Attached to Pauncefote's despatch was a draft convention for the mixed Tribunal. Salisbury took objection to Blaine's contention that Canadian vessels were acting *contra bonos mores* and he argued that this applied in times of peace against pirates. If it was a crime under United States law, then the American courts could only have jurisdiction over its citizens and not foreigners. Fur-seals were *res nullius* and *ferae naturae* animals – they did not constitute property until taken into possession. As for the American claims founded upon the Russian Ukase of 1821, this could not be justified; there was no *mare clausum* as contended by Russia in 1821; in any event it was never enforced.[49] The High Seas were open to all nations, but Russia had placed exclusive possession on the fisheries of the Behring Sea which contradicted this principle of international law. Although the United States was anxious to reach agreement as delay would 'result in the elimination of the seal population',[50] Britain and the United States had reached an impasse created by Lord Salisbury's proposition in 1888, Pauncefote's approach in 1890 and the change in approach

[44] *Ibid* 18. Salisbury had consulted the Russian Government and they had agreed to include the area to the Sea of Okhotsk to latitude 47°.

[45] *Oral Argument of the United States* (n 1) 25.

[46] The rights of American and Canadian fisherman off Newfoundland had been disputed since the War of Independence but temporarily agreed by 1888. *Oral Argument of the United States* (n 1) 21, 29–30.

[47] *Ibid* 39. *Blaine to Pauncefote* (22 January 1889).

[48] *Ibid* 44–46 and *Pauncefote to Blaine* (29 April 1890).

[49] *Ibid* 51–52.

[50] *Ibid* 58.

by the Harrison administration.[51] Not only this but in June 1890 Pauncefote was of the view that the matter could not be settled by an expert commission but had to be resolved through arbitration because the matter concerned legal questions of seizure of vessels and compensation for the vessels that had been arrested.[52]

Carter was at pains to distinguish the United States' argument from that argued by Blaine who had based the question on Russia's exclusive rights over the Behring Sea. He had argued that such rights were not affected by the treaties of 1824 and 1825. But the problem was that America had opposed the Russian Ukase as much as Britain had and therefore the United States' case was contradictory. Not only that, but as will be noted, the reliance on a mistranslation of the Russian treaties would cause further embarrassment to the American case.[53] Furthermore, Blaine had tried to equate pelagic seal fishing with piracy because it injured the commercial interest of the United States and then argued the matter on the basis of a right to protect United States' property.[54]

Eventually the parties reached agreement on a treaty for a mixed commission of experts to report and if possible, agree the issues and whilst the parties agreed that the seal colony was being diminished by pelagic sealing, they could not agree the cause(s).[55] Under the Treaty signed and ratified on the 7 May 1892 the parties then referred the matter to arbitration and separate reports were submitted.

i. Legal Argument – Authorities

Carter then went on to make his submissions on applicable law which in his view was international law or, as he put it, 'a general standard of justice recognised by the nations of the world'. It was a law based on moral standards, a general standard of justice.[56]

This was a *tour de force* referring to Ulpian; Sir William Blackstone who said it was the law of nature dictated by God from which all law is derived;[57] Sir Robert Phillimore who said it was 'common rules of right approved by nations'; and Chief Justice Marshall, who held in *Church v Hubbart* that a state may exercise its power to secure itself from injury which may be exercised beyond the limits of its territory.[58] Carter submitted that it was not difficult to uphold an exclusion on a remote a coast as Alaska was in 1821. That was 70 years before, and commerce and population had increased, but more importantly the Russians

[51] Salisbury maintained that he had only agreed a scheme with Bayard on a provisional basis, but it is not clear from the exchanges that Canada was an inhibition.

[52] *Oral Argument of the United States* (n 1) 62–64.

[53] FO 97/544 (Preliminary Draft 8) and see above *Oral Argument of Great Britain* (n 2).

[54] *Oral Argument of the United States* (n 1) 71.

[55] *Ibid* 74.

[56] *Ibid* 76–80.

[57] *Commentaries*. Book I (Library of Alexandria, 2009) 11; *Oral Argument of the United States* (n 1) 81.

[58] *Church v Hubbart* (1804) 6 US 187 (1804).

had not sustained their Ukase.[59] Carter described property as either *dominium emineus* where the state was the absolute owner of property and could displace the individual's right or *dominium utile* the right to use and enjoy. Thus, he submitted that if such property was attacked or its citizens were attacked it had a right to defend them by such means and methods as were necessary 'fully and perfectly to protect itself'. There was no limitation or boundary-line in this; it was a matter of necessity: it was the necessity of self-defence. He was not arguing a case on jurisdiction, sovereignty or territorial dominion, nor he suggested, relying on the Russian claim but what Blaine had put to Lord Salisbury,[60] was an argument that the United States owned the fur-seals which went to and fro to the breeding islands. Russia's exclusion of vessels within 100 Italian miles of the coast was not declaring the Behring Sea *mare clausum*: it was simply a matter of self-defence.[61] He submitted that Russia had a sealing industry on the Pribilof Islands and claimed exclusive right to protect its interests under the Ukase of 1821. These rights were not abandoned by the treaties of 1824 or 1825 and no one challenged or disturbed this exclusivity of Russia or the United States up to 1883, thus Great Britain was estopped from denying this position. Thus, such rights as were vested in Russia were passed to the United States by virtue of the Treaty of the 30th March 1867. This seems contradictory in that the United States was resting part of its case on the Russian position, but the United States was going further in claiming property rights in the fur-seals in the sea, alternatively, a property interest in the industry which they had a right to protect.[62] The British argument was that fur-seals were *res communes* and were not recognised in law as property. Carter went to great lengths quoting Gaius, Blackstone, Savigny, Locke, Heutefeuille, Vittel, Felice and Levi, arguing that the United States held these fur-seals on trust for all mankind in the sense that by the United States having property rights in the fur-seals they were protected and could increase for the benefit of all.[63] He described property as a utility or desire of man, of limited supply and capable of exclusive appropriation. In interpreting the nature of the property in fur-seals, he relied on the characteristics of the seal; their nature and habits as described by the American Commissioners.

Carter rejected the findings of the British Commissioner's report, stating that the only common ground was the fact that the seal population had diminished but the cause could not be agreed.[64] Carter submitted that the Commissioners were witnesses of fact because of what they observed and recorded during their investigation. He complained that the United States had served their witness statements on the British, but they had not exchanged their statements.

[59] *Oral Argument of the United States* (n 1) 81–100.

[60] *Blaine to Lord Salisbury* (30 June 1890); *Oral Argument of the United States* (n 1) 106.

[61] *Oral Argument of the United States* (n 1)115–17.

[62] *Ibid* 138–41.

[63] *Ibid* 145–77.

[64] *Ibid* 178–79. In 1872, pelagic sealing accounted for 1,029 fur-seals being killed and in 1881, 13,541.

He further complained that the British Commissioners were asked to investigate what methods must be pursued in order to preserve the fur-seals. His submission that the terms of reference of the Commissioners was so restricted was not correct: what was agreed was that the terms of reference encompassed the facts relating to seal life in the Behring Sea and measures necessary for its proper protection and preservation.[65]

Whilst the Joint Commission had sat for more than 30 days, it was adjourned without agreement on 4 March 1893. The British Commissioners had rejected the American claims of exclusivity in favour of the rights of all nations to pursue fur-seals at sea just as the United States had a right to take them on their land. The American commissioners concluded that the United States could take 100,000 young male fur-seals each year without danger to the stock.[66]

ii. Legal Argument – Property

The idea of protection and property interest was questioned by the Tribunal President, de Martens, and Carter was asked to explain whether the American Company, as lessees of the islands had a legal or moral right to insist on a right of property and protection. He replied at length admitting only an interest, not an absolute title, but a qualified one. He had difficulty explaining authority for this proposition based on United States municipal law, having to fall back on regulations the Tribunal would establish providing the basis for such an Act of Congress.[67]

On the 21st April, Day 13 of the proceedings, Carter expanded on his argument on property as to things which are either not possessed or cannot be possessed. He argued that the law recognised a right of property in things incapable of absolute and permanent possession which could be exclusively appropriated wherever there was a social good. Further, he submitted that wherever wild animals were captured to the extent of the annual increase so as to preserve the stock, any taking of it by others risking extinction would give those who capture it or them property in the animal.[68] He applied Blackstone's classification of property that was *per industriam* to the fur-seals on the islands and suggested that there the company practised self-denial by a restricted culling. In passing he distinguished pelagic sealing from the 'industry' on the islands in that the former was an unregulated attack on the stock, whereas the latter was regulating the increase. This it seems would be a stronger argument than an assertion of property in a seal swimming in the High Seas. What Carter was trying to do was to suggest that the United States was not acting in any selfish interest, but to protect the animals as property in which mankind had

[65] *Ibid* 180–83.
[66] *Ibid* 183–92.
[67] *Ibid* 204–206.
[68] *Ibid* 217.

an interest: all mankind having a right to enjoy, albeit limited in that enjoyment by employing the instrumentality of the United States in its industry on the Pribilof Islands.[69] The President interrupted Carter as to his definition of property, as did other members of the Tribunal and Carter explained that although it was not absolute property it was property in the sense that the United States is entitled to the exclusive custody and management of it and to prevent any interference with it from any quarter as well as to the direct profits of it; but as to beneficial enjoyments it meant the interest of the whole world.[70] When tested on this by Senator Morgan as to property rights during migration, Carter's answer was not convincing as he simply said that the way the industry worked on the islands was for the benefit of mankind and since that was the case 'they should be awarded the property in the animal, not only while he is on land, but while he is at sea'. But how could an animal be your property when it was not in possession and swimming about on the High Seas? Carter's answer was that the fur-seal returned to its breeding grounds and because of this natural instinct of return the property subsists, and that 'where their (United States) right of property in an industry is injured by an act on the High Seas which is, in itself, a wrong, then they have a right to interfere and defend themselves against that wrong'.[71]

iii. Legal Argument – Protection or Self-Defence

Carter next considered the question of protecting those rights. He equated the right to defend property in fur-seals by the executive's exercise of a self-defence power on the principle of necessity subject to limitations. He equated this right with belligerent rights of blockade and acts committed on the High Seas outside the jurisdiction as a means of self-defence.[72] He also referenced the English statutes against hovering and transhipping of goods as an example of extra-territorial jurisdiction and enforcement of property interests.[73] He quoted other cases from the US Supreme Court, but all these authorities referred to the seizure of ships, not animals *ferae naturae* such that the application of such principles to fur-seals is difficult to comprehend.

Following this frangible argument, the Tribunal then discussed the regulations in general with Carter leaving his colleague, Coudert, to deal with in detail. Just before that there was some controversy over the status of any Award the Tribunal produced, Senator Morgan making it very clear he would withdraw if the Award were not to be binding.[74] The question as to the extent and scope of the concurrent regulations was unlimited in that it was left to the arbitrators to

[69] *Ibid* 232.
[70] *Ibid* 232.
[71] *Ibid* 236–37.
[72] *Ibid* 245.
[73] *Ibid* 247. He also referred to Chief Justice Cockburn in *R v Keyn* (1876) 2 Ex D 63 and Chief Justice Marshall in *Church v Hubbart* (n 58).
[74] *Oral Argument of the United States* (n 1) 262.

decide the extent of those regulations.[75] Carter submitted that what they needed to consider was the nature and habits of the animal, the methods by which it was pursued and captured, and the perils to which it was exposed, as well as the means to protect it.[76]

The fact was that according to Carter 160,000 fur-seals were taken every year from the herd; probably more than 100,000 on the islands and 60,000 to 70,000 in pelagic sealing, plus unknown numbers that were lost at sea, injured or disabled.[77]

J. The British Argument

The American argument concluded on Day 19, 9 May 1893 so that Sir Charles Russell opened the argument for Britain the next day. Russell opened the case for Britain by setting out the structure of his argument with reference to questions regarding assumed exclusive jurisdiction and purported legal rights according to Article VI of the Treaty of Arbitration, the question of regulations under Article VII, followed by the claim for damages under Article VIII and finally the claim for damages under the fifth article of a *modus vivendi* of 1892.

Russell's command of the case was clear from the outset in its focus, structure and detailed critical analysis. His argument was simple – an absolute and complete denial of any exclusive right of property, jurisdiction or protection of the fur-seals by the United States save whilst on the Pribilof Islands subject to Britain's desire for it to approach the question of regulations in a fair, just and equitable spirit in a common interest of mankind.[78]

Russell referred to Coudert's arguments on the regulations as being full of 'intellectual allurements', a great many of those arguments being remote from any of the relevant legal questions and so far as Carter was concerned Russell said it was 'astounding that it should be thought necessary to dig, as my learned friend Mr. Carter did, down to the foundations of human society in order to try and discover those upon which the institution of property rest'. Nor could he understand how the Tribunal determining 'questions of right to be determined according to law (… could) derive much assistance from courageous ascents into the mists and clouds of metaphysical and ethical discussion, such as my learned friend has made'.[79]

Russell was quick to point to the contradiction in the American diplomatic exchanges and the case presented to the Tribunal.

[75] *Ibid* 266.
[76] *Ibid* 272.
[77] *Ibid* 275
[78] *Oral Argument of Great Britain* (n 2) 3–4.
[79] *Ibid* 4.

i. Contradiction between United States Diplomacy and Legal Submissions

The first inconsistency was regarding the first four questions of Article VI dealing with the assertion of a claim of exclusive jurisdiction and exclusive rights derived from Russia, which it was asserted Russia exercised, and which it was further asserted passed unimpaired to the United States. It had submitted that such title as the United States derived from Russia was of no moment; the United States was not relying on its exclusive jurisdiction, but the executive protective acts rightfully exercised in defence of its property interests. Russell submitted that it was impossible to explain the four questions in the context of a mere inherent right of protection of property or of interest, for the simple reason that each of those questions was a question of exclusive jurisdiction in a defined area of the Behring Sea. The acts of Russia had been acts in defence of property – a right which is inseparable from the possession of property. Russell argued that right would not be confined to a defined area, namely the eastern part of the Behring Sea, but would be a right which would exist and follow the property wherever the property itself existed. The United States advanced its argument on that basis and its municipal laws to justify the seizure and confiscation of vessels of British subjects.[80]

The next inconsistency was the definition of the 'Pacific Ocean' and whether it included the Behring Sea as used in the Treaty of 1825. Russell argued that

> if it were true that, under the operation of the Treaty of 1825, Russia, the predecessor in title of the United States in the Alaskan territory, had recognised the general right of fishing in the North Pacific Ocean including the Behring Sea, it would go a long way to negative the existence of any right to limit the right of fishing to citizens of the United States or to those authorised by the Executive of the United States.[81]

However, Carter suggested that this was a comparatively unimportant question. This was not the view of Blaine, the United States Secretary of State. In his despatch dated 17 November 1890, he stated that if Britain could establish that the definition of 'Pacific Ocean' included the Behring Sea in the Treaty of 1825, the United States could have no well-founded cause of complaint against Britain. In other words, Blaine was relying on Britain's acquiescence of an assertion of American exclusivity in the region. This was far different from Carter's reliance on a right of property, and a right of protection of property, or of an industry founded upon property.[82]

In this respect the United States case contradicted the stated diplomatic position. Russell argued that it was more perplexing than that because the Tribunal was told that although the United States could in point of law insist upon its claim of property to the individual fur-seals or seal herd, wherever they may be found, 'whether it was three thousand miles south of the Aleutians, off the

[80] *Ibid* 5.
[81] *Ibid* 5.
[82] *Ibid* 5–6.

southern part of California, or elsewhere the needs of the United States case did not require so high a position as that'. Ultimately Russell said it came down to a very extraordinary position:

> that even if it be found that neither in the seal as an individual, nor in the herd as a collection of individuals, did any legal property exist in the United States, yet they maintained a legal right to claim, and a legal right to exercise, a power of protection over an industry founded upon the skinning of the fur-seals upon the Pribilof Islands.[83]

Russell's argument was that such assertions lacked legal authority.

ii. Property in and Right to Protect Animals

Carter had suggested that the right of protection of the property and interests of a nation were the same in time of peace and war in that ships of a friendly power could be searched, seized and confiscated when they were pursuing pelagic sealing, although there had been no diplomatic expostulation or warning. His proposition that the moral law and the law of nature were international law enabled the United States to conclude that pelagic sealing was a crime – a grave moral wrong, and an indefensible act akin to piracy. The property in the fur-seals were said to be animals *ferae naturae*, and that the property in them was vested in the United States because they bred upon the islands, and have the *animus revertendi* to them.[84] Thus, because the fur-seals naturally by animal instinct returned to the breeding islands they, like domestic animals, were property. This was a far-fetched argument, based by Carter on some highly respected legal opinions.

However, Russell countered that authority with what he called 'a remarkable confusion' in Carter's analysis. He submitted that in respect of animals *ferae naturae* which the owner of the soil has, *ratione soli*, this amounted to a right to kill those animals when they were on his soil and the right to exclude all others from access to it. That he said was a distinct, clear, legal conception; a right recognised by the law as incident to property, and it was properly called the right *ratione soli*. But that did not affect the question of property in those animals when they are not on the soil of the owner. If they were domestic animals, or if they were animals which by the industry, care and art of man have become assimilated as domestic animals, then a property could exist in them. The right to possession would follow that property even when they were off the land and out of the physical control of the owner. But the right *ratione soli* which is exclusive of everybody else, and which is exercisable only on the soil of the owner, did not give the property in animals *ferae naturae* when they are on the land – much less when off the soil of the owner.[85] Thus, Carter's argument based on *ratione soli* was flawed.

[83] *Ibid* 6.
[84] *Ibid* 7.
[85] *Ibid* 7.

The other misperception here was Carter's reference to *animus revertendi* as if the mere fact of *animus revertendi* gave property because if *animus revertendi* gave property in animals *ferae naturae*, then Russell argued that the law of every civilised country would have given property in pheasants, rabbits, hares – in almost every class of animal which was recognised as coming under the head of game. The law of every civilised country recognized that there was merely an exclusive right to take game when it was upon the land of the owner. When the game was off the land, although it has the *animus revertendi*, the law did not recognise the right of property on account of that *animus revertendi*, although in that case it was to some extent produced by the art and care of man himself.[86]

iii. Russell's Focus on International Law

Russell summarised the case of the United States put by Carter in these terms:

1. That as the United States owns the Pribilof Islands, and as it can kill the fur-seals upon the Pribilof Islands, more or less as it liked, the United States is the owner of the fur-seals.
2. That no one is entitled to more than the usufruct of property; therefore, pelagic sealing on the High Seas, which may be, or is, wasteful of the stock, is an offence against international law.
3. That although neither the municipal law of the United States, nor the municipal law of England nor the municipal law of any civilised country would recognise property in the fur-seals as between individuals (even supposing this were a case of private assertion of right, and the Pribilof Islands belonged to a private person) yet the United States claimed that international law could be invoked to declare the property in the United States.[87]

Russell explained why some of these propositions were such in which the right conclusion was drawn from erroneous premises; where the wrong conclusion was drawn from correct premises; and, some, where both the premises and conclusion were wrong.

In putting his argument, Russell gave a rather philosophical direction to the Tribunal, one which perhaps arbitrators should bear in mind, in his case acknowledging that the Tribunal was acting as judges and jurists. He opined

> … that your duty is not to make the law, but to declare the law: not to speculate what the law ought to be, but to say what the law is: not to formulate or try to formulate novel rights, but to adjudge what are existing rights.[88]

Bearing in mind the unprecedented nature of this case, that task would be challenging and in making such international regulations revolutionary.

[86] *Ibid.*
[87] *Ibid* 7–8.
[88] *Ibid* 8.

Before asserting his main argument, Russell gave an opinion on what international law was. He put it thus:

> It may be admitted that all systems of law prevailing, I care not in what country, profess to be founded upon principles of morality, and upon principles of justice. Does it follow from that that every principle of justice, as one nation or another may view it, or every principle of morality, as one nation or another may view it, forms part of international law? By no means. International law, properly so called, is only so much of the principles of morality and justice as the nations have agreed shall be part of those rules of conduct which shall govern their relations one with another. So far as they have by agreement incorporated into the rules which are to regulate their mutual arrangements, relations and conduct, and so far only, can there be said to be an incorporation of the rules of morality and of justice, as to which nations as well as men differ: so far and so far only can they be said to be incorporated into international law. In other words, international law, as there exists no superior external power to impose it, rests upon the principle of consent. In the words of Grotius, *Placuit ne gentibus*? Is there the consent of nations? If there is not this consent of nations, then it is not international law: and I think it is very easy to illustrate that that must be so – that without that consent there cannot be said to be an *imprimatur* which can give force and efficacy to international law. If it were not so, international law would be in a constant state of flux and uncertainty.[89]

He then gave two examples on the question of consent in this context. The first example was the Treaty of Paris 1856 and the declaration as to the illegality of privateering which was discussed here earlier in the Geneva Arbitration, and the other the slave trade. Most countries in the world had condemned slavery by 1848, but in 1893 it was not against international law.[90] Russell said that whatever Chief Justice Marshall and Baron Parke decided was of no consequence to international law as they were the *interpreters* of international law and there was 'no necessary consensus of nations stamping with its imprimatur the traffic in slaves as an offence and crime against international law'.[91] He also quoted Lord Chief Justice Coleridge in *R v Keyn*,[92] a case in which 13 judges took part espousing the proposition that international law was nothing more nor less than the collection of usages which the civilised states have agreed to observe in their relations with one another. The Court held that the Law of Nations incorporated by agreement many principles of ethics and natural law. In Russell's view the phrase of Grotius, *placuit ne gentibus*, encapsulated the true idea of the Law of Nations. When text book writers, theorists and diplomatists made assertions as to those laws, the test in each case was not whether the rule so expressed, or the usage or the right so asserted, was humane, or was just, or was moral, the sole question was whether it had received the assent and consent of civilised

[89] *Ibid* 8–9.
[90] *Buron v Denman* (1848) 2 Ex 167.
[91] *Oral Argument of Great Britain* (n 2) 10.
[92] *R v Keyn* (1876) 2 Ex D 63.

nations: *placuitne gentibus*. That consent could be express or inferred from conduct by custom and usage.[93]

Russell went on to suggest that the United States had not been so much concerned with sealing in the Behring Sea and quoted from a report of the United States Committee of Ways and Means to show that the value of the seal islands was not considered because Russia had derived extraordinarily little benefit from them. Quoting Senator Sumner, he referred to an 'extraordinary ignorance at home and abroad relative to the Pribilof Islands'.[94] When Senator Morgan alluded to the British claims of exclusivity off the north American coast of 100 miles, Russell replied:

> I do not care where they were, with great deference; it is entirely immaterial to the point I am upon. Then came the American rebellion, and the independence of America. It thereupon became a sovereign Power, and it claimed that as it had borne its part when a colony in acquiring these rights and in exercising these rights, it was entitled, as an independent Power, to a continuance of those rights which as a colony it had previously enjoyed. The contention on the part of Great Britain was that it had lost its right by what it was pleased to call its act of rebellion, and that it had no right to share in those rights at all; and that matter was ultimately arranged by Treaties, only one of which you have referred to, (Treaty of Peace 1783) but which I will have to discuss at a later stage.[95]

This is a good example of how Russell dealt with interventions from Morgan who frequently intervened with counsel, pre-empting in many cases what counsel was going to address or making comments that were not directly relevant. It serves as a hint that too many interruptions sometimes defeat the purpose. Morgan was trying to suggest that Britain claimed the property in the fish in that region; this Russell firmly rejected. Russell agreed that while there was an assertion of rights of exclusive property undoubtedly, this was a quite different matter. Nations such as Spain and Britain, whilst claiming exclusive control of large stretches of the sea, had never claimed the property in free swimming animals in that area, or that they were the property of either government, or of any individual subjects of that government.[96] To underline his argument Russell referred to a Report of the Board of Trade of Port Townsend, a port in Washington Territory,[97] defining the terms of the lease of the 'Pribilof Islands and adjacent waters'. This was never meant or intended to mean the waters of the Behring Sea as a whole; but that the limit of one marine league from the shore as the recognised limit, outside of which were the High Seas.

As far as the definition of 'pelagic sealing' was concerned, the fact was pelagic sealing was the oldest pursuit of the fur-seal historically known. Russell

[93] *Oral Argument of Great Britain* (n 2) 11.
[94] *Ibid* 14–15.
[95] *Ibid* 17.
[96] *Ibid*.
[97] *Ibid* 18.

charged that it was not this practice at sea that had brought about the extermination of the seal species in its accustomed rookeries, but the slaughter upon the land.[98] This enabled him to make an effective argument and introduce evidence of American practices on the islands. He referred to the cruel conditions of the fur-seals on the Pribilof Islands in various reports, in particular those of Mr Elliott, which described the 'panting torture of travel' that fur-seals endured in being forced to the killing grounds on the islands.[99] Russell also pointed to the monopoly in trade, and the income generated from rent of the islands and taxes levied on each seal skin which the United States enjoyed to the exclusion of all other states and yet proclaimed it for benefit to all mankind.

At one point in his speech, we find hints of Russell's impassioned speech in defence of Parnell in the 1888 Special Commission in the context of America's fight for independence:

> I think America ought to be the last country, its representatives the last people, to seek to limit the rights of expostulation and of action on the part of colonists. They held a very free and very correct view of their rights in that regard while they were still colonists; and in the time of Lord North, the Lord Salisbury of that day, they showed very clearly, very plainly, and, as I believe, most justifiably, that they were the best judges of what their own interests as colonists demanded.[100]

Russell defended the role of the British Commissioners who investigated the actual facts as regards the alleged serious diminution of seal life on the Pribilof Islands, the date at which the diminution began, the rate of its progress, and any previous existence of a similar occurrence; as well as the causes of such diminution, whether and to what extent it was attributable to a migration of the fur-seals to other rookeries, method of killing pursued on the islands themselves, to the increase of sealing on the high seas, and the manner in which it is pursued.[101]

Having defended the Commissioners, Russell supported his argument by reference to a lease to the Hudson's Bay Company from Russia, before the sale of Alaskan territory to the United States, and for a number of years, the Hudson's Bay Company had a lease of an important part of Alaskan territory from Russia. It secured by barter from the natives all the pelts on that coast, including, to a limited degree, the fur-seal. In his view there was no limitation of pelagic sea.[102]

The United States never legislated to make pelagic sealing a crime or a wrong if committed by its own nationals outside a given area. Russell submitted that this was the first time in the history of the world that a nation or an individual

[98] *Ibid* 22.
[99] *Ibid* 23.
[100] *Ibid* 32. His speech in defence of Parnell was discussed in the author's article 'Indictment of a Nation' in (1982) 33 *Northern Ireland Law Quarterly Review* 277–85.
[101] *Oral Argument of Great Britain* (n 2) 33.
[102] *Ibid* 35.

had ever claimed property in a free-swimming animal in the ocean. It was the first time that an attempt had been made to differentiate one animal from all the other animals that dwelt in the ocean.[103]

In the context of international and municipal law, Russell argued that the United States had no right of sovereignty to apply its municipal legislation to the eastern part of the Behring Sea, or to base that right upon a derivative title from Russia. It could not be done upon the sole authority of one nation.[104] Russell could find no legal authority to support this proposition.[105] The ordinary right to defend property did not apply; it was a matter of freedom of the seas and equality of all nations.

Russell then referred to the case as to the seizure of British vessels and the question of liability, under Article IV of the Treaty; the derivative right from Russia, and propositions advanced on that authority. He compared the legislation of other nations as affording some foundation for the contentions advanced by Carter but could not accept the argument in such analogy that the legislation of other civilised countries could justify the claims under international law. On seizures he asked the Tribunal to find as fact that the British vessels were seized, unlawfully according to international law, albeit with the authority of the United States' Government.[106] The Tribunal enquired as to power to award damages but the parties agreed that the Tribunal would rule on liability only so the parties could agree damages and agree a statement of facts.[107] In respect of the claims by British fishermen, they claimed damages for loss of catch, probable catch, balance of probable catch, reasonable earnings and loss of profits.

Britain alleged that the number of fur-seals killed had increased following the American acquisition. The methods and management to sustain the population was inadequate.[108] Britain contested the figures submitted by the United States as to the killings, the seal herds had altered their behaviour, their habitats and their breeding islands.[109] The British Commissioners concluded that the primary reason for the reduced population of fur-seals was the disturbance by man.[110] In the Appendix to the British Argument, a comparison was drawn between statements given to the American and the British lawyers which were contradictory and mostly unreliable.[111]

[103] *Ibid* 39.
[104] *Ibid* 41.
[105] *Ibid* 44.
[106] *Ibid* 48.
[107] *Ibid* 49–57.
[108] *Case Presented on the Part of the Government of Her Britannic Majesty to the Tribunal of Arbitration Constituted under Article 1 of the Treaty Concluded at Washington on the 29th February 1892 Between Her Britannic Majesty and the United States of America* (Government Printing Office, 1895) (hereinafter '*British Case*') 77.
[109] *Ibid* 93–108.
[110] *Ibid* 112.
[111] *Ibid* 123–31.

Russell then dealt with the diplomatic correspondence passing between Washington and London concerning the proceedings in the Sitka District Court and the judgment of Mr Justice Dawson. He remarked on the change in approach when in March 1889, President Harrison succeeded President Grover Cleveland and Mr Blaine succeeded, as Secretary of State, to Mr Bayard. The policy became more antagonistic and further ships were arrested.[112]

iv. The Derivative Title Claim

Russell's most effective attack was on the question of the derivative title of the United States from Russia and the proposition asserted by the United States, unknown to international law, of the property right in fur-seals on the High Seas. He submitted that the United States had no right to proclaim that pelagic sealing by Britain was *contra bonos mores* in time of peace whatever the rights were in cases of belligerency. There could be no exclusive right to *mare clausum* in the Behring Sea: the right of freedom of the seas was a right given to all mankind and to all nations in common.[113] He analysed a number of United States' statutes referring to 'the waters of the territories ceded', 'within the waters of Alaska territory', 'extended to the Territory of Alaska and the waters thereof' or 'in the waters adjacent thereto'. He submitted that

> a Judge or a lawyer would construe them, still to mean (unless there was something in the context which showed a different meaning was intended), the marginal belt of three miles; the principle being, *terrae dominium finitur ubi finitur armorum vis.*

In other words, none of the United States statutes could be recognised as giving the United States exclusive territorial jurisdiction over that sea.[114]

As to the proceedings of Judge Dawson, he asked Sir Richard Webster to read the brief that was purportedly submitted by the Government of the United States to the judge. Mr Phelps disputed it. Whilst this brief was apparently not used in the Court, its references to Vattel's, *The Law of Nations* and the Treaty of Cession are enlightening in the context of the United States case. Vattel wrote:

> When a nation takes possession of certain parts of the sea, it takes possession of the empire over them as well as of the domain on the same principles which are advanced in treating of the land. These parts of the sea are within the jurisdiction of the nation and a part of its territory; the Sovereign commands them; he makes laws and may punish those who violate them; in a word, he has the same rights there as on the land, and in general every right which the laws of the State allow him.[115]

[112] *Oral Argument of Great Britain* (n 2) 63–70.
[113] *Ibid* 66–77.
[114] *Ibid* 71–82.
[115] E Vattel, *The Law of Nations, or, Principles of The Law Of Nature, Applied To The Conduct And Affairs of Nations And Sovereigns, With Three Early Essays on The Origin and Nature of Natural Law and on Luxury* (edited by B Kapossy and R Whatmore) (Liberty Fund, 2008) 130.

Further, the Treaty of Cession 1867 between Russia and the United States stated in Article 6:

> … the cession of territory and dominion therein made is declared to be free and unencumbered by any reservations, privileges, franchises, grants or possessions and conveys all the rights, franchises, and privileges now belonging to Russia in the said territory or dominion and the appurtenances thereto.

There is doubt as to whether this brief was used in Court but Russell used it to describe the position of the United States.

Russell's further argument as to the findings of Judge Dawson was the fact that because the Court was a municipal court it had no international jurisdiction. Mr Phelps argued that it had Prize Court jurisdiction, but Russell persisted in his argument.[116] He then reverted to the property issue. What was this exclusive jurisdiction and what exclusive rights in the seal fisheries did Russia assert and exercise? It could not be a right in relation to property or property interest as was claimed; it was not a right which had any legal circumscription at all. It was a right which existed wherever the property was to be found. It was the right to defend possession of property against anyone who attacked that property wherever it was. He submitted that such a right as the one which the United States sought to defend a special property interest, was not a right exercisable in a defined area; it was a right which, if it existed, would exist and be exercisable wherever the property to be defended at the time the right was asserted: it would have no local area of circumscription at all.[117]

Following these persuasive arguments, Russell then exposed several forged translated documents submitted by the United States. The United States had maintained a strong case based on derivative title without direct and detailed knowledge of the contents of certain Russian documents said to support their claim. When the documents were submitted in evidence, neither Mr Blain, nor United States' counsel knew that the translations were forgeries. They were only subsequently discovered. When they were, the United States radically altered its argument and case. The Russian evidence contained no reference to the fur-seals, no assertions by Russia in respect of jurisdiction or territorial control over the waters of the Behring Sea, in fact no acts of interference asserted or suggested by Russia in that sea at all.[118]

The argument as to protection of property was countered by Russell's claim that this was an assertion of territorial jurisdiction.

Summing up Russell's argument he answered the reference as to the first four questions under Article VI as follows:

1. That in 1821 only Russia asserted exclusive jurisdiction over a part of the Behring Sea along its coasts, but that she withdrew the assertion, and never

[116] *Oral Argument of Great Britain* (n 2) 99–109.
[117] *Ibid* 124.
[118] *Ibid* 114–19.

afterwards asserted or exercised such jurisdiction. That Russia exercised no exclusive rights in the seal fisheries in the Behring Sea prior to 1867; that in 1821, only, Russia claimed exclusive rights, as included in her claim of jurisdiction extending to 100 miles from the coast, but that she withdrew the assertion and never afterwards asserted or exercised such rights. The only exclusive right which Russia subsequently exercised was the right incidental to her territorial ownership.

2. That Great Britain neither recognised nor conceded any claims by Russia of jurisdiction as to seal fisheries, either (a) of exclusive jurisdiction in the Behring Sea, or (b) exclusive rights in the fisheries in the Behring Sea.
3. That the Behring Sea was included in 'Pacific Ocean' in the Treaty of 1825; that Russia neither held nor exclusively exercised any rights in the Behring Sea after the Treaty of 1825, save only such territorial rights as were allowed to her by international law.
4. That no rights as to jurisdiction or as to the seal fisheries in the Behring Sea east of the water boundary in the Treaty between the United States and Russia of the 30th March 1867, passed to the United States under that Treaty, except such as were incidental to the islands and other territory ceded.[119]
5. The fifth question on property right led Russell to attack Mr Carter's submissions in point and use the reports of Mr Elliott and the British Commissioners to good effect. He argued that the United States acquired property in the fur-seals on land when the seal was hit on the head and killed then acquiring property in the animal on the ground of reclamation, or *per industriam*. The municipal law of the United States gave no such right of property in the fur-seals. Mr Carter had relied too much 'on theories of a metaphysical writers as to that the law ought to be instead of what the law is'.[120] Thus, his submission in answer to question 5 of Article VI was thus:
6. That the United States have no right (a) of protection, or (b) of property in the fur-seals frequenting the islands of the United States in the Behring Sea when they are outside the ordinary three-mile limit.[121]

K. Diplomatic Discussions

During the hearings, diplomatic discussions continued with the interested parties. Rosebery informed Tupper that an arrangement had been reached with the Russian Government to prohibit sealing within a zone of 10 miles from the Russian coasts in the Behring Sea and other parts of the North Pacific Ocean,

[119] *Ibid* 179–80.
[120] *Ibid* 202–208.
[121] *Ibid* 401.

and within 30 miles around the Commander Islands and Robben Island. This was a provisional measure for a year without prejudice to the rights of either Power.[122] Tupper also attempted to reach agreement with Mr Foster as to the British claims concerning British ships owned by United States' citizens. Aside from the diplomacy, on the 31 May Russell and Phelps agreed that they would not be asking the Tribunal to make any finding on damages under Article V of the Treaty, nor under the *modus vivendi* of 18 April 1892.[123]

L. Close of Hearing

Towards the close of the British argument, the President praised Sir Charles Russell, the Attorney General, and Sir Richard Webster on their 'brotherly association' where their country's national interest was at stake. They were followed by Mr Robinson who made some humorous criticism of the assumption by the United States as to its position as trustees of the seal industry.[124] On the 8th of June the United States' Agent presented suggestions for regulations. These prohibited the killing or capturing of fur-seals in the North Pacific Ocean or the Behring Sea excluding the activities of Indians who used traditional methods of sealing and provided that any ship or boat belonging to either British or American citizens engaged in such pursuits could be sized by US or British naval vessels. Draft regulations were also proposed[125] which were later incorporated into the regulations by the Tribunal.

M. The Award of the Tribunal

The Tribunal's Award was published on 15 August 1893. After reciting references to the arbitration treaty and confirmations of ratification and the process of appointment of the arbitrators, it recited the questions referred to the Tribunal for answer and the request concerning regulations.

As to question 1: *What exclusive jurisdiction in the sea now known as the Behring Sea, and what exclusive rights in the seal fisheries therein, did Russia assert and exercise prior and up to the time of the cession of Alaska to the United States?*

The Tribunal answered this question by a majority decision. The arbitrators referred to the Russian Tsar's Ukase of 1821 which claimed a jurisdiction that extended 100 Italian miles from the Russian coast and its islands, at that time

[122] FO 414/289 *Minute of Meeting* (31 May 1893).
[123] *Ibid.*
[124] FO 414/289 No113 *Mr Tupper to The Earl of Rosebery* (8 June 1893).
[125] FO 414/289 No113 *Minutes of Meeting* (8 June 1893).

including Alaska and the Aleutian Islands. The treaties of 1824 with the United States and 1825 with Britain referred to the Russia's territorial rights as extending only within the reach of cannon shot from the shore. This was the legal position until the cession of Alaska to the United States. The Tribunal found that Russia never asserted in fact or exercised any exclusive jurisdiction in seal fisheries beyond the ordinary limits of its territorial waters.

As to question 2: *How far were these claims and jurisdiction as to the seal fisheries recognised and conceded by Great Britain?*

On this point the Tribunal by majority held that Britain did not recognise or concede any Russian claim as to the exercise of exclusive jurisdiction in the Behring Sea outside Russian territorial waters.

As to question 3: *Was the body of water known as the Behring's Sea included in the phrase 'Pacific Ocean', as used in the Treaty of 1825 between Great Britain and Russia; and what rights, if any, in the Behring's Sea were held and exclusively exercised by Russia after said treaty?*

The Tribunal decided that the Behring Sea was part of the Pacific Ocean for the purposes of the 1825 Treaty between Russia and Britain. Furthermore, it decided that Russia did not exercise any exclusive rights of jurisdiction in the Behring Sea nor any exclusive seal fishery rights other than those exercised in its own territorial waters.

As to question 4: *Did not all the rights of Russia as to jurisdiction and as to the seal fisheries in Behring's Sea east of the water boundary, in the Treaty between the United States and Russia of the 30th of March 1867, pass unimpaired to the United States under that Treaty?*

The Tribunal decided unanimously that such rights did pass unimpaired to the United States under that Treaty.

As to question 5: *Has the United States any right, and if so, what right of protection or property in the fur-seals frequenting the islands of the United States in the Behring Sea when such seals are found outside the ordinary three-mile limit?*

The Tribunal decided that the United States had no rights of protection or property in the fur-seals.

In addition to the questions answered, the Tribunal unanimously agreed the following regulations applicable to the Behring Sea.

Article I provided that the governments should:

> forbid their citizens and subjects respectively to kill, capture or pursue at any time and in any manner whatsoever, the animals, commonly called fur-fur-seals, within a zone of 60 miles around the Pribilov Islands, inclusive of territorial waters. The miles referred to were geographical miles, being 60 miles to a degree of latitude.

Article II provided that the governments should:

> forbid their citizens and subjects respectively to kill, capture or pursue, in any manner whatever, during the season extending each year, from the 1st of May to the 31st of July,

> both inclusive, the fur-fur-seals on the high sea, in the part of the Pacific Ocean, and inclusive of the Behring Sea, which is situated to the north of the 35th degree of North latitude, and eastward of the 180th degree of longitude from Greenwich till it strikes the water boundary described in Article 1 of the treaty of 1867 between United States and Russia and following that line up to Behring Straits.

Article III provided that:

> … only sailing vessels shall be permitted to carry on or take part in fur seal fishing operations. They will, however, be at liberty to avail themselves of the use canoes or undecked boats, propelled by paddles, oars, or sales, as are in common use as fishing boats.

Article IV provided that:

> Each sailing vessel authorized to fish for fur-fur-seals must be provided with a special licence issued for that purpose by its Government and shall be required to carry a distinguishing flag to be prescribed by its Government.

Article V provided that:

> The masters of the vessels engaged in fur seal fishing shall enter accurately in their official logbook a date and place of each fur seal fishing operation, and also the number and sex of the fur-seals captured upon each day. These entries shall be communicated by each of the two Governments to the other at the end of the fishing season.

Article VI provided that:

> The use of nets, firearms and explosives shall be forbidden in the fur seal fishing. This restriction shall not apply to shot guns when such fishing takes place outside of Behring's Sea, during the season when it may be lawfully carried on.

Article VII provided for the control of persons authorised to engage in fur-seal fishing.

Article VIII excluded application of rules to Indians living in the coastal territories of the United States and Britain and carrying on fur-seal fishing for themselves in canoes or undecked boats. The exclusion did not extend to the Behring Sea or the Aleutian Passes.

Article IX provided that these regulations would remain in force until the parties abolished or modified them by further agreement. They would be reviewed every five years.

Finally, the Tribunal found that the allegations and claims made by Britain in its case in relation to the searches and seizures of British vessels were true. There were 20 vessels in question that were seized or warned by United States revenue cutters in the period between 1886–1890.

N. A Milestone in Anglo-American Relations

Unlike the Geneva Arbitration, when tensions ran very high between the former colonial power and its former colonies this case marked the beginning of a closer diplomatic relationship between the countries of the Old and New Worlds. Perhaps because Britain, although the greatest sea power at that time, was realising that one day the United States would overtake it. But also, because they were both English speaking, had developed the same Common Law, held the same respect for the rule of law and sought an extension and promotion of that law internationally. Where Britain and America led, the world might follow. Here the fundamental argument of Britain was that the law of nations was recognised as such because all nations consented to it. This was a critical point because the whole case had turned upon international law not municipal law. It could only be resolved by this international tribunal by and with the consent of the states involved with regulations accepted by those states and then possibly by all others. This was a determination which both Britain and America supported.

In procedural terms, with it being in public, the arbitration was quite revolutionary in terms of conventional arbitration; perhaps more like an ad hoc international court than an arbitration although it did not hear witnesses or permit cross examination, all oral evidence having been taken on deposition. It reflected a desire for such disputes between states to be transparent in order to develop a greater understanding between them. Distrust was a problem in relation to Britain not exchanging witness statements simultaneously and America exhibiting forged documents.

As to advocacy this narrative has concentrated on Carter and Russell. Both were highly skilled advocates and no doubt Carter had a much harder task. Russell thought Carter tended to be caught in 'the mists and clouds of metaphysical and ethical discussion'. Russell was blunt and had little time for niceties, although he seemed to mellow as the case progressed. What comes through though, as per his other great feats of advocacy, was his total command of the case. He intervened numerous times to correct omissions on the other side but did not always get it right. However, he undoubtedly impressed the Tribunal and his American colleagues to the extent that he received invitations to speak in America and one of his finest speeches was at Saratoga. FE Smith considered it to be 'one of the greatest of his triumphs at the Bar'.[126]

II. THE ANGLO-VENEZUELA ARBITRATION

The Anglo-Venezuela Arbitration of 1898 involved an inquiry into rival territorial claims between Britain and the United States of Venezuela. In each case the parties relied on historical evidence as to the claims of competing Powers that settled, colonised and governed certain tracts of land at various times. By no means was this a simple exercise as there were competing claims and allegations

[126] FE Smith and NW Sibley, *International Law as Interpreted During the Russo-Japanese War* (T Fisher Unwin, 1905) 268.

based on prior Dutch and Spanish occupation. The Treaties of Münster, London and Utrecht were cited and interpreted, historical maps produced together with reports of missionaries, surveyors and various officials of interested parties providing altogether a complex territorial dispute involving an analysis of the history of European settlement and colonisation of the lands in question. It is no wonder that the argument of the British Attorney General, Sir Richard Webster, took 55 days.[127]

A. Overview of the Case

The result of the proceedings was that Britain succeeded in maintaining most of the land enclosed by the Schomburgk line drawn by Sir Robert Schomburgk, an engineer in 1840, which it had claimed since 1840.[128] A stretch along the coast of 30 square miles was taken out of Schomburgk's line which was of no particular value. The key point was that it did not affect the gold fields worked by British subjects within the boundary of the Schomburgk line.

The outcome was that Britain succeeded in getting access through the Barima and Amakuru Rivers, as well as a line along the north bank of the Cuyuni gaining the islands and the other tributary of the Cuyuni as far as the river Wenamu as an extension to the Schomburgk line. The arbitrators took no notice of the inhabitants' status under rule (a). This was a victory for Britain and once again demonstrated the effectiveness of arbitration and its promotion by Britain and America.

B. How the Dispute Arose

The case involved complex issues of fact and international law and delved into the history, examining the system established by King Philip II of Spain, the efforts of Catholic missionaries and even the expeditions of Sir Walter Raleigh. It considered how Spain traded and exploited the native population and excluded the Dutch (Project of Para) using natives in order to possess the gold mines. Those Dutch settlers who colonised the coast of Guiana worked hard to clear the forests and drain the land in order to grow crops supplying sugar and rum. The Dutch ruled Guiana for 30 years, but under increasing pressure from Spanish missionaries. The Dutch colony was seized by the British and French which substituted the growing of cotton for sugar cane.[129]

[127] 'The Anglo-Venezuelan Arbitration Commission: British Case, Counter Case, and Argument' (1900) *The Edinburgh Review* 191, 391.
[128] *Ibid.*
[129] *Ibid.*

The Spanish were beaten back by Venezuelans and Britain took Guiana from the Dutch in 1814.[130] Much of the history of this dispute was contained in a letter from Mr Olney, the United States Secretary of State, who wrote to Mr Bayard, the British ambassador in Washington, for Lord Salisbury's information.[131] Britain, it said, acquired the territory by a treaty with the Netherlands which granted Britain the establishments of the Demerara, Essequibo and Berbice. But Britain had no clearly defined western boundary of the territory. On the other hand, the Venezuelans claimed that their territory extended to the line of the Essequibo as the true boundary between Venezuela and British Guiana. According to Mr Olney, Britain had been indifferent to the question until 1840 when Sir Robert Schomburgk was commissioned to demarcate its true boundary.[132] This seemed to be corroborated by the fact that although Britain claimed the land the British never occupied the hinterland, but concentrated on the coastal region where the plantations were. These establishments were dependent on the slave trade and when that was abolished British interests were sustained by the discovery of gold.[133] The problem then was that there were no defined boundaries and the British miners working in the gold districts had to be protected. The Schomburgk line was marked out by posts and other symbols, but these had to be removed on the express instructions of Lord Aberdeen following vigorous protests from Venezuela.[134] Lords Granville, Rosebery and Salisbury attempted to reconcile differences with Venezuela notwithstanding the fact that the British boundary was unilaterally moved further west in succeeding years.[135] Thus, the Granville line commenced 29 miles from the Moruka River in the direction of Punta Barima and the Rosebery Line of 1886 placed it west of the Amacuro as far as the source of the Cumano River and the Sierra of Usupamo. The effects of these changes meant an enlargement of the British possession to 76,000 square miles in 1885 and 109,000 square miles in 1887.[136] In 1876, Venezuela offered to resolve the dispute by accepting the Morocco line, but Lord Granville rejected the proposal.[137] In 1886 there were further discussions to settle this and other matters with Mr Gladstone's administration by referring the dispute to a third Power or several Powers in amity with both.[138] But this was not agreed. In 1890, the Salisbury line fixed the starting point at the mouth of the Amacuro west of the Punta Barima on the Orinoco. Then in 1893 the Rosebery Line took the

[130] Previously Britain and Holland had had a close relationship in the 18th century, Britain guaranteeing Holland's frontiers and the succession to the Dutch throne. *Index to Sir Robert Schomburgk's Reports which Form Vol. II of Annex to the British Case* (Foreign Office, Harrison & Sons, 1904).

[131] Letter dated 21 July 1895 sent on behalf of the President of United States giving some views about the dispute between Britain and Venezuela as published in the *London Gazette* on 17 December 1895.

[132] *Ibid* 1.

[133] See Map on p 115 of British Guiana.

[134] Letter in *London Gazette* (n 131) 1.

[135] *Ibid.*

[136] *Ibid* 2.

[137] *Ibid.*

[138] *Ibid.*

boundary from a point to the west of the Amacuro as far as the source of the Cumano River and the Sierra of Usupamo. Such claims and boundary changes made it difficult for the parties to the dispute to reach agreement on how to settle the matter and it took some time for them to agree a reference to arbitration.

C. Diplomatic Overtures for Settlement – Intervention by the US

When Gladstone's administration fell over Irish self-government in 1886, Lord Salisbury, his successor, rejected the arbitration clause of a draft treaty Gladstone had considered to resolve the boundary issue. Venezuela however continued to press for arbitration but broke off diplomatic relations in 1887. Negotiations continued from 1890 until 1893 but reached another impasse in that year. It was at this point the United States intervened in that Mr Evart, then Secretary of State (formerly one of the United States Counsel in the Geneva Arbitration),[139] responded to Venezuela's concern by declaring that the United States' Government could not 'look with indifference to the forcible acquisition of territory by England'.[140] Mr Evart's successor, Mr Frelinghuysen, informed the United States Minister at Caracas that the United States would suggest arbitration to resolve the question and would

> cheerfully lend any needful aid to press upon Great Britain in a friendly way the proposition so made … and the United States, while advocating strongly the recourse to arbitration for the adjustment of international disputes affecting the United States of America, does not seek to put itself forward as their arbiter … and that, regarding all such questions as essentially and distinctively American, the United States would always prefer to see such contestations adjusted through the arbitrament of an American rather than an (sic) European Power.[141]

In 1884 the US Secretary of State instructed his Minister in London, Mr Lowell, to inform Lord Granville that the United States was not 'without concern as to whatever may affect our sister Republic'.[142] This was followed in December 1886 by a further intervention by the United States when Mr Bayard, the Secretary of State, instructed the United States Minister in London to tender his country's good offices to Britain to 'promote an amicable settlement of the respective claims …' It is clear from the instruction that the United States was keen on an accommodation with Britain in accepting that such matters would be amicably resolved. This *demarché* offering a form of mediation was declined as Britain preferred to resolve through direct diplomatic negotiations.[143] This was

[139] *Ibid.*
[140] Mr Evarts to Venezuelan Minister at Washington in *ibid* 2, 3.
[141] Letter in *London Gazette* (n 131) 3.
[142] *Ibid* 3.
[143] *Ibid* 4.

not resolved and the United States made a further *demarché* in February 1888 when the British proposed the construction of a railway (according to the Colonial Office List[144] outside the apparent western boundary of British Guiana) from Ciudad Bolivar to Guacipati. As before, Mr Bayard was very careful in his instructions but warned that if Britain's expansionist policy was unlimited then it would be a matter of grave concern. Matters came to head in 1889 when Barima at the mouth of the Orinoco was declared a British port. Mr Blaine was then the Secretary of State and Mr Lincoln the United States Minister in London.[145]

On 1 May 1890, Lincoln was instructed to use his good offices to promote the resumption of diplomatic relations between Britain and Venezuela and to suggest that the matter be resolved by arbitration, the attitude of the United States being one of 'impartial friendship towards both litigants'.[146] President Grover Cleveland authorised the Secretary of State to instruct Mr Bayard to put into effect the President's Annual Message to Congress of the 3 December 1893 that the United States desired the re-establishment of diplomatic relations between Venezuela and the United States, as well as to induce the disputants to resolve their differences by arbitration. This was subsequently endorsed by the Congress in a Joint Resolution of the 22 February 1895.[147] This was understandable in the context of the Pan-American Conference, when 17 out of the 19 American states met in Washington to establish a Tribunal of Arbitration for all inter-American disputes.[148]

D. Application of the Monroe Doctrine

The President was trying to apply the Monroe Doctrine by defining the United States' national interest in accordance with what it felt was its national honour and interpret the doctrine in relation to its sister American Republics.[149] President Washington in his Farewell Address had warned his countrymen against European entanglements. The Monroe administration concluded that this meant non-intervention in European matters and that European Powers should not interfere in the Americas.[150] In his Message to Congress of 2 December 1823, President Monroe had warned foreign Powers that 'any attempt on their part to extend their system to any portion of this hemisphere as dangerous to

[144] In particular the land defined in the List for 1877 was quite different from that described in 1887. Letter in *London Gazette* (n 131) 4.

[145] *Ibid.*

[146] *Ibid* 5.

[147] *Ibid.*

[148] FH Hinsley, *Power and the Pursuit of Peace* (Cambridge University Press, 1963) 266, 267.

[149] Letter in *London Gazette* (n 131) 5.

[150] *Ibid* 6.

our peace and safety'.[151] In essence, this declaration gave notice that any colonisation of the Americas by a European Power would be seen as an unfriendly act towards the United States.[152] This doctrine was advanced in argument by Mr Olney to Lord Salisbury, although the doctrine as Lord Salisbury advised Sir J Pauncefote, the British Ambassador in Washington,[153] had never before been advanced against any other state.[154] Lord Salisbury, writing to Pauncefote, took the view that Britain had sympathised with the doctrine in 1823 and supported those states in South America that sought independence of European Powers.[155] However, in this case as Lord Salisbury pointed out to his Ambassador the position of Britain was quite different: no system of government was being imposed on Venezuela and nor was Britain interfering politically. It was not a matter of colonisation but of delineating the boundary.[156] Interestingly, Lord Salisbury did not seem to have much faith in arbitration. As he opined:

> It is not always easy to find an Arbitrator, who is competent, and who, at the same time, is wholly free from bias; and the task of ensuring compliance with the Award when it is made is not exempt from difficulty.[157]

Salisbury considered that the Law of Nations did not provide that a third country could impose arbitration on two states in dispute with each other.[158] No such principle had ever been known to international law and Salisbury was quite correct in emphasising the point to Sir J Pauncefote that such matters rested on consent. Salisbury disputed that 'American questions are for American decision'.

He also took exception to Mr Olney's view that 'But with the Powers of Europe permanently encamped on American soil, the ideal conditions we have thus far enjoyed cannot be expected to continue'.[159]

The union of Britain with Canada, Jamaica, British Guiana and Honduras, was not, he said, 'inexpedient and unnatural' as Mr Olney had suggested. In ending his despatch Salisbury hoped that some reasonable arrangement could be made at an early date. Clearly his argument rested on international law whilst respecting the Monroe Doctrine as he interpreted it. In a second despatch of the same date,[160] Lord Salisbury corrected some of the erroneous impressions that Venezuela had given the United States as relayed by Mr Olney. The dispute did not

[151] *Ibid.*

[152] *Ibid.*

[153] Then British Ambassador in Washington but previously he was the Permanent Under-Secretary of State at the Foreign Office from 1882 until 1889.

[154] Letter in *London Gazette* (n 131) 11. *Lord Salisbury to Sir J Pauncefote* (26 November 1895). FO 420/238 *Boundary between British Guiana and Venezuela Further Correspondence.*

[155] Letter in *London Gazette* (n 131) 11. *Lord Salisbury to Sir J Pauncefote* (26 November 1895).

[156] Letter in *London Gazette* (n 131) 12. *Lord Salisbury to Sir J Pauncefote* (26 November 1895).

[157] Letter in *London Gazette* (n 131) 12. *Lord Salisbury to Sir J Pauncefote* (26 November 1895).

[158] Letter in *London Gazette* (n 131) 12. *Lord Salisbury to Sir J Pauncefote* (26 November 1895).

[159] Letter in *London Gazette* (n 131) 13. *Lord Salisbury to Sir J Pauncefote* (26 November 1895).

[160] Letter in *London Gazette* (n 131) 13. No 2 *Lord Salisbury to Sir J Pauncefote* (26 November 1895).

arise in 1814 but after 1840. The British title derived from the Dutch conquests of Demerara, Essequibo and Berbice. Indeed, the relationship between Britain and Venezuela was friendly. No evidence of the Venezuelan claims could be found regarding their boundaries being bordered by the Amazon and the Atlantic. The Dutch territory could be proved by reference to the Treaty of Münster 1648, the Dutch remonstrances to the Spanish Court in 1759 and 1769 as to the Dutch regions of the Cuyuni and Essequibo.[161] Venezuela also founded her claim upon a Papal Bull of Pope Alexander VI in 1493 which granted the whole American continent to Spain. Venezuela appeared to argue that lands to the north of the Amazon and west of the Atlantic were her inheritance.[162]

Lord Salisbury explained the circumstances of an expedition by Sir Robert Schomburgk into the interior of British Guiana between 1835 and 1839. He was instructed to survey the boundaries and the result was given to the neighbouring states that could raise objection. Schomburgk did not discover or invent anything; he relied on actual surveys and evidence of the native Indians and Dutch possessions.[163] He concluded that the Government could claim the Cuyuni and the Yuruari basins, ie that territory where the rivers flowed into the Essequibo. In consideration of the retention of Point Barima, Britain should renounce its claim to 'a more extended frontier inland'.[164] Lord Salisbury pointed out that Mr Olney was right to the extent that the Schomburgk line, as it was called, was simply a matter of 'convenience and expediency'. Britain could have claimed a greater extent of territory but the Schomburgk line was proposed as a 'speedy and friendly arrangement'.[165]

In January 1844, Britain started negotiations with Venezuela. Venezuela failed to produce any persuasive evidence as to its entitlement, but as a friendly gesture Britain offered a line starting from the mouth of the Morocco to the junction of the River Barima with the Waini, thence up the Barima, the point at which that stream approached nearest to the Acarabisi, and thence following the Schomburgk line from the source of the Acarabisi onwards.[166] This offer lapsed in 1850 as Venezuela never replied to it, however in that year Venezuela declared that it had no intention of making incursions on British territory.[167]

In 1876 Venezuela appeared to break the understanding of 1850 by granting licences to timber merchants in Barima. In 1879 Venezuela renewed its claim up to the Essequibo as her eastern boundary.[168] This was rejected by Britain, but it was prepared to negotiate. In February 1881 Venezuela proposed a settlement along the lines of Lord Aberdeen in 1844. This in turn was also rejected because

[161] Letter in *London Gazette* (n 131) 14. No 2 *Lord Salisbury to Sir J Pauncefote* (26 November 1895).
[162] Letter in *London Gazette* (n 131) 14. No 2 *Lord Salisbury to Sir J Pauncefote* (26 November 1895).
[163] Letter in *London Gazette* (n 131) 14. No 2 *Lord Salisbury to Sir J Pauncefote* (26 November 1895).
[164] Letter in *London Gazette* (n 131) 15. No 2 *Lord Salisbury to Sir J Pauncefote* (26 November 1895).
[165] Letter in *London Gazette* (n 131) 15. No 2 *Lord Salisbury to Sir J Pauncefote* (26 November 1895).
[166] Letter in *London Gazette* (n 131) 15. No 2 *Lord Salisbury to Sir J Pauncefote* (26 November 1895).
[167] Letter in *London Gazette* (n 131) 15. No 2 *Lord Salisbury to Sir J Pauncefote* (26 November 1895).
[168] *Lord Salisbury to Sir J Pauncefote* (26 November 1895).

it included many British subjects, although the Lieutenant Governor and Attorney General of British Guiana suggested adjustment to the Schomburgk line.[169] Lord Granville proposed this modification in September 1881, but this was again ignored by Venezuela. Worse, Venezuela breached the understanding or 'Agreement of 1850' by attempting to set up settlements on British territory and by their Minister Señor Guzman Blanco proposing arbitration over all the territory up to the left bank of the Essequibo.[170]

E. Sir Francis Bertie's Memorandum

According to a Memorandum prepared by Francis Bertie[171] dated 23 January 1896, notes were exchanged regarding arbitration between November 1883 and March 1884 when Britain rejected the suggestion but suggested 'other means'.[172] Discussions took place between Pauncefote and Señor Guzman Blanco when Lord Granville the Foreign Secretary was not available.[173] Such discussions took place when Señor Guzman Blanco came to England in October 1884. He persisted in his claim for a boundary arbitration or a mixed Anglo- Venezuelan Commission, but this was again rejected by Lord Granville on 13 February 1885 on the ground of 'constitutional difficulties'.[174] There was however some progress towards a commercial treaty which contained an arbitration clause to the effect that anything that could not be decided by 'friendly negotiation' should be submitted '… to the arbitration of a third power in amity with both, without resorting to war'.[175] In his memorandum dated 13 December 1884, Señor Guzman Blanco had suggested settlement of the boundary question by 'the Judgement of a Court of Law' but this was rejected. It is difficult to see what Court of Law would have had such jurisdiction in those days which both sides could have accepted. It appears that the reason for the British objection to arbitration was the difficulty in selecting a tribunal and a procedure.[176] Señor Guzman Blanco then suggested the adoption of 'Power' instead of 'Arbitrators' and that the clause should cover 'all differences which may arise between the High Contracting Parties, and not those only which arise on interpretation of the Treaty'.[177] However, the draft Commercial Treaty containing the

[169] *Ibid.*

[170] Letter in *London Gazette* (n 131) 16. No 2 *Lord Salisbury to Sir J Pauncefote* (26 November 1895).

[171] Later Sir Francis Bertie, British Ambassador to the French Republic, who played a crucial role in the July 1914 crisis, as discussed in chapter 7.

[172] FO 881/6725 *Memorandum respecting Lord Granville's Views as to referring to Arbitration the Dispute with Venezuela in regard to the Boundary of British Guiana* (23 January 1896) (Mr F Bertie) 1.

[173] *Ibid* 2.

[174] *Ibid* 1.

[175] *Ibid* 3. Art XVI Commercial Treaty.

[176] *Ibid* 3. Reference was made by Lord Granville to the arbitration clause contained in the Protocol to the Treaty dated 15 June 1883 between Britain and Italy.

[177] This closely followed the wording of Art 109 of the Federal Constitution of the Republic of Venezuela.

arbitration clause was considered too wide when Lord Salisbury succeeded Lord Granville.[178] 'Any difference' could well be interpreted as including the payment of British claims against Venezuela.[179] A way to avoid the problem was to exclude such matters concerning any question of sovereign territory or rights. Thus, on the 27 July 1885 Lord Salisbury informed Señor Guzman Blanco[180] that Britain was unable to concur in the previous assent given to agree to arbitrate any matters. His government could only assent to those arising out of the interpretation of the Treaty or any alleged violation of it excluding matters of sovereignty.[181] Lord Rosebery succeeded Lord Salisbury on 6 February 1886 and with Lord Granville, then Colonial Secretary, agreed that the British territory should be delineated along the lines advised by the Colonial Office in 1881.[182] This was a more westerly boundary and more natural in terms of the topography, and Granville suggested a concession of territory on the right bank of the Orinoco and territory beyond the boundary they then marked out.[183] As a precautionary measure the Admiralty was instructed to order the West India Squadron to cruise off the mouth of the Orinoco.[184]

F. Discussions about Arbitration

On 1 July 1886, Lord Rosebery proposed that the area of the unsettled lands between the Schomburgk line and Britain's rightful boundary should be the subject of a reference to arbitration or to a joint commission for the purpose of an equal division of territory, due regard being had to natural boundaries.[185] Some negotiation along these lines was conducted whilst the Venezuelan Minister Señor Guzman Blanco remained in London. Lord Rosebery separated the boundary dispute with Venezuela from the proposed Commercial Treaty negotiations. He suggested that Venezuela be given a 'Most Favoured Nation' clause and that Britain accept the arbitration clause in that Treaty limited to differences arising at the date of the signature of the Treaty, excluding the boundary question and that of the Isle of Patos.

[178] On 24 June 1885.

[179] This was Art XV which was criticised by Foreign Office advisers, including Sir F Pauncefote who wisely advised reference to the Law Officers.

[180] FO 881/6725 (n 172) 5.

[181] *Ibid.*

[182] *Ibid* 6.

[183] *Ibid.*

[184] Letter to the Admiralty (8 June 1886) as cited in *ibid.*

[185] FO 881/6725 (n 172) 6. Britain maintained its claim for all the territory within the Schomburgk line but to consider referring the unsettled lands between that line and Britain's rightful boundary to arbitration.

Britain declared that the Schomburgk line was the 'irreducible boundary of the Colony'.[186] Relations deteriorated when agents of the Venezuelan Government were sent into the British territory and Venezuela demanded the evacuation of the territory from the mouth of the Orinoco to the Pomeroon River failing which diplomatic relations would be broken off.[187] Diplomatic relations were suspended on the 21 February 1887. In December of that year a formal notice was served on the Venezuelan Government by the Governor of British Guiana formally reserving the British claim. Further discussions took place in 1890, 1891 and 1893 to renew diplomatic relations without progress.[188]

The dispute therefore crystallised in terms of an area of the coast line up to the River Amacura (Amakuru) and the whole basin of the Essequibo River, one area of which Britain could submit for arbitration, another within the boundary of the Schomburgk line, which she could not.[189]

Finally, Lord Salisbury concluded his despatch by arguing that Britain could not submit the matter to foreign jurists where it involved 'claims based on extravagant pretensions of Spanish officials in the last century' and which involved the transfer of British subjects who would be subjected to little protection from a country whose institutions were unstable.[190]

G. The Treaty of General Arbitration

A month after Lord Salisbury's despatches to Sir J Pauncefote, public opinion in the United States was stirred by President Cleveland's bellicose message to Congress calling for $100,000 for an investigatory commission to report on the divisional line between the Republic of Venezuela and British Guiana.[191] It appears that the American Minister in his despatch to Mr Bayard of 20 July 1895 misrepresented the position since it was entirely based on exaggerated Venezuelan allegations that Britain had ambitions to acquire large areas of South America in contravention of the Monroe Doctrine.[192] The President was supported in Congress by some Senators but received a condemnation from

[186] In the words of Lord Salisbury, see: Letter in *London Gazette* (n 131)16. No 2 *Lord Salisbury to Sir J Pauncefote* (26 November 1895).

[187] *Lord Salisbury to Sir J Pauncefote* (26 November 1895).

[188] *Ibid.*

[189] Letter in *London Gazette* (n 131) 17. No 2 *Lord Salisbury to Sir J Pauncefote* (26 November 1895).

[190] *Lord Salisbury to Sir J Pauncefote* (26 November 1895). Venezuela had been subject to considerable disturbances since gaining independence and this had also affected the course of negotiation.

[191] FO 881/6810/ *Part XII Further Correspondence Respecting the Boundary Between British Guiana and Venezuela also Correspondence Respecting Proposals for A Treaty of General Arbitration between Great Britain and The United States* (January to June 1896) 1–2.

[192] *Ibid* 2.

most eminent American jurists.[193] The *New York Herald* went so far as to state that: 'there is grave reason to fear that it [war] is coming'.[194]

Unlike the controversy over the Confederate cruisers, Britain was not showing any ill will towards the United States and so far as Britain's position was concerned it enjoyed the support of the European Powers.[195] The extraordinary effect of the message was that if Britain did not agree to the Commission, the United States would declare war.[196] Mr Morse, a Congressman from Massachusetts, reminded the House of Representatives that earlier that year he had presented a memorial to the Congress from the House of Commons to refer all questions of international dispute to arbitration.[197] He also, in passing, made reference to the dispute over the fur-seals in the Behring Sea which was not 'worth a day's war'.[198] Despite such reservations Congress voted the sums that President Cleveland required for a Commission.[199] In January 1896 it was suggested to Lord Salisbury by the former Lord Chief Justice of British Guiana, DP Chalmers, that the boundary-line be determined by international law.[200] The American jurist Wheaton was quoted to the effect that 'the acquisition of vacant territory by possession' should be the basis and primary condition for arbitration.[201] In *The Science of International Law* published just three years earlier, Walker opines that: '... But the main path of territorial aggrandisement undoubtedly lies in the occupation by civilised people of lands previously untenanted or tenanted only by persons little advanced in civilisation'.[202]

Chalmers' opinion based on Wheaton also alluded to the case of the Oregon boundary settled on the basis of the contiguity of vacant territory to the territory that was already settled and occupied by either party, and the facilities in place, as well as the natural boundaries.[203]

On 14 January 1896 the Colonial Secretary, Joseph Chamberlain, wrote to the Administrator of British Guiana requesting information as to the extent of concessions and grants of land within the Schomburgk line from Barima Point to the Dutch Guiana and to what extent they had actually been occupied and settled.

[193] *Ibid* 2.

[194] *Ibid* 2. Enclosure 2. Extract from the *New York Herald* of 22 December 1895. The consequences of the President's message was to spread panic in the financial markets and losses on them of $1,000,000,000. *Ibid* 4.

[195] *Ibid* 6. Article in the *New York Herald* by George W Smalley of 22 December 1895.

[196] *Ibid* 12. Speech of Hon Elijah A Morse, Mass. House of Representatives (26 December 1895).

[197] Congressional Record 53 Congress, Third Session, 2408. 19 February 1895.

[198] FO 881/6810/ (n 191) 13. Speech of Hon Elijah A Morse, Mass. House of Representatives (26 December 1895).

[199] FO 881/6810/ (n 191) 16. It was the view of a leading American jurist, Professor von Holst, that the President's approach was a perversion of the Monroe Doctrine which had been promoted by George Canning when he was British Foreign Secretary.

[200] FO 881/6810/ (n 191) 16. No 10 *Sir D Chalmers to the Marquess of Salisbury* (7 January 1896).

[201] *Ibid.*

[202] TA Walker, *The Science of International Law* (CJ Clay and Sons, Cambridge University Press, 1893).

[203] FO 881/6810/ (n 191) 17. No 10 *Sir D Chalmers to the Marquess of Salisbury* (7 January 1896).

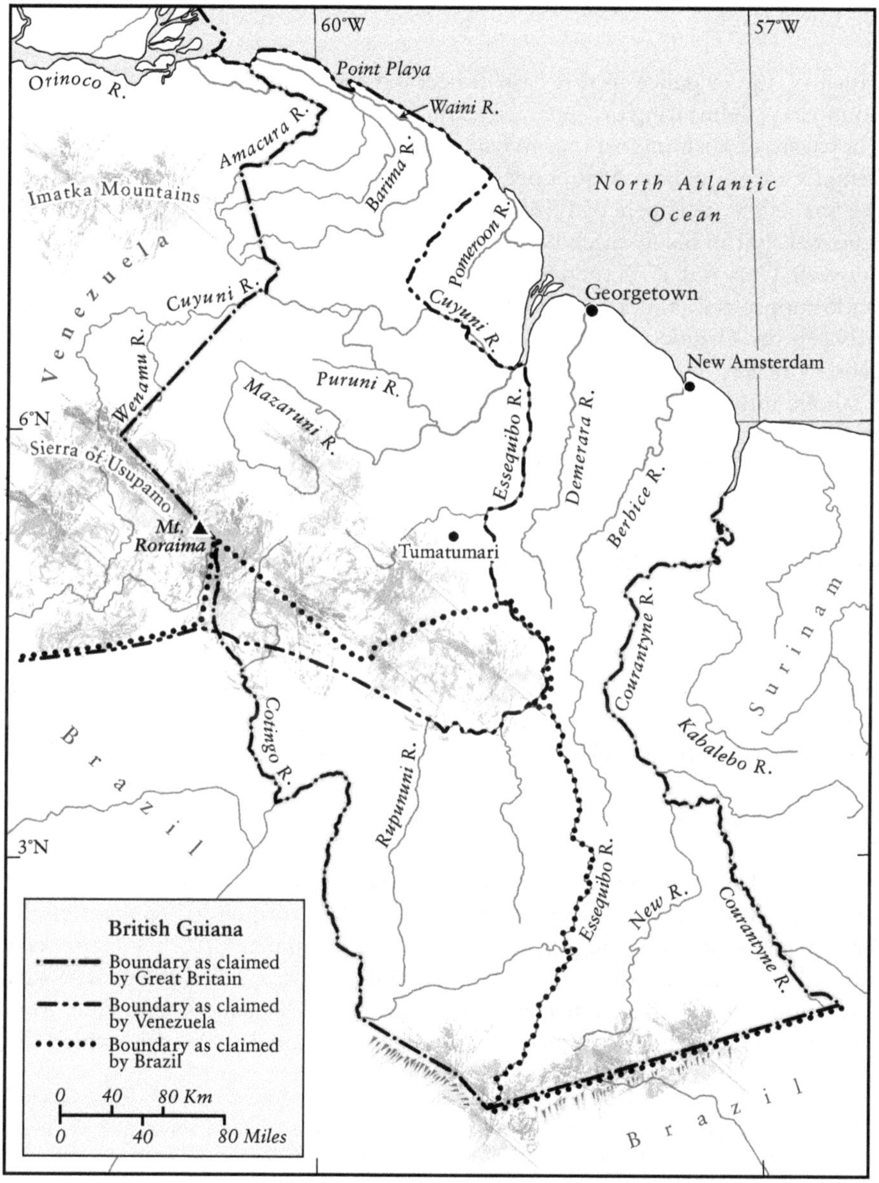

Figure 3.2 Map illustrating Venezuela-Guiana boundary
Credit: Mina Moshkeri

H. Cartography

Much of the evidence in this case concerned the position and the line of the boundaries delineating the separate territorial claims as found on various maps. They were of such importance in determining the respective claims that coincidentally, on 14 January 1896, Lord Salisbury received a letter from the Editor of the Spanish State Papers of Elizabeth at the Public Record Office. The archivist reported that in his research of the old Spanish records he had discovered that between 1766 and 1777 the Dutch had been dislodged from Guiana, the slave trade suppressed, and a large number of Spanish settlements were established between the Orinoco and the Essequibo. He stated that in the late eighteenth century it was reported that there were 1,800 inhabitants administered by the Catholic missionaries (Observant Fathers and Catalan Capuchins) in addition to the Barima Missions conducted by the Dominican Fathers who founded six new towns.[204] According to one of his sources, a large number of new towns were inside British claimed territory.[205] The day before that letter was received, Joseph Chamberlain suggested that information be obtained from the British Consul at Ciudad Bolivar as to how far Venezuela had occupied territory on their side up to the Schomburgk line.[206] Chamberlain's enquiries were essential in assessing the rival claims.[207] For this purpose an expedition into the interior was undertaken to the Upper Cuyuni.[208] Reports were received by the Administrator that there had been some incursions in the valley of the Barima and some Venezuelan threat at El Dorado opposite the Uruan police station. Despite such threats, Chamberlain took the view that conflict should be avoided and if the Venezuelans committed any aggression then they would be in the wrong. This would certainly counter the allegations made earlier by the United States against British actions.[209]

Research carried out in the Madrid Foreign Office confirmed that a map drawn by Major F von Bouchenwroeder in 1798 corresponded to most of the British maps of the same period. Besides this a number of other maps were studied with varying descriptions of the Dutch territory, but there were very few Spanish maps of the late eighteenth century.[210] The Cano y Olmedillo Map provided the clearest exposition of the maps examined in Madrid which did

[204] *Historia Corographica de la Nueva Andalucia, Provincias de Cumaná, Guyana y Vertientes del Orinoco, por el R.P. Antonio Caulin, Provincial de los R.R.P.P. Oberservantes en el Reino de la Nueva Granada*. Published 1779.

[205] FO 881/6810/ (n 191) 19. No 11 *Martin AS Hume to the Marquess of Salisbury* (14 January 1896).

[206] FO 881/6810/ (n 191) 19. No 12 *Colonial Office to Foreign Office* (15 January 1896).

[207] FO 881/6810/ (n 191) 19. No 12 *Mr Chamberlain to the Administrator of British Guiana* (14 January 1896).

[208] FO 881/6810/ (n 191) 19. No 15 *Colonial Office to Foreign Office* (18 January 1896).

[209] FO 881/6810/ (n 191) 19. No 15 *Colonial Office to Foreign Office* (18 January 1896) paras 6–9.

[210] FO 881/6810/ (n 191) 61–64. Enclosure in No 66. *Notes by Mr Houghton on Maps in the Madrid Foreign Office*.

not assign as much territory to Spain as Venezuela claimed regarding the right bank of the Orinoco and the mouths of the Essequibo and Cuyuni. The map of Major F von Bouchenwroeder made in 1798 showed extensive Dutch settlements along the banks of the estuary of the Essequibo at the mouth of the Cuyuni and other rivers even a little above Cape Nassau.[211]

I. Negotiations about the Constitution of the Tribunal

Following such enquiries, it was timely that the American Ambassador to Britain, Mr Bayard, wrote to Lord Salisbury on 27 February 1896 with a view to reaching 'a well-defined agreement for a basis of negotiation to constitute a tribunal for the arbitration of the boundary between British Guiana and Venezuela …'[212] For this purpose it was suggested that the British Ambassador in Washington have discussions with the American Secretary of State as to the reasons why Britain wanted to exclude the definition of 'settlements' by individuals in the territory in dispute. During this time, it appears that President Cleveland appointed a commission to investigate the dispute. The Venezuelans had little evidence and inquiries had to be made in London, at The Hague and in Spain.[213] This was corroborated by a further Memorandum from Mr Houghton[214] which dealt with analogies and differences between the boundary dispute between Colombia and Venezuela and the Venezuela-British Guiana dispute.

Mr Houghton had the opportunity of studying the arbitration proceedings between those South American Republics in the Spanish archives. Both disputants had sought evidence from Madrid as to the delimitation of the boundaries between the former Spanish provinces. More interestingly, the Award in that case published on the 17 March 1890 dealt with the case in six parts. The sixth part was the most relevant to the British case. This was based on the Venezuelan right to possession and *bona fide* possession of the territories to the west of the Orinoco.[215] This was the same ground that Holland had invoked in her claim against Spain. Although the jurisdiction of the Spanish Arbitration Commission was limited by the Treaties of the two Republics to a frontier line of 1810, the arbitrators considered the position a century before. In doing so they went deeper into the evidence of 'audiencia de Caracas', considering communications between the provincial Governors and the Spanish Government.[216]

[211] FO 881/6810/ (n 191) 64. Enclosure in No 66. *Atlases and Maps at the Madrid Foreign Office.*

[212] FO 881/6810/ (n 191) 65. No 68 *Mr Bayard to the Marquis of Salisbury* (27 February 1896).

[213] 'The Anglo-Venezuelan Arbitration Commission' (n 127) 191, 391.

[214] FO 881/6810/ (n 191) 75. No 88. Enclosure 2. *Memorandum on the Analogies and Differences that Exist between the question of the Limits of British Guiana and Venezuela, and similar cases in which Spanish American Republics have likewise sought in Spanish records and precedents data for the settlement of their disputes* (hereinafter 'No 88. Enclosure 2. *Memorandum*').

[215] FO 881/6810/ (n 191) 76. No 88. Enclosure 2 *Memorandum* (n 214).

[216] FO 881/6810/ (n 191) 76. No 88. Enclosure 2 *Memorandum* (n 214).

There was a paucity of detailed information and a lack of evidence which suggested that the Spanish authorities attached very little importance to the outlying districts and the coastal areas.[217] Another telling point he made was that when Britain succeeded to the Dutch territory in 1814, Spain made no objection or when Holland had assumed Spanish rights over the area if indeed Spain had any.[218] Thus, Houghton suggested it would be advantageous to the British case if it made reference to the Spanish Award of 1890 and the *bona fide* occupation of those lands by the Dutch from 1648 to 1800, as well as the natural frontiers.[219]

On the 5 March 1896, Lord Salisbury received a despatch from Sir Horace Rumbold in Geneva stating that the Commission appointed by President Cleveland to enquire into the boundary between British Guiana and the Venezuelan Republic had sent an envoy to Madrid to access the Spanish State archives.[220] That same day Lord Salisbury wrote to the British Ambassador in Washington, Sir J Pauncefote, saying that it was a favourable time to discuss the question of arbitration over the Venezuelan-British Guiana boundary.[221] Matters of national honour or integrity would be excluded.[222]

J. Lord Salisbury's Draft Arbitration Treaty

What is remarkable here is that Lord Salisbury attached to his despatch draft heads for an Arbitration Treaty in certain cases and that he looked upon this as an experiment. This could be interpreted as an instrument to resolve the Venezuelan crisis or of more general application. It is odd perhaps that he did not refer to the earlier Treaty of Washington of 1872 discussed in chapter 2. But he knew enough to distinguish between arbitration affecting a state's subjects and one concerning a claim regarding sovereign rights and territory. So far as the first category was concerned this was analogous to private arbitration. As to the second it was more difficult because the second category concerned the 'collective capacity' of the state.[223] The problem was that a state could lose its prestige through such a process and much depended on the choice of tribunal. Lord Salisbury was sceptical about this and feared that 'rival challenges would pretty well exhaust the catalogue of the nations from whom competent and suitable Arbiters could be drawn'.[224] He said there was no Court of Appeal to correct his law, no jury to find his facts and it was tantamount to accepting a foreign rule.[225]

[217] FO 881/6810/ (n 191) 77. No 88. Enclosure 2 *Memorandum* (n 214)
[218] FO 881/6810/ (n 191) 77. No 88. Enclosure 2 *Memorandum* (n 214).
[219] FO 881/6810/ (n 191) 77. No 88. Enclosure 2 *Memorandum* (n 214).
[220] FO 881/6810/ (n 191) 77. No 89 *Sir Horace Rumbold to the Marquis of Salisbury* (4 March 1896).
[221] FO 881/6810/ (n 191) 78. No 90 *The Marquis of Salisbury to Sir J Pauncefote* (5 March 1896).
[222] An important reservation in most such cases where the sovereignty of the state may be in question.
[223] FO 881/6810/ (n 191) 78. No 90 *The Marquis of Salisbury to Sir J Pauncefote* (5 March 1896).
[224] FO 881/6810/ (n 191) 78. No 90 *The Marquis of Salisbury to Sir J Pauncefote* (5 March 1896).
[225] FO 881/6810/ (n 191) 78. No 90 *The Marquis of Salisbury to Sir J Pauncefote* (5 March 1896).

This is surprising because of the earlier Geneva Arbitration of 1871 which Lord Salisbury must have known about and its multi-national tribunal of jurists who were eminent lawyers. But what he suggested in his draft was a novel approach. He appeared to have less confidence in arbitrators than judges and proposed a somewhat novel approach to the arbitration process.[226]

In his heads of a Treaty for Arbitration Lord Salisbury provided for the appointment of two or more permanent judicial officers, and in the event of any difference between the two Powers these officers would sit as arbitrators.[227] The arbitrators would then select an umpire who would decide any matter upon which they would disagree. Either the two arbitrators or the Umpire's determination would be regarded as the Award. The jurisdiction of the Tribunal would extend to: all claims or groups of claims amounting to not more than £100,000against either Power, by the nationals of the other, whether based on the alleged rights by treaty or agreement or otherwise; all claims for damages or indemnity under the said amount; all questions affecting diplomatic or consular privileges; all alleged fishery rights; access to navigation or commercial privilege; and all questions referred by special agreement between the two parties referred in accordance with the treaty. The Award was to be final.

However, the proposed Treaty made a curious provision for appeal on a matter of fact as well as one of international law. In respect of any question of fact or of international law involving the territory, territorial rights, sovereignty or jurisdiction by either Power or any pecuniary claim or group of claims of any kind involving a sum in excess of £100,000 referred to such arbitration, either party could apply within three months of the Award being published on the ground of an error of fact or issue of international law for the Award to be reviewed by a court comprising three judges from the Supreme Court of England and Wales and three judges of the Supreme Court of the United States. Such court was required to give judgment by a majority of five to one. In that case the Award would be final and binding. If the judges did not come to such a judgment by that means then the Award would be void. The venue and timing of the arbitration was a matter to be decided by the arbitrators or by the umpire if appropriate.[228]

This was an extraordinary constitution for such a tribunal whose Award would not be final, but subject to an appeal on law and fact to a superior judicial tribunal. The novel aspect was that of the two Powers involved, only Britain would be represented by a nominated officer as arbitrator in the event of unsuccessful negotiations and Venezuela would not be represented by one

[226] To this day there is a procedure under the Civil Procedure Rules 1996 for the Lord Chancellor to grant permission for a TCC judge to sit as an arbitrator, although such appointments are rare.

[227] FO 881/6810/ (n 191) 79. Enclosure in No 90 *Heads of a Treaty for Arbitration in Certain Cases.*

[228] FO 881/6810/ (n 191) 79–80. Enclosure in No 90 *Heads of a Treaty for Arbitration in Certain Cases.*

of its judicial officers but by one from the United States. Furthermore, in any appeal Venezuela would not have its judges on the court. This underlines a point that may have escaped Lord Salisbury in his reading of Mr Olney's despatch of the 20 July 1895 that Olney was accepting Britain's argument on prescriptive and historical rights to the detriment of Venezuela.[229] Venezuela's key argument based on 'historical right' was thus removed. In effect Venezuela's position was subservient to the American interpretation of the Monroe Doctrine to the benefit of Britain and America.[230]

Despite the belligerent tone of the earlier communications between Washington and London, by March 1896 the tone was very polite as between the American Ambassador in London, Mr Bayard, and Lord Salisbury; although Lord Salisbury's approach had consistently been polite and diplomatic.

On 10 March 1896, Mr Chamberlain received a despatch from the Acting Governor in Georgetown Demerara enclosing a copy of the American Consul's request for information as to British settlements and grants between the Essequibo and the Schomburgk line, and interestingly those grants to United States' citizens.[231] Responding to Lord Salisbury's proposed draft treaty, Mr Olney informed Sir J Pauncefote in Washington that the treaty should be amended to provide that the decision of the arbitral Tribunal should be final if given unanimously.[232] In other cases there could be an appeal against the Award which would be reviewed by six Supreme Court judges, their decision to be final whether by a majority or by unanimous decision. If this 'Court of Review' was equally divided, then Britain and the United States should appoint three jurists to be selected by agreement and the extended court's Award should be final if rendered by a majority.[233]

Whilst these diplomatic exchanges were taking place, Mr Houghton was continuing his enquiries in Spain but reported that this had been very thorough and little was left to examine.[234] At the same time, a Venezuelan Special Agent was reported to be seeking evidence from the Vatican archives. Lord Salisbury instructed his Ambassador to the Holy See to report any information.[235]

[229] JAS Grenville, *Lord Salisbury and Foreign Policy at the Close of the Nineteenth Century* (The Athlone Press, 1964) 60.

[230] It may well be regarded perhaps as an endorsement of a closer relationship that was developing between Britain and America.

[231] FO 881/6810/ (n 191) 82. Nos 97 and No 97. Enclosures 1 and 2 *Colonial Office to Foreign Office* (Downing Street, 9 March 1896).

[232] FO 881/6810/ (n 191) 93. No 113 *Sir J Pauncefote to The Marquis of Salisbury* (21 March 1896).

[233] FO 881/6810/ (n 191) 93–94. No 113 *Sir J Pauncefote to The Marquis of Salisbury* (21 March 1896).

[234] FO 881/6810/ (n 191) 93. *Memorandum by Mr Reddan on Mr Houghton's Searches in Spain* (21 March 1986).

[235] FO 881/6810/ (n 191) 94. No 115. *The Marquis of Salisbury to Sir Clare Ford* (Foreign Office, 21 March 1896).

K. Wider Implications for the Resolution of International Disputes

Subsequently there were further exchanges between Sir J Pauncefote and Mr Olney which not only considered further refinements to the draft Arbitration Treaty but laid the foundation for further discussion between Britain and the United States as to a 'general system of arbitration of disputes between the two Governments'.[236] In his despatch Mr Olney remarked that a 'general arbitration scheme not perfected through repeated arbitration experiments' entailed the risks of erroneous awards.[237] Perhaps he had in mind a permanent system of international inter-state arbitration such as was conceived later in the Permanent Court of Arbitration.

So whilst Olney's objective was to propose a means to resolve the Venezuelan dispute he had a wider objective with the idea of a general treaty of arbitration which could be adapted to deal with the British Guiana boundary.[238] Lord Salisbury replied to Mr Olney's remarks on 18 May 1896 welcoming the approach of the United States to resolve 'all differences of opinion'.[239] Not only that but he agreed with Mr Olney that they should agree general principles applicable to disputes 'not just between Great Britain and the United States, but between either of them and any other government'.[240]

This was of considerable significance for the dispute but more importantly for the future of world peace and the work that was subsequently undertaken by international jurists. Lord Salisbury suggested that the United States and Britain could agree a General Arbitration Treaty which would facilitate such a treaty dealing with territorial disputes. Whereas the United States was prepared to refer all territorial claims to arbitration, Britain was not. Arbitration for such matters was never obligatory.[241] Furthermore, whereas costs in arbitration was usually a deterrent to the losing party that did not apply in the case of governments that might be prepared to submit speculative claims. Lord Salisbury was also concerned that the threat of arbitration would disturb the inhabitants who might become exiles or be forced to change allegiance. On the other hand, arbitration might prevent a war, but it was an untried system and there might be doubts as to the impartiality of arbitrators and their competence.[242]

There were other problems such as the interpretation in international law in respect of international prescription, territorial property and constructive occupation and control.[243] Such a measure might encourage numerous cases but would also have to be adopted to suit Britain's constitutional usages.[244]

[236] FO 881/6810/ (n 191) 111. No 135 *Mr Olney to Sir J Pauncefote* (11 April 1896).
[237] FO 881/6810/ (n 191) 113. No 135 *Mr Olney to Sir J Pauncefote* (11 April 1896).
[238] FO 881/6810/ (n 191) 114. No 135 *Mr Olney to Sir J Pauncefote* (11 April 1896).
[239] FO 881/6810/ (n 191) 129. No 149 *The Marquis of Salisbury to Sir J Pauncefote* (18 May 1896).
[240] FO 881/6810/ (n 191) 129. No 149 *The Marquis of Salisbury to Sir J Pauncefote* (18 May 1896).
[241] FO 881/6810/ (n 191) 130. No 149 *The Marquis of Salisbury to Sir J Pauncefote* (18 May 1896).
[242] FO 881/6810/ (n 191) 130. No 149 *The Marquis of Salisbury to Sir J Pauncefote* (18 May 1896).
[243] FO 881/6810/ (n 191) 130. No 149 *The Marquis of Salisbury to Sir J Pauncefote* (18 May 1896).
[244] FO 881/6810/ (n 191) 131. No 149 *The Marquis of Salisbury to Sir J Pauncefote* (18 May 1896).

Overall fear of a miscarriage of justice would discourage parties but they might be assured of remedy where there could be recourse to an appellate court if the award was 'manifestly unjust'.[245] Despite these reservations Lord Salisbury considered that territorial disputes could not be arbitrated unless 'the safety and practicability of this mode of settlement are first ascertained by a cautious and tentative advance'. Sir Julian Pauncefote asked Lord Salisbury whether he could suggest a new clause as an alternative to Article V that where a party disputed the Award it could be reviewed by a court composed of not less than five judges of the 'Supreme Court of the Power protesting'.[246] This would seem to undermine the independence of the arbitral Tribunal and lead possibly to a charge of bias by the complainant's national court, but this, according to Sir J Pauncefote, would be acceptable to Mr Olney. In response to that Mr Olney acknowledged the proposal but made it clear that the Venezuelan boundary dispute could not be part of a General Treaty of Arbitration between Great Britain and the United States.[247]

Following further consideration by the United States' Government, Mr Olney raised some 'minor criticisms' of the 22 May proposal. The United States had difficulty in accepting a restriction on the arbitrator's jurisdiction to define a boundary that excluded any territory occupied by a British subject.[248] The point argued by Mr Olney in his communication of 12 June 1896[249] was that mining licences, grants and concessions had been given to British subjects with notice that such might be within the area claimed by Venezuela. In such a case it had been suggested by the Governor of British Guiana that compensation might then be claimed from Venezuela. Mr Olney strongly objected to this on the basis that such persons may well have been deceived by the British Government and that this was no matter for Venezuela but for Britain.[250] He argued that Britain could not assert this point because such permissions as were given were made with full notice of the Venezuelan claims. He relied on the evidence of the Governor of British Guiana who in June 1887 gave notice of the Venezuelan claims to the Court of Policy of the Colony.[251] In order to resolve this argument Olney suggested that the Tribunal be empowered to 'give such weight and effect … to such occupation as reason, justice, the rules of international law, and the equities of the particular case may appear to require'. In other words, the impasse might be overcome by granting the Tribunal a wide discretion.[252]

[245] FO 881/6810/ (n 191) 131. No 149 *The Marquis of Salisbury to Sir J Pauncefote* (18 May 1896).
[246] FO 881/6810/ (n 191) 130. No 167 *Sir J Pauncefote to The Marquis of Salisbury* (2 June 1896).
[247] FO 881/6810/(n 191) 185. Enclosure 3 in No 193 *Mr Olney to Sir J Pauncefote* (6 June 1896).
[248] FO 881/6810/ (n 191) 130. No 149 *Sir J Pauncefote to The Marquis of Salisbury* (15 June 1896).
[249] FO 881/6810/ (n 191) 186. Enclosure in No 194 *Mr Olney to Sir J Pauncefote* (12 June 1896).
[250] FO 881/6810/ (n 191) 187. Enclosure in No 194 *Mr Olney to Sir J Pauncefote* (12 June 1896).
[251] FO 881/6810/ (n 191) 187. Enclosure in No 194 *Mr Olney to Sir J Pauncefote* (12 June 1896).
[252] FO 881/6810/ (n 191) 188. Enclosure in No 194 *Mr Olney to Sir J Pauncefote* (12 June 1896).

L. Colonial Office Reservations

In a Colonial Office file[253] there is a handwritten note dated 26 January 1897 to the effect that the question of any concessions had to be carefully considered. It did not want another 1850 situation to arise and that the status quo was the Schomburgk line stated in the file to be 'a provisional boundary'. It was considered that the agreement had to be drafted so as 'to avoid fresh disputes and contingencies' and that areas in dispute in the land unoccupied at the date of the arbitration agreement between Britain and Venezuela should remain unoccupied until the date of the Award.[254] This would preclude the construction of any road or railway between the Essequibo and the Orinoco, and the opening of any new mine in the Gold region. Neither government should occupy or grant land or make any road or railway on the side of the Schomburgk line further from its own undisputed territory and all grants made on the disputed territory should be subject to the Award. It was said: '… this will be bad enough for capitalists who will find themselves under a semi-burdensome state like Venezuela'.[255] The note then went on to warn that the Foreign Office did not appreciate the problems of British Guiana. It stated: 'The F.O. do not appreciate the difficulties of the colony and I am afraid the Attorney General will brief for unqualified paralysis pending the arbitration'.

Mr E Wingfield who wrote that note advised there be a conference with the Foreign Office and that he had so advised Joseph Chamberlain.[256] The British Ambassador in Paris, Edmund Monson, informed Lord Salisbury on the 23rd January 1897 that France would be willing to hold the arbitration hearings in Paris. The hearings would be held in the splendid offices of the French Foreign Ministry. Mr Monson could not confirm that and asked Lord Salisbury for instructions. The French Government understood that a General Treaty of Arbitration had been signed between Britain and the United States, as well as an arbitration agreement between Britain and Venezuela.[257] The French were a little presumptuous since the Treaty was not signed until the 2nd February 1897. So far as Mr Chamberlain was concerned the proposal for non-occupation of the unoccupied, undeveloped and un-utilised areas were such that no adverse possession could be permitted. The status quo had to be maintained so that neither government should occupy or permit its subjects to occupy any such territory on either side of the Schomburgk line furthest from Georgetown and Caracas pending the Award.[258]

[253] Colonial Office (CO) 111/499 *Venezuelan Arbitration Treaty-Question of Status Quo Pending Arbitration Proceedings* (1897).

[254] CO 111/499. File Note (26 January 1897).

[255] CO 111/499 File Note (27 January 1897).

[256] *Ibid.*

[257] CO 111/499. No 1 (22 January 1897).

[258] CO 111/499 No 1 *Colonial Office to Foreign Office*. Downing Street. E Wingfield. Secret and Confidential (7 January 1897).

On 29 January 1897 Sir J Pauncefote sent a copy of the draft Anglo-Venezuelan Treaty as finally agreed between him and Señor Andrade to Lord Salisbury.[259] It then only needed the assent of the King of Sweden and Norway and the designation of the arbitrators to complete.

M. The Anglo-Venezuelan Treaty of Arbitration 1897

The Anglo-Venezuelan Treaty of Arbitration 1897,[260] Article I provided for the immediate appointment of an arbitral Tribunal to determine the boundary between Venezuela and British Guiana. Article II provided for the constitution of the Tribunal of five jurists. Two to be nominated by the Judicial Committee of the Privy Council, two for Venezuela one nominated by the President of Venezuela and one by the Justices of the Supreme Court of the United States. Within three months of the exchange of ratifications of the Treaty the arbitrators were to agree a fifth nomination, failing which the nomination was to be made by the King of Sweden and Norway.

Article III described the scope of the jurisdiction:

> to investigate and ascertain the extent of the territories belonging to, or that may be lawfully claimed by, the United Netherlands or by the Kingdom of Spain respectively at the time of the acquisition by Great Britain of the Colony of British Guiana–and shall determine the boundary-line between the Colony of British Guiana and United States of Venezuela.

Like the Geneva Arbitration, this Treaty of Washington also contained three rules in Article IV. These provided that the Tribunal decide title by the principles of international law not inconsistent with:

a) Adverse holding or prescription during a period of 50 years[261] shall make a good to title and the arbitrators may deem exclusive political control of the district as well as an actual settlement thereof sufficient to constitute adverse holding or to make title by prescription.
b) The arbitrators may recognise and give effect to rights and claims resting on any other ground whatever valid according to international law, and on any principles of international law or to which the arbitrators may deem to be applicable to the case, and which are not in contravention of the foregoing Rule.
c) In determining the boundary-line, if territory of one party be found by the Tribunal to have been, at the date of this Treaty, in the occupation of

[259] CO 111/499 *Sir J Pauncefote to The Marquis of Salisbury* (29 January 1897).
[260] Signed at Washington on 2 February 1897. Ratifications exchanged in Washington on 14 June 1897.
[261] Sir Richard Webster for Britain later argued that the 50 years related back from the date of the Treaty to 1821, but the Venezuelans argued that it related back 50 years before the Treaty of London of 1814, ie back to 1764.

> the subjects or citizens of the other Party, such effect shall be given to such occupation as reason, justice, the principles of international law, and the equities of the case shall, in the opinion of the Tribunal, require.

Article V provided that the venue of the hearing be in Paris or elsewhere if the Tribunal so decided and that the Tribunal meet 60 days after delivery of the Arguments.

Article VI provided for the delivery of the parties' printed cases eight months from the date of exchange of the Treaty ratifications.

Article VII provided for the delivery of any counter-case four months after the delivery of the printed case. This provision gave the Tribunal specific power to order disclosure of a copy or original of any report or document referred to in its case provided notice was given within 30 days of service of the case.

Article VIII provided for the submission of points of argument within three months of the service of the counter-case of both sides. The Tribunal could require further elucidation of such arguments by written or oral submission.

Article IX empowered the Tribunal to grant extensions of time regarding the process of Articles VI-VIII.

Article X provided for the signing and publication of the Award[262] within three months of the close of argument on both sides.

Articles XI and XII related to the record of the proceeding's costs and expenses, with each side to pay its own costs of counsel and the arbitrators appointed by it or on its behalf.

N. Rules of Procedure

The Rules of Procedure[263] provided that the agents of the two governments had a right to appoint special secretaries for the purposes of reporting on the proceedings, but not any private discussions by the Tribunal behind closed doors.[264] Such reports had to be signed by the President, the respective government agents and countersigned by the Principal Secretary.[265] The proceedings were to be conducted in French or in English and the final report in three languages: English, French and Spanish.[266] The public were to be admitted provided they had tickets.[267] This was a departure from the general rule that all arbitration proceedings are conducted *in camera*. The President of the Tribunal, M de Martens,

[262] The Treaty refers to 'decision of the Tribunal'. Arbitrators make Awards and this would be regarded as a Final Award. In some cases, however, international tribunals may be asked to give a decision and then to follow it up with a reasoned award.

[263] See FO 420/397 *Hotel Du Ministère Étrangères, Paris. Arbitration Between the Governments of Her Britannic Majesty and the United States of Venezuela. Rules of Procedure* (14 June 1899).

[264] *Ibid* Rule 1.

[265] *Ibid* Rule 2.

[266] *Ibid* Rule 3. The Final Award was to be in the same three languages. Rule 19.

[267] *Ibid* Rule 5.

had control of the proceedings.[268] The rules further stipulated that as the preliminary proceedings had closed the Tribunal had the right to refuse the production of any further enactments or documentary evidence.[269] It also had the right to demand production of any such documents it may be invited to consider and to communicate them to the other party.[270] Furthermore, it had power to require production of any act or document and further require explanation as it might deem necessary.[271] Counsel could make oral arguments and make any motion or amendment but that the ruling given by the Tribunal would be final and binding.[272] The Tribunal could put any questions to the agents or counsel and demand further and more detailed explanations of any doubtful points. Any such observations by the Tribunal were not to be regarded as expressing a particular view of the Tribunal in general.[273] Importantly, the Tribunal had the power to determine its own jurisdiction on the basis of the Treaty of Washington 1897 and international law.[274] However, the approach adopted by the Tribunal was viewing the proceedings as a debate with counsel giving explanations and proofs.[275] The idea of a debate is very much a civil law aspect not a common law one but demonstrates the fusion of approaches in agreeing a fair process to both sides. During these 'debates' the Tribunal could proceed *in camera*.[276] The procedure was decided by a majority of the arbitrators.[277] The rules stipulated that the Final Award would be read to the parties and that counsel should assist at that meeting.[278] Three copies of the award were to be made; one for Britain's agent, one for Venezuela's agent and one to be deposited in the archives of the French Republic.[279] The Final Award would be decisive as to the lines of the frontiers between the respective parties.[280] These rules were adopted by the Tribunal sitting in Paris on 14 June 1899.

These rules are interesting in that they had to accommodate lawyers from different jurisdictions and apply common rules of natural justice and fairness in their deliberations. Influences such as the common law tradition of full disclosure of documents has some bearing on Rules 8–10 and the power to order production. The rules generally follow the practice in the courts, eg, Rule 13 questioning counsel to elucidate a point. Remembering what happened at the end of the Geneva Arbitration when Sir A Cockburn refused to sign the Award,

[268] *Ibid* Rule 6.
[269] *Ibid* Rule 8.
[270] *Ibid* Rule 9.
[271] *Ibid* Rule 10.
[272] *Ibid* Rules 11 and 12.
[273] *Ibid* Rule 13.
[274] *Ibid* Rule14.
[275] *Ibid* Rule 15.
[276] *Ibid* Rule 16.
[277] *Ibid* Rule 17.
[278] *Ibid* Rule 21.
[279] *Ibid* Rule 22.
[280] *Ibid* Rule 24.

these rules provided that any such refusal would be noted.[281] By pre-empting such problems embarrassment could be saved and avoid that which occurred at Geneva.

O. The United States Special Commission

Before the Arbitral Tribunal convened in Paris, President McKinley of the United States submitted the report of the Special Commission enquiring into the Venezuela-British Guiana boundary. Its reports presented findings from enquiries of the disputants as well as evidence gathered from sources in Caracas, Georgetown, London, Madrid and the Holy See. It was assisted by experts from leading universities in America; Harvard College, Wisconsin and John Hopkins, as well as the Library of Congress and the Geological and Hydrographic Office. They studied original and copy documents, as well as 300 maps of the region. They also examined the Treaty of Münster and treatises on international law as well as the disputes over the Texas border and the boundary with British Colombia. The Treaty was not helpful and no clear description of the boundary was found. This was the case with most of the evidence they analysed: the position of the boundary had never been precisely defined or agreed. They also discovered certain international law norms in dealing with such cases which were generally accepted by countries, but not in this case. There was no attempt to define the exact boundary-line over the course of diplomatic exchanges. Neither were the maps providing any consensus of the demarcation line. The documents were inconclusive. In the end the Commission produced 76 maps, several historical reports, cartographical reports, five volumes of British Blue Books, three volumes of Venezuelan documents and other Venezuelan documents.[282]

Whilst Britain might not have welcomed this United States' initiative at first, it probably hastened and facilitated the negotiations towards an arbitration treaty. Certainly, the gathering of evidence would have shortened the time the Tribunal might otherwise have to spend in studying documents of little consequence. Much of it was vague, but it may be concluded from that and the lack of a prescribed boundary-line that judicial analysis was the only way to define a permanent line.

P. The Tribunal

The Tribunal was composed of Lord Herschell and Lord Justice Richard Henn Collins, both appointed by Britain. Melville Fuller, the United States Supreme Court Chief Justice, and Justice David Brewer were appointed by Venezuela

[281] *Ibid* Rule 20.
[282] *Venezuelan Boundary Commission*, 27 February 1897, published Washington 24 May 1897.

with its Chairman Frederic de Martens, the leading international jurist who was much in demand at the Hague Conference.[283] They held their first meeting on the 25 January 1899 at the French Ministry of Foreign Affairs. Unfortunately, due to the enforced absence of Lord Herschell and the Hon Melville Weston Fuller the Tribunal had to postpone its meeting to the 25 May 1899. The Tribunal was unable to meet on the appointed date due to the death of Lord Herschell and Lord Russell of Killowen, the Lord Chief Justice of England, was appointed in his place.[284] This first meeting was held on 21 June 1899 and the proceedings were opened by a welcome from the French Foreign Minister.[285] In reply, de Martens referred to the initiative of the Russian Tsar Nicholas II in calling nations to the First Hague Conference which was then in session in order 'to come to an understanding as to the most efficient means of avoiding international conflicts, and of establishing firm basis for the maintenance of peace among nations'.

De Martens said that this was 'the greatest honour of his life'. The Tribunal confirmed the appointment of its Secretary, Mr RW Martin, Secrétaire d'Ambassade, an attaché at the French Foreign Office and Mr Lucas D'Oyly Carte and Mr Perry Allen as Assistant Secretaries to the Tribunal.[286] The Chairman then announced a further adjournment of a few days subject to which sittings would take place on the first five working days of every week thereafter. This however was rejected by counsel as it was more realistic to sit the first four days each week. This was agreed. Sir Richard Webster then applied by motion to introduce some diplomatic correspondence, but in view of the fact that it omitted a private letter from Mr Olney to Sir Julian Pauncefote, this was withdrawn so that a complete bundle could be submitted. The meeting was then adjourned.

This early exchange prefaced some subsequent consideration of the matter of disclosure of diplomatic communications which Webster opposed. What Webster introduced at the first day's hearing related to the diplomatic exchanges between Britain and the United States relating to the arbitration agreement but what Webster later objected to was the disclosure of very sensitive state communications in the matter of Sir Henry Light's (Governor of British Guiana) despatch to the Lord Aberdeen on 25 March 1842.

[283] De Martens was a famous international jurist, Professor of International Law at the University of St Petersburg and author of *The International Law of Civilised Nations* (1883). He won the Nobel Peace Prize in 1902. He wrote scientific studies, compiled 15 volumes of treaties between Russia and other states, and represented Russia at several international conferences between 1874 and 1907. He greatly promoted arbitration as an alternative to war, embodied in the Convention for the Peaceful Settlement of International Disputes.

[284] Charles Russell, Lord Russell of Killowen, was one of the great advocates of his time. He had acted in defence of Charles Parnell the Irish Nationalist leader and had pioneered Gladstone's Home Rule legislation. Sir Richard Webster QC was his opponent in that case. See the author's articles on Russell: *Never a Greater Man at the English Bar* (*Law Society Gazette*, 1985) and *Indictment of a Nation. Russell's Defence of Parnell before the Special Commission* (1982) 33 *Northern Ireland Law Quarterly Review* 277–85.

[285] Minutes of Meeting. Protocol II 15 June 1899.

[286] *Ibid*.

Venezuela argued that this document induced Lord Aberdeen to prepare a boundary along the line of the Moruka River close to the Essequibo, instead of the Amakuru close to the Orinoco, but in the light of the open correspondence he had supported the Schomburgk line. Mr Reid, on behalf of Britain, in reply to a question from the US Chief Justice suggested that no international arbitral tribunal would consider production of state communications relating to 'high policy as between the central government of the country and its administration in distant parts'.

Then, as now, such diplomatic discussions were and are privileged from disclosure in court and inadmissible as evidence protected by national and international law. Sir Richard Webster's subsequent view was such disclosure would put an end to all diplomatic negotiations and arbitration if that was the norm.[287] Although the Tribunal requested production Sir Richard Webster refused it on the ground of high state policy.[288] When Venezuela attempted to assert argument as to political control over the borderlands, Russell questioned the efficacy of such submission which had been delayed for over a year. Counsel for Britain opposed such submission because he asserted that Venezuela had deliberately withheld evidence. Although there were certain difficulties, these were in large part overcome by the adoption of 24 of the rules agreed at the first Hague Conference. This is significant in that this arbitration was a contemporaneous test of what was being debated and agreed at The Hague.

Q. The British Case

The British case was tersely and persuasively drafted referring to the key arguments in the case cross-referenced to specific documents. Having taken considerable pains to produce the written submissions, it was reported that counsel, Sir Robert Reid and Mr Askwith, had distinguished themselves by their forceful presentation and focussed argument, pressing their key arguments to the Tribunal from the beginning. On the other hand, those acting for Venezuela, Generals Tracy and Harrison, were reported as being less effective, reserving their best argument until the concluding submissions. As was said: 'Criticism without an affirmative case is apt to pall; the affirmative case, too long delayed, comes to jaded minds and tired ears'.[289]

The Attorney General for Britain, Sir Richard Webster QC MP, directed the Tribunal's attention to the Treaty. In the first instance their task was to investigate and ascertain the extent the territories belonging to or that might lawfully be claimed by the United Netherlands or the Kingdom of Spain respectively at

[287] 'The Anglo-Venezuelan Arbitration Commission' (n 127) 191, 391, Attorney General's Statement. Day 13 of the Hearing.
[288] *Ibid.*
[289] *Ibid.*

the time of the acquisition by Britain of the colony of British Guiana.[290] Britain claimed through the United Netherlands, whereas Venezuela claimed through Spain. The extent to which, at the date of the acquisition of the colony by Britain, the territory in Guiana had been actually acquired by the United Netherlands or Spain respectively was the first step in examining the respective rights of the parties.[291] Any claims either by the United Netherlands or Spain as at the date of the acquisition of the colony by Britain was not sufficient in itself to enable the Tribunal to determine the boundary line. What happened during the nineteenth century regarding possession of the Dutch and Spanish Territories was important in ascertaining the rights of the parties under Article IV of the Treaty.[292]

R. Submissions under Article IV Rules

As far as the 50-year period for prescriptive title was concerned under Rule (a), the arbitrators could deem exclusive political control of the district as well as the actual settlement sufficient to constitute adverse holding or to make title by prescription. Thus, once the period of 50 years was established all further argument ceased whatever may have been the origin of the possession because exclusive political control constituted possession.

As to Rule (b), applying international law Webster submitted possession by one nation, however recent, and further good title unless a superior title were shown by some other state. If you applied that principle it could not be excluded by the prescriptive rule of 50 years adverse possession as prescription conferred an absolute title.

As to Rule (c) in determining the boundary-line at the date of the Treaty, the arbitrators had to give effect to such occupation by the subjects or citizens of the other party as reason, justice, the principles of international law and equity demanded. But this rule was not intended to override the previous rules of prescription or international law where it contemplated the case of subjects or citizens of one nation being an occupation in a territory which would belong to the other party.[293] This rule enabled the arbitrators to deal with all the questions

[290] *British Guiana Boundary Arbitration with the United States of Venezuela. The Case (and Appendix) on behalf of the Government of Her Britannic Majesty* (Foreign Office 1898) (hereinafter '*British Guiana Boundary Arbitration: British Case*') Ch 1, 1, lines: 10–13.

[291] *Ibid*, lines: 19–25.

[292] These provided that the Tribunal decide title by: a prescriptive right of 50 years based on political control of the district, as well as settlement thereof constituting actual holding or to make title by prescription; by international law principles deemed applicable subject to the prescriptive rule; if the territory of one party was occupied as at the date of the Treaty, 2nd February 1897, in occupation of the other party's subjects then the matter was to be decided by reason, justice and principles of international law and the equities of the case.

[293] *British Guiana Boundary, Arbitration with the United States of Venezuela. The Argument on behalf of the Government of Her Britannic Majesty* (Foreign Office, 1898) 3 (hereinafter '*British Argument*').

likely to arise in determining where the boundary-lines were to be drawn and where necessary to arrange for suitable compensation and adjustments to be made.[294]

So far as the pre-treaty negotiations were concerned, it was submitted that whatever might have been suggested by way of concession or otherwise during the negotiations had no bearing whatsoever on the proceedings.

S. Venezuelan Counter-Case

At the root of the case of Venezuela was the contention that Spain, by virtue of a Papal Bull of 1493 and the first discovery of America by Columbus followed by the establishment of a settlement at Santo Thomé, became entitled to the whole territory between the rivers Orinoco and Amazon, and the Atlantic.[295] In their case the Venezuelans repeatedly referred to the Dutch settlers as trespassers, smugglers, or raiders and robbers. But they alleged that such actions by the Spanish constituted proof of ownership and exercise of a lawful authority. Where the Dutch may have settled then the Venezuelans submitted that the Dutch were only entitled to the actual spots settled and occupied and to no more. They also asserted that apart from these 'spots' occupied by the Dutch, Venezuela as the successor of Spain was entitled to all that territory excluding those particular Dutch occupied areas.[296]

i. Alleged Rights of Spain under the Papal Bull

The origin of the Venezuelan claim rested on a Papal Bull *Inter Caetera* which was the invention of Rodrigo De Borgia, Pope Alexander VI, a Spanish Pope who divided America between Spain and Portugal after its discovery. This was given further legal expression in the Treaty of Tordesillas of 1494. This was contrary to the English doctrine of 'effective occupation' which was applied in the reign of Henry VII and restated during the reigns of Mary and Elizabeth Tudor.[297] In the view of many, the Pope exceeded his spiritual jurisdiction in attempting to partition the world so that *Inter Caetera* was subsequently disputed by

[294] Such adjustment was made in relation to the occupation of the Catholic missionaries.

[295] *British Guiana Boundary, Arbitration with the United States of Venezuela the Counter-Case of the United States of Venezuela Before the Tribunal of Arbitration to Convene at Paris Under the Provisions of The Treaty Between the United States of Venezuela and Her Britannic Majesty signed at Washington 2 February 1897*. (New York, 1898) (hereinafter '*Venezuelan Counter-Case*') 116.

[296] *British Guiana Boundary, Arbitration with the United States of Venezuela the Case of the United States of Venezuela Before the Tribunal of Arbitration to Convene at Paris Under the Provisions of The Treaty Between the United States of Venezuela and Her Britannic Majesty signed at Washington 2 February 1897* (New York, 1898) (hereinafter '*Venezuelan Case*') 61–74; *Venezuelan Counter-Case* (n 295) 13.

[297] Not least contested by the expeditions of Drake, Raleigh and Hawkins.

many states, not least by Francis I of France.[298] In subsequent years a number of international treaties superseded the papal declaration: the Truce of 1609 whereby Spain acknowledged the right of the United Netherlands to trade, settle, and occupy those parts of America which were not in the actual possession of Spain.[299] Again in the Treaty of Münster, Spain acknowledged the right of the United Netherlands to settle and occupy any territory not in the actual occupation or possession of Spain. This Treaty was confirmed by the Treaty of Utrecht in 1714.[300] Apart from this, at no point during the negotiations between the United Netherlands and Spain did Spain raise any argument based upon the Papal Bull, nor did the Dutch ever take a grant from Spain. For the remainder of the seventeenth century, after the Treaty of Münster, Spain made no attempt to prevent or hinder Dutch colonial expansion in Guiana. Indeed, it was argued by Webster that Spain acquiesced in Dutch colonisation west of the Essequibo and that Spain had accepted the status quo at Utrecht in 1713 because it followed that Articles V and VI of the Treaty of Münster were incorporated in the Treaty of Utrecht.[301] Apart from that no Spanish remonstrance was ever made against such extension of Dutch settlement or jurisdiction between the Essequibo and the Orinoco. The argument about an entitlement under the Papal Bull was resurrected in the mid-nineteenth century by Venezuelan diplomats; an argument that the Spanish Government had never utilised in 300 years. Spain, in effect, had recognised the Dutch settlements.[302] These facts and the evidence clearly refuted such a claim by Venezuela.

ii. Rights of Spain as First Discoverer

The other Venezuelan argument appeared to be that Spain was entitled to the whole territory from the Orinoco to the Amazon as first discoverer of America and the settlement at Santo Thomé thus to the whole of Guiana.[303] Both Twiss and Vattel in their works argued that possession of a point which could not be separated from the whole meant possession of the whole. But the territory between the Orinoco and the Amazon was not an indivisible unit. The area was interwoven with rivers and mountain ranges, natural barriers and it was not feasible to suggest that occupation of Santo Thomé was the equivalent of taking possession of the whole territory.

[298] *British Guiana Boundary Arbitration: British Case* (n 290) 157; *British Guiana Boundary Arbitration with the United States of Venezula. The Counter-case on behalf of the Government of Her Britannic Majesty [and Appendix] (Printed at the Foreign Office by Harrison and Sons, 1898)* (hereinafter '*British Counter-Case*') 44–45.

[299] *British Counter-Case* (n 298) 45.

[300] *Ibid* 37–52.

[301] *Proceedings*. Days 4 and 5. *British Counter-Case* (n 298).

[302] *British Guiana Boundary Arbitration: British Case* (n 290) *App VII*, 91.

[303] *Ibid* 149. Day 15, Proceedings; WE Hall, *A Treatise of International Law*, 8th edn (Oxford University Press, 1924) 127.

Venezuela argued that the second owner (Britain) could not enjoy the right of the discoverer (Spain). The extent of settlement Venezuela argued was irrelevant because the second owner could only take what was left, and, according to Twiss, 'title by settlement superseded title by discovery'. An analysis of the evidence revealed there was but little evidence of Spanish settlements over the three centuries in question. Britain argued that discovery gave an 'inchoate title' which could be perfected by actual occupation over a reasonable time.[304] This theory of 'inchoate title' was adopted by Twiss, Phillimore, Creasy and Hull. The key point was however that discovery alone did not give permanent dominion or sovereignty over the territory. According to Webster quoting Vattel, 'things' belonged to the person who first took possession of them. Thus, when the land was found uninhabited it could be taken into possession.[305] But could the territory then be populated and sustained? Vattel's view was that the land had to be occupied and put to use, and only then could sovereignty be acquired. Grotius took the view that title did not amount to ownership, but also required possession. Webster argued that territorial possessions could only depend on size and population of the settlement as well as the extent of occupation and cultivation.[306]

Britain effectively argued that Venezuela's rights based on Spanish discovery would lapse de jure if there was no occupation.[307] In his treatise, Twiss argued that the right of discovery could be waived de jure by a non-user or the right of occupancy renounced de facto by abandonment. Title by reason of discovery was recognised at the time of the hearing, but it had to be supported by actual or effective occupation. That proposition is supported by Grotius, Vattel, Pufendorf, Wolff, Martens, Kluber, Twiss, Wheaton, Halleck, Phillimore, Hall and John Bassett Moore.

There was abundant evidence of Spain's recognition and acceptance of the Dutch colonial acquisition. Both Spain and the United Netherlands had acquired territory, settled it, and brought it under their control. Similarly, it will be seen how Britain and Venezuela acquired title in succession to Spain and the United Netherlands. By such process it was submitted that Britain acquired possession and title.

T. Case Analysis

The British case was clearly presented on four key points:

1. That Venezuela can show no title to any part of the territory to the east of the Schomburgk line.

[304] *British Guiana Boundary Arbitration: British Case* (n 290) 1, 51.
[305] Vattel (n 115) III, Section 2017, 84.
[306] This was argued on Day 14 Proceedings.
[307] *British Guiana Boundary Arbitration: British Case* (n 290) 153.

2. That to the west of the Schomburgk line there is a great extent of territory which Venezuela can show no title.
3. That Britain has established her title to the whole of the territory east of the Schomburgk line and to a considerable extent of the territory to the west of that line.
4. That the existing occupation by Britain is only the natural sequel to a long course of acts of dominion and controlled by the Dutch and British.[308]

As to legal title, Britain's claim was based on acquisition by right of conquest, whereas Venezuela's claim was based on the right of discovery. It was said that discovery gave 'a primary and exclusive right to it … the second owner enters rightfully only when there has been an abandonment, *de facto* or *de jure* by the discoverer'.

The area in dispute encompassed the whole of that part of Guiana which lay between the Schomburgk line and the Essequibo and considerable tracts to the west of that line. Britain submitted that Spain had never occupied, possessed, or controlled any part of this territory; nor did Venezuela, with the exception of some small part of the territory to the west of the Schomburgk line, for example, the Venezuelan police stations on the Rivers Uruan and Amakuru. According to the British case, Spanish occupation and control were confined to the settlement of the Santo Thomé adjacent to the River Orinoco and the Capuchin Missions in that region. Santo Thomé in effect guarded the entrance to the Spanish provinces of New Granada, Cumana, Barcelona and Venezuela.[309] As far as Spanish settlements in the River Essequibo were concerned, there was no evidence of any continued Spanish occupation since the Dutch settled and occupied the Essequibo from 1623.[310] Santo Thomé was the only Spanish settlement in the region from the early seventeenth century. The old settlement was destroyed by Sir Walter Raleigh.[311] Reports from the Governors of Trinidad and Guiana in 1640 and 1662 respectively and also a further report from the Governor of Trinidad in 1671 demonstrated that up to the end of the seventeenth century no Spanish settlements had been established in Guiana except Santo Thomé. Spanish control was solely confined to the River Orinoco in the vicinity of Santo Thomé.[312] This position was confirmed by the Treaties of Utrecht and Münster.

[308] *Ibid, Scheme of Argument*. See Map by Robert H Schomburgk, London 1840. Parliamentary Papers 1840, Vol 34. Printed by Order, House of Commons 11 May 1840.

[309] The existence of Santo Thomé depended upon the Dutch Colonies of the Essequibo. *British Guiana Boundary Arbitration: British Case* (n 290) *App II*, 20; *British Counter-Case* (n 298) *App* 196.

[310] *British Guiana Boundary Arbitration: British Case* (n 290) 21. *Venezuelan Case* (n 296) 42–43; *Venezuelan Counter-Case* (n 295) 14.

[311] *British Guiana Boundary Arbitration: British Case* (n 290) *App I*, 104; *British Counter-Case* (n 298) *App* 10.

[312] British Guiana Boundary Arbitration: British Case (n 290) *App I*, 104, 152, 32; *British Counter-Case* (n 298) *App* 10, 15, and 44.

The Spanish position in the river Orinoco was tenuous and did not afford any protection against Dutch or other foreign incursions.[313] Only one Spanish town was in existence in Guiana in 1733.[314] At the time of the British invasion in 1742, Santo Thomé was the only Spanish settlement on the Orinoco.[315]

Before the Capuchin Missions had established certain mission stations on the upper tributaries of the Cuyuni, the Dutch had taken possession of the Essequibo, its tributaries, including the Cuyuni and the Massaruni.[316] Such settlements as the missionaries established were within Dutch territory. They had no rights over the Cuyuni. Indeed, they did not reach the Cuyuni and consequently Venezuela found no claim under international law.[317] Despite various Spanish attempts to survey the extent of the boundary between 1781 and 1813, no action was taken to make any further settlements apart from Santo Thomé.[318] There were some communications between the Spanish authorities in regards to protecting the Capuchin Missions by establishing a Spanish post at the junction of the Cuyuni and the Curumo. This was thought to be the extent of the Spanish Territory.[319] Up to 1847 no settlements had been attempted by the Spanish because the Spanish did not have sufficient forces to make any incursion against the Dutch, apart from a raid on the Dutch post on the Cuyuni in 1758.[320] The Venezuelans alleged that the Spaniards during the whole period of their occupation of Santo Thomé controlled the whole of the Orinoco down to the mouth of that river prohibiting trade with the Dutch and others. However, there was no evidence of this save for an attempt in 1760 which was abortive.[321]

When the Spanish colony of Venezuela revolted in 1817 the insurgents destroyed the mission settlements. Soon after the region was abandoned until gold was discovered in 1850 in the upper reaches of the Yuruari. In 1891 Venezuela established a police station and subsequently two more on the left bank of the Amakuru. In 1892 it established a police station on the River Uruan.

On any analysis of this evidence, it became clear the Venezuelan claims were unfounded to the extent they relied on Spanish acquisition. The claims could not be sustained in the Venezuelan case.

What Britain had established was:

1. That neither Spain or Venezuela was ever occupier to or controlled any territory to the east and the Schomburgk line.

[313] *Report of the Council of the Indies 1723*; *Venezuelan Counter-Case* (n 295) *App III*, 10.

[314] *British Counter-Case* (n 298) *App*, 161. *Further Report of the Council of the Indies 1733*.

[315] *Report of Iturriaga 1747*. *British Guiana Boundary Arbitration: British Case* (n 290) *App II*, 52. Corroborated by a *Report of Don Jose Diguja* appended to the *British Guiana Boundary Arbitration: British Case* (n 290) *App III*, 1–77.

[316] This is better seen on the Barrington Brown Map 1876, clearly delineating the rivers in question.

[317] *British Guiana Boundary Arbitration: British Case* (n 290) *App V*, 117.

[318] *Ibid App IV*, 210, 211 and 218: and *App V*, 18, 20, 57–63, 203 and 214.

[319] *Ibid* 60, 61 and *App V*, 114, 116 and 119.

[320] *Ibid* 42, 44. *British Counter-Case* (n 298) 83 and 84. *British Guiana Boundary Arbitration: British Case* (n 290) *App II*, 145.

[321] *British Guiana Boundary Arbitration: British Case* (n 290) *App II*, 187, 190–192 and 194.

2. That west of that line there is a great extent of territory, which Spain never attempted to occupy and over which they exercised no control.
3. That the effective occupation control of Spain and Venezuela was limited to Santo Thomé and to the mission settlements situated west of a line drawn under the junction of the Uruan and Yuruari.

U. The Dutch and British Titles

The key question for the Tribunal was to determine the delimitation of the boundary-line between Venezuela and British Guiana. To maintain British claims, it was necessary for counsel to demonstrate that from time to time the Dutch and British continuously and as a matter of legal right traded with, occupied, settled, and controlled those districts claimed as British Guiana. To accomplish that it was necessary to consider the extent of those rights by reference to the Rivers which traversed the disputed territories: the Amukuru, the Barima, Waini, Moruka, Pomeroon, Cuyuni, Massaruni and Essequibo. From their stations the Dutch and British exercised dominion and control over the districts in which they were situated. It was demonstrated that as early as 1657 the establishment of colonies was regulated on the wild mainland coast between 1° and 10°.[322] In 1669 the Hanau Grant treated the Dutch Territory as extending to the River Orinoco.[323] This was supported by authoritative statements from the Council of War of the Indies and others.[324] There was little doubt that the Dutch were settled on the Amakuru of which the Spanish were aware.[325] In 1684, the Dutch proposed to build a small station on the Barima. By 1752 it was treated as under Dutch jurisdiction.[326] By 1762, the River Amakuru was regarded as the limit of the Dutch colony.[327] In 1767 the Spanish and Dutch regarded the east bank of the Barima as being under Dutch control[328] and in 1804 as extending to Cape Barima.[329] Furthermore, the reports of Mr Crichton, the Superintendent of Rivers, confirmed that as a magistrate he exercised continuous jurisdiction up to the Barima.[330] The Venezuelans had never come east of the Amukuru.[331] The River Waini was similarly used by the Dutch and regarded as Dutch territory from 1768.[332] From 1803 the British exercised jurisdiction in

[322] *Ibid App I*, 67.
[323] *British Counter-Case* (n 298).
[324] *British Guiana Boundary Arbitration: British Case* (n 290) 29 and *App I*, 177–78; and *British Counter-Case* (n 298) *App I*, 16; *British Guiana Boundary Arbitration: British Case* (n 290) *App II*, 41.
[325] Dutch Declaration sent to Spanish Government in 1657. *British Guiana Boundary Arbitration: British Case* (n 290) *App I*, 91, 99, 109 and 110.
[326] *British Guiana Boundary Arbitration: British Case* (n 290) *App II*, 42 and 61.
[327] *Ibid App II*, 12.
[328] *Ibid App III*, 141,191.
[329] *Ibid App V*, 186.
[330] *British Counter-Case* (n 298) 283.
[331] *Ibid App VII*, 208–32.
[332] *Ibid App III*, 181.

this area. The evidence of settlement and control by the Dutch in the Pomeroon and the Moruka is practically continuous from 1659.[333] By this time the Dutch colony was passing to the British a whole seaboard westward of the Moruka, as well as the land for a considerable distance to the Pomeroon and its tributary the Wakepo had been surveyed and laid out in agricultural lots.[334] British missions were established on the Pomeroon before 1840 and on the Moruka in 1845.[335] The influence of these British missions spread southward to the district source of the Cuyuni and the Caroni.[336] So far as the Cuyuni was concerned this was always regarded by the Dutch and British as an integral part of the colony. The formal Remonstrance of 1769 stated in most explicit terms the right of the Dutch to all the tributaries of the Essequibo and especially the Cuyuni.[337] So far as the river Massaruni was concerned there is no evidence of any Spanish occupation on that river. The Dutch occupied and traded upon it making use of its resources which was sufficient to give them title to the territory traversed by it.[338]

The Venezuelans claimed territory up to the left bank of the Essequibo. As early as 1685 there were private settlements along the river and subsequently Dutch settlers created plantations up to the Falls.[339] The Dutch established a trading post on the river in 1737. The Arinda post was established there by the Dutch as trading in red slaves and dye.[340] The Arinda post was transferred to a higher position at the junction of the Rupununi in 1764 and this became a centre of control in that region.[341] From that point the Dutch were able to explore the interior of the country and evidence was produced that the Dutch Postholder had asked the Carib Indians to protect Dutch plantations, the Caribs being under the control of the Dutch.[342] The position appears to have been recognised by the Spanish in 1799 who took great care not to allow any of their people to enter any part of the area between the Massaroni and the Essequibo for fear the Dutch would arm the Caribs.[343] In 1837 Sir R Schomburgk planted the British flag in the latitude 0° 41' at the sources of the Essequibo. A mission was subsequently established on the eastern side of the Rupununi near the Ura Rapids, and in 1841 a detachment of British troops was dispatched to Pirara with the objective of protecting the Indians.[344]

According to the evidence, the whole of this region was unknown to the Spanish and, so far as the Arinda was concerned, in 1769 the Spanish Governor

[333] *British Guiana Boundary Arbitration: British Case* (n 290) *App I*, 148.
[334] *British Counter-Case* (n 298) *App* 381 and 386.
[335] *Ibid App VI*, 6, 116 and 137.
[336] *Ibid App* 301, 302, 304 and 306–12.
[337] *Ibid App VI*, 29.
[338] *British Guiana Boundary Arbitration: British Case* (n 290) 31.
[339] *Ibid App* 8, 192. *British Counter-Case* (n 298) *App* 47–58, Venezuelan Case (n 296) 59.
[340] *British Guiana Boundary Arbitration: British Case* (n 290) *App II*, 227.
[341] *Ibid App II*, 71.
[342] *Ibid App III*, 112, 113, 176.
[343] *Ibid App V*, 121. The Dutch armed them in 1804 according to evidence in *ibid App V*, 185,187.
[344] *Ibid App VI*.

of Guayana confirmed that he had never heard of the station and of the country between the Orinoco. He stated that it was unknown to the Spanish and was inaccessible to them and their Indians.[345]

From this evidence it could be concluded that the waterways of all these Rivers were from at least the commencement of the seventeenth century under the control of the Dutch and subsequently the British; that at no time did the Spaniards or the Venezuelans have any control of the waterways of any of these Rivers; that the Dutch and British proved in different ways continuous occupation, settlement and enjoyment, as well as control of these territories or drainage of the areas through which various rivers flowed. Any intrusion or encroachment on the territory was the occupation of the Spanish missions of the Savannah country in the neighbourhood of the upper tributaries of the Cuyuni which was west of the line drawn due north from a junction of the Uruan and the Yuruari.

V. Political Control

Underpinning the British case was the fact that the Indians habitually turned to the Dutch and British for protection. The original policy of the Dutch by virtue of the 1621 Charter granted to the West India Company enabled the Company to make contracts and alliances with the natives of the lands within the limits of the Charter.[346] This alliance benefited the Spanish in so far as the Dutch prevented the Caribs from attacking the Spanish missions.[347] It would appear that the Dutch recognised the Spanish Missions de facto. The British adopted the Dutch regime of employing the Carib Indians and keeping records of those Indians in government service employed in the region between the Barima and the Essequibo.[348] To all intents and purposes it appears that the British colonial government had complete control over the various Indian tribes in British Guiana.[349]

Counsel submitted that at the time of the arbitration the northwest district as far as the right bank of the Amakuru was subject to British rule: it had courthouses, police stations, post offices, regular steam boat services to the Morawhana and thence up the Barima. There were hotels, hospitals, farming and mining under the complete political and administrative control of Britain. The Moruka and the Pomeroon Rivers were inhabited by British subjects. There were police stations, post offices with a daily post, hospitals, churches and missions. The Dutch plantations were maintained and along the Pomeroon River farming had continued. There were sugar estates and cattle farms along

[345] *Ibid App IV*, 43.
[346] *Ibid App I*, 44.
[347] *Ibid App II*, 46, 58.
[348] *Ibid App V*, 214–16. The Dutch employment of the Indians was confirmed in a letter from the Acting Governor to Lord Bathurst in 1813.
[349] *Ibid App VI*, 22–35.

the Arabian Coast which stretched from the Pomeroon to the Essequibo. The three large rivers: Cuyuni, Massaruni and the Essequibo united in a confluence some 40 miles from the sea. This estuary was thickly populated up to the first falls. British governance was evident in the Commissioner's regular visits to the Cuyuni as far as the Uruan and the Massaruni, to the Essequibo and the Rupununi to the borders of Brazil.

W. Gold Mining

Along these rivers, gold mines were worked by British subjects under licences issued by the British Government. The gold workings on the Cuyuni extended to the Waiamu, also there were workings on the Puruni and the Essequibo. The British had built road communications linking these areas and industries. A railway was built from the Demerara River to the Essequibo. The gold industry was centred on Tumatumari.[350]

The Venezuelan Government in its case and counter-case did not define the extent of its occupational control at the date of the treaty of arbitration.[351] The facts on the British case were that since 1850 Venezuela had occupied parts of the territory to the extreme west including Tumeremo. It had established stations at the junction of the Uruan with the Cuyuni on the left bank of the Amakuru. Subject to those exceptions and some small police stations set up on the north bank of the Cuyuni as at the time of the arbitration, there were not and never had been any Venezuela settlements east of the Tumeremo. In effect, there was an unoccupied region between the area occupied by Britain and that of Venezuela.[352]

X. Conclusion of the Proceedings

The Tribunal concluded its hearings on the 3rd October 1899. The Award was executed in duplicate by the five arbitrators; the decision of the Tribunal was unanimous. At this final meeting the material parts of the Award were read and following the President's speech two executed copies of the Award were handed to the agents of the respective governments.[353]

Despite the complexity of this case, it had taken the Tribunal three months of very hard work to complete oral evidence and review more than 2,650 documents.

[350] *Venezuelan Case* (n 296) 50.
[351] *Ibid* 51.
[352] *Ibid* 52.
[353] FO 420/397 *Minutes of Meeting* (3 October 1899) Protocol LVI.

Y. The Award

In a despatch of 3 October 1899,[354] Mr Buchanan, the British Ambassador in Paris, confirmed to Lord Salisbury that the Tribunal had made the following Award:

> The boundary-line, starting from the coast at Point Playa will run in a straight line to the River Barima at its junction with the River Murrumba, and thence along the mid-stream of the latter river to its source, and from that point to the junction of the River Haiowa with the Amakuru, and thence along the mid-stream or of the Amakuru to its source in the Imataka Ridge, and thence in a south westerly direction along the highest ridge of the spur of the Imataka Mountains to the highest point of the main range of such Imataka Mountains opposite to the source of the Barima, and thence along the summit of the main ridge in a south-easterly direction of the Imataka Mountains to the source of the Acarabisi, and thence along the mid-stream of the Acarabisi to the Cuyuni, and thence along the northern bank of the River Cuyuni westward to its junction with the Wenamu to its westernmost source, and thence in a direct line to the summit of mount Roraima, where it re-joins the Schomburgk Line.[355]

The Ambassador went on to explain that the district between the Wenamu and the Upper Cuyuni became Venezuelan Territory, while that between Point Playa and Point Barima, the Amakuru, and the line indicated above was awarded to Venezuela, subject to the condition that the Rivers Barima and Amakuru were to be absolutely free to navigate.[356]

The form of the Award was quite simple. It recited the Treaty of Washington, some further recitals as to the constitution of the Tribunal and then its decision. No reasons were published with the decision, but it simply indicated that with regard to the navigation of the Amacuro and the Barima no customs duties would be charged either by the Republic of Venezuela or by the colony of British Guiana in respect of any goods carried on board ships, vessels or boats passing along the river. Customs duties would only be chargeable in respect of goods landed in the territory of Venezuela or Britain respectively.

Z. Conclusions

This seminal case gives rise to a number of conclusions in the context of contemporary controversy at the time and an analysis of the process in terms of avoiding hostilities between states.

[354] FO 420/397 *Mr Buchanan to Marquis of Salisbury* (Paris, 3 October 1899).

[355] FO 420/397 *Award of The Tribunal of Arbitration Constituted Under Article I of the Treaty of Arbitration Signed at Washington on 2 February 1897* (October 1899).

[356] FO 420/397 *Mr Buchanan to Marquis of Salisbury* (Paris, 3 October 1899). The Award was entirely without prejudice to any questions as between Britain and Brazil or between Brazil and Venezuela regarding their respective boundaries.

The first questions whether the Award was the product of judicial analysis or diplomatic negotiation? The question has to be addressed because of the extraordinary request made by Venezuela's Director General of the Ministry of External Relations at the seventeenth session of the General Assembly of the United Nations on 20 August 1962 just before the world teetered on the brink of a major international crisis that might otherwise have resulted in nuclear Armageddon. Venezuela claimed that it had been forced to accept the Treaty of Washington in 1897 to its disadvantage. This arose out of a controversial memorandum written by one of the counsel for Venezuela, Mr Mallet-Provost, who alleged that after the close of submissions and oral argument he was called in to see the two American arbitrators; Justice Brewer and Chief Justice Fuller. He claimed that the President, de Martens, told Brewer that the British arbitrators, Chief Justice Russell and Lord Justice Collins, favoured the Schomburgk line starting at Point Barima, giving Britain control of the mouth of the Orinoco.

De Martens had then suggested that if Venezuela was given a boundary starting on the coast at the River Mocura, further to the east, he would support the British judges and approved the Schomburgk line as the true boundary. De Martens, who was a diplomat, wanted a unanimous decision, then allegedly said that he was proposing a line some distance southeast of Point Barima to give Venezuela control of the Orinoco. Such a line would cross the Schomburgk line giving Venezuela 5,000 square miles of territory at the head of the Orinoco.[357] This suggestion or allegation may no doubt be true. It is difficult to contradict. It may be likely that where the judges were evenly divided as to their decision, that the President's job as Chairman of the Tribunal would be to seek an accommodation between the American and English judges despite their holding entirely contradictory opinions. This is to an extent corroborated by the public statement made by Justice Brewer as reported in *The New York Times* on 5 October 1899.[358] He said:

> Until the last moment I believed a decision would be quite impossible, and it was by the greatest conciliation and mutual concessions that a compromise was arrived at. If any of us had been asked to give an award, each would have given one differing in extent and character. The consequence of this was that we had to adjust our different views, and finally to draw a line running between what each thought right.

He went on to point out that European lawyers did not look upon questions of prior rights resulting from a right of discovery in the same way as American lawyers. Also, the question of nature of control and extent of influence and relationship with the native races and many such matters were not viewed in the same manner on either side of the Atlantic. He said that the Americans had a keener appreciation of what he termed 'the whole situation' than the Europeans.

[357] CL Joseph, 'The Venezuelan Boundary Arbitration 1899: Part 1' (1970) 10 *Caribbean Studies* 56–61.

[358] 'Judge Brewers Opinion: Venezuela's Arbitrator Tells How the Verdict was Reached' *The New York Times* (5 October 1899).

Such comments were perhaps better left unsaid by an arbitrator, but they highlight the dilemma that confronts such an international tribunal where there will be cultural divergencies and understandings. In this case it must be said that if Mallet-Provost was right then it does say something about the skillful diplomacy of M de Martens and the reasonableness of the judges who were faced with a complex and difficult task. Chief Justice Russell was noted in England for his great skill as a cross-examiner and dominant personality. It would be most unlikely that he would agree the Award unless he considered there were strong reasons for it. Be that as it may, Justice Brewer, despite his misgivings about European and American approaches, was welcomed on the bench of the Court of Appeal in London on 3 February 1899 before the start of the proceedings in Paris. He therefore had some understanding of English procedure in that he later suggested that if it had been applied in the arbitration it would have curtailed the case.[359]

The second question to consider in conclusion is whether it was fair that Venezuela was not represented on the Tribunal and that she was represented by American judges albeit eminent jurists. On the one hand it can be argued that Venezuela opted to choose an American Supreme Court judge, but on the other hand, as we have seen in the diplomatic negotiation for the Treaty of Washington, this was largely carried on between Britain and the United States. The fact of *realpolitik* was that Venezuela was in no position to exert much influence over the British Empire without the support of the United States. In that context Venezuela had some understandable anxiety about the arbitration reflected 63 years later at the United Nations.

i. Was the Tribunal's Decision Arbitral or Political?

Whilst the President may well have counselled his co-arbitrators in reconciling differing approaches to settling the delineation of the boundary, it is characteristic of arbitration that it is not litigation which follows the procedure of a court of law. Whilst sometimes arbitrators adopt the rules of evidence applied in the courts and the applicable law of procedure and substance applied in a particular jurisdiction, it is considered that it is a quasi-judicial process. It is not an exact judicial science, but a process. Whilst the arbitrators carefully considered the evidence and the legal rights of the opposing state parties, based on their claims and counter-claims; whether founded on assertions as to the validity and effect of a Papal Bull, or rights of acquisition and settlement, or rights of conquest, or various Treaty rights, or questions of natural boundaries and naturalisation of the indigenous population, underlying all that would be the practicality of the Award.

As in commercial arbitration whilst applying the applicable law and rules of natural justice, arbitration recognises commercial sense and in this international

[359] *Ibid.*

state context we learn how diplomacy plays an essential part. The American jurist Eliah Root distinguished the role of arbitrators in such circumstances as:

> Arbitrators too often act diplomatically rather than judicially; they consider themselves belonging to diplomacy rather than to jurisprudence; they measure their responsibility and their duty by the traditions, the sentiments, and the honourable obligation which have grown up in centuries of diplomatic intercourse, rather than by the traditions, the sentiments, and the sense of honourable obligation which characterise the judicial departments of civilised nations.[360]

Another consideration that must have weighed heavily with the arbitrators was whether the Award would be sustainable. The fact that judges may have had to compromise their conflicting opinions was overtaken by perhaps a need to give a sustainable result that both countries could accept. In that sense they had to take judicial notice of political facts and consequences just as they would if they were sitting in court assessing an award of damages in the context of the economic consequences for a business. The Award, whatever the misgivings of Mr Mallet-Provost were, was sustained and settled the boundary. The purpose of the arbitration was achieved and hailed at the time as a success underpinning the interest demonstrated at the First Hague Conference held that year in Geneva. More than that whilst Britain might easily have used force it surely gained more respect internationally by its appeal to the arbitral process.

Perhaps the most significant point to be taken from this arbitration was the observation of General Harrison, a former President of the United States and the leading counsel for Venezuela, who concluded his submissions and case for Venezuela by reference to the proceedings of the First Hague Conference which had then recently concluded:

> If conventions, if accommodations, and if the rule of give and take are to be used, then let the diplomatists settle the questions. But when these have failed in their work, it seems to me necessarily to imply the introduction of a judicial element into the tribunal.[361]

By such a 'judicial element in the tribunal' he appears to have been referring to proposals for a permanent international tribunal which was discussed at the Geneva deliberations.

Whilst both Root and Harrison have understandable reservations as to the role of diplomacy in international state arbitration, it is surely arguable that arbitrators in such matters must pay respect to the norms of diplomacy just as they respect the rules of equity and international law, if only because without an understanding of the diplomatic and international relations consequences their deliberations may be in vain.

[360] *Proceedings*, National Arbitration and Peace Conference 15 April 1907, 44.

[361] Reference made by John W Foster in *Proceedings of the American Society of International Law* 1909, 27.

4

Forms of Dispute Resolution as Instruments of Prevention: Part II

THIS CHAPTER GIVES a selection of dispute resolution processes between states. The first is a reference to the Permanent Court of Arbitration as a result of the Hague Conference of 1899. The second is an inquiry into the sinking of British trawlers off the Dogger Bank by the Russian Baltic Fleet. The third concerns a diplomatic dispute between Britain and the United States over reciprocal rights of passage through the Panama Canal, and the final matter concerns diplomatic tensions over French and German rivalry in Morocco.

I. THE PIOUS FUND CASE

The first case to come before The Permanent Court of Arbitration at the Hague was *United States of America v The Republic of Mexico*. This was brought as a result of Mexico's default in honouring the Award of an earlier Mixed Commission decision of 11 November 1875 as amended on 24 October1876. That Award, by the umpire Sir Edward Thornton, was in favour of the United States on behalf of the Pious Fund which was originally established as an express private charitable trust by deed of gift. The objectives of the trust were for the purposes of establishing, supporting and maintaining the Catholic Church missions in California and converting the indigenous population. Essentially it was for the advancement of religion not for political or military purposes.

A. The United States–Mexican Claims Commission 1868

To understand the reference to the Permanent Court of Arbitration it is necessary to consider the US–Mexico Claims Commission and the history of the Pious Fund, as well as Sir Edward Thornton's Award which was the subject of the reference to the Court in 1902 – the first reference under the Hague Convention of 1899.

Donations of money and property were given to the Fund in the early eighteenth century and given to the Jesuit missionaries. They were expelled by the Spanish rulers of the Californias in 1773 and, with the Fund being administered by the Spanish colonial Government, the Franciscan order became the beneficiary.

The Spanish were later expelled, and the Mexican governor Santa Anna sequestrated the properties of the missions, placing the funds in the Mexican Treasury. It was later restored to the Bishop of California in 1836 but was again seized by the Mexican Government by decree in 1842. This decree acknowledged the obligation to pay an amount of six per cent per annum on the total proceeds of sale of the properties and other income. The Mexican Government never paid this sum. By the date of the Commission this amounted to a debt of $1,809,401.58.

According to the Mexican arbitrator, Mr Zamacõna, the claim was misconceived.[1] The missionaries were 'delegates' of the Spanish Government whose object was the conquest of the Californias. Hence, they had military, civil and political duties on which the Spanish Government, and later the Mexican Government, relied. It appears that once the Jesuits were expelled, the Spanish effectively controlled the Fund allegedly for the benefit of Spain and then Mexico. Property was sold and an annuity paid to the missions. In 1848, the United States by the Treaty of Guadeloupe acquired the Mexican territories of Upper and Lower California. The missionaries became citizens of the United States and were subject to its laws.[2] The Mexican bishoprics ceased to exist and became American corporations sole. The Mexican argument was that the missions were established for the 'Catholic Church of the Californias' and for 'the civil and political objects'. They were established in their view as 'delegates' for the conquest of northwest Mexico[3] and were more temporal than religious. The 'American Catholic Church of Upper California' was not the 'heirs or continuation' of the 'Mexican Catholic Church'.[4] Accruing to Mexico the missionaries were military chiefs and magistrates perceived by Spain as the instruments of colonisation and conquest. Early historical records referred to them as 'conquerors'.[5] The problem with this argument was that such evidence as the Mexican counsel produced dated from 1697, decades before the trust was established as the American case proved. Furthermore, the terms of the deed of gift establishing the trust made no reference whatsoever to civil, military or political duties. This was clearly the conclusion of Sir Edward Thornton as umpire in assessing the Opinions of the American and Mexican members of the Mixed Tribunal. It was the Mexican view that the problem of Mexico was the number of revolutions 'which used to have the arsenal in the barracks and the banker in the ecclesiastical administration.'[6]

[1] *The Hague Court Reports Comprising the Awards, Accompanied by Syllabi, the Agreements for Arbitration, and Other Documents in Each Case Submitted to the Permanent Court of Arbitration and to the Commissions of Inquiry Under the Provisions of the Conventions of 1899 and 1907 for the Pacific Settlement of International Disputes*, Carnegie Endowment for International Peace Division of International Law (Pranara Books. Reprint, 2020) 24.

[2] *Ibid* 25–26.

[3] *Ibid* 27–28.

[4] *Ibid* 29–30.

[5] *Ibid* 33.

[6] *Ibid* 38–39.

B. Sir Edward Thornton's Award

The nationality of the Pious Fund was hotly disputed, but Thornton was clear: the Fund was that of the Roman Catholic Church of Upper California which became a corporation sole on 30 May 1848, the day when ratifications of the Treaty of Guadalupe Hidalgo, were exchanged. Being that none of the missionaries elected to remain citizens of Mexico they automatically became US citizens under the Treaty after a year.[7] Thus the American Roman Catholic Bishop of California and his successors were lawful beneficiaries.

As to the suggestions that the missionaries were 'delegates' of Spain and had military, civil and political roles, all of a national character, this was rejected. No evidence was produced that the Spanish Government provided any support to the missionaries. Quite the reverse: they expelled the Jesuits, and took over the management of the fund, paying annuities to the Franciscans and Dominican Orders but sequestrating their property, selling and leasing it and thereby assuming control of its administration. A decree of Santa Anna of February 1842 declared that the Fund's objects were the religious conversions.[8]

Thornton concluded that the classes of beneficiaries of the trust fund were not just the Catholics of Upper California, but all Californians and all United States' citizens and that all the interest outstanding since the date of default over a 21-year period was to be paid to the United States' Government on behalf of the Pious Fund trust. His Award was made on the 11 November 1875 as later amended on 24 October 1876 in the sum of $904,070.79 plus interest.[9] The interest on the capital sum was never paid and consequently reference was made to the Permanent Court.

C. Reference to the Permanent Court of Arbitration

The Church appealed to the United States State Department for assistance in recovering the unpaid interest on the Award. In 1898 diplomatic discussions commenced culminating in an Agreement for Arbitration dated 22 May 1898. This contained rules of procedure as to appointments, submissions and evidence which meant the record of the proceedings of the Mixed Tribunal and submissions on law. On the one hand, the United States would claim that Thornton's Award be recognised as it was *res judicata*, and on the other hand, Mexico would argue that the claim be dismissed as the claimants were not acting for the same beneficiary since they did not recognise the claim. In short, the question the Permanent Court had to decide was whether the US claim founded on the Mixed Claims Tribunal Award was *res judicata*, and, if not, was it just?[10]

[7] *Ibid* 48–49.
[8] *Ibid* 49–52.
[9] *Ibid* 52–54.
[10] Permanent Court of Arbitration under the Hague Convention 1899. *United States v Republic of Mexico*. Statement and Brief on behalf of the United States of America (1902) 2–10.

The proceedings took place in The Hague from 15 September 1902 to 1 October 1902, with the Award being published to the parties on 14 October.[11] The Hague Court (the Permanent Court of Arbitration) was composed of Henning Matzen,[12] Edward Fry,[13] Dr Martens,[14] TMC Asser[15] and AF De Savornin Lohman.[16]

D. Case of the United States

The case put by the United States on behalf of the Fund was very clear. It was an express private charitable trust by deed of gift dated 8 June 1735 of land and property valued at $408,000 with land at Los Alamos, San Pedro Gudalcazar, San Antonio, and San Pedro de Ibarra. The trust was for 'the maintenance of the religious and to provide for the ornament and decent support of divine worship …'.[17] It also provided that '… the estates aforesaid shall be perpetually inalienable and shall never be sold'. The deed excluded the jurisdiction of the courts and specified that the purposes and objects were 'the propagation of our holy Catholic faith'.[18]

After the expulsion of the Jesuits in 1767 three of the missions were suppressed. The Franciscans took over missions in northern California and a beneficial interest under the trust. On 25 May 1832, the Government leased some trust property and applied the income to the Mexican Federal Mint in accordance with Article 6 of the Law of 25 May 1832.[19] In 1836 Mexico formed bishoprics in California making the last President of the missions the first Bishop of California. He was granted $3,000 for expenses and $6,000 from public revenues

[11] Report of Jackson H Rolston, Agent of the United States and Counsel in the Matter of the Case of the Pious Fund of the Californias Part 1, 13.

[12] LLD, Professor at the University of Copenhagen, Counsellor Extraordinary to the Supreme Court, President of the Landsthing, member of the Permanent Court of Arbitration.

[13] Edward Fry was born in Bristol, and educated at University College, London. He was called to the Bar in 1854, and became a Lord Justice of Appeal in 1883. He resigned in 1892, and then served as chairman of various commissions. He was listed as a member of the Hague Permanent Arbitration Court.

[14] Fyodor Fyodorovich Martens, born 27 August 1845, taught public law in St Petersburg between 1872 and 1905 and became a Russian jurist and diplomat, international arbitrator and an historian. He appears in this context in the Pious Fund case and in the Digger Bank case where he was negotiator in the Treaty of Portsmouth settling the Russo-Japanese War. He represented his country at the Second Hague Conference and was an authority on International and Maritime Law. His *magnum opus* was the 15 volume *Recueil des traités et conventions conclus par la Russie* (1874–1909), a combination of international law and history.

[15] TMC Asser LLD was a Member of the Council of State of the Netherlands, Former Professor of the University of Amsterdam and Member of the Permanent Court of Arbitration.

[16] AF De Savornin Lohman was former Minister of the Interior of the Netherlands, former Professor of the Fee University of Amsterdam, member of the second Chamber of the States-General and Member of the Permanent Court of Arbitration.

[17] Statement and Brief on behalf of the United States of America (n 10) 9.

[18] *Ibid* 9.

[19] *Ibid* 10.

and given management of the properties of the Fund. By 1841 the income from the Fund was $34,000.[20] Contrary to the express terms of the trust and decrees of the Mexican Government Santa Anna took over the Fund decree dated 5 February 1842. The Fund then stood at $1,656,125.33 leaving only the income from tobacco revenues for the Church. Santa Anna sold assets and property of the Fund, but some capital was returned to the Church by the law of 3rd April 1845. There was no evidence of any property being returned.[21]

Counsel argued on behalf of the Fund that the matter had been arbitrated and umpired and that Mr Thornton's Award must be regarded as *res judicata*. These issues had been tried and the questions answered. As matters stood at common law and civil law there could be no reopening of the case of the same matter between the same parties. Article 1351 of the French Civil Code was in point. The Mixed Tribunal was a competent tribunal authorised by the state parties to determine its own jurisdiction. Counsel alluded to the British threat over the issue of consequential and indirect damages claims in the Geneva Arbitration. There was no reviewing or appeal process in the 1868 Treaty; no right of rejection was reserved and Mexico at no stage declined or refused to proceed. Whilst Mr Zamacõna's submission may be construed as a motion to dismiss or to strike out because of the character of the Catholic Church in the United States, he suggested it was not the same legal entity as when under Mexican rule, nevertheless by his action, submissions of evidence and participating in the hearing he submitted to the jurisdiction of the tribunal. He had taken steps in the proceedings. No subsequent objection before The Hague Court could revive a defunct right of objection to jurisdiction which never existed in the first place. Mexico consented to this process and took part in it so would be estopped from denying the jurisdiction of the Mixed Commission and The Hague Court in any event.[22] The Award of the Mixed Tribunal of 1868 was conclusive and the matter was final and binding and there was considerable legal authority that Mexico had waived any right to object to its jurisdiction. The 1868 Treaty implied a positive obligation on the part of Mexico to comply with the Award and the same applied to its submission to The Hague Court.[23] There was no ground of challenge here, there was no '*erreur essentielle*', no abuse of process or irregularity, only a minor numerical transposition which was corrected.[24] The Hague Court had no power to review the Award of the Mixed Tribunal, only power to consider whether Thornton's Award was *res judicata* and the consequences if it was not.[25]

[20] *Ibid* 14–15.

[21] *Ibid* 16–19.

[22] *Ibid* 20–22. It is interesting to note that the Anglo-American Commission formed under the Jay Treaty of 1794 at the conclusion of America's war of secession from Britain that British commissioners attempted to deny the Commission jurisdiction. The British Government to its credit acknowledged the Commission's right to determine its own jurisdiction.

[23] Opinion supported by M Chevalier Descamps, *Revue de Droit International* (1900) 225.

[24] Statement and Brief on behalf of the United States of America (n 10) 33.

[25] *Ibid* 43.

Based on the applicable civil and common law authorities, the findings of fact of the Mixed Tribunal were decisive as to every material allegation or statement which was binding and final so far as any such questions arose. There was no doubt as to the charitable nature of the trust despite the interventions of Spain and Mexico and accordingly Mexico had to account. The debt amounted to $1,420,682.67 plus future annuity payments of $43,050.99 in perpetuity. The Hague Court found that 33 annuities had not been paid and of them 21 would have to be paid in gold and the remaining 12 in Mexican silver dollars.

E. The Importance of the Case

The importance of this case was the recognition of the binding nature of the Award of an international tribunal and the jurisdiction of The Hague Court. International law in terms of the Agreement of Arbitration under the Treaties was recognised and proved its value in ending this dispute. It also demonstrated the emerging role of the United States as a world leader in the cause of international arbitration and support for an international rule of law through The Hague Court. It was also interesting that Britain's umpire Sir Edward Thornton played an important part in the Mixed Commission, demonstrating his independence and fine judgment. Such support by Britain and the United States for the Hague process and arbitration underpins perhaps a closer relationship founded on the rule of law as an alternative to war. It was also interesting that the doctrine of *res judicata*, so often recognised in national courts, was for the first time given international recognition in The Hague Court. Of course, the legal argument of the United States was well founded in national laws that both the parties and the subject matter as between the referral to The Hague Court and the Mixed Tribunal were one and the same. There was no difference in terms of any claim for payment of right as between the Catholic missionaries under Mexican rule and under American: the church was one and the same carrying out the objects of the trust.

The members of the Hague Court drew some procedural lessons from their experience. In a note to the Foreign Minister of the Netherlands dated 14th October 1902, they addressed certain issues that had arisen which could improve the process.[26] Under Article XXII, the International Bureau was the intermediary for communications to the Court. Upon the Bureau being informed that the parties had agreed to arbitration it should immediately take steps to establish the Tribunal and having received the names of those participating should

[26] Matzen, Fry, Martens, Asser and Savorin Lohman, 'Note from the Members of the Arbitral Tribunal in the Pious Fund Case to The Netherlands Minister for Foreign Affairs, Making Some Suggestions as to the Conduct of Future Arbitrations' (1911) 5 *American Journal of International Law* 73–78.

send copies of the *compromis* to the parties and at the same time confirm the members' appointments.

In relation to Article XXXIII and the selection of an umpire, members suggested that in order to avoid difficulties and an umpire's refusal to act as chairman or president, he should be chosen by the arbitrators. In relation to Article XXXVIII – choice of language – this should be agreed between the parties before the proceedings so that the agent and counsel were conversant with it. As to Article XXXIX regarding the two phases of the process: preliminary examination and discussion, such examination consisted of disclosure of the printed records, evidence and arguments in the case. It was essential that disclosure be given before the commencement of proceedings and discussions before the Tribunal. A longer period to ensure that all relevant documents were disclosed was advisable. Once the hearing or discussion ended no further evidence should be admitted.

Under Article LV, the Convention reserved the right of a party to demand a revision of the award if 'some new fact' would have 'decisive influence' on the award. The Hague Court was empowered to rule on that, but this was inconvenient. If such a short period was intended it would be unlikely to result in a new finding of fact, and if it was a longer period it would cause concern as the suspension would make the Award moribund. In the context of a dispute between nations this would be dangerous. The Tribunal's opinion was that such a provision should be very rarely used. The Tribunal may have had in mind the delay of Sir Edward Thornton in correcting his Award; whether or not that had any consequences on Mexico's default in paying interest is speculative.

II. THE DOGGER BANK INQUIRY

As has been considered earlier, the divergent imperial interests of Russia and Britain collided at several points of the Asian boundaries in Persia, Afghanistan and India – the Jewel in the British Imperial Crown. Where those interests conflicted some became the subject of diplomacy and others were resolved through mediation and arbitration. The Penjdah dispute was one such example, but perhaps a more dangerous crisis occurred over the mistaken action taken by the Russian fleet bound to attack Britain's ally Japan.

A. Russo-Japanese War

Following a period of isolationism, Britain, although an imperial power which held supremacy on the High Seas, found it in her interest to enter into friendly arrangements with other Powers. In Asia, Britain found it in her interest to preserve the status quo in China and Korea with the Anglo-Japanese Treaty of 1902 which would secure the British interest against further Russian expansion and deterred France from interference in the Russo-Japanese war. In Europe and North Africa, Britain found it in her interest to enter friendly relations with France in 1904. By such means Britain reconciled her differences with France over Morocco and Egypt; each country recognising the other's interest. But despite these efforts tension between Russia and Britain was high. Britain, an ally of Japan, was seen by Russia as a possible enemy when Japan demanded that Russia withdraw from Korea and Manchuria. At the time France was an ally of Russia and thus there was a risk war between the two alliances. Russia and Britain had rivalled each other in Asia in what historians called the Great Game.[27] Japan and Russia started negotiations in July 1903 with France undertaking mediation in January 1904. Russia regarded Korea as necessary for her defence, but nevertheless proposed withdrawing her troops from Manchuria. These negotiations were protracted and the Japanese lost patience with Russia. Mediation was dead and Japan attacked Port Arthur on 8 February 1904 without warning.

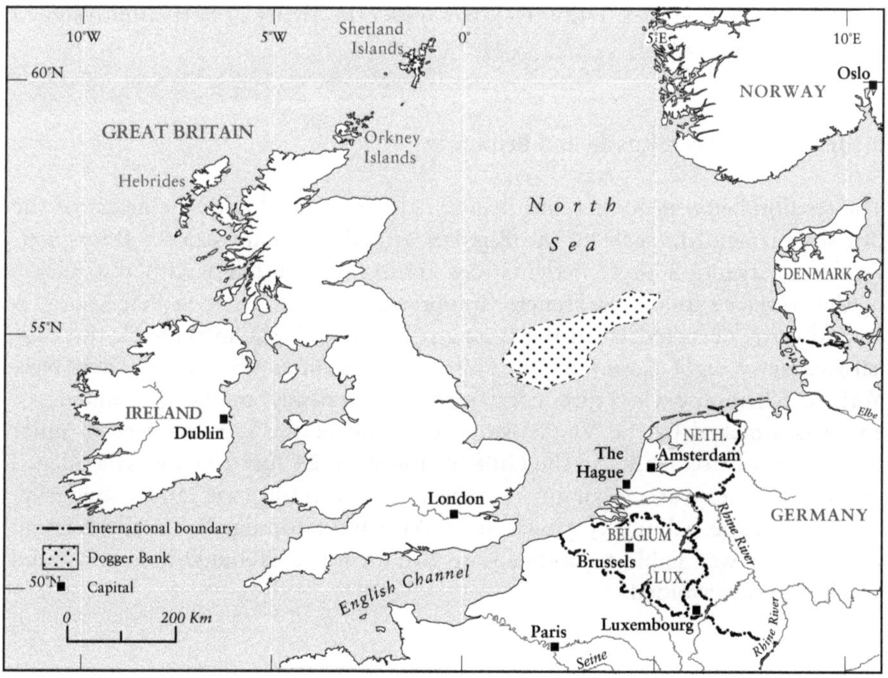

Figure 4.1 Map illustrating the location of the Dogger Bank
Credit: Mina Moshkeri

[27] See generally P Hopkirk, *The Great Game* (John Murray, 1990).

Britain and France were concerned at the outbreak of this war in the Far East, as it threatened both their interests. France did not want to risk a war with Britain and attempted to persuade Britain to urge her new ally towards moderation. In doing so France suggested that Britain and France settle their colonial differences, and this eventually led to the *Entente Cordiale* settling all outstanding differences in Egypt and Morocco. In addition, they expressed a desire that the Russo-Japanese war be limited. The British interest would be threatened if France and Russia joined forces, enabling Russia to expand its empire in Central Asia or worse perhaps, that Russia and Japan might become allies. In 1905 Russia suffered a severe blow at the siege of Port Arthur and subsequently at the battle of Tsushima. The impact in Europe undermined the interests of Britain and France because Russian prestige had been damaged and its great Power status diminished by the defeats in 1905. It was left to President Theodore Roosevelt to mediate a settlement whereby Russia suffered less than might otherwise have been the case resulting in anti-American feeling in Japan. As a result, Russia evacuated Manchuria and surrendered the Lease on the Liaotung peninsula including Port Arthur to Japan under the Treaty of Portsmouth signed on 5 September 1905.

B. Tension between Russia and Britain

The tension between Russia and Britain came to a head with the arrest of the British steamer *Malacca* by the Russian armed merchant cruiser *Petersburg*. French intervention prevented matters getting out of hand with the release of the *Malacca* following French diplomatic intervention at St Petersburg. A second crisis occurred when the Russian Vladivostok squadron sank the British steamer *Knight Commander*. This British steamer was sailing from New York to Chemulpo via Japan carrying general railway engineering materials. She was attacked by the Vladivostok Squadron of the Russian fleet 75 miles south-west of Yokohama in the Gulf of Tokyo on 24 July 1904. Russia alleged that the steamer was carrying contraband of war, in this case railway material. Fortunately, the Admiralty Court at St Petersburg adjudged that the Russian Government was liable to compensate Britain for a £100,000 indemnity and hostilities were avoided.

C. *'La nuit, sur mer, tout est possible'*[28]

In October 1904, during the Russo-Japanese war, the Admiral of the Russian Baltic fleet, Admiral Rozhdestvensky, received reports from several sources of

[28] M De Lanessan, Minister of Marine comment to *The Times* (1 March 1905) 5 Issue 37,643.

the presence of Japanese torpedo boats in the vicinity of his ships' position off the coast of Norway, where the fleet was coaling. As a result, he ordered the fleet to set sail for the Far East 24 hours ahead of schedule. On the night of the 24 October,[29] the Russian Baltic fleet *en route* to attack the Japanese fleet in the Pacific by mistake fired upon British fishing trawlers *The Gamecock* off the Dogger Bank, believing they were being attacked by Japanese torpedo boats. As a result, one trawler was sunk, two fishermen were killed, and others wounded. *The Times* reported that Captain Klado witnessed 'two torpedo boats going towards the *Kniaz Suvaroff* ready to launch torpedoes against her'.[30] The *Frankfurter Zeitung* suggested that the Russian fleet fired on and sank a Swedish steamer the *Ares*. Conjecture may suggest that this was mistaken for a torpedo destroyer which is what Lieutenant Ott of the *Anadyr* who ordered the firing may have seen.[31] It appears that Rojdestvensky and his officers ignored the lights and signals on the trawlers because of the difficulty in recognising them. The night was slightly foggy and cloudy. Rojdestvensky was suspecting some attack after leaving the coaling station but not expecting to sail through an English fishing fleet.

The Russian action appeared to be a deliberate attack and worse the Russian fleet made no attempt to pick up survivors or report the incident to the British authorities. Rojdestvensky initially defended his fleet's action, claiming that there were two unidentified foreign torpedo boats in the area and action was taken accordingly. Two reports by telegram were sent, both claiming the presence of two torpedo boats, the second cable suggesting the presence of several other steamers.[32] Lord Lansdowne, the British Foreign Secretary, could not accept such an extraordinary story. Lansdowne made enquiries of his consular officials on the continent and in Japan, all of whom confirmed reports that there were no torpedo boats in the area at that time.

Lord Lansdowne demanded an apology, reparations, an inquiry into the circumstances and punishment for those responsible. He made inquiry of Sir Charles Hardinge, the British Ambassador, at St Petersburg on 24 October.[33] Hardinge met Count Lamsdorff, the Russian Minister of Foreign Affairs that day who expressed his 'horror' at the reports and promised a full inquiry 'with prompt punishment and full reparation'.[34] Tsar Nicholas sent Lamsdorff to see Hardinge the next day to apologise and confirm that compensation would be paid to the victims. It was also echoed by Count Benckendorff on his return from Russia to London when he met Lansdowne on 25 October. When Lansdowne

[29] In an obituary published in *The Times* on 16 January 1909, it states that the incident occurred on 21 October 1904.*The Times* (17 December 1904) 7 Issue 37,580.

[30] *The Times* (21 December 1904) 3 Issue 37,583.

[31] *The Times* (14 November 1904) 3 Issue 37,551.

[32] N Bar-Yaacov, *The Handling of International Disputes by Means of Enquiry* (Oxford University Press, 1974) 51.

[33] GP Gooch and H Temperley (eds), *British Documents on the Origins of the War 1898–1914* (BD) Vol IV 'Anglo-Russian Rapprochement' (Her Majesty's Stationery Office, 1929) 6, No 6.

[34] *Ibid* 7.

saw Benckendorff again on the 26th October, he demanded a statement along the lines discussed and warned Benckendorff that 'if it (The Baltic Fleet) were allowed to continue its journey without calling at Vigo, we might find ourselves at war before the week was over'.[35] Lansdowne proposed a Commission of Inquiry under Articles IX and XIV of the Hague Convention composed of high ranking officers representing the Powers concerned, as well as representatives from three other Powers. Lansdowne wanted to see the officers responsible tried and punished and was not persuaded by the explanations provided by Admiral Rojdestvensky. Hardinge warned him that Russian feeling was sensitive, and they had suffered humiliation in the Russo-Japanese war as well as the serious social unrest in the country.[36]

D. British Fleet Dispositions

Russia was alarmed at the British reaction despite the Tsar's agreement to a Commission. The Admiralty gave orders on 27 October to the Commander in Chief, Mediterranean Fleet that battleships, armoured cruisers and destroyers should be assembled at Gibraltar. Further instructions were given to the Vice Admiral, Channel Fleet to concentrate on Gibraltar and to stop the Baltic Fleet. The navy was to 'try persuasion or by force if necessary' but no action was to be taken until ordered to do so. As a precaution the British cruisers were to shadow the Baltic Fleet. The Home Fleet was ordered to concentrate on Portland.[37] The next day Benckendorff told Lansdowne that the Baltic Fleet would remain at Vigo pending the inquiry and those responsible be sent on to St Petersburg for a court of inquiry. They would be tried if found guilty by the Tribunal. He disclosed that the Baltic Fleet whilst at Libau had been given an order to fire on any boat coming near the squadron. This was an extraordinary order but accounts for the reckless action taken against defenceless trawlers. Lansdowne was alarmed at this and sought an undertaking from Russia that on no account would such action be taken for the rest of the Baltic Fleet's voyage.

E. Diplomacy Takes Over

At this point M Paul Cambon, the French Ambassador to London, became involved and since France had an alliance with Russia and an entente with Britain it was important that the matter was resolved amicably. Cambon emphasised how quickly Russia had acceded to Britain's demands.[38] Lansdowne later

35 *Ibid* 11–13, No 13 *Lansdowne to Hardinge* (26 October 1904).
36 *Ibid* 12, No 14 and 15, No 15.
37 *Ibid* 18, No 19 Encl 2 and 3.
38 *Ibid* 22–23, No 22.

acknowledged Cambon's efforts in a speech in Berlin on 10 November 1904 as a tribute to the *Entente Cordiale* which in his words proved to be 'an instrument of peace.[39]

In St Petersburg, Hardinge met with Lamsdorff who confirmed orders to the Baltic Fleet to stop at Vigo and remove those responsible. He said that punishment would depend on the inquiry and praised Lansdowne's moderate language but criticised the bellicose tones of the British press.[40] The Tsar was also critical of the British press in his audience with Hardinge on 31 October and alarmed at the British navy's action. He did not want war with Japan's European ally.[41] Nicholas expressed the view that the press had become 'a tyranny which in foreign politics was capable of great mischief and for which it was difficult to escape'. Nicholas agreed the composition of the Tribunal and remarked on the disposition of the British fleet. He remarked that a fortnight before he had stopped a Russian division from moving on the Orenburg-Tashkent line. This dispatch was seen by King Edward VII who remarked that it was 'an admirable and interesting dispatch'. What perhaps it demonstrated, as did Hardinge's despatches, was Russia's concern to have a good relationship with Britain.

F. Risks

Russia would not accept any apportionment of guilt, nor would it accept its officers being tried in Russia.[42] The officers who were apprehended were not those directly involved but were selected because they were multi-lingual.

Lord Lansdowne wanted an inquiry into all the circumstances of the disaster, where responsibility lay and the degree of blame. Russia wanted the inquiry to 'give a decision on the question of responsibility, in accordance with results of the enquiry'. That there was no reference to 'where the responsibility for the disaster lies' or 'to the degree of blame which attaches to those upon whom responsibilities are found to rest'.

The Russian fleet sailed from Vigo before any undertaking was given and as Lansdowne foresaw the risk of the Russians taking prizes, raised questions of international law.[43] Two ships were sunk and others arrested during the course of the war.[44] Reference to a tribunal was not however without its risks. Headlam-Morley suggested that such process 'made a peaceful settlement appreciably more difficult and might well have brought about rupture'.[45] Lansdowne

[39] *The Times* (11 November 1904) 3 Issue 37,549.
[40] BD Vol IV (n 33) 23, No 22.
[41] *Ibid* 25–28, No 24.
[42] Bar-Yaacov (n 32) 56.
[43] BD Vol IV (n 33) 23–24 No 23.
[44] FE Smith and NW Sibley, *International Law as Interpreted During the Russo-Japanese War* (T Fisher Unwin, 1905) Appendix K.
[45] J Headlam-Morley, *Studies in Diplomatic History* (Methuen & Co, 1930) 28.

would have preferred a reference to the Permanent Court of Arbitration at The Hague. Whilst this was happening the Kaiser, ever watchful for an opportunity to take advantage, sought the possibility of an alliance between Germany and Russia. Nothing came of this because Russia wanted to consult France first.[46] Benckendorff told Lansdowne that the inquiry would take time to establish responsibility which must be the subject of an admiralty investigation.[47]

G. Draft Terms of Reference

On 31 October, the day of the Tsar's audience with Hardinge, Lansdowne wrote to Hardinge saying that the officers as witnesses would be sent to The Hague. He also enclosed the draft terms of reference for the inquiry for Russian agreement. The draft referred to Articles 9–14 of the Hague Convention 1899 and Article 1 provided that the Tribunal consist of one Russian and one British Admiral, one French and one American Admiral, and a president elected by the four appointees. Article 2 set out the object of the inquiry and it was that that led to some differences of opinion later. Article 2 stated:

> The Commission shall enquire into and report upon the circumstances attending the disaster in the North Sea, and particularly as to where responsibility for the disaster lies, and that the degree of blame which attaches to those whom at that responsibility is found to rest.

Count Lamsdorff objected to the inclusion of reference to the degree of blame. He therefore proposed alternative text:

> The Commission shall investigate all the circumstances connected with the North Sea incident and particularly elucidate the facts relating thereto, and give a decision on the question of responsibility, in accordance with the results of enquiry.

There was a difference of opinion as to whether the Tribunal would 'decide' or whether it would 'pronounce' on the question of responsibility in accordance with the results of inquiry. In arbitration, arbitrators publish an award which is a reasoned judgment. Here it would appear that the intention was to simply give a view more in the way of a technical assessment than a judgment of the court. Lansdowne and Lamsdorff also disagreed over whether the Tribunal could make a finding of liability. To make matters more difficult, Hardinge sent a further warning to Lansdowne on 7 November reporting serious concern over Russian opinion and the prospect of war as a result of the British cruisers shadowing the Baltic fleet from Vigo to Tangier. Hardinge said that the Russians perceived

[46] RJ Sontag, European Diplomatic History 1871–1932 (Appleton-Century-Crofts, 1933) 102. See also R Albrecht-Carrie, *A Diplomatic History of Europe Since the Congress of Vienna* (Methuen, 1965) 246.

[47] Bar-Yaacov (n 32) 50.

England as more of an enemy than Japan. Russia's position was difficult as there was widespread discontent, poverty and suffering. The War Party led by the Grand Dukes would seek to deflect problems at home by prospect of a successful war in Central Asia. There was a real threat of Russian incursions in Afghanistan and India via Orenburg and the Caspian.[48]

Lansdowne had a further meeting with Cambon on 15th November when Cambon expressed the view that the word 'blame' in Article 2 did not conform with The Hague Convention. It had a different meaning in French meaning punishment but in England it meant censure. The problem was that Lansdowne could not alter the wording because he had spoken publicly of it in his speech at the Guildhall.[49] The final text of Article II as agreed and signed in St Petersburg on 25 November 1904 was:

> The Commission shall enquire into and report on all the circumstances relative to the North Sea incident, and particularly on the question as to where the responsibility lies, and the degree of blame attaching to the subjects of the two high contracting parties or to the subjects of other countries in the event of their responsibility being established by the enquiry.

This is a curious form of words for an inquiry which was constituted under the Hague Convention of 1899 which restricted such processes to matters of fact, although as an international tribunal it was surely bound to consider national and collective responsibility, not individual.

The Commission held sessions at Paris from 22 December 1904, to 26 February 1905, on which date its report was rendered. It was comprised of Admiral Baron Spaun of Austria-Hungary, Vice-Admiral Fournier who was elected by the other members as President of the Commission, Admiral Doubassoff of Russia, Admiral Sir Lewis Beaumont of Great Britain and Admiral Charles Davis of the United States. The British agent was Sir Edward Fry and the Russian agent was Michael Taube. The Tribunal proceeded on the basis that sessions would be in public unless matters were confidential or of a security sensitive nature.[50] Agents could present statements of fact and be assisted by legal advisers and counsel provided that such counsel notified the commissioners and were approved by them. Counsel could only ask questions of witnesses provided that the questions were previously submitted to the President. Once information had been submitted only agents were entitled to submit their conclusions and observations in writing which could be read in the public sessions.[51] Among the principal witnesses were the fisherman, sailors from Norway, the Shetland Islands and Denmark and also agents belonging to the Intelligence Department of the Russian Admiralty, as well as officers from the Russian fleet including Captain

[48] BD Vol IV (n 33) 33–35 No 26.
[49] *Ibid*. Text of Convention 37 No 29.
[50] Bar-Yaacov (n 32) 61.
[51] Bar-Yaacov (n 32) 62.

Klado who was the agent of Admiral Skrydloff, the Commander in Chief of the Russian Naval forces in the Pacific.

H. Inquiry Report

The Commissioners' Report found[52] that the Second Russian Squadron of the Pacific Fleet, under the command of Vice-Admiral General Rojdestvensky, anchored on the 7 October 1904, off Cape Skagen, with the purpose of coaling before continuing its voyage to the Far East. Evidence to the inquiry confirmed that from the time of sailing from Reval, Admiral Rojdestvensky ordered the squadron to be ready for any night attack by torpedo boats, either at sea or at anchor. These precautionary measures were based upon intelligence reports of Russian agents suggesting attack by torpedo boats. But just how torpedo boats in those days could reach the Baltic or the North Sea from Japan is perplexing.

Whilst at Skagen, in Norway, Admiral Rojdestvensky had been warned of the presence of suspect vessels in the area. He received a report from the commander of the transport *Bakan* steaming south that four torpedo boats were sighted. The Admiral decided to sail at once ahead of schedule in six divisions, the last being four battleships and a transport vessel. The fleet sailed at 12 knots and 10 knots for the respective first four divisions in two sections. Progress was delayed however because one of the transports, the *Kamchatka*, developed engine trouble. Having received warning the *Kamchatka* opened fire on a Swedish ship, the *Aldebaran*, and other unidentified ships mistaking them for torpedo boats. At 8:45 pm the commander of the *Kamchatka* sent a signal to Admiral Rojdestvensky that he was 'attacked on all sides by torpedo boats'. The Admiral considered that if the *Kamchatka* was being attacked 50 miles from his position, he could expect an attack at 1 pm the next morning.

In making this assessment and in giving orders to his officers in wartime the Commission found nothing unwarranted in his actions based on the information he was given at the time. Rojdestvensky deemed it essential that one of his two superior officers should keep watch on the captain's bridge during the night to warn him at once if any incident occurred. Importantly since they were at war stations the Admiral's standing orders to the officer of the watch were to open fire if they came under imminent attack by torpedo boats. If the attack came ahead of the squadron, senior officers were ordered to open fire on their own initiative, but in all other cases they should defer to the commanding officer. Most of the Commissioners considered that these orders were in no way excessive in time of war, and particularly in the circumstances, in which Admiral

[52] Reference submitted to them for Inquiry under the terms of the Declaration of St. Petersburg 12th November 1904 (1931) 2 *American Journal of International Law* 931. Carnegie Endowment for International Peace Division of International Law, *The Hague Reports* (edited by James Brown Scott) (Oxford University Press American Branch, 1916) 403–12.

Rojdestvensky 'had every reason to consider very alarming, seeing that it was impossible for him to verify the accuracy of the warnings that he had received from the agents of his Government'.[53]

The Report continued as follows:

> 9. Toward 1 o'clock in the morning of the 9th (22d) October 1904, the night was rather dark, a slight, low fog partly clouding the air. The moon only showed intermittently between the clouds.
>
> A moderate wind blew from the southeast, raising a long swell, which gave the ships a roll of 5° on each side. The course followed by the squadron toward the southwest would have taken the last two divisions, as the event proved, close past the usual fishing ground the Dogger Bank of the fleet of Hull trawlers, which was composed of some thirty of these small steamboats, and was spread over an area of several miles. It appears from the concordant testimony of the British witnesses that all these boats carried their proper lights, and were trawling in accordance with their usual rules, under the direction of their 'admiral,' and in obedience to the signals given by the conventional rockets.
>
> 10. Judging from the communications received by wireless telegraphy, the divisions which preceded that of Admiral Rojdestvensky across these waters had signalled nothing unusual. It became known afterward, in particular, that Admiral Fulkerson, having been led to pass round the fishing fleet on the north, threw his electric searchlight on the nearest trawlers at close quarters, and, having seen them to be harmless vessels, quietly continued his voyage.
>
> 11. A short time afterwards the last division of the squadron, led by the *Souvoroff* flying Admiral Rojdestvensky's flag, arrived in its turn close to the spot where the trawlers were fishing. The direction in which this division was sailing led it nearly toward the main body of the fleet of trawlers, round which and to the south of which it would therefore be obliged to sail, when the attention of the officers of the watch on the bridges of the *Souvoroff* was attracted by a green rocket, which put them on their guard. This rocket, sent up by the 'admiral' of the fishing fleet, indicated in reality, according to regulation, that the trawlers were to trawl on the starboard tack. Almost immediately after this first alarm, and as shown by the evidence, the lookout men, who, from the bridges of the *Souvoroff*, were scanning the horizon with their night glasses, discovered 'on the crest of the waves on the starboard bow, at an approximate distance of eighteen to twenty cables,' a vessel which aroused their suspicions because they saw no light, and because she appeared to be bearing down upon them. When the suspicious-looking vessel was shown up by the searchlight, the lookout men thought they recognized a torpedo boat proceeding at great speed. It was on account of these appearances that Admiral Rojdestvensky ordered fire to be opened on this unknown vessel. The majority of the commissioners express the opinion, on this subject, that the responsibility for this action and the results of the fire to which the fishing fleet was exposed are to be attributed to Admiral Rojdestvensky.
>
> 12. Almost immediately after fire was opened to starboard, *Souvoroff* caught sight of a little boat on her bow barring the way and was obliged to turn sharply to the

[53] *The Hague Reports* (n 52) 406.

left to avoid running it down. This boat, however, on being lit up by the searchlight, was seen to be a trawler. To prevent the fire of the ships being directed against this harmless vessel, the searchlight was immediately thrown up at an angle of 45°. The admiral then made the signal to the squadron 'not to fire on the trawlers.' But at the same time that the searchlight had lit up this fishing vessel, according to the evidence of witnesses, the lookout men on board the *Souvoroff* perceived to port another vessel, which appeared suspicious from the fact of its presenting the same features as were presented by the object of their fire to starboard. Fire was immediately opened on this second object, and was, therefore, being kept up on both sides of the ship, the line of ships having resumed their original course by a correcting movement without changing speed.

13. According to the standing orders of the fleet, the Admiral indicated the objects against which the fire should be directed by throwing his searchlight upon them; but as each vessel swept the horizon in every direction with her own searchlights to avoid being taken by surprise, it was difficult to prevent confusion. The fire, which lasted from ten to twelve minutes, caused great loss to the trawlers. Two men were killed, and six others wounded the *Crane* sank; the *Snipe*, the *Mino*, the *Moulmcin*, the *Gull*, and the *Majestic* were more or less damaged. On the other hand, the cruiser *Aurora* was hit by several shots. The majority of the commissioners observe that they have not sufficiently precise details to determine what was the object fired on by the vessels; but the commissioners recognize unanimously that the vessels of the fishing fleet did not commit any hostile act; and, the majority of the commissioners being of opinion that there were no torpedo boats either among the trawlers nor anywhere near, the opening of the fire by Admiral Rojdestvensky was not justifiable. The Russian commissioner, not considering himself justified in sharing this opinion, expresses the conviction that it was precisely the suspicious-looking vessels approaching the squadron with hostile intent which provoked the fire.

14. With reference to the real objectives of this nocturnal firing, the fact that the Aurora was hit by several 47-millimeter and 75-millimeter shells would lead to the supposition that this cruiser, and perhaps even some other Russian vessels, left behind on the route followed by the *Souvoroff* unknown to that vessel, might have provoked and been the object of the first few shots. This mistake might have been caused by the fact that this vessel, seen from astern, was apparently showing no light, and by a nocturnal optical illusion which deceived the lookout on the flagship. On this head the commissioners find that they are without important information which would enable them to determine the reasons why the fire on the port side was continued. According to their conjecture, certain distant trawlers might have been mistaken for the original objectives, and thus fired upon directly. Others, on the contrary, might have been struck by a fire directed against more distant objectives. These considerations, moreover, are not in contradiction with the impressions formed by certain of the trawlers, who, finding that they were struck by projectiles and remained under the rays of the searchlights, might believe that they were the object of a direct fire. The time during which the firing lasted on the starboard side, even taking the point of view of the Russian version, seems to the majority of the commissioners to have been longer than was necessary. But that majority considers that, as has already been said, they have not before them sufficient data as to why the fire on the portside was continued. In any case, the commissioners take pleasure in recognizing, unanimously,

that Admiral Rojdestvensky personally did everything he could, from beginning to end of the incident, to prevent trawlers, recognized as such, from being fired upon by the squadron.

16. Finally, the *Dmitri Donskoi* having signalled her number, the Admiral decided to give the general signal for 'cease firing.' The line of his ships then continued on their way and disappeared to the southwest without having stopped. On this point the commissioners recognize, unanimously, that after the circumstances which preceded the incident and those which produced it, there was, at the cessation of fire, sufficient uncertainty with regard to the danger to which the division of vessels was exposed to induce the Admiral to proceed on his way. Nevertheless, the majority of the commissioners regret that Admiral Rojdestvensky, in passing the Straits of Dover, did not take care to inform the authorities of the neighbouring maritime Powers, that, as he had been led to open fire near a group of trawlers, these boats, of unknown nationality, stood in need of assistance.

17. In concluding this report, the commissioners declare that their findings, which are therein formulated, are not, in their opinion, of a nature to cast any discredit upon the military qualities or the humanity of Admiral Rojdestvensky, or of the personnel of his squadron.[54]

I. Analysis

The conclusion reached was that there were no torpedo boats either among the trawlers or anywhere near and that the opening of fire by the Russian Admiral was not justified. His action under the circumstances was not, however, such as to cast discredit upon his military abilities or humanity or that of the personnel of his squadron. This rather begs the question that if the action was not justified was it contrary to international law? The Commission could not answer that question as it was not an arbitral tribunal, although its procedure was similar. Russia accepted the result and paid damages to the extent of about $300,000. From its point of view, Russia had preserved the reputation of its fleet and from the British point of view compensation was paid. On the other hand, the officers responsible for the incident escaped prosecution principally because the error of judgement that was made was excusable given the particular circumstances and naval practice at that time.

The holding of the Commission was a considerable achievement for those who upheld the rule of international law because this dispute related to national interests and national honour, something which President Taft subsequently proposed in his international arbitration treaties with England and France. It is therefore a credit to the Russian and British governments at that time that had the foresight to accept the jurisdiction of a mixed international tribunal. Russia alleged collusion between the British trawlers and the Japanese since Japan was

[54] *Ibid* 406–10.

a British ally, but Britain had declared neutrality in the matter. So far as British foreign policy was concerned, an expanding Russia was a threat in Asia which the Japanese Alliance had checked, but in the European context Russia might be a block on German domination.

The success of the Commission was mainly due to the efforts of M Paul Cambon who used his good offices in London with the Russian ambassador Count Benckendorff to facilitate agreement between the Russians and the British to establish the Commission. The alternative of each state having its own investigation risked different outcomes and the continuation of the dispute which might easily result in war.

Another unique feature of the Commission was the power to examine questions of responsibility and apportion blame. The Commission found the cause stemmed from the engine failure on the *Kamchatka* and the standing order to open fire on sighting torpedo boats. At the same time the Commission excused Admiral Rojdestvensky from blame because, according to the naval experts, the precautions he ordered were justified in times of war. The Commission also found that the *Gamecock* was not hostile, and the attack was not justified. It also found that no blame should fall upon the Russian fleet commander as Count Lamsdorff had requested. The reason why the Commission never apportioned blame was because in its view it was conforming to Article 9 of the Hague Convention 1899. Legally, this is somewhat difficult to understand bearing in mind the Admiral's admission. In this sense Russia was settling the dispute without admission of liability.

Questions arose as to whether Admiral Rojdestvensky was justified in thinking that the trawlers were Japanese torpedo boats. Did he see them? Did he give proper instructions? Were reasonable efforts made to identify the targets? Not only did the squadron fire on the British trawlermen, but also on their own ships. There may have been some difficulty in recognition because torpedo boats in those days might resemble small or light cruisers. Indeed, the views of admiralty experts including Sir John Fisher of the Royal Navy was that such a failure was not unusual and there had been many other incidents.[55]

The Report was essentially a factual account with technical analyses of the key facts. It was written by the Commissioners themselves without input from the legal advisers. They dealt with some questions of causation but were hampered because they could not ascertain certain other facts by the means at their disposal. The Commissioners concluded that Admiral Rojdestvensky gave orders to fire on the fishing fleet because he believed that he was being attacked by Japanese torpedo boats. The question is whether that was a reasonable belief at the time in relation to the information he had been given. This might certainly provide sound justification for mistakenly firing on Russian warships which were out of range of the searchlights and not expected to be where they were, but it

[55] A Hershey, *The International Law and Diplomacy of The Russian Japanese War* (The Macmillan Company 1906) 243.

is more difficult to understand in relation to the proximity of British trawlers illuminated by powerful searchlights. The British trawlers were unarmed private neutral vessels sailing on the High Seas carrying out their lawful rights under international law. To all intents and purposes, they were totally innocent and unaware of any belligerent war risk. They were showing appropriate international signals and had no reason to precipitate any attack. It was no defence for the Russian Baltic Squadron to say they were acting as a matter of precaution, or in accordance with orders, or by mistake. To attack unarmed private trawlers from a neutral state thinking they were enemies was no defence under international law. It may also be argued that to attack in these circumstances was an act of piracy.[56] It could not have been a matter of inevitable necessity in time of war where what we now call 'collateral damage' may occur. In 1904 it was a case of right of angary whereby compensation would be payable by the belligerent, but then the Gamecock (name of the fishing fleet) was not hampering any naval defensive disposition nor aiding any Japanese attack. The Russian Baltic Squadron simply had no defence.

The squadron's recklessness was compounded in that having identified the trawlers the fleet sailed on. The reason given for this is the suspicion that the torpedo boats could have been hiding amongst the fishing fleet or the fishing fleet might have been in collusion or giving cover to the Japanese since Japan was an ally of Britain. But the problem with such argument is simply that there was no evidence whatsoever of Japanese torpedo boats in the North Sea apart from allegations made by Russian naval officers, and those ships that had been attacked were all neutral. Whilst the naval experts opined that such events were not uncommon and therefore Admiral Rojdestvensky was acting in accordance with his duty to protect the fleet in sailing away, it is arguable that although the obligation to search for and rescue survivors is not an absolute one, nevertheless a belligerent should take all possible measures to rescue survivors consistent with its own security. Were such firing to have been directed at defenceless survivors of the two sunken trawlers then there could be no justification on operational grounds.[57]

The Commissioners did not give any ruling on international law. Their Report was accepted by both states and had the effect of an arbitration award. The process was similar to litigation which Lord Lansdowne had wanted. Each state agent argued their respective case but used Counsel to examine the witnesses. They read conclusions and made observations, but they were not jurists. There were no pleadings or submissions, no procedure had been agreed beforehand and much time was spent arguing about procedure. This was remedied by the Second Hague Conference.

[56] Smith and Sibley (n 44) 298.

[57] RW Tucker, *The Law of War and Neutrality at Sea* (Naval War College, 1955) and see Article 23 paras c and d Regulations annexed to Hague Convention IV (1907). Article 23 expressly forbids: *(c)* To kill or wound an enemy who, having laid down his arms, or having no longer means of defence, has surrendered at discretion; *(d)* To declare that no quarter will be given.

Whilst the procedure and the outcome may not have been recognised as a judicial proceeding, it nevertheless served the purpose of satisfying both parties and succeeded in facilitating a peaceful settlement in what might otherwise have resulted in hostilities. In addition, it saved France and Britain embarrassment and a potential conflict between two alliances; France and Russia on the one hand, and Japan and Britain on the other. It would appear that the composition of the Commission representing the parties, but with a majority of neutral representatives undoubtedly facilitated the moderate tone of the report which was acceptable to both parties avoiding any suggestion of dishonour. Above all the Commission demonstrated that where there was a conflict of national interest and national honour a suitably constituted tribunal could succeed. In that sense it reinforced President Taft's argument for international arbitration treaties to resolve such disputes. Whilst the United Sates undoubtedly performed a great service to the cause of world peace and championed the cause of arbitration, yet in the case of the Panama Canal where her own national interests were at stake, President Taft expressly objected to the differences between Britain and the United States being referred to arbitration.

III. THE PANAMA CANAL DISPUTE

A. Nature of the Dispute

The dispute between Britain and America over the construction and management of the Panama Canal arose out of a series of treaties and differing interpretations of those treaties. To understand the dispute, it is important to consider the terms of such treaties in relation to the duties and obligations of Britain and the United States and the conflicting national interests of Britain and the United States. The principal treaties referred to here include: The United States and the Republic of Colombia or New Granada Treaty 1846, the Clayton-Bulwer Treaty 1850, the Constantinople Convention 1888, the Hay-Pauncefote Treaty 1901, the Anglo-American Arbitration Treaty 1908, and the General Peace Treaty 1914. So far as the United States was concerned all these international treaties were subject to the Panama Canal Act 1912 and the advice by way of a Memorandum to the Congress by President Taft in that year. So far as Britain was concerned the United States was bound by the treaty of 1901 but especially the obligation that Britain would be treated equally as expressly provided in the Clayton-Bulwer Treaty 1850. Here there were conflicting approaches.

Britain had acquired its interest in Belize prior to the United States gaining its independence. Britain claimed such interest under two treaties between Britain and Spain made in 1783 and 1786.[58] The legal title was limited to a

[58] See D Waddell, 'British Honduras and Anglo-American Relations' (1957) 5 *Caribbean Quarterly* 50.

right to cut wood: it was not a sovereign right[59] yet Britain exercised rights of sovereignty over British Honduras and the port of Belize for the purposes of trade. The United States projecting its own imperial ambitions sought hegemony of Central America under its Monroe Doctrine following the aspirations of Thomas Jefferson and John Quincy Adams.[60]

The issue in dispute eventually crystallised into a dispute over the imposition of tolls on vessels passing through the Panama Canal. Britain protested that the United States had no right to levy tolls on foreign ships if its coastwise traffic was exempt from tolls. Britain argued that the United States was bound by the rules under Article VIII of the Clayton-Bulwer Treaty of 1850 prohibiting the imposition of tolls and the rules under Article III of the Hay-Pauncefote Treaty 1901. Britain further argued that it should be treated fairly and equally with the United States under those provisions, as well as by the incorporation of the Constantinople Convention 1888 rules governing passage through the Suez Canal whereby the canal should be free and open to 'all nations'.

B. Policy of the United States

The idea of an interoceanic passage through the Central American isthmus was suggested by Henry Clay, US Secretary of State to the US representatives to the Panama Congress on the 8th May 1826.[61] It is significant that from an early stage in the discussion he suggested that if the work could be executed

> to admit the passage of sea vessels from ocean to ocean, the benefits of it ought not to be exclusively appropriated to any one nation, but should be extended to all parts of the globe upon the payment of a just compensation or reasonable tolls.

This was followed in March 1835 by a Senate Resolution regarding the opening of discussions with the Central American states for a ship canal through the isthmus 'securing forever, by such stipulations the free and equal right of navigating such canal to all such nations'. In 1839, the House of Representatives passed a Resolution unanimously 'securing forever' by suitable treaty stipulations 'the free and equal right of navigating such canal to all nations'.[62] Thus, the basis of any future negotiation in principle had been considered. In 1846 the United States and New Granada (Colombia) signed a treaty whereby New Granada guaranteed to the United States the right of passage across the isthmus of Panama and that it would be open and free to the US Government and its

[59] RW Van Alstyne, 'British Diplomacy and the Clayton-Bulwer Treaty 1850–60' (1939) 11 *The Journal of Modern History* 149, 160.
[60] RW Van Alstyne, *The American Empire* (Historical Association, 1960) 13, 14.
[61] Proceedings of the American Society of International Law at its Annual Meeting (1907–1917) Vol 7 International Use of Straits and Canals with Especial Reference to the Panama Canal (24–26 April 1913) 93.
[62] *Ibid* 94.

citizens. No tolls would be levied on the United States' ships or citizens. Perfect neutrality, the rights of sovereignty and property of New Granada would be guaranteed.[63] President Polk's objective was to secure to all nations the free and equal right of passage over the isthmus.[64]

Figure 4.2 Map illustrating Central America and the Panama Canal zone
Credit: Mina Moshkeri

[63] *Ibid* 96.

[64] President Polk's Annual Message to the Senate. 'International Use of Straits and Canals with Especial Reference to the Panama Canal' (24–26 April 1913) 7 at Proceedings of the American Society of International Law (n 61) 96.

C. Rival Interests

At the time of the Clayton-Bulwer Treaty, the relative bargaining strengths of Britain and the United States were imbalanced. Britain had the strongest navy in the world and a great empire. The United States was a growing country expanding to the west and as result of war with Mexico had gained California and New Mexico. Its movement was west towards the Pacific and the canal was seen as enhancing its interoceanic communications with its western states and commercial interests in the Pacific region.

The Clayton-Bulwer Treaty was also perceived as an international alliance whereby the former colonial power was jointly obliged with the United States to protect the construction and operation of a canal. From the British point of view, the Treaty halted United States expansion to the south. From the American side Britain was still regarded with suspicion in certain quarters of the press and the political establishment typified by papers such as the *New York Herald* which in late 1849 published bellicose attacks on Britain suggesting that the United States would absorb Canada, Cuba, Puerto Rico and the British West Indies in the American Union.[65] John M Clayton, the Whig Secretary of State, recognised a chief cause of concern was the Mosquito Coast. He knew that Palmerston did not want Britain entangled in Central America and why Palmerston felt a moral obligation towards protection of the Mosquito Indians.[66] Clayton did not foresee a problem over Belize and the Bay Islands and had to contend with much criticism at home of Britain's controlling interests in Yucatan, Belize, Jamaica, the Mosquito Coast[67] and Guiana, with its navy controlling the Caribbean. His critics failed to understand that this was a partnership with Britain with the aim in Clayton's mind of securing the 'independence and neutrality of Nicaragua, Costa Rica, Honduras and the whole of the British Mosquito coast'.[68] Clayton considered the question would never be settled unless both countries withdrew their claims on Nicaragua and Costa Rica because if the two governments held possession of the country on either side of the canal there might be some unfair advantage of one over the other.[69] There was an important conversation between Palmerston and Rives on 24 September 1849.[70] First Rives, the newly appointed American Minister in London, reassured Palmerston that President Taylor was anxious to preserve the most cordial good understanding with Britain. Rives referred to a letter published by the British consulate in New York which asserted very positively an exclusive claim for the Mosquito Indians of ownership and sovereign jurisdiction of the mouth and lower part

[65] *New York Herald* (1 and 24 November and 19 December 1849). Van Alstyne (n 59) 149,151.
[66] Van Alstyne (n 59) 149, 151.
[67] Britain's de facto title to Belize was disputed by the United States.
[68] H Miller, *Treaties and Other International Acts of the United States of America* (Department of State, 1937) V, 715–24.
[69] *Ibid.*
[70] *Ibid* 719–20.

of the San Juan River. He assured Palmerston that the United States had no intention of intermeddling in the slightest degree with that but emphasised that it was of the highest importance that both governments should be acquainted with the intentions of the other to prevent any misunderstanding. He said that they were pursuing a common end and the United States sought no exclusive privilege or preferential rights of any kind regarding the proposed canal. What was significant about this meeting was Rives' declaration that the United States was dedicated to 'the common use by all nations on the most liberal terms of perfect equality' for guarding against any unreasonable and oppressive exactions of use by either state's requisition of territory. The United States would not obtain any exclusive right or privilege in a great highway which naturally belonged to all mankind. However, he went on to say that with regard to the Mosquito coast Britain would appreciate that it had given rise to some dissatisfaction and distrust on the part of other commercial powers.[71]

Britain granted a protectorate to the native Indians on the Mosquito Shore on the eastern coast of Nicaragua and annexed the Bay Islands in order to establish a settlement at the mouth of the San Juan River.[72] A settlement was established there renaming San Juan, Greytown. Contrary to American concerns, Britain did not want to establish a deeper involvement in Latin American states.

Before Rives came to London he was instructed to go to Paris via London to freely discuss the Mosquito question.[73] Palmerston was at pains to explain the British interest in the Mosquito coast and that Britain had no intention whatsoever of colonising Central America. Britain already had more colonies than it could manage; it had no intention of preventing any passage of the isthmus, on the contrary, he hoped that Britain and America could unite in promoting by their joint influence and mutual cooperation the opening of the canal to the benefit of all nations. Palmerston regarded the case of the Mosquito Indians as *sui generis*.[74] Britain regarded this as outside the Treaty and in any event, as Palmerston opined, no dominion was exercised over the Mosquito Indians, but its government was carried on 'under the Mosquito [King's] authority by British subjects'.[75] Palmerston drew a distinction between voluntary colonisation by British subjects and governmental colonisation. The former was not illegal, nevertheless Palmerston withheld his approval for any colonisation not only of Belize but also of Costa Rica which, as Richard Van Alstyne explained, became settled policy of the British Government.[76]

[71] Miller (n 68).

[72] GF Hickson, 'Palmerston and the Clayton Bulwer Treaty' (1931) 3 *The Cambridge Historical Journal* 295.

[73] Miller (n 68) 714.

[74] *Ibid.*

[75] *Palmerston to Clarendon* (18 September 1855); also *Bulwer to Clarendon* (24 January 1854); *Argyll to Clarendon* (23 August 1854); *Russell to Clarendon* (31 October 1854), Clarendon Papers. Cited in Van Alstyne (n 59) 149, 159.

[76] Van Alstyne (n 59) 149, 162.

The intentions of both were thus incorporated in the treaty which prohibited both parties from any further territorial acquisition or political control in the region.[77] Britain was in a position of 'static desuetude' although it required markets for its industrial revolution, whereas America required more space for its expanding population.[78]

As Palmerston said 'the safest course for English authorities to pursue seems to be to abstain rigidly from all interference in the internal dissensions of those republics'.[79] Lord Aberdeen believed the British title to the Mosquito Coast was based on usage and that of the Bay Islands on 'little better than manifest usurpation'.

The British interest concerned communication with its empire, protection of its trading interests and halting United States' southern expansion. American objections to British occupation of the Mosquito Coast were dismissed on the basis that Britain acquired its interest there before the War for Independence and did not regard the Monroe Doctrine as binding.[80]

So far as the Central American republics of Guatemala and Mexico were concerned, they had rival claims to British Honduras based on the doctrine of *uti possidetis*,[81] an argument supported by the United States. Palmerston argued the contrary that the Latin American revolutions gave the revolutionaries a right of independence and self-government over the territory they occupied. They did not inherit any rights from Spain; they only acquired rights over the territory they possessed or occupied. In 1821 Central America became independent. British Honduras was not occupied by Mexicans or Guatemalans so whatever the rights of Spain such rights remained with Spain and not with Mexico or Guatemala.[82]

D. American and British Imperial Proclivities

The negotiation and the Treaty may be seen against the emergence of the United States as an imperial power having just expanded its frontiers to the Pacific Ocean and looking beyond it joining with Britain in a mutual treaty to benefit both old and new empires. Commercial interest was uppermost in both countries' aims but underlying that a conflict of interest with Britain wishing to retain Belize and America wanting to uphold the Monroe Doctrine by

[77] *Ibid* 149.

[78] LM Keasbey, 'The Terms and Tone of the Clayton-Bulwer Treaty' (1899) 161 *The Annals of the American Academy of Political and Social Science* 8.

[79] Hickson (n 72) 296.

[80] *Ibid*. See also: British Parliamentary Papers 1856, LX 2052, 276. *To Earl of Clarendon* (6 January 1854).

[81] Such doctrine, not recognised by Britain, regarded the boundaries of the Mother Country as the boundaries of the new state.

[82] Waddell (n 58) 52.

excluding Britain from America. Despite such conflicts of interest, negotiations for the treaty were successfully conducted by Sir Henry Lytton Bulwer for Britain and John M Clayton for the United States. Bulwer was a professional diplomat with considerable experience in diplomacy having been ambassador at Madrid, Washington and Constantinople, while John Clayton was a lawyer by profession and had some legislative experience. Even before the treaty was signed there was scepticism in the United States and criticism from those who sought enforcement of the Monroe Doctrine. Thus, when George Bancroft[83] wrote to James Buchanan[84] on 16th November 1849, he said that he had read every scrap of paper whilst in Paris relating to the negotiations in 1783 by which England pledged itself to evacuate the Mosquito territory.[85] Writing to Burke, a congressman from New Hampshire, a lawyer and a newspaper joint editor, on 3rd December 1849, Buchanan confirmed that the intention of the United States was to prevent further incursions in Central America by Britain especially in Costa Rica, but this was never intimated to Britain.[86] On 2nd April 1850 Buchanan wrote to a lawyer named McClernand, commenting on articles published in the *New York Tribune* as to British encroachment. In his view, Britain was the protector of Guatemala, Honduras, San Salvador, Nicaragua and Costa Rica so that with British Honduras and Belize, Jamaica and Trinidad, Britain could command the Caribbean area. According to him the Clayton-Bulwer Treaty placed the United States 'in the power of Great Britain'.[87] There was no need to treat with Britain at all; the United States and the New Granada Treaty of 1846 was sufficient.[88] Buchanan also said that the Treaty reversed the Monroe Doctrine as against the interests of the United States in favour of European governments.[89] A month later Buchanan was even more antagonistic towards Clayton's diplomacy. In a further letter to Burke dated 30th May 1850 Buchanan complained that the Treaty did not remove the British protectorate over the Mosquito Coast. President Polk's policy was to avoid political connections with Europe. The Clayton-Bulwer Treaty of 1850 reversed this principle and made Britain the protector of Central America so that strategically it could cut off California and Oregon by blocking the canal.[90]

The British Government was not so much, as Palmerston indicated, interested in possessing Central America as in trading with it. Britain's interest in the canal was ensuring it had use of it. From the United States' point of view, having recently acquired California, its interest was incentivised by the discovery of

[83] Former diplomat and US Secretary of the Navy.
[84] US President 1857–61.
[85] 'Letters of Bancroft and Buchanan on the Clayton-Bulwer Treaty 1849, 1850' (1899) 5 *The American Historical Review* 95.
[86] *Ibid* 98.
[87] *Ibid* 100.
[88] *Ibid*.
[89] *Ibid* 101.
[90] *Ibid* 102.

gold in that territory and it was necessary to open up a quicker route avoiding by sea Cape Horn and by rail the Rockies. Bulwer was instructed to acquire trading rights for British vessels in the American intercoastal trade and to secure reciprocal trading privileges for Canada.[91]

Bulwer appreciated that there were three British objectives: first, to counter anti-British sentiment in the United States; second, to thwart United States' ambitions in Central America; third, to facilitate construction of the canal and to resolve the Mosquito question.[92] Overriding this was the commercial objective: balancing British territorial possessions in Central America with the trade benefits of a more direct route to the Pacific.

E. The Clayton-Bulwer Treaty 1850

Article I of the Treaty declared that neither the United States nor Britain would ever obtain or maintain exclusive control over the ship canal. They would jointly protect it. More importantly it went on to state that neither party would erect or maintain any fortifications commanding the canal or in the vicinity, or fortify, or colonise the area, or assume, or exercise any dominion over Nicaragua, Costa Rica, the Mosquito Coast, or any part of Central America.

Article V provided that when the canal was completed Britain and the United States would protect it from interruption, seizure, or unjust confiscation and they would guarantee its neutrality so the canal would remain open and free. As it then stood the United States and Britain could protect the canal, but Article V also provided that the parties could withdraw that obligation if those building the canal discriminated in favour of one state on giving six months' notice. Article VI provided that the canal should be for the benefit of all on equal terms and any differences between the parties should be resolved by them using their good offices. Article VIII provided that no other charges other than those which were just and equitable should be levied and canals and railways should be open to the United States and British citizens and subjects on equal terms and on like terms for other states.

The Treaty was underpinned by the mutual understanding that the project should be neutralised and that neither one nor the other power would obtain or maintain for itself any exclusive control over the canal.[93] It was this provision that would lead to tension later, but at this time neither party wanted to build the canal and it was thought that some corporate joint venture might be promoted. HU Addington, the Permanent Under Secretary of State for Foreign Affairs at the time, considered that Britain would abandon Greytown and the Mosquito Coast except for the British possessions in the region.[94] Belize was retained but

[91] Van Alstyne (n 59) 149, 154.
[92] *Ibid* 149, 156.
[93] Hickson (n 72) 296–97. This was explicit in Article 1 of the Treaty.
[94] FO 56/3 *Memorandum* (11 October 1850).

the Mosquito Coast and the Bay Islands[95] were later abandoned. Clarendon, the Foreign Secretary, was cautioned by Bulwer in March 1854. Bulwer advised that British interests in Central America could be protected by either a harmonious and friendly conjunction with the United States or by establishing a counterpoise to them. The counterpoise was possible because of the friendliness of Guatemala, the largest and richest state in Central America. This enabled Britain to pursue a conciliatory course and then take a different line if necessary. This could be achieved without raising the Mosquito Shore Question.[96] But Clarendon confirmed the policy of disengagement in an undated Memorandum to Bulwer (possibly 1 August 1854). Britain's policy towards America was tempered also by public opinion which had been bitterly divided at the time of America's secession from the United Kingdom. Public opinion was against any hostilities with the United States and commercial interests were against it as Hickson states that Lord John Russell opined at the time: 'There is room for both of us on the globe'.[97] What Lord Palmerston said was:

> My noble Friend (Lord J. Russell) has, however, expressed a hope that the instructions which Her Majesty's Government have given to the naval force which was recently dispatched from this country to the coast of America, are not such as are likely to bring about any unnecessary collision between the American and British squadrons.[98]

There was risk of Britain drifting into war with America again at a time when Russia and Turkey were at war with Britain and France.[99] Foreseeably, the French alliance could be strained over Greytown and the Mosquito Coast.

As evidence of the success of the Clayton-Bulwer Treaty in 1857, Palmerston wrote to Clarendon stating that the Clayton-Bulwer Treaty was '... stopping the Yankees out of Central America, and therefore they all hate and detest the treaty'.[100]

i. Benefits of the Treaty: Beginnings of a Special Relationship

Palmerston's objectives for the Treaty were first, that each end of the canal was to be controlled by an independent Central American state which had the means and authority to keep the peace, second it would be achieved by joint Anglo-American diplomatic action, and third, this would entail a withdrawal of influence of both Powers in Central American politics.[101] According to Bourne, British public opinion would not countenance any further colonisation

[95] These became a Crown colony in 1852.

[96] 'Anglo-American Relations, 1853–1857: British Statesman on the Clayton Bulwer Treaty and American Expansion' (1937) 42 *The American Historical Review* 496; *Bulwer to Clarendon* (March 1854).

[97] Hansard, HL Deb (series 3) 16 June 1856, vol 142,1508. Hickson (n 72).

[98] *Ibid.*

[99] 'Anglo-American Relations, 1853–1857' (n 96) 497. *Graham to Clarendon* (24 October 1854).

[100] 'Anglo-American Relations, 1853–1857' (n 96) 500. *Palmerston to Clarendon* (31 December 1857).

[101] Van Alstyne (n 59) 149, 165. FO 5/525 No 55 *Palmerston to Bulwer* (2 May 1851).

in Central America or conflict with the United States and accordingly it would be unwise to oppose American expansion.[102] On the other hand, no progress had been made on the canal, disputes continued and the filibusters from the southern states were causing a nuisance. By 1857 there was agitation in America for abrogation of the Treaty. Lord Napier, the British Minister in Washington, advised the Foreign Secretary Lord Clarendon to either grant American demands or acquiesce in friendly abrogation.[103] This was not an easy decision but was eventually considered by Clarendon's successor Lord Malmesbury.[104] According to the Law Officers abrogation would simply restore the status quo ante.[105] Gradually, the British attitude towards American expansion in Central America changed fundamentally as Britain now welcomed the possibility of the American acquisition of Mexico and the other central republics,[106] recognising American imperial ambitions. Palmerston went so far as to suggest that one day the whole of the American continent North and South would come under 'the mastery of the Anglo-Saxon Race'.[107]

By the late 1890s there appeared to be a greater understanding of the mutual benefits in Anglo-American relations between the governments[108] and also a realisation by Britain that its former colony was not so much a rival as an ally in imperial ambitions. The United States had defeated Spain in the Caribbean and was looking to develop interoceanic communications and improve communications with its interests in the Pacific as part of its westward expansion.[109] Strategically, access to the Pacific was important for the United States linking its eastern coastal states.[110] Britain wanted to strengthen her eastern and western sea-trade routes. It was said by William Paterson that it '... will enable his proprietors to give laws to both oceans and become arbitrators of the commercial world'.[111] According to Keasbey, American independence enabled the Americans to extend their influence westward and become the self-appointed guardians of the Latin American states.[112] The United States presumed not to interfere with European dependencies in the New World and thwarted British ambitions into 'static desuetude'. By the Treaty of Versailles in 1783 and the Treaty of Madrid in 1814, Britain agreed to abandon her interests in Central America save Belize, although later Palmerston forced Nicaragua to cede the Mosquito Coast as the

[102] K Bourne, 'The Clayton Bulwer Treaty and The Decline of British Opposition to The Territorial Expansion of The United States, 1857–60' (1961) *The Journal of Modern History* 287.

[103] FO (America)/675 No 279 *Napier to Clarendon* (13 December 1857) and *Napier to Clarendon* Private (14 December 1857), Clarendon Papers as cited in Bourne (n 102) 288.

[104] Bourne (n 422) 288.

[105] Bourne (n 102) 291, fn 14.

[106] *Ibid* 289.

[107] *Palmerston to Clarendon* (31 December 1857) Clarendon Papers.

[108] Keasbey (n 78) 2.

[109] *Ibid*. See also see Van Alstyne (n 60) 3–28.

[110] Keasbey (n 78) 3.

[111] *Ibid* 4.

[112] *Ibid* 6.

gateway to the Pacific to Britain.[113] But the Americans secured the Pacific end of the interoceanic causeway in 1850 increasing tension as between Britain at one end and the United States at the other.[114] Under the Clayton-Bulwer Treaty, Britain and America agreed jointly to protect the interoceanic canal and importantly agreed the canal would be open to both parties' vessels without charge, so the parties would enjoy free and equal access to the waterway under Article VIII, with their subjects being treated equally. In terms of protection afforded by both states, this Treaty resembled an alliance or at least a partnership and in that sense was a remarkable improvement in Anglo-American relations. Contrary to the scepticism of Buchanan, the United States was placed on an equal footing with the greatest Sea Power in the world, and obtained exclusive control over the ship canal jointly with Britain.[115] While the United States had no substantial fleet, it had the benefit of a promise of British capital investment; Britain benefitted by recognition of its interest in Belize, contrary to the Monroe Doctrine although this was not mentioned in the Treaty. In the words of John F Crampton, the British Minister in Washington, who was dismissed by President Pierce on 28 May 1856, the doctrine amounted to nothing less than:

> an attempt to establish a principle of Public Law applicable to this Quarter of the World analogous to that prevailing to a certain extent in Europe:-with this difference however, that while in Europe such principles were established with the consent and by the agreement of all the Parties concerned and consigned in solemn Treaties: here the attempt is made to lay down a Law of a much more sweeping nature by the *ipse dixit* of a single power over two whole Continents and the adjacent Islands, not only without the agreement of the other powers who hold them but notoriously contrary to their wishes and interests in a manner inconsistent with their independence.[116]

Like all negotiations it ended in a compromise and like some there was ambiguity: Americans thinking Britain was withdrawing from Central America and the British understanding that further colonisation was barred.[117] Their respective interests were equally recognised. The negotiation was carried out against a backdrop of increasing tensions between the northern and southern states in the United States. This culminated in 1861 in the Civil War, a pressure recognised by Crampton in his report to Clarendon on 7 February 1853 where he referred to 'the inextinguishable struggle between North and South, Free States and Slave States' which, in his view, paralysed US foreign relations.[118]

Despite these benefits, both sides were in breach of Article I in influencing the neighbouring states: America by southern filibusters and northern concessionaires and Britain by its government agents. The United States could insist upon

[113] *Ibid* 8.
[114] *Ibid*10.
[115] Waddell (n 58) 54.
[116] 'Anglo-American Relations, 1853–1857, (n 96) 494. *Crampton to Clarendon* (7 February 1853).
[117] Waddell (n 58) 55.
[118] 'Anglo-American Relations, 1853–1857' (n 96). *Bulwer to Clarendon* (March 1854).

the immediate abrogation of the Clayton-Bulwer Treaty because both parties had interfered in Central American affairs.[119] The United States did not recognise the British occupation of the Mosquito Coast and the Bay Islands. In its view it violated the original agreement. To this extent, as Keasbey concludes, it appears that Britain had established the *status quo ante conventum* and America simply reverted to the *status quo post conventum*.[120] Britain by its Declaration had made it clear that: 'Her Majesty does not understand the engagements of that Convention to apply to Her Majesty's settlement at Honduras or to its Dependencies.'[121]

This Declaration was dated 29th June 1850 (five days before the exchange of ratifications) when Bulwer met Clayton that day. Clayton acknowledged this on the 4th July confirming that British Honduras was not included in the Treaty, but as he said:

> at the same time carefully declining to affirm or deny the British title in their settlement or its alleged dependencies. After signing my note last night, I delivered it to Sir Henry & we immediately proceeded without any further or other action to exchange the ratifications of said treaty.[122]

A further reply was allegedly made by Bulwer dated 4th July, but possibly on 5th July, which caused considerable controversy.[123] Neither Clayton nor his assistant Fisher appeared to have had any knowledge of it and nothing further from Bulwer was received before exchange after Clayton's counter-declaration of 4th July.[124] Whatever the recollections of Clayton and his clerk Fisher, undoubtedly correct from their best knowledge and belief, it does appear on the balance of probabilities that Bulwer's note was delivered to the State Department but not read as it was entered in the record of subject or contents, communications from and communications to the British Legation.[125]

Be that as it may, the fact is that in acceding to the British Central American claims, despite reservations as to the legal title of such acquisitions, or controversy over declarations and notes between Bulwer and Clayton, President Buchanan waived such objection allowing Britain to argue that whatever the question of title the United States was estopped from denying it by its acquiescence. The definition of 'Central America' could have been more precise and although this was considered by Bulwer and Clayton in a possible joint declaration stating to

[119] Keasbey (n 78) 16.
[120] *Ibid.*
[121] Miller (n 68) 681.
[122] Miller (n 68) 682.
[123] J Bigelow, *Breaches of Anglo-American Treaties* (Sturgis & Walton Company, 1917) who, after examination of only part of the evidence, calls the note 'bogus' and 'spurious' and says that it 'was smuggled into the archives of our Department of State' (at 124–25; the argument is at 121–38). The question remains as to whether such note was brought to Clayton's attention.
[124] *Clayton to William L Marcy, Secretary of State, Washington* (21 May 1856).
[125] Miller (n 68) 702–703. The Department of State archives Vol.59/Index/to/Correspondence/with/British Legation /Department/ of State.

what states or territories the Treaty did apply, it was thought better to omit it as this would promote further difficulty in the Senate.[126] However, it was clear to both plenipotentiaries that the Treaty was intended to apply to future and not present possessions.[127] So far as the United States was concerned in point of law, the declarations of the negotiators, not submitted to the Senate, were of no validity and could not affect the Treaty.[128]

Buchanan went so far as to say: 'the discordant constructions of the Clayton-Bulwer Treaty between the two governments ... have resulted in a final settlement entirely satisfactory to this government'.[129] Despite this, arguments persisted over Belize and some adjoining islands which Britain declared a Crown colony. The United States disputed this under Article I of the Clayton-Bulwer Treaty as to what was known as British possessions at the time of the Treaty. The new colony included the islands of Ruatan, Bonacca, Utifla, Barbarat, Helena and Morat, all designated as the colony of the Bay of Islands. Article I was explicit in stating that neither party would ever assume, or exercise any dominion over Nicaragua, Costa Rica, the Mosquito Coast, or any part of Central America. Was this a breach of Article 1? What did Clayton know at the time? He would have known that under Article IV of the Treaty of London 1786 it stated, 'the English shall be permitted to occupy the small island known by the names of Casina, St. George's Key, or Cayo Cafina'. Reverdy Johnson, who was Attorney General in the Cabinet of Zachary Taylor at the time of the negotiation of the Clayton-Bulwer Treaty, confirmed this to be the case.[130] These were the only known 'dependencies' of British Honduras known to the United States' government on the 4th July 1850.

At one point Britain had been prepared to abandon Greytown but not the rest of the Mosquito Coast. The Bay Islands inhabited by British colonists were declared a Crown colony in 1852 and brought into question by the new American Minister James Buchanan.[131] His intention was to drive Britain out of the Bay Islands and the Mosquito Shore, quite possibly out of Belize altogether. Britain's desire for a settlement may have been increased by the Crimean War so that it was more prepared to make concessions reverting to the Spanish Treaty position. An American bombardment of Greytown put that out of the question.[132] The position between British Honduras and Nicaragua, Honduras and Guatemala was settled between Britain and those countries just before the outbreak of the American Civil War, British Honduras then being given colonial status.[133]

Towards the end of the nineteenth century, British statesmen realised that their former colony would become a great Power through industrialisation, vast natural resources and huge population. As Keasbey remarked, Europe's

[126] Miller (n 68) 686.
[127] *Ibid* 688.
[128] *Ibid* 689.
[129] Keasbey (n 78) 17.
[130] Senate Executive Document Nb 13, 33d Congress, 1st session, serial 694, 14–19.
[131] Waddell (n 58) 56.
[132] *Ibid* 56–57.
[133] *Ibid* 58.

dominance depended on imports of raw materials and exporting the products of manufacture from that, but the tide was turning so that the United States could become a major exporter and rival. Britain therefore gradually changed its approach, enhanced by a deeper respect and understanding of Americans exemplified perhaps by the marriage of many wealthy Americans and members of the English aristocracy. This included some prominent English politicians such as Randolph Churchill and Joseph Chamberlain.[134] Britain had been reluctant to leave America in the forlorn hope that America would return to the Crown and was technically in breach of its Treaty obligations for being slow to abandon New York and some of its forts. Despite this, these English-speaking peoples not only had a common inheritance, a Common Law, language and religion, an historical connection and regard for a parliamentary system of government, but also imperial dreams.

Before examining the negotiations that led to the Hay-Pauncefote Treaty in 1901 having considered the concerns raised by Buchanan and others the relationship has to be seen in the context of the drafting and interpretation of the Clayton-Bulwer Treaty, in particular, the controversy over Article VIII. As has been seen with other differences between Britain and the United States, it was one of the new nations asserting its independence and freedom of action on the American continent restrained by British interests in Canada, the Caribbean and Central and South America.

F. The Hay-Pauncefote Treaty 1901

There were two treaties under which the United States made guarantees of neutrality to Colombia. The first, between the United States and the Republic of Colombia or New Granada in 1846, and the second the Clayton-Bulwer Treaty of 1850. Under the 1846 Treaty the United States guaranteed 'perfect neutrality' of Panama and New Granada's sovereignty. Under the Clayton-Bulwer Treaty of 1850, Britain and the United States rejected any exclusive control but gave a bilateral guarantee of neutrality and joint protection.[135] In giving joint protection Britain wanted equal treatment. Britain would not guarantee Colombian sovereignty (Nicaragua was part of Colombia) over Panama but would respect it. The United States thought that if it gave a guarantee it should enjoy some benefit.[136]

Efforts were made to reconcile the controversy. Treaty negotiations were concluded between Britain and the United States – the Clarendon-Dallas Treaty – on 17th October 1856 placing the absolute independence and sovereignty of

[134] CS Campbell, Jr, *Anglo-American Understanding. 1898–1903* (The John Hopkins Press, 1957) 9.
[135] GF Howe, 'The Clayton-Bulwer Treaty: An Unofficial interpretation of Article VIII in 1869' (1937) 42 *American Historical Review* 484.
[136] *Ibid* 485.

Nicaragua over its territory on a clear footing. Britain rejected an amendment to the Treaty, so it was never ratified.[137] The two governments continued to adopt different interpretations of the Clayton-Bulwer Treaty. When President Buchanan met Lord Napier in Washington on the 6th May 1857, he denounced the Clayton-Bulwer Treaty as one which had been 'fraught with misunderstanding and mischief from the beginning'. 'It was', he said, 'concluded under the most opposite constructions by the contracting parties'.[138] Britain suggested arbitration, but this was rejected by the United States. Britain even went so far as to suggest that it would consider abrogation of the Clayton-Bulwer Treaty by mutual consent.[139] Between 1850 and 1858 there were three proposals for arbitration as well as suggestions for modification and abrogation but deadlock remained.[140]

This impasse led to further apparent breaches of the Clayton-Bulwer Treaty when the United States sought to negotiate treaties with Colombia in 1869 and 1870, giving the United States a veto on any construction of a railway or canal across the isthmus.[141] The problem was that Article III of the 1869 Colombian Treaty seemed contrary to Article VIII of the Clayton-Bulwer Treaty of 1850. This apparent repudiation of the Clayton-Bulwer Treaty was disavowed by President Grover Cleveland in December 1884, notwithstanding the fact that the Preamble to the Clayton-Bulwer Treaty referred to a different route through the isthmus and not through Colombian territory.[142]

With the changing balance of power between Britain and America, it was obvious that the arrangement over a canal should be reviewed. On the 19 November 1881, Mr Blaine, the Secretary of State, wrote to Mr Lowell, the United States Ambassador in London, referring to the remarkable expansion of America's Pacific coast since the Clayton-Bulwer Treaty in 1850 argued that the Treaty conceded to Britain practical control of a canal.[143] Britain and America were not on a plane of 'perfect equality' because Britain had a far superior naval force capable of dominating such a canal. The United States was restricted from using her military force but Britain was unrestrained in deploying its naval units. If American troops were excluded from the canal zone, then British ships should also be excluded.[144] Britain controlled all the strategic points en route to India at Gibraltar, Malta, Cyprus, Aden and Perim. The Red Sea was the British *mare clausam*. Britain could therefore hardly object to American demands. The Suez Canal was barred to every vessel in time of war, and that should also

137 US Department of State, Foreign Relations 1st Session, 47th Congress 1880–81 (1881–1882) 564.

138 *Lord Napier to Lord Clarendon* (6 May 1857). Also, US Department of State, Foreign Relations 1st session, *ibid*.

139 US Department of State, Foreign Relations 1st session (n 137) 567.

140 *Ibid* 569.

141 Howe (n 135) 485.

142 Bureau of Claims, State Department Paper by E Peshine Smith, 15 April 1869, cited in Howe (n 135) 487–89.

143 US Department of State, Foreign Relations 1st session (n 137) 555.

144 *Ibid* 555.

be the case with the Panama Canal.[145] Much of this objection was met in the Treaty of November 1901 where the parties agreed expressly to adopt the rules of the Constantinople Convention 1888 which Convention stated '... the principle of equality as regards the free use of the canal'.[146] The United States would construct the canal and was best placed to maintain 'the absolute neutralisation' of the canal as it was not likely to be engaged in a war with any European Power. Britain and America had had a monopoly of trade in the area, but since 1877 France and Germany were increasingly trading in the Caribbean area.[147] The United States now faced competition from these Powers but was restrained by the Clayton-Bulwer Treaty of 1850. The restriction on fortifications should be removed but not that against acquisition of territory.[148] Free ports at either end of the canal could be maintained. Joint protection was obsolete and should be removed.[149] Some rights, privileges, tolls and obligations should be applied impartially to all merchant ships of all nations.

These circumstances crystallised the American case for rectification of the Treaty or the framework for a new treaty. Westward expansion of the United States and its growing strength in production, population and prestige after its victories over Spain and Mexico made it an emerging international state actor altering the power balance.

On 1 December 1884 the United States signed a Convention with Nicaragua repudiating Articles I–VII of the Clayton-Bulwer Treaty, but this was withdrawn by President Cleveland.[150]

Richard Olney, a former Secretary of State, argued that since the canal was owned by the United States it could charge tolls. The treaty with New Granada in 1846, then the Republic of Colombia gave its citizens equal treatment and granted perfect neutrality of the isthmus. Since Britain held the eastern coast, an accommodation had to be made with Britain in 1850. The basis of the Clayton-Bulwer Treaty was that neither Britain nor the United States had to build or control it but facilitated its construction by their joint protection. Olney identified two key points: first, a self-denying ordinance by Britain and America not to build or control it, and second, that a state building it on its own territory could dictate conditions of use giving protection to it or denying its use. In 1869 Seward[151] declared that no foreign government or capitalists would build it.

[145] *Ibid* 556.

[146] Article XII the Constantinople Convention of 1888.

[147] US Department of State, Foreign Relations 1st session (n 137) 557.

[148] *Ibid* 558.

[149] This had covered the construction of a railway, but since America had already constructed one the provision was outdated. Article VIII of the Clayton-Bulwer Treaty of 1850 referred to joint protection of canals or railways.

[150] Howe (n 135) 490.

[151] William Seward (1801–1872), a lawyer by profession, was a politician who served as Governor of New York, as a US senator and as Secretary of State during the Civil War (1861–65). He was Secretary of State in Lincoln's Cabinet and also served as Secretary of State under President Andrew Johnson.

By 1889 he was proved right: de Lesseps'[152] attempt had failed. The United States therefore had to build and control it. No change of sovereignty could affect obligations under the Hay-Pauncefote Treaty 1901 as finally agreed on 18th November 1901. Its main purpose was for the United States to acquire the canal territory. The canal was to be built in a territory excluding foreign influence or control except for use on equality of terms. It was free and open to the vessels of commerce and of war of 'all nations'. What precisely these words meant in context was a matter of interpretation. Olney argued it excluded the United States. Professor Oppenheim argued to the contrary.[153]

In summary the Hay-Pauncefote Treaty 1901 provided:

- Article I: that the Treaty would supersede the Clayton-Bulwer Treaty of 1850.
- Article II: that the canal would be constructed under the auspices of the government of the United States and the United States would have and enjoy all the rights incident to such construction. As well as the exclusive rights providing for the regulation and management of the canal.
- Article III incorporated a set of rules from the Convention of Constantinople 1888 for the free navigation of the Suez Canal, such rules provided:
    1. The canal would be free and open to vessels of commerce and of war of all nations observing the rules on terms of entire equality; there would be no discrimination against any nation in respect of conditions or charges for use of the canal and such charges would be just and equitable.
    2. The canal would never be blockaded, or hostilities committed within it. The United States would police it to prevent disturbances.
    3. Warships of any belligerent would not be able to revictual but they would be able to transit through the canal in accordance with the regulations.
    4. Belligerents would not embark troops or munitions of war or warlike materials.
    5. These provisions applied to the waters adjacent the canal and within three miles of either end. Belligerent vessels would not remain in the waters longer than 24 hours except if in distress. The vessel of one belligerent would not depart within 24 hours from the departure of a vessel of war of another belligerent.
    6. Buildings and establishment of the works enjoy immunity from attack by any belligerent.

[152] Ferdinand de Lesseps was a French career-diplomat who served in Tunisia, Spain, Italy and Egypt. De Lesseps was responsible for the Suez Canal project which proved a success and later for an abortive attempt to create a Panama Canal which proved a failure due to insurmountable technical difficulties caused by the terrain, geological conditions and the inhospitable climate.

[153] Whewell Professor of International Law, University of Cambridge, formerly of the London School of Economics and author of *International Law A Treatise*, vol I (Longmans, 1948) and *The Panama Canal Conflict*, 2nd edn (Cambridge University Press, 1913).

- Article IV: that no change of territorial sovereignty of the international relations of the country or countries traversed by the canal would affect the general principle of neutralisation or the obligation of Britain or the United States.
- Article V: that ratification of the Treaty take place within six months of signing.

G. The Panama Canal Act Controversy

The Hay-Pauncefote Treaty of 1901 led to intense debate in the United States, in particular the discussions held by the American Society of International Law at its Annual General Meeting in 1913.[154] The views expressed there by Richard Olney, Rear Admiral Stockton, Lewis Nixon, Professor Eugene Wambaugh, John Latané, Albert Hart, Roswell Hoes, Crammond Kennedy and William Collier presented the problems of interpretation and tensions between national interests and international law norms.

In interpreting this Treaty, Professor Wambaugh of Harvard Law School opined that the Hay-Pauncefote Treaty 1901 had to be examined in context as a whole, the general intention of the parties, other similar treaties, the history of the negotiations, and the general principles of law and its purpose. The contentious clause had three elements: the guarantee to 'all nations' of rights of use; the guarantee to be protected against inequality and injustice, and the duty to obtain no unjust enrichment.[155] This was arguable because Article VIII of the Clayton-Bulwer Treaty provided that the canal be open to citizens of the United States and subjects of Great Britain on equal terms and since 'all nations' included the United States and under Article II: 'subject to the provisions of the present treaty', ie the rules of Article III the United States was bound. The rules also incorporated the provisions of the Convention of Constantinople 1888.[156] Wambaugh did not think that the position changed just because America built the canal. The sovereignty argument was defeated by the express exclusion or reservation in Article IV of the Hay-Pauncefote Treaty 1901 that included neutralisation or obligations under the Treaty, although it begs the question as to what each party intended. Wambaugh acknowledged that ships engaged in engineering or construction works of the canal would not be subject to tolls, but private vessels were another matter. The general principle was one of equality. He recounted the management of the canal as a business not the exercise of a government function.[157] 'All nations' covered the right of use, right of equality

[154] Proceedings of the American Society of International Law at its Annual Meeting (n 61) 81–150.
[155] *Ibid*.
[156] *Ibid* 129–30.
[157] *Ibid* 132.

and the duty of observing the right of others to similar equality. The key points of Wambaugh's argument were as follows:

1. Extraordinary language would be required for Britain to give up the right to use the canal on equal terms with the United States.
2. The United States was bound by the provisions of the Treaty.
3. The United States adopted the rules therefore it must observe them.
4. The Hay-Pauncefote Treaty 1901 referred to the Constantinople Convention of 1888 so that such inequality would be repugnant to it.
5. Extraordinary language would be required to indicate any departure from the doctrine of equality as interpreted under the laws of the United States and England.
6. A treaty had to imply equality unless there is an express country indication.[158]

Professor Albert Bushell Hart of Harvard University observed that the Hay-Pauncefote Treaty 1901 was a residuum – 'a deliberate alteration of a previous status'. The United States was the weaker power in 1850.[159] The Clayton-Bulwer Treaty of 1850 was a division of empire in his view. Britain was then the greatest maritime power in the world; the United States was the second commercial power in the world and the Clayton-Bulwer Treaty made them equal regarding the canal project. Britain did not need Central America or Panama; it had Suez.[160] Another contributor to the debate, Mr Crammond Kennedy, wondered how neutralisation could be maintained by any one nation alone.[161] Olney argued that the Treaty was a contract between two countries permitting third parties to have rights of passage.[162] The United States as sovereign had absolute title: it held the territory for the benefit of United States' commerce and its merchants; it was not a customer. The Hay-Pauncefote Treaty in his view compelled the United States to reverse its established policy and devise a plan for subsidising its own vessels in order that they may have free use of the canal. On the contrary, ownership of the canal meant that the legal and beneficial owner could use its property as it may determine. Olney cited the case of *The Avon*[163] that under international law a state which constructed an artificial channel could apply whatever conditions of use it pleased. He suggested that Article VIII of the Hay-Pauncefote Treaty 1901 regarding neutralisation was used to deny the United States its ownership rights. Britain placed the United States in the position of a customer. Under Article III of that Treaty, both parties accepted just and equitable charges, the canal being free and open on terms of entire equality to 'all nations'. The original idea of neutralisation came from Article VIII of the Clayton-Bulwer Treaty 1850, but Olney interpreted it in the light of the

[158] *Ibid* 133.
[159] *Ibid* 136.
[160] *Ibid* 137.
[161] *Ibid* 146.
[162] *Ibid* 129.
[163] *The Avon* 18 Int Rev Record, 165.

Hay-Pauncefote Treaty as simply meaning that the United States as owner would fix reasonable and equitable charges to vessels of 'all nations'. He said that that followed the Constantinople Convention of 1888 as provided in Article III.[164] Under Article X of the Constantinople Convention, Egypt had the right to secure Egypt's defence. By Article XIII of that Convention the sovereign rights of the Sultan of the Ottoman Empire were protected. Thus, the Hay-Pauncefote Treaty 1901 did not inhibit the exemption of coastwise traffic from tolls.[165] But Article IV of the Hay-Pauncefote Treaty excluded any change in obligation by transfer of sovereignty so that the general principle of neutralisation and obligation persisted, although Article I of the Hay-Pauncefote Treaty provided that it superseded the Clayton-Bulwer Treaty of 1850. Hence the room for argument. Olney said that the Hay-Pauncefote Treaty 1901 assumed that the United States would be the owner of the canal built on its own territory. America had complete ownership and control excluding all foreigners.[166] The Clayton-Bulwer Treaty, in his view, had contradicted the Monroe Doctrine when it gave Britain a joint protectorate although Lewis Nixon, a delegate of the Fourth Pan American Conference, thought that the Clayton-Bulwer Treaty refuted the United States and New Granada Treaty of 1846.[167]

More definitive arguments were made at the conference as to the meaning of 'all nations' in Article III, Rule 1 of the Hay-Pauncefote Treaty 1901. Nixon, strongly argued that all nations could not include the United States because the United States had control allowing others access subject to observation of the rules.[168] Lord Lansdowne, the British Foreign Secretary, confirmed in a despatch dated 3 August 1901 that the British intention was that Britain would not be placed in any position less advantageous to any other power.[169] Nixon argued that Lansdowne did not mean to include the US in 'all nations'. Senator Elihu Root rejected this, agreeing with the British interpretation that American and British ships be treated equally.[170] At the time of the negotiations Hay had understood that the Treaty would relieve the United States of 'vague, indefinite and embarrassing obligations' imposed by Article VIII of the Clayton-Bulwer Treaty.[171] Nixon was quick to point out that it would make nonsense of Article III of the Hay-Pauncefote Treaty 1901 if the US allowed enemy ships through the canal which would follow if 'all nations' included the US in Article III, Rule 1.[172] Nixon also cited Sir Edward Grey's admission in his despatch that the US was 'the practical sovereign of the canal'. Nixon said that Professor Oppenheim was

[164] Proceedings of the American Society of International Law (n 61) 88.
[165] *Ibid*.
[166] *Ibid* 89–90.
[167] *Ibid* 123.
[168] *Ibid* 105.
[169] *Ibid* 106.
[170] *Ibid* 106 and 109.
[171] *Ibid* 110.
[172] *Ibid*.

wrong, the US could administer and regulate the canal's commerce as an incident to the benefit of its construction. He also noted the breaches committed by Britain of the Clayton-Bulwer Treaty, the occupation of Greytown from 1848 until relinquishment in 1894.[173] Legally Nixon opined that the US owned the fee title in perpetuity which excluded all other proprietary rights and was sovereign. He cited Chief Justice Marshall's Opinion to President Jefferson on the legality of the Louisiana Purchase.[174] Constitutionally, he opined that the US Government was empowered to make war and treaties; consequently, that Government possessed the power of acquiring territory, either by conquest or by treaty.

Whilst Professor Wambaugh did not accept the arguments of Olney and Nixon as to the effect of the Hay-Pauncefote Treaty, he did accept that a sovereign state had a right to fortify its territory. The Constantinople Convention 1888 acknowledged the rights of Egypt subject to the suzerainty of the Ottoman Sultan to protect the canal.[175] The grant of territory clearly came from Panama, not from Britain, and under the Hay-Pauncefote Treaty 1901 the United States had the right to manage and regulate the canal, adopting the formula of neutralisation in the Constantinople Convention.[176]

Section 5 of the Panama Canal Act 1912 provided for the prescription of tolls by the President of the United States.[177] President Taft said that no tolls could be levied on the coastwise traffic of United States' vessels. The Act established an Interstate Commerce Commission to determine questions of unfair competition between railway operators and other common carriers in the United States. The Commission regulated the rates of charge preventing any unfairness. The Act was supported by a Memorandum from Taft in order to counter opposition. In the Memorandum, Taft explained that was a domestic matter for the United States Congress which could regulate its own domestic and foreign commerce. The United States had adopted the rules of the Constantinople Convention of 1888, Article I of which provided for the free and open use of the canal and 'charges of traffic which were just and equitable'. Taft argued that the United States built the Panama Canal. It had an absolute right of ownership and the Hay-Pauncefote Treaty 1901 permitted free passage and remission of tolls of United States' coastwise traffic. He considered that the United States had granted privilege to all nations of the world without any discrimination, inferring that the United States was not 'all nations'. Neutralisation did not mean the United States was so restricted – it was sovereign and could use the Panama Canal as it sought fit. It would be absurd if the United States in competition with

[173] *Ibid* 119–21.

[174] *Ibid* 125.

[175] Turkey's rights were restricted by Articles I, II, VIII, IX, XI, XII and XIII of the Constantinople Convention 1888.

[176] Proceedings of the American Society of International Law (n 61) 617.

[177] The President to Congress, 24 August 1912. Foreign Relations of the United States. Great Britain Panama Canal Tolls. File No 811f.812/296 and see: Office of the Historian, *Papers Relating to the Foreign Relations of the United States* with the Annual Message of the President transmitted to Congress, 3 December 1912, Panama Canal Act.

other nations was restricted whilst other nations would be free to subsidise their own vessels which would be absurd. The US Government was simply granting a subsidy to oceanic coastwise traffic as it had previously given railroads. Taft suggested that any British subject who wanted to challenge this could do so in the US Supreme Court, the Congress having declined to accept arbitration or any further negotiation. In his State of the Union message of the 2nd December 1911, Taft had been forthright: 'We own the canal. It was our money that built it. We have the right to charge tolls for its use.' The reason was quite clear, he said: 'to secure from the canal tolls a sufficient amount ultimately to meet the debt which we have assumed and to pay the interest'. On the point of British claimants acceding to the jurisdiction of the Supreme Court of the United States, Professor Oppenheim in *The Panama Canal Conflict* responded:

> It is true that, according to Article VI of the American Constitution, all international treaties of the United States shall be the supreme law of the land, but in case an Act of Congress contains rules not in agreement with stipulations of a previous international treaty, the American Courts consider themselves bound by the Act of Congress, and not by the stipulations of the previous treaty. It is obvious that, according to the practice of the Courts of the United States, International Law and Municipal Law are of *equal* force, so that on the one hand new rules of International Law supersede rules of previous Municipal Law, and on the other hand, new rules of Municipal Law supersede rules previous International Law. For this reason, the American Courts cannot be resorted to in order to have the question decided whether or not the enactments of Section 5 of the Panama Canal Act are in conformity with Article III, No. 1, Hay-Pauncefote Treaty.[178]

H. The Diplomatic Discourse

On the 8th July 1912 in the absence of James Bryce, the British Ambassador at Washington, the British Chargé d'Affairs[179] wrote to the Secretary of State[180] protesting at the proposal to exempt all American shipping from the payment of tolls.[181] In substance this amounted to breaches of the Hay Pauncefote Treaty in that the Bill before the Senate provided that:

1. American shipping generally should be exempted from the payment of tolls.
2. The tolls collected from American ships should be refunded.
3. American ships engaged in coastwise trade should be exempted from the payment of tolls.
4. The tolls collected from the American ships engaged in coastwise trade should be refunded.[182]

[178] Oppenheim, *The Panama Canal Conflict* (n 153) 19.
[179] Mr A Mitchell Innes.
[180] PC Knox.
[181] Office of the Historian. File No 811f.812/300.
[182] PF Neary, 'The Panama Canal Tolls Dispute' (1966) *The Journal of Transport History* 173.

These proposals amounted to a subsidy. On 15 July, the American Ambassador in London, Mr Reid, had a meeting with Sir Edward Grey at the Foreign Office. Grey acknowledged that the Hay-Pauncefote Treaty 1901 had replaced the Clayton-Bulwer Treaty of 1850 in reliance that there be no discrimination against British vessels using the canal. Grey considered the Panama Canal Act 1912 to be a violation and discrimination against steam ships owned by railway companies especially those that were Canadian. Reid argued that the United States had built the canal and would not make a profit. It was United States' sovereign territory. Grey said that if the United States did not use it, it would derive profit from the great commercial nations in any event and have the strategic advantage of use by the US Navy.[183] On the 24th August 1912, the British Chargé d'Affairs, Mr Innes, wrote to the Secretary of State confirming that Britain was considering the Treaty and giving notice that if there was dispute the matter ought to be referred to arbitration under the Anglo-American Arbitration Treaty 1908.[184] This was acknowledged by the Assistant Secretary of State on 30th August 1912.[185] The Secretary of State did not reply to the protest until his despatch to the Chargé d'Affairs in London on 17 January 1913. In the meantime, on 13 November 1912 President Taft signed a Proclamation prescribing the tolls to be paid on vessels using the canal. Merchant vessels would be charged $1.20 per tonne carrying passengers or cargo, and vessels without cargo or passengers 72 cents per tonne; naval vessels $0.50 per tonne, army and Navy transports $1.20 per tonne. The proclamation was transmitted to Congress on the 3rd December 1912.[186]

I. Sir Edward Grey's Objection to the Panama Canal Act 1912

Without knowledge of the Proclamation, Grey had instructed the British Ambassador in Washington, James Bryce,[187] to make formal objection to the Panama Canal Act 1912 and President Taft's Memorandum. Grey regarded the equality of all nations as fundamental as it was in the Constantinople Convention 1888. There were limits to America's freedom of action under the Hay-Pauncefote Treaty 1901 which Grey regarded as a corollary to the Clayton-Bulwer Treaty 1850. The general principle under Article VIII of the Clayton-Bulwer Treaty was not to be impaired. The 1850 Treaty facilitated the construction of the canal without prejudice to the reservations of Article VIII

[183] Office of the Historian. File No 811f.812/304.
[184] Office of the Historian. File No 811f.812/320.
[185] *Ibid.*
[186] *Papers Relating to the Foreign Relations of the United States, Great Britain. Panama Canal Tolls Exemption of Vessels in the Coast-Wise Trade of the United States from Payment of Tolls, and Other Features of the Panama Canal Act of August 24, 1912. Objections thereto of the British Government* 481.
[187] Academic, historian, jurist and Home Ruler.

of the 1850 Treaty, namely, the principle of neutralisation.[188] This was subject to the condition that neither party was to 'obtain any exclusive control over the contemplated ship canal'. The general principle of protection was implicit in the Hay-Pauncefote Treaty 1901,[189] also no change of sovereignty would affect the obligations of the parties[190] and as Grey admitted the United States had become the 'practical sovereign' of the canal.[191] Grey argued that if the canal was built under the Clayton-Bulwer Treaty both the United States and Britain would pay the same tolls. Taft's interpretation ignored the restriction of Article VIII of the Clayton-Bulwer Treaty which provided that both countries should understand that 'those who constructed it should impose no other charges or conditions than the two governments considered just and equitable …' Grey asserted that Britain did not intend to protect the canal,[192] and referred to the preamble of the Hay-Pauncefote Treaty under which the United States recovered its right to construct the transisthmian canal upon terms that when constructed the canal was to be open to British and United States' ships on equal terms and since 'neutralisation' included both joint protection and equal treatment the United States must have intended to exclude joint protection, but preserve equal treatment.[193] Grey did not mean that Britain merely had equality with other states but with the United States.[194] In Grey's view, Hay-Pauncefote was identical in principle to the Boundary Waters Treaty of 1909 between Britain and the United States.[195] Article III, in Grey's opinion, meant 'neutralisation' in the sense of equal rights which extended to ships of all nations. If Britain only obtained 'Most Favoured Nation Status' treatment this was 'not apparent to His Majesty's Government'.[196]

No reservation was included in the Hay-Pauncefote Treaty 1901 because the United States was not the owner at that time, but Britain did not question America's right to protect it. Grey construed 'all nations' in Rule I of Article III of the Hay-Pauncefote Treaty as including the United States so the same tolls were chargeable on each states' ships.[197] 'Just and equitable' treatment meant that the tolls would represent the fair value of services rendered to compensate the United States for the interest on capital expended and the cost of operating and maintaining the canal. There could be no fair share Grey argued, unless tolls were levied on all ships as there could be no calculation of a fair value if some US ships were exempt. Furthermore, by exemption the United States created an unfair

[188] *Papers Relating to the Foreign Relations of the United States* (n 186) 482.
[189] *Ibid* 483.
[190] As stated in Lord Lansdowne's Memorandum on 3rd August 1901.
[191] *Papers Relating to the Foreign Relations of the United States* (n 186) 486.
[192] *Ibid* 483.
[193] *Ibid.*
[194] Neary (n 182) 173, 174.
[195] *Papers Relating to the Foreign Relations of the United States* (n 186) 483.
[196] *Ibid* 485.
[197] *Ibid* 486.

burden on 'all nations' ships.[198] Grey argued that there was a conflict between the Panama Canal Act 1912 and the Hay-Pauncefote Treaty 1901. The effect of Section 5 of the Panama Canal Act 1912 and Article XIX of the Panama Canal Treaty 1904 was that US vessels would not contribute to the upkeep of the canal nor would vessels of the Republic of Panama. This conflicted with Article VIII of the Clayton-Bulwer Treaty 1850 which provided for equal treatment for both US and British ships and that the tolls would not be unjust or inequitable which would be a breach of Rule I of Article III of the Hay-Pauncefote Treaty 1901.[199] In effect this meant that foreign vessels would bear all the costs for the working and maintenance of the canal: this was a violation of equal treatment and gave the US coastwise trade preferential treatment. American ships could take advantage of this by their coastwise traffic taking on foreign trade.[200] In view of the difference of opinion, Grey suggested that the matter be submitted to arbitration if the United States agreed or otherwise withdraw the matters of objection by Britain.[201]

James Bryce, the British Ambassador in Washington, discussed the matter with Taft on the 5th October 1912 when Taft hinted at an appointment of six commissioners of eminent jurists to examine, consider, and report upon the points of difference between the countries. Bryce was in favour of the suggestion because he perceived that the Commission would disclose the true facts to the public knowing that the American public had certain sympathy with the British case. He also thought that it might be easier to induce the Senate to agree to this as a means of resolving the dispute by arbitration.[202] Bryce received the Law Officer's opinion on the 14th November 1912 but found it too detailed and advised that it could be more persuasive and gain more support in America by putting the British case more generally.[203]

J. Mr Knox's Reply and President Wilson's Resolution

On the 17th January 1913, Secretary of State, Mr Knox, instructed the American Chargé d'Affairs to respond to the British objections which in his view was hypothetical and anticipatory. As to the question of the United States imposing tolls and exempting its own vessels for alleged breaches of the Clayton-Bulwer and Hay-Pauncefote Treaties; in so far as Section 5 of the Panama Canal Act 1912 provided for US coastwise traffic paying no contribution and other US vessels paying a lower toll rate than foreign ships (less than this proportion of operational and maintenance costs of the canal) this was a matter between the

[198] *Ibid* 487–88.
[199] *Ibid* 487.
[200] *Ibid* 488.
[201] *Ibid* 489.
[202] Neary (n 182). FO 371/1418,43435 *Bryce to Grey* (5 October 1912).
[203] FO 371/1419 *Bryce/Grey* correspondence (25 November 1912 to 4 December 1912) cited in Neary (n 182) 173, 176.

United States and Panama under the Treaty of 1904.[204] If the coastwise traffic was bona fide then Britain could not object. There could not be a submission to arbitration since no question had arisen for resolution. There was no dispute, no coastwise traffic had passed through the canal and been granted exemption. For the same reason the objection on the ground that the US ships would transport foreign commerce through its coastwise traffic was precipitate.[205] Grey's objection as to the power to fix tolls under the Panama Canal Act predated the President's proclamation fixing the tolls. In fact, the tolls fixed by President Taft did not exceed the cost of interest on the capital expenditure for the construction of the canal plus the operating and maintenance costs. The United States would likely be subsidising not only all coastwise traffic, but foreign vessels as well.[206] The Congress could empower the President to renounce the Hay-Pauncefote Treaty 1901 if it chose to as a matter of municipal law. In short Grey had no complaint; there was no improper exercise of power, the tolls were not unfair or inequitable and, in any event, no such power had been exercised. There would be no dispute referable to arbitration, but the United States would not object to adopting an inquiry and report procedure under the unratified Arbitration Treaty of 3rd August 1911. The United States would ratify that Arbitration Treaty or proceed by way of a special arbitration reference if Britain agreed.[207]

Bryce responded to the Secretary of State on the 27th February 1913.[208] He argued that the United States passed an Act directly contrary to the Hay-Pauncefote Treaty 1901 and to international law. It constituted a breach because the President's Proclamation distinguished US coastwise vessels from other nations' vessels, ie from all nations. This amounted to a denial of Britain's right to equality of treatment. Bryce argued that this was 'inconsistent with the treaty irrespective of the particular way in which such power has been so far actually exercised'.[209] Britain, he said, was in favour of settling the matter before 'the great waterway' was opened.[210] Bryce was against any compromise and advised that Britain should maintain its position. Arbitration would not be necessary since the tide of public opinion so strong in the United States would turn against the Act and it would be repealed. In America he said this had raised a 'grave and moral issue'. The feeling in America he said was: 'They censure Congress for having arrogantly taken the law into its own hands and for us to yield before that arrogance would appear to rehabilitate Congress'.[211] The matter remained

[204] Office of the Historian, Foreign Relations of the United States. File No 812/355.
[205] *Ibid.*
[206] *Ibid.*
[207] *Ibid.*
[208] Office of the Historian, File No 812/400.
[209] Interesting statement in the light of Professor Oppenheim's opinion in *The Panama Canal Conflict* (n 153) 41–42 where he stated that in international law the municipal law overrules previous international law. On such basis the 1914 Act of the Congress would prevail over the Hay-Pauncefote Treaty 1901.
[210] Office of the Historian, File No 812/400.
[211] Neary (n 182) 173, 177–78.

unresolved since the United States would not submit to arbitration or withdraw the exemption. He considered an agreement on arbitration with the United States would set an excellent precedent.[212]

Fortunately for Grey, and as Bryce predicted, wiser counsel prevailed when the new President, Woodrow Wilson, addressed the Congress on the 5th March 1914 saying that the exemption of the coastwise traffic constituted 'a mistaken economic policy from every point of view' and was, in his opinion, in plain contravention of the Hay-Pauncefote Treaty 1901. He said that the 'large thing to do' was the only thing America could afford to do which was 'voluntary withdrawal from a position everywhere questioned and misunderstood'.[213] Britain had suggested arbitration of the dispute under the General Arbitration Treaty of 1897 which provided for the appointment of six arbitrators, three from each side, with a decision of five. A decision of the majority would be binding. The Tribunal was to be chosen from the House of Lords in England and the Supreme Court in Washington. This had been previously rejected and in this case was not necessary as the matter would be resolved internally in the United States.

A Bill was immediately introduced into the House of Representatives and passed.[214] When the Bill reached the Senate it was opposed by formidable opposition. On 24 March 1913 Bryce had an urgent meeting with President Wilson who had assumed office and urged him to expedite the matter. Wilson was supportive but did not have time to go into the matter. Bryce then saw William Jennings Bryan, Secretary of State, on the 1st April and again pressed for a quick resolution.[215] On the 15th April Wilson's cabinet debated the matter and conceded that Britain would not grant any extension of the Arbitration Treaty of 1908 until the tolls matter had been settled. Wilson, it is reported, was inclined to think that under the Hay-Pauncefote Treaty America had no right to charge tolls on British or other vessels more than their own coastwise trade. No action however could be contemplated during the special session.[216] Bryce advised Grey that the matter would still take more time because Wilson had to persuade Congress but he was confident that Wilson would be fair to Britain.[217] The repeal Bill was debated for three months with the insertion of a proviso aimed at preserving any rights the United States might have to discriminate in favour of its own vessels.[218] On 13 November 1913, Sir William Tyrrell, Grey's

[212] WS Coker, 'The Panama Canals Controversy: A Different Perspective' (1968) *The Journal of American History* 555, 558.

[213] Woodrow Wilson, 1856–1924, 'Address to Congress' 5 March 1914, Cary T Grayson Papers, Woodrow Wilson Presidential Library and Museum, Staunton, Virginia.

[214] Editorial Comment, 'The Repeal of the Provision of the Panama Canal Act Exempting American Coastwise Traffic Vessels from the Payment of Tolls' (1914) 8 *American Journal of International Law* 592–97.

[215] FO 371/1702, 16742 *Bryce to Grey* (24 March 1913); Neary (n 182) 173, 178. This differs from Coker's account as to the date when Bryce met Bryan. Coker states it was a few days after Wilson's cabinet meeting on the 15 April.

[216] Coker (n 212) 555, 558.

[217] FO 800/83.4 *Bryce to Grey* (15 April 1913).

[218] 'The Repeal of the Provision of the Panama Canal Act' (n 214) 593–94.

Private Secretary, had a meeting with Wilson and reported to Grey the following day that the President was in entire agreement with Grey's view on the matter of the Panama Canal tolls.[219] It was said by Grey's biographer GM Trevelyan that: 'Wilson would not have won the battle of the Panama dues against the Senate if Grey had not aided him by the concession on the other troublesome matter of Mexico'.[220] Between Wilson's election and the passing of the repeal it was a case of quiet diplomacy. Britain had to wait on this as on the extension to the Arbitration Treaty which was ratified in February 1914.

On the 5th March 1914, the President addressed a joint session of the Congress and called for an amendment to the Panama Canal Act because it violated the Hay-Pauncefote Treaty. He said:

> We consented to the treaty, its language we accepted, if we did not originate; and we are too big, too powerful, too self-respecting a Nation to interpret with too strained or refined a reading the words of our own promises just because we have power enough to give us leave to read them as we please.[221]

As a result of the President's encouragement for repeal of the offending exemptions from tolls for American vessels in the Act and recognition of the obligations owed to Britain under the Hay-Pauncefote Treaty obligations, Britain ratified the Arbitration Treaty extension provisions on 11th March 1914. Following this a General Peace Treaty was signed with Britain on the 11th November 1914.

On the 15th June 1914 the Act received the approval of the President and it became law. A proviso to the Act provided that it would not be construed or held as a waiver or relinquishment of any right the United States might have under the Hay-Pauncefote Treaty 1901 and would not waive, impair, or affect any right of the United States under the Treaty with respect to its 'sovereignty over or the ownership, control, and management of the canal and regulation of conditions or charges of traffic through the same'.[222] The action taken by President Wilson was given support by Sir Edward Grey in the House of Commons on the 29th June 1914 when he confirmed 'any line President Wilson has taken was not because it was our line, but his own'. He confirmed this was not due to any diplomatic bargain, and that:

> it has not been done to please us or in the interests of good relations, but I believe from a much greater motive-the feeling that a government which is to use its influence among the nations to make relations better must never, when the occasion arises, flinch or quail from interpreting treaty rights in a strictly fair spirit.[223]

In hindsight it is arguable that the best solution would have been an arbitration between Britain and the United States to determine a purely legal question

[219] Coker (n 212) 555, 560.
[220] GM Trevelyan, *Grey of Falloden* (Longman's Green and Co, 1937) 208.
[221] Congress Record, 63 Cong, Sess 4313 (5 March 1914).
[222] 'The Repeal of the Provision of the Panama Canal Act' (n 214) 594.
[223] *Ibid* 595.

of interpretation of treaty rights and obligations; one which would have been encompassed within the terms of the General Arbitration Treaty of 1908 which had been renewed for another five years. Arbitration was desired by a majority in Congress but prevented by Senate opposition: a resolution was unable to secure a two-thirds majority.[224]

Whilst the Clayton-Bulwer Treaty had led to difficulty between Britain and the United States, chiefly through rival interpretations of the Treaty terms and conflicting national interests of a commercial nature, the rivals managed to resolve their differences through successful negotiation and diplomacy. Whilst Clayton may have been criticised in America, he was a realist and he achieved a rank of equality for the United States with the most powerful naval power at that time. He raised America's profile and gave it recognition as an imperial state. Bulwer, on the other hand, was an accomplished diplomat who managed to preserve Britain's interest in Belize, especially its commercial interest. Palmerston also managed the matter well in standing by Britain's moral commitment to the Mosquito Indians and ensuring if a canal were built Britain would have the same rights of passage and benefit as America. Eventually Britain made treaties with Nicaragua, Guatemala and Honduras dispensing with the Mosquito Shore, the Bay Islands and delimiting the boundaries of Belize.

Hay and Pauncefote overcame the earlier difficulties arising from the Clayton Bulwer episode and produced an acceptable compromise so that Britain avoided involvement in the construction, but preserved its right to equal treatment obtaining a benefit without sharing the construction risks. The United States obtained exclusive control over the construction and maintenance of the canal and sovereignty over the canal zone ceded by Panama, thus enhancing its position in the area.

The Clayton Bulwer Treaty has rightly been described by Richard W Van Alstyne as

> a unique instrument of American diplomacy. It was a *permanent alliance* entered into by the two countries to affect a common settlement in an area which concerned the vital interests of each other. It made of the United States an American power, equal in every respect to the only other first-class American power, Great Britain. To it, rather than to the Monroe Doctrine the United States owes this position.[225]

Thus, after decades of controversy arising from opposing legal interpretations of obligations under the Clayton-Bulwer and Hay-Pauncefote Treaties as affected by the Panama Canal Act 1912, President Wilson judiciously settled this issue on the eve of the First World War. If this had not been resolved it would possibly have made Anglo-American relations more difficult at a time when the Mother Country, which had imperilled the young republic at birth, was herself imperilled by the German onslaught on Belgium. It will not escape observation

[224] *Ibid.*
[225] Van Alstyne (n 59) 149, 168.

that Grey's statement to the House was made a day after the assassination of Archduke Ferdinand in Sarajevo.

In the final analysis it may be that these Treaties were more than a partnership between two English speaking countries. They might be regarded as a rekindling of the familial relationship which evolved into what has been termed 'the special relationship'. It has rightly been said that 'certainly no treaty of the United States made during the nineteenth century has been the subject of more diplomatic correspondence, of more extensive legislative debates, or of more voluminous literature, than has the Clayton-Bulwer Treaty'.[226] Also it may be suggested that there can be little doubt that Clayton, Bulwer, Palmerston, Hay, Pauncefote, Grey, Bryce, and Presidents Roosevelt, Taft and Wilson all contributed to an historic relationship that had significant consequences in the twentieth century for the international rule of law.

IV. THE CASABLANCA CASE

Since 1871, relations between Germany and France had gradually been deteriorating and reached crisis during the first and second Morocco crises described in chapter six. It became more severe when deserters from the French Foreign Legion were arrested before embarking for Germany on board the *Cintra*, a German vessel moored in the harbour at Casablanca.[227] The deserters: two Germans, one Austrian, one Swiss and one Alsatian[228] were in the custody and under the protection of the German consular authorities at the time of their arrest. They were arrested by French soldiers and sailors and those giving them safe conduct to the ship, the German consular officials and their diplomatic agents were threatened. Their guard, a Moroccan soldier and employee of the German consulate, was injured and detained for a short time. Despite protests from the German consul the deserters remained in detention of the French military authority at Casablanca. It appeared that the consulate issued the Letter of Safe Conduct without knowing the nationality of all the legionnaires. The German Government demanded the release of the German deserters and an apology for violating German consular rights and privileges. As a result of this, tensions grew between the states, but eventually on the 24th November 1908 a submission to arbitration was settled by Messrs Renault and Kriege, jurisconsults of the French and German Foreign Offices.[229]

[226] Miller (n 68) 802.

[227] RL Bindschedler and others, *Encyclopaedia of Public International Law, Max Planck Institute Vol 2 Decisions of International Courts and Tribunals and International Arbitrations* (North-Holland Publishing Company, 1981) 45.

[228] The Alsatian's nationality was disputed between France and Germany.

[229] Editorial Comment, 'The Casablanca Incident and Its Reference to Arbitration at The Hague' (1909) 3 *American Journal of International Law* 176.

A. Submission to Arbitration

The French and German governments had previously agreed on the 10th November 1908 to submit the dispute to arbitration regarding the events which occurred at Casablanca on 25th September 1907. The Tribunal was empowered to deal with questions of law and fact arising from the event between the agents of the two countries at Casablanca.[230] The Tribunal was composed of five arbitrators chosen amongst members of the Permanent Court of Arbitration at The Hague. Within 15 days, each government was to present a *compromis* whereby each government chose two arbitrators of whom one could be its national. Four arbitrators chosen would then select an umpire within 15 days from the date of notification of their appointment.[231] By the 1st February 1909 each government was to submit to the Bureau of the Permanent Court 18 copies of its *memoire* with certified copies of all papers and documents supporting their case. Each arbitrator would be given two copies and three copies for each party. Two copies were lodged in the Bureau.[232] By the 1st April 1909, the parties would deposit their respective *contre-memoires*. The hearing was fixed for the 1st May 1909 with power to proceed to any place to obtain information.[233] Both languages were used in the proceedings and for the Award.[234] Each party could appoint a special agent as in the Geneva and other tribunals.[235] Following its decision the Tribunal was empowered to determine the situation of those arrested.[236]

B. The Composition of the Tribunal

The arbitrators appointed by the parties were: for Germany Dr Kriege[237] and Mr Fusinato;[238] for France Professor Louis Renault[239] and Sir Edward Fry.[240] The arbitrators then chose a Swedish diplomat as the President, KH von Hammarskjöld.[241]

[230] Article 1 of Agreement for Arbitration Compromis of arbitration relative to the questions raised by the events which occurred at Casablanca, 25 September 1908. Signed at Berlin on 24 November 1908.

[231] Article 2 *ibid.*

[232] Article 3 *ibid.*

[233] Article 5 *ibid.*

[234] Article 6 *ibid.*

[235] Article 7 *ibid.*

[236] Article 8 *ibid.*

[237] Doctor of Laws, counsellor and solicitor with the Department of Foreign Affairs.

[238] Professor of International Law, Member of the Institute, formerly Minister of Public Instruction and prominent figure at the Second Hague Conference.

[239] Member of the Institute of France, Minister Plenipotentiary, Professor in the Faculty of Law of Paris, Solicitor of the Ministry of Foreign Affairs and Member of the Permanent Court of Arbitration.

[240] Distinguished Lord Justice of Appeal in England, judge of the Hague Court and former member of Dogger Bank International Commission of Inquiry, arbitrator in the Pious Fund case. British Representative at the Second Hague Conference. Member of HM Privy Council.

[241] Doctor of Laws, Former President of the Court of Appeals of Jönköping, former Law Professor, and former Minister of Justice in Sweden.

Mr Andre Weiss, Professor in the Faculty of Law at Paris and Assistant Solicitor in the Ministry of Foreign Affairs, submitted to the Tribunal that it was wrong for the German consul and consular officers to grant their protection and assistance on French occupied territory to three members of the French Foreign Legion whom they thought or might have thought to be Germans. In doing so they disregarded the exclusive right of jurisdiction claimed by the occupying power in a foreign territory (Morocco) which had given France extra territorial jurisdiction.[242] Weiss denied that the arresting party had breached consular inviolability as against the Chancellor of the consulate Herr Just or of the Moroccan soldier Abd-el-Kerim ben Mansour, but had simply acted in self-defence.[243]

In reply, the German advocate Dr Albrecht Lentze[244] submitted that on the facts the three individuals who had previously served in the French Foreign Legion, namely, Walter Bens, Heinrich Heinnemann and Julius Meyer were all Germans. On 25th September 1908 at Casablanca while they were being accompanied by German agents, they were violently arrested by a contingent of French soldiers and sailors. Lentze alleged that the German agents were attacked, maltreated, outraged, and threatened by the French. As to the points of law, the three individuals in question were subject exclusively to the jurisdiction and protection of the Imperial German Consulate at Casablanca and that the arresting party had no authority to interfere with the German deserters because the Consul had granted them safe conduct and protection,[245] nor had the French a right to exclusive jurisdiction. As to the status of those individuals arrested on the 25th September 1908 the French should release them as soon as possible to the German Government.[246]

The proceedings closed on the 17th May 1909 and the Tribunal considered its award. This was published on the 22nd May 1909. The Tribunal considered that the extraterritorial jurisdiction in Morocco meant that the German Consulate exercised exclusive jurisdiction over all German subjects in that country. On the other hand, the French forces also exercised exclusive jurisdictions over all French citizens. This as such was their right of jurisdiction which should be recognised as a rule even in countries granting extraterritorial jurisdiction. This caused a conflict of jurisdiction. On the one hand, the French Government did not make known the composition of their Expeditionary Corps (Foreign Legion) and did not declare the fact of military occupation. On the other hand, the German Government made no protest regarding the employment of the Foreign Legion which was composed in part of German subjects.[247]

[242] *France v Germany: The Casablanca Arbitration Award, 22 May 1909* (The Hague Court Reports) 112–113.
[243] *Ibid* 113.
[244] Privy Counsellor of the Legation, Reporting Counsellor at the Department of Foreign Affairs.
[245] Presumably correct so far as the German nationals were concerned.
[246] *France v Germany: The Casablanca Arbitration Award* (n 242) 113.
[247] *Ibid* 114.

Such a conflict of jurisdiction could not be decided by an absolute rule which would in a general manner accord preference to either of the two concurrent jurisdictions and in each particular case account had to be taken of the actual circumstances which tended to determine the preference. The French jurisdiction extended to legionnaires within the territory which was under its immediate, lasting and effective control.[248] The city of Casablanca was occupied and guarded by French military forces which constituted the garrison of the city which were stationed in or about the city. In these circumstances the deserters of German nationality who belonged to the camps were subject to the French Foreign Legion's exclusive military jurisdiction. On the other hand, in a country (Morocco) granting extraterritorial jurisdiction, the question of the respective competency of the consular and military jurisdiction was complex and unprecedented. The Tribunal therefore considered that the German consular authority did not incur any blame for having granted protection to the deserters. The German Consulate in Casablanca did not grant the protection of the consulate to deserters of non-German nationality.[249]

The Tribunal also held that the Consul did not exceed the limits of his authority when he signed the safe conduct for six people instead of three without reading it: it was an unintentional error. The Moroccan soldier at the consulate, in aiding the deserters to embark, acted only in accordance with his orders and incurred no personal responsibility. The Secretary of the Consulate intentionally sought to embark the deserters of non-German nationality. He deliberately induced the Consul to sign the safe conduct and then conducted the deserters to the port of embarkation. He exceeded the limits of his authority and committed 'a grave and manifest violation of his duties'.[250] The German Consulate's protection was given to the deserters of German nationality at the port; it was not manifestly illegal. The situation should have been respected by the French, but the German deserters were arrested despite protests made by consular officers. They ought to have confined themselves to preventing the embarkation and escape of the deserters. Before proceeding to their arrest and imprisonment, the French soldiers should have directed that the deserters be confined to the German consulate until the question of competent jurisdiction could be decided.[251] This, in the Tribunal's Opinion, would have tended to maintain the prestige of the consular authority in the interests of all Europeans living in Morocco. Even if the arrests were lawful the assaults made by the French soldiers were not, but considering the acts of violence on both sides the exact nature of events could not be properly determined.[252] The deserters of German nationality should have been returned to the Consulate.

[248] *Ibid* 114.
[249] *Ibid* 115.
[250] *Ibid*.
[251] *Ibid* 116.
[252] *Ibid* 116.

Thus, the Court of Arbitration declared:

1. That it was wrong and a grave and a manifest error for the Secretary of the Imperial German Consulate at Casablanca to attempt to have embarked on the German steamship *Cintra* deserters from the French Foreign Legion who were not German.
2. The German consul and consular officers were not responsible in this regard but in signing the safe conduct which was presented to him the consul committed an unintentional error.
3. The German consulate did not under the circumstances of the case have a right to grant its protection to deserters of German nationality. This error of law was committed by officers of the consulate and could not be imputed against them either as an intentional or unintentional error.
4. It was wrong for the French military authorities not to respect as far as possible the actual protection granted to these deserters by the German consulate.
5. The circumstances did not warrant the French soldiers' assaults or shooting at the Moroccan soldier.[253]

C. An Expedient Decision

When the Tribunal was formed it was not clear whether it was a commission of inquiry or a court. As its terms of reference in the *compromis* provided, it was not confined to investigating facts but determining the law. It followed the example of the Dogger Bank Inquiry where Britain and Russia agreed to a determination of the question of responsibility and also followed the proposal of Russia at the Second Hague Conference in 1907 for such determination of responsibility as well as matters of fact.[254] Interesting that at the conference in 1899 Germany had opposed a Permanent Court but acceded to that jurisdiction in two international arbitrations at The Hague in the cases of Japan and Venezuela so that they seem to have accepted the concept of a court.[255]

The Tribunal had to determine a question of priority in competing jurisdictions; that of the occupying forces of the French Government or that of the German consul. Under Article 123 of the Treaty of Algeciras[256] which approved the continuing applicability of the Convention of Madrid of the 3rd July 1880, the German consul in Morocco was entitled to exercise exclusive jurisdiction over German nationals. Whilst that was acknowledged by the French Government, the Tribunal concluded that the French authorities had jurisdiction over

[253] *Ibid* 117.
[254] 'The Casablanca Incident' (n 229).
[255] *Ibid*.
[256] Algeciras Conference 1906.

members of the French military occupation forces. That position was not meant to follow a general principle of international law but was based on the particular facts of this case.

The award was accepted with approval by the countries involved and led to a certain easing of tensions. Both governments expressed their regret about the wrongful acts found by the Tribunal. It was reported that the deserters were condemned to death, but later the sentence was commuted, and they were released by an act of clemency in 1909. In retrospect this was more in the nature of an expedient political compromise, not so much a legal reasoned decision. Some regretted that the Tribunal did not differentiate between different kinds of occupation: belligerent and pacific. Also, it did not clarify the applicable law regarding the jurisdiction of other countries whose nationals were members of the Foreign Legion and where that country had some jurisdiction over its citizens. The decision ignored the question of extradition of German deserters and whether the interference and obstruction of German protection was unlawful.[257]

As with other arbitrations discussed, this Award was made quickly without any untoward delay which again demonstrates the efficiency of these tribunals but also the weighty problem that could have otherwise resulted in hostilities between two Great Powers and their allies.

[257] Bindschedler and others (n 227) 46.

5

Towards a Code of International Arbitration: Instruments of Peace and Diplomacy

THE QUESTION CONSIDERED in this chapter is the extent to which states could accept a common framework of arbitration to resolve international disputes and to avoid war.

The evolution of international law through the treatises and writings of international jurists is considered as influencing The Hague Conferences for the resolution of international disputes between states and providing a code or framework for an international forum to resolve such disputes.

I. EVOLUTION OF AN INTERNATIONAL LAW TO RESOLVE DISPUTES BETWEEN STATES

Prior to the First Hague Conference, delegates were given a copy of a special study of international law and arbitration drafted by the Special Committee of the International Law Association appointed by the Brussels Conference of 1895 and dedicated to the Tsar of Russia, Nicholas II.

Throughout history, since the time of the ancient Greeks, there have been schemes to reduce the risk of conflict. Perhaps, the earliest scheme was that of the Amphictyonic Council, an assembly or league, founded in ancient Greece in the Pass of Thermopylae as early as the fourteenth century BC. This was a defensive alliance formed from a religious union; it was not an arbitration body as such; but it encouraged peace between the tribes by use of 'friendly correction'. Many centuries later when Grotius wrote his *de arbitris*, he opined that there were three ways of preventing war: by conference, lot and arbitration.[1] Arbitration he considered was an equitable process decided on the merits.[2]

Another example was that given by the Grand Design of Henry IV of France in 1603. His idea was a balance of power in Europe so that no Power would envy

[1] H Grotius, *On the Law of War and Peace* (Book II) (edited by SC Neff) (Cambridge University Press, 2012) Ch xxiii (xlvii).

[2] *Ibid.*

another. A General Council was to represent the 'States of All Europe'. In 1693, William Penn proposed a diet, parliament for the 'States of Europe'. Such an assembly's object was to establish rules of justice for mutual observance based on international law. Later, Henry IV's scheme was elaborated by the Abbé Saint Pierre who suggested a union of Christian sovereigns to preserve the unbroken peace of Europe by supporting them against sedition or rebellion. In Pufendorf's the *Law of Nature* he opined that before war was declared 'milder methods' should be attempted by means of 'friendly discussion' by them or their agents. If discussions failed, reference was made to arbitration which would be final and binding unless the parties agreed to be bound by a particular municipal law.[3] Vattel in Book II of *The Law of Nations* recognised several forms of dispute resolution between states: amicable accommodation, compromise, negotiation by way of conference, mediation and arbitration. As he wrote:

> When sovereigns cannot agree about their pretensions and are nevertheless desirous of preserving or restoring peace, they sometimes submit the decision of their disputes to arbitrators chosen by common agreement. When once the contending parties have entered into articles of arbitration, they are bound to abide by the sentence of the arbitrators: they have engaged to do this; and the faith of treaties should be religiously observed.[4]

In Jeremy Bentham's scheme, *The Fragment of An Essay on International Law*, he opined that to preserve the peace some organisation resembling that of the German Diet, the Swiss League, or the American Confederation should be promoted having two representatives from each Power, but limited to giving and publishing its opinions and the use of a court. Kant, on the other hand, believed in a Permanent Congress of Nations. He considered 'perpetual peace' was an impractical idea, but thought that states could voluntarily unite in a 'Federal State of Europe' based on the success of the early eighteenth-century diplomatic conferences. The law of nations would provide the instrument for resolving disputes through judicial proceedings.[5]

John Locke in his *Treatise of Government*[6] advocated a federal union like the United States or the Swiss Confederation. Thus, he suggested a Supreme Court of Justice and a system of subordinate courts in every state of such union. Its jurisdiction, Mill suggested, being confined to federal matters so that both federal government and state governments could be liable for failing to enforce federal rights or for exceeding their powers or for non-performance of federal duties. The Supreme Court would have a similar role to that of the US Supreme Court to nullify legislation. Courts would act as umpires in disputes between

[3] W Evans Darby, *International Tribunals* (FB&Co Ltd, 2015).

[4] E Vattel, *The Law of Nations, or, Principles of The Law of Nature, Applied To The Conduct And Affairs of Nations And Sovereigns, With Three Early Essays on The Origin and Nature of Natural Law and on Luxury* (edited by B Kapossy and R Whatmore) (Liberty Fund, 2008) s 329.4.

[5] Kant, *Rechtslehre Part II*, s 61.

[6] J Locke, P Laslett (ed), *Two Treatises of Government* (Cambridge University Press, 1988).

federal and state governments. War would be precluded by virtue of the union. The Supreme Court would dispense international law.

Dr JC Bluntschli, a Swiss Jurist, proposed a traditional type of arbitral tribunal appointed by the parties which could propose settlement and determine its own jurisdiction.[7] It would give awards by majority decision and this would be equivalent to a binding treaty. Such award had to comply with international law and the treaties provided rules for procedure and mode of appointment. Like Locke and Kant, this was predicated on a European Union for 'the careful preservation of the independence and freedom of the associated states'. But he went further in advocating a code of international law, international legislation and the international administration of justice.

Between 1873 and 1878, eight conferences were held by the Association for Reform and Codification of the Law of Nations: at Brussels in 1873; at Geneva in 1874; at The Hague in 1875; at Bremen and Philadelphia in 1876; at Antwerp in 1877; at Frankfurt in 1878; and in London in 1879.

In 1875 the Institute of International Law proposed the appointment of sovereigns or heads of state and 'all persons who are competent according to the law of their country to exercise the function of arbitrator'.[8]

In 1876 at the Association for Reform and Codification of the Law of Nations' meeting in London, a Codification of Public International Law was suggested by AP Sprague, the Secretary of the International Code Committee of America, and for a Tribunal of Arbitration and a High Tribunal of Public International Judicature. The main purpose being to provide an International Codification and Arbitration providing peaceful means of settling international controversies. Some writers such as Emery de la Croix (Nouveau Cynée) and Castel de St Pierre (Projet de la Paix) agreed with this approach in line with that taken earlier by Jeremy Bentham.[9]

At the convention of the Alumni Association of Haverford College in 1883, an Arbitration League was proposed with an international police force at the disposal of a tribunal 'to execute any orders it may think fit to issue'.[10]

At this time America reduced its standing army from one million men in 1865 to 25,000 in 1874. Organisations such as the Universal Peace Union and other peace societies in America promoted international arbitration. President Ulysses S Grant became an advocate of arbitration and two eminent American lawyers, David Dudley Field and James Bassett Moore supported it.

In England, Field attended a meeting of the British Association for the Promotion of Social Science in Manchester in September 1866 and proposed the appointment of a committee to prepare and report to the Association on the outlines of an international code. This was eventually published in New York in 1872.[11]

[7] Evans Darby (n 3) 102.
[8] *Ibid* 270.
[9] *Ibid* 228.
[10] *Ibid* 267.
[11] D Dudley Field, *Draft Outlines of An International Code* (Diossy & Company, 1872).

This code provided under Article 532 for the service of a formal Notice of Dissatisfaction or Cause of Complaint by the aggrieved nation on the nation against whom redress was sought. Under Article 533 every nation that received such a Notice of Dissatisfaction or Cause of Complaint was given three months in which to give a full and explicit answer. If the nations did not agree between themselves as to the matters complained of, they could each appoint five members to a Joint High Commission who would discuss the differences and endeavour to reconcile them within six months of their appointment and report the result accordingly. The draft outlines also included provision for a High Tribunal of Arbitration where the Joint High Commission failed to agree a resolution (Article 535). Further under Article 536 each nation was bound by the decision of the Tribunal of Arbitration. Article 537 provided that if any party were to begin a war in violation of the code the other parties bound themselves to resist the offending nation by force. In order to preserve the peace Article 538 provided that a conference of representatives of the nations would be held every year at a capital in rotation for the purposes of discussing any amendment to the code, averting war, and facilitating the causes of peace.[12] A variation of this project was produced by Leon Levi.

M Leon Levi, a member of Lincoln's Inn, and Lord Hobhouse produced a draft project for a Council and High Court of International Arbitration in October 1889.[13] Sir Edmund Hornby suggested a Permanent International Tribunal of Arbitration whereby the enforcement of an award would be by means of withdrawal or suspension of diplomatic relations, imposition of damages or by seizure and occupation of territory and as a last resort recourse to war. The Tribunal of Arbitration would consist of 13 senators who would be statesman or diplomats or former judges. On acceptance, office members would have to renounce allegiance to their state of origin. Countries had to demonstrate that the dispute could not be resolved through diplomacy and then they would be able to refer to the Tribunal. Hornby designated the Tribunal as a College of International Law.[14]

A similar idea was taken up by The International American Conference with representatives from North, Central and South America who proposed a plan for a Permanent Tribunal of Arbitration in April 1890. The aim of this Tribunal was to preserve peace and goodwill amongst the American republics with arbitration being adopted as a principle of American international law. Arbitration was mandatory upon all member states. A jurisconsult, Professor the Marquis Corsi, suggested that there should be rules for international arbitration which should disbar any person who was a subject of a contending state, or had a personal interest in questions arising, or had published an opinion on the same

[12] *Ibid* 369–71.

[13] Levi produced the original draft in October 1887 and Lord Hobhouse amended it and it was published in October 1889.

[14] Evans Darby (n 3) 124–26.

question referred to the Tribunal, or pamphlets and speeches that might prejudice his independence. On the other hand, Corsi's proposed rules had a wider perspective in that the arbitrator could be a faculty of law, a local authority, or a religious or a learned society or a head of such. Such a tribunal would not be bound by any state laws as to jurisdiction which the tribunal would settle itself *de novo*. Under his rules, governments would pay the costs of the arbitration in equal shares. W Evans Darby, the author of the compendium of treatises and proposals referred to here, as Secretary of the Peace Society, put forward his own proposals for statesman, diplomats, former senior judges or others having a high reputation and standing to be nominated by disputant governments as arbitrators. The tribunal he suggested had the status of a diplomatic mission with all the immunities appertaining thereto. It would be a permanent tribunal for the life of the members. Such tribunal would give extra judicial opinions on any question of law or interpretation of a treaty in order to prevent differences arising. It would also give advice to conferences of sovereigns or statesman.

Following all these proposals, further rules relating to a Permanent Tribunal of International Arbitration were presented by the Special Committee of International Law on 10th October 1893 at its conference on the 1st and 2nd October 1895 and accepted at a later meeting in Buffalo, New York on the 31st August 1899. This was a significant event which added weight to the inter-parliamentary conference proposals leading to the formation of the Permanent Court of Arbitration in 1899.[15]

In 1893 the Chicago Congress proposed rules for the organisation of an International Tribunal of Arbitration which would operate by virtue of a Notice of Complaint seeking redress of any member state. A Joint Commission of three commissioners for each party would be appointed to report. If the report was not accepted the Notice of Complaint would be referred to a Tribunal of Arbitration. If a party ignored the Tribunal's award, then all other members would declare such default an infraction of the treaty and after 30 days close their ports to the defaulting state until such time as it complied with the award.[16]

A Code of International Arbitration was approved by the Peace Conference at Antwerp in August 1894. The Code was drafted so as not to interfere with the autonomy or independence of disputant states. This was to be enabled by bilateral convention general or limited. Rules of procedure, in default of any special stipulations, provided that the Tribunal formulate the award on special international law applicable to the enabling treaty; the general international law formulated or used by civilised nations and the public or private law of the disputed nations or of other civilised nations.[17]

[15] *Ibid* 364–68.
[16] *Ibid* 282.
[17] *Ibid* 234–40.

A resolution was passed by the Inter Parliamentary Conference in Brussels in 1895 proposing a Permanent Court of Arbitration. It was this event which was the touchstone for the most successful outcome of the first Hague Conference. The Parliamentary conference proposed that this Court should have a fixed abode. Member state representatives were disqualified from representing their government and there was a right of appeal against an award. In that year Signor P Fiere[18] published his scheme for an Arbitration Tribunal to 'decide any particular difference arising between two or more states'. The Tribunal would apply the principles of Public Law or any agreed special law under the treaty enabling the proceedings.[19]

A Memorial of the Bar Association of the State of New York dated 22 January 1896 proposed an Anglo-American Arbitration Tribunal, but this was opposed in favour of other European countries being admitted. They proposed The International Court of Arbitration with nine members of high judicial rank to hold office for life. This would first deal with Anglo-American disputes and avoid war.[20]

II. ANGLO-AMERICAN TREATY DISCUSSIONS

It was against the background of increasing harmony between Britain and America that a treaty was negotiated between the two countries and signed in Washington on the 11th January 1897. This grew out of diplomatic discussions in 1895 over a possible international arbitration treaty between the two English speaking countries. There was much debate over what would be included within such a treaty in which John Wodehouse, the Earl of Kimberly, then Secretary of State, and Sir Julian Pauncefote, Britain's Ambassador in Washington, were in discussions with the United States' Government. In July 1894 the Senate and the House of Representatives passed a Resolution requesting the President to negotiate a treaty with Great Britain providing for arbitration of disputes. It was proposed that the parties enter into an arbitration treaty for a term of 25 years terminable on six months' notice. These discussions took some time because Pauncefote was awaiting confirmation from the Senate committee on the resolution. There was some debate in Congress on the questions of national honour, territorial integrity and vital interests of both nations. These were matters which could not be arbitrated as they directly affected the question of national sovereignty. Whilst the United States was still wary of imperial ambitions, circumstances had changed and the old enmity stemming from the American Revolution was disappearing. More significantly the natural ties between Britain

[18] Professor at the University of Naples and Jurisconsult.
[19] Evans Darby (n 3) 290.
[20] *Ibid* 167–71.

and America were becoming closer.[21] A feeling of mutual respect and friendship was displayed in certain events, for example, in March 1898, in the New York theatres, they played 'God Save the Queen' after 'The Star-Spangled Banner' (national anthem of the United States);[22] and in July 1898 Pauncefote reported the flying of the Union Jack and Stars and Stripes together at the American army base in Tampa, Florida. Perhaps a more telling indication was the redeployment of a British naval squadron in Manilla Bay preventing threatening manoeuvres against the American fleet by a German fleet.[23] Far from thwarting American imperial designs, Britain supported them. Both countries had analogous ambitions.

Against such background Pauncefote drafted a treaty having in mind the Clayton-Bulmer Treaty 1850 which is discussed in chapter four.[24] The draft arbitration treaty provided for a large choice of arbitrators who met the required qualifications and were respected by both governments, but it was to be subject to certain exceptions regarding 'political offences'. The British exceptions were not agreed by the United States but were replaced with classes of cases to which the treaty could apply. The respective government's positions were reserved as to what 'might imperil the national independence'.

It is clear from these discussions and negotiations that the sticking point even between friendly states like the United States and Great Britain was the difficulty in referring to an international tribunal sensitive matters affecting state sovereignty, vital state interest, or national honour.[25] Those matters however did not include adjustment of unsettled and disputed boundaries.[26] The final draft submitted by the American Government provided the following:

> Article I
>
> The High Contracting parties agree to arbitration all questions of difference which may arise between them, and which they may fall to adjust by diplomatic negotiation, concerning diplomatic and consular privileges, boundaries, indemnities, the right of navigation, and publicity, construction, and enforcement of treaties. But questions which, in the judgement of either High Contracting Party, involve or imperil its independence are not embraced in such agreement.

Other provision followed what had been agreed as to arbitrators, but the most innovative provision was Article III which provided:

> Article III
>
> The enumeration in Article 1 of the present Treaty of certain subjects of difference in respect of which arbitration shall be obligatory upon the High Contracting Parties

[21] For a more detailed analysis, see CS Campbell, *Anglo-American Understanding* (The John Hopkins Press, 1957).

[22] *The Times* (16 March 1898).

[23] Campbell (n 21) 50–55.

[24] This Treaty provided for joint protectorate by England and the United States of any transisthmian canal.

[25] Lawyers may take the view that in practical terms states do not surrender sovereignty, they exercise it by virtue of the treaty or agreement to arbitrate.

[26] Foreign Office Papers (FO) 414/131 Article III British draft.

> is not to be understood as excluding the submission of other subjects of difference to arbitration by agreement, it being the desire and object of the High Contracting Parties by the present Treaty to recognise and establish in the arbitration of international differences as a general principle.[27]

This may have been something of a turning point in Anglo-American relations and contributed to a 'special relationship'. The first point of significance is that apart from the exclusionary provisions of Article I the United States and Great Britain had agreed to settle a wide variety of disputes, but furthermore the second point was of greater significance in so far as both Powers were recognising arbitration as a means of settling all international differences. This great aspiration was a commitment that had considerable support amongst international jurists. An immediate product of this treaty was the establishment of the Anglo-Venezuelan Arbitration which is discussed in chapter three.

Subsequently, Randal Cremer MP, promoted an Anglo-American arbitration treaty and was introduced by Andrew Carnegie to President Grover Cleveland.[28] British MPs presented a Memorandum to President Cleveland on 31st October 1887 which was supported by France, Ireland, the Quakers in England and by Canada and the United States. In June 1880 the Senate Foreign Relations Committee reported the resolution which authorised President Cleveland to negotiate an arbitration treaty and in February 1890 the resolution passed the Senate. In 1893 the House of Commons passed a similar resolution. The First International American Conference convened in October 1889 with American states agreeing a convention to settle all their disputes which diplomacy could not settle save questions of independence by arbitration. This was hailed by Mr Blaine, the American Secretary of State, as 'the new Magna Carta'. This was a premature declaration as nothing was ratified but it encouraged an Anglo-American arbitration agreement. On the 16th June 1893 Randall Cremer introduced the debate in the House of Commons on an Anglo-American arbitration agreement and it was resolved that the Government should cooperate with the United States in such a measure.[29] Cramer then led a delegation to Paris to make an appeal with Frédéric Passy to Britain, France and the United States to negotiate an arbitration treaty. An Inter-Parliamentary Union was formed and in 1895 one of its committees presented a plan for a permanent international court which influenced The Hague Peace Conference in 1899. Thomas Bayard, the United States Ambassador, supported arbitration and President Cleveland declared that: 'Without arbitration, diplomacy. If that fails, war and sacrifice of life, and retrogression in civilization.' Despite this America did not proceed with an arbitration treaty, although President McKinley gave some encouraging signs in December 1897 to treaties of arbitration. Such a treaty would have dealt

[27] FO 414/131 Article III United States counter-draft.

[28] C DeArmond Davis, *The United States and the First Hague Conference* (Cornell University Press, 1962) 2–17.

[29] *Ibid* 20.

with all matters incapable of resolution through diplomatic channels and would have resolved claims up to £100,000 excluding territorial claims. In April 1898, however, McKinley's Government declared war on Spain as a result of the sinking of the *USS Maine*.

III. THE INFLUENCE OF AMERICAN JURISTS

Following the American Civil War and the settlement of the Geneva Arbitration Award, relations between the United States and Britain gradually developed. This relationship facilitated discussions of the issues that confronted the delegates at The Hague who were concerned with sovereignty and the rights of states to accept the jurisdiction of an international court whose authority would be mandatory. In understanding this approach, the influence of certain other American jurists Brown Scott, Taft and Root is worthy of note.

A. James Brown Scott

In his address on international law,[30] Brown Scott considered that international law was appealed to by a belligerent to validate their cause. Likewise, the enemy also appealed to international law norms. He referred to the opinions of John Bassett Moore and Elihu Root that the foundation of international law stemmed from the Treaty of Westphalia at the end of the Thirty Years War. A concept endorsed by Henry Kissinger describing international order with prescribed limits for state actors.[31] It is worth noting that the Peace of Westphalia was regarded as a turning point[32] by Kissinger which established the concept of state sovereignty and acknowledged the right of each state to choose its own domestic structure and religious orientation respecting the rights of minority faiths.[33] The Westphalian settlement gave rise to the system of conferences between ambassadors and diplomats along the Venetian model and was later extended at the conclusion of the Napoleonic wars into the Congress System or Concert of Europe which lasted until 1914. Brown Scott envisaged a similar form of international dispute settlement after the First World War.[34] The problem Brown Scott tried to address was what type of international dispute was justiciable. He averred that the US Supreme Court provided a model in that it refused to accept

[30] J Brown Scott, 'The Nature and Form of the Agreement for the Submission of Justiciable Disputes to an International Court' (1907–17) *Proceedings of the American Society of International Law at its Annual Meeting* 81–95.

[31] Henry Kissinger, *World Order* (Penguin Books, 2015) 43.

[32] *Ibid* 26.

[33] Religious toleration was not given to Catholics in Ireland or England until the Roman Catholic Relief Act 1829.

[34] Brown Scott (n 30) 88.

matters of political dispute.[35] Brown Scott suggested that states could accept the jurisdiction of an international tribunal for certain types of references for a fixed period of time.[36] He also gave the example of Russia, which taking advantage of the Franco-Prussian War of 1870, abrogated the provision of the Treaty of Paris 1856 preventing Russian warships from entering the Black Sea. The London conference declared that '… no Power can repudiate Treaty arrangements or modify treaty provisions, except with the consent of the contracting parties amicably obtained'.

Thus, what Brown Scott was concerned about was the enforcement of treaty obligations. If state parties were in breach, how were they to be enforced? The answer lay in the reference to arbitration, for example, the Postal Convention signed in Rome in 1906.[37] That provided that each state become a member of the Postal Union which was a justiciable union, judicial union and a juridical union.

> ARTICLE 23
>
> *Disputes to be settled by arbitration*
>
> 1. In case of disagreement between two or more members of the Union as to the interpretation of the present Convention, or as to the responsibility resting on an Administration by the application of the said Convention, the question in dispute is decided by arbitration. To that end each of the Administrations concerned chooses another member of the Union not directly interested in the matter.
> 2. The decision of the arbitrators is given by an absolute majority of votes.
> 3. In case of an equality of votes the arbitrators choose, with the view of settling the difference, another Administration equally uninterested in the question in dispute.
> 4. The stipulations of the present Article apply equally to all the Agreements concluded by virtue of the foregoing Article 19.

Brown Scott's example permitted states to submit their dispute either to a court or to arbitration. It was also the fact that he could not recall any reference where the parties had not accepted the award by the tribunal of their own choice. The sanction for acceptance of an award according to opinion was that of public opinion itself or a 'league of peace' to enforce the award before a recourse to arms.[38]

B. William Howard Taft

President Taft was unique amongst twentieth century jurists in that he held the highest executive and judicial posts in his country. In so doing he commanded

[35] *Ibid* 89.

[36] *Ibid* 90.

[37] Convention and final protocol signed at Rome on 26 May 1906. Ratified and approved by the Postmaster General of the United States on 13 October 1906. Terminated by convention of 30 November 1920.

[38] Brown Scott (n 30) 92–93.

considerable authority for his support of international arbitration as a means to prevent disputes between states that might otherwise result in war. In hindsight observers can say that neither the League of Nations, nor the Permanent Court of Arbitration prevented the conflagrations of 1930s Europe. But it is arguable, and argued here, that the intellectual contribution of international jurists such as Taft enabled mankind to consider what might be. He is seen here in the context of the American movement which believed that it might be possible to settle and resolve disputes between states as lawyers might resolve them between claimant and defendant. At this time America had many organisations devoted to this object. These groups and societies included the Interparliamentary Union, the American School Peace League, the American Society for the Juridical Settlement of International Disputes, the World Peace Foundation, and the Carnegie Endowment for International Peace. Taft held the Vice Presidency of the American Society for the Judicial Settlement of International Disputes formed in 1910 and later he was appointed as the Honorary President of the International Law Association.

In many respects these factions followed the earlier abolitionist movement before the American Civil War.[39] They set the scene and gave Taft the encouragement to find a better way imbued perhaps by optimistic narratives such as *The Great Illusion*[40] which argued that interdependence through international trade and commerce rendered war illogical and counterproductive. If that were true, then international commerce held the key and Taft readily imbibed the idea of commercial diplomacy.[41]

In 1896 Taft was appointed to the American Conference on International Arbitration to promote a proposed permanent system of arbitration between the United States and Great Britain. Following his term as President of the United States, Taft headed the League to Enforce Peace which promulgated his bilateral arbitration treaties by submitting justiciable disputes to an International Court and providing for military intervention for those who opted for war before going to the Court.[42] Taft also supported the United States' accession to the League of Nations and the Permanent Court of Arbitration. He was 'dedicated to building world peace by legalising the conduct of international relations.'[43] Although Taft was a Republican he was a proponent of progressive developments in international law. He had sound legal practice experience in dealing with international and diplomatic matters from the times when he was a Governor General of the

[39] E Mead, *The Literature of the New Peace Movement* (World Peace Foundation Pamphlets, 1912) 7, 9.

[40] N Angell, *The Great Illusion* (The Knickerbocker Press, 1910).

[41] J Campbell, 'Taft Roosevelt and the Arbitration Treaties of 1911' (1966) 53 *The Journal of American History* 290.

[42] JE Noyes, 'William Howard Taft and the Taft Arbitration Treaties' (2011) 56 *Villanova Law Review*, 535, 536.

[43] *Ibid* 535, 537 and M Weston Janis, *America and the Law of Nations 1776–1939* (Oxford University Press, 2010).

Philippines and Secretary of War. It was his judicial experience and qualities as a lawyer which prompted him to advance the application of the rule of law universally. His approach was positivist, in line with the views of Kelsen adopting a scientific approach to law much in keeping with the approach adopted by Dean Langdell at Harvard Law School. As Solicitor General he argued the Behring Sea case before the Supreme Court against the British Government.[44] He was a good negotiator and successfully resolved matters after the Cuban insurrection by promoting a solution which was accepted by the Cuban people.[45] He was instrumental in overseeing the completion of the Panama Canal project influencing its methods of construction.[46] He was an advocate of international dispute resolution by arbitration and the rule of law and could argue strongly in favour of such a system. Taft's views were supported by the religious community in America which believed that international legal mechanisms could contribute to peace.[47] Taft did not believe in disarmament; he was a realist who understood that America required sufficient forces to deter a potential aggressor and that international arbitration treaties could not guarantee this. What arbitration might do was prevent war in certain cases. He wanted to extend the jurisdiction of the process to include vital interest and national honour. This was opposed in Congress and his key provision for reference to a Joint High Commission of Inquiry was defeated by only two votes in the Senate.[48] That was fundamental and fatal. What might have been was an extraordinary advance in the Comity of Nations albeit between two culturally similar English-speaking countries holding equal respect for the rule of law.

C. Elihu Root

One of the leading proponents of international dispute resolution by application of international law was the lawyer and statesman Elihu Root. In his Address on International Subjects in 1916[49] he spoke of how the American people achieved liberty and schooled themselves to the service of liberty and justice.[50] He thought that peace and liberty could only be preserved by the authority and of observance of rules of national conduct founded on principles of justice and humanity by the establishment of law where nations were responsible to the 'enlightened public opinion of mankind'.[51] He was deeply critical of the

[44] T Burton, 'The Claims of the Candidates: William Howard Taft' (1908) 187 *The North American Review* 641–83, 679.

[45] *Ibid* 682.

[46] *Ibid.*

[47] Noyes (n 42) 535, 540.

[48] *Ibid* 535, 547.

[49] E Root, *Addresses by Elihu Root on International Subjects* (James Brown and Robert Bacon, Gaunt, 1997).

[50] *Ibid* 440.

[51] *Ibid* 441.

United States indifference to the German attack on Belgium which destroyed the independence, liberty and life of a peaceful country in repudiation of the treaties and Law of Nations. He denounced those who would remain silent and neutral when international law and the rights of man and progress of humanity and liberty were threatened. Root said

> … opinion was powerless and brute force rules and will rule the world … If no difference is recognised between right and wrong then there are no moral standards. There are times in the lives of nations as of man when to treat a wrong as if it were a right is treason to the right.[52]

Root argued that under the Constitution of the United States, the Federal Government could not enforce a Supreme Court judgment against a state of the Union.[53] At this time there was no means of enforcement. James Brown Scott saw no effective means to enforce but thought that the moral force of public opinion (provided it was sufficiently educated) would be the means of accomplishment. In this Root agreed with Brown Scott that the weight of public opinion could make a state respect an arbitration award.

D. Politis

In his treatise on international commissions of inquiry, Nicolas Politis questioned whether inquiries were simply arbitral tribunals.[54] He opined that arbitral tribunals dealt with legal matters and gave binding awards, whereas inquiries simply confirmed the facts. But often matters of fact affect legal rights and obligations and law and fact overlap.

E. Nissim Bar-Yacoov

Professor Bar-Yacoov[55] discussed the efforts made by states to resolve their disputes through means of inquiry and report, a process not unknown to the English Legal system.[56] Bar-Yacoov followed the thinking of Professor Roling,[57] rapporteur of the Committee on Judicial Questions who pointed out the shortcomings of negotiation as a peaceful method of settling international disputes.

[52] *Ibid* 442.

[53] Brown Scott (n 30) 93.

[54] Politis, 'Les Commissions Internationales d'enquette' (1912) 19 *Revue Générale de Droit International Public* 152, fn1.

[55] N Bar-Yacoov, *The Handling of International Disputes by Means of Enquiry* (Oxford University Press, 1974).

[56] See MP Reynolds, *Caseflow Management: A Rudimentary Official Referee Process 1870–1970* (London School of Economics, Law Department Thesis, 2009).

[57] International lawyer and jurist, Professor Utrecht University. Rapporteur, UN Committee on Judicial Questions 1956.

Roling considered the impediments to such resolution as being reluctance to surrender sovereignty to the International Court of Justice, limitations of the League of Nations and the UN whose members were motivated by their own national interest rather than the merits of the case. Bar-Yacoov's framework encompassed mediation, conciliation, arbitration and judicial settlement within his concept of 'inquiry'. He defined that as 'a specific category of investigation conducted by an international body'. He distinguishes these types of process in categories of type and scope and questions their purpose.

IV. THE HAGUE CONFERENCE AND CONVENTION 1899

The First International Peace Conference was held at The Hague in 1899. Essentially, it was an extension of the concert system and aimed at 'seeking, by means of international discussion, the most effectual means of ensuring to all peoples the benefits of a real and durable peace, and above all, or putting an end to the progressive development of the present armaments'.[58] It was soon realised that this objective was unrealistic and that a more modest objective namely 'the maintenance of general peace' should be adopted in the light of the arms race. This seems to have begun when the Reichstag passed the first German naval laws in 1898 and portentously passed another series of laws one year after The Hague Conference in 1900. It is interesting to note that it was the German Government that opposed a Russian plan for inclusive and compulsory arbitration.[59] However, the establishment of a Permanent Court of Arbitration was adopted despite further German objections. The Court would function as a court of arbitration 'in questions of a judicial character, and especially regarding interpretation of treaties.[60]

According to William Langer,[61] the idea of a conference of the Great Powers was inspired by an increasing desire for peace amongst the Free Church leaders and labour organisations in England, and they, through means of a petition signed by 35,000 people including a number of MPs, inspired Lord Rosebery the Foreign Secretary to make the suggestion to Russia. Russia and especially Count Witte, the Finance Minister, was receptive to the idea because Russia could not afford to keep pace with the cost of armaments. It is extraordinary that at a time of rearmament amongst the Great Powers and an enthusiasm for imperial ambitions exemplified by the Spanish American war, the Boer war and the Sino-Japanese war such a movement could gain acceptance for what was termed 'a true Parliament of Man'. Whilst such high-minded ideals were

[58] Rescript of the Russian Emperor 24 August 1898, see: J Brown Scott (ed), *Texts of the Peace Conferences at the Hague,1899 and 1907* (Boston and London, 1908) 1–2.

[59] A Hershey, 'History of International Law Since the Peace of Westphalia' (1912) 6 *American Journal of International Law* 30, 57.

[60] Art 16 of the Arbitration Treaty and First Convention.

[61] William Langer, *The Diplomacy of Imperialism 1890–1902* (Alfred A Knopf, 1956) 582–83.

laudable they were not the essential reason for Russia's invitation to the Powers. The fact was that Russia could not afford to keep up with the arms race by spending $50 million on a new gun to rival the French 75mm and the new German gun which could fire six rounds a minute to the one round of a Russian gun.

Lord Salisbury was curious as to the Russian plan and what was entailed. Was it armaments, or issues such as Afghanistan, Constantinople or Egypt and how would matters be considered by population, area or wealth?[62] The French saw the invitation as an opportunity to reconcile differences between Britain and France especially as rivalry existed over Sudan and the confrontation at Fashoda.[63] It was considered contrary to French prospects of recovering Alsace and Lorraine[64] but alarms may have been raised by the Kaiser's excursions into the Near East via Constantinople, Jerusalem and Damascus planting the seeds of subsequent infiltration and influence.[65]

Contrary to the subsequent opposition taken in Berlin to the Conference, Lascelles reported to Salisbury that the Chancellor of the German Empire, Bernhard von Bülow, favoured it in terms of the status quo and some discussion about the Balkans.[66] There were no preliminary conditions, it did not seem overtly political nor secret but the invitation seemed open to consultation and suggestions of military, financial and commercial matters. The British Ambassador at Vienna, Horace Rumbold, reported opposition from Austria-Hungary to Salisbury and told Salisbury that there was no proposal for immediate disarmament from Austria-Hungary.[67] Satow told Salisbury that Japan was willing to follow the lead of America and England whilst Rumbold told Salisbury that Germany and Italy thought this was an opportunity for an 'exchange of ideas'.[68] An ominous report was sent by MacDonald in Serbia. He was told by the Serbian Foreign Minister that 'We live in hope of getting security for ourselves out of the general conflagration, whenever it takes place'.[69] Salisbury was pleased to accept participation in the Conference, believing that there was a constant tendency by nations to expend vast sums on the instruments of war which could only result in 'unrest and discontent'.[70] However, there were those in the Admiralty who objected to the imposition of restrictions on naval armament saying that '... any such restriction would favour the interests of Savage nations, and be against those of the more highly civilised. It would be a retrograde step ...'.[71]

[62] P Gooch and H Temperley (eds), *British Documents on the Origins of the War 1898–1914* (BD) Vol I 'The End of British Isolation' (Her Majesty's Stationery Office, 1927) 215 *Marquis of Salisbury to Sir C Scott* (30 August 1898).

[63] *Ibid* Vol I, 215–16 *Monson to Marquis of Salisbury* (1 September 1898); DeArmond Davis (n 28) 48.

[64] DeArmond Davis (n 28) 40.

[65] *Ibid* 48.

[66] BD (n 62) Vol I, 216–17 *Lascelles to Marquis of Salisbury* (2 September 1898).

[67] *Ibid* Vol I, 218 *Rumbold to Marquis of Salisbury* (8 September 1898).

[68] *Ibid* Vol I, 218–19 *Satow to Marquis of Salisbury* (8 September 1898) and Vol I, 219–20 *Rumbold to Marquis of Salisbury* (14 September 1898).

[69] *Ibid* Vol I, 220 *MacDonald to Marquis of Salisbury* (15 September 1898).

[70] *Ibid Marquis of Salisbury to Sir C Scott* (24 October 1898).

[71] FO General 1702. BD (n 62) Vol I, 224 *Admiralty to Foreign Office* (16 May 1899).

As far as the War Office was concerned, they said it was undesirable to give any undertaking as to the numbers or cost of military forces or to agree to any restrictions on the development of armaments or to assent to any international code as to the laws and customs of war but that they would undertake to consider issuing general guidance to British forces.[72]

Despite the Admiralty's and War Office reservations Lord Salisbury was very much in favour of the Conference. He said that he had '... an earnest desire by all possible means to promote mediation and arbitration for the prevention of war'.[73] He therefore supported Pauncefote's idea for a Permanent Court of Arbitration with three-fifths of the arbitrators being appointed by a vote of the whole college.[74] This was opposed by the Kaiser who tried to inveigle Austria-Hungary to oppose the British, French and Russian efforts to establish the court. Salisbury instructed Rumbold to influence the Austro-Hungarian Foreign Minister Goluchöwski as to the merits of such a court.[75] The British Military attaché at The Hague, Lieutenant Colonel Charles, concluded that while all powers wanted peace 'there was not the slightest chance of any agreement of the kind'. He went on to say that '... No power can cry a halt while the one next below him on the scale continues to arm, and that the latter will not cease to arm until he has reached an equality with the rival above him'.[76] Pauncefote was more optimistic and felt that the Conference was changing its approach to a common understanding.[77]

Whilst progress was difficult on armaments it was not so regarding codes of humanising the laws of war on land and at sea. Jurists and diplomats were able to produce a document containing processes for use of good offices, mediation and arbitration: *Project of a Convention for the Pacific Settlement of International Conflicts*. Its most interesting innovation was the Permanent Court of Arbitration.[78] Whilst there was progress in the suggested regulation of the laws of war it was obvious to Sir E Mason and the President of France that it was not possible to prevent war by arbitration. Each nation had to judge its honour where a wilful act or misconduct of another would render arbitration inapplicable.[79]

When Rumbold discussed this with Goluchöwski, the latter explained that the objection was to a mandatory jurisdiction and the inference of an obligation to refer. Germany wanted an option to accept or reject arbitration.[80]

[72] BD (n 62) Vol I, 225 *War Office to Foreign Office* (17 May 1899).

[73] FO General 1694. BD (n 62) Vol I, 225 *Lord Salisbury to Sir J Pauncefote* (1898).

[74] BD (n 62) Vol I, 215 *Marquis of Salisbury to Sir J Pauncefote* (31 May 1899).

[75] *Ibid* Vol I, 227 *Marquis of Salisbury to Sir C Rumbold* (12 June 1899).

[76] *Ibid* Vol I, 231 *The Hague* (29 July 1899).

[77] *Ibid* Vol I, 215 *Pauncefote to Marquis of Salisbury* (31 July 1899).

[78] *Ibid* Vol I, 232 *Report of M Descauys*. As referred to in *Pauncefote to Marquis of Salisbury* (31 July 1899 (n 77).

[79] *Ibid* Vol I, 232 *Sir E Mason to Marquis of Salisbury* (24 October 1899).

[80] This is a matter that obstructed negotiations between Sir E Grey and Bethmann-Hollweg in July 1914 when Germany considered Grey's plan for a conference of ambassadors, an arbitration interfering with a sovereign state.

Thus, it was that the First Hague Peace Conference was initiated by a *Rescript* of Tsar Nicholas II of Russia which sought:

> ... by means of international discussion, the most effectual means of insuring to all peoples the benefits of a real and durable peace, and above all, of putting an end to the progressive development of the present armaments.

His invitation of the 24th August 1898 to ambassadors was to make 'the great idea of universal peace triumph over the doubts of trouble and discord'.[81] The invitation had two themes; the first, the question of limitation of armaments, and the second, the use of pacific means of resolving disputes through international diplomacy. The Tsar suggested that the Conference consider such matters as: changes to the laws of war at sea regarding neutrals and small navy powers; the laws and customs of war; and an improvement in extension of arbitration and mediation.[82] Underlying the invitation might have been the Russian need to divert attention away from her encroachments in Manchuria and the Chinese Eastern Railway project opening a more direct approach to Vladivostok.[83] The Tsar was anxious to avoid any conflict on that question with Britain as he said: 'Peace is more important than anything else, unless our honour is touched'.[84] Strategically, Russia may have been considering the prospect of Germany siding with Japan, England and America regarding Far Eastern rivalries, but secondly might want to unite the continent against the moral supremacy of the Anglo Saxons.[85] This invitation was accepted by Germany, Austria, Belgium, China, Denmark, Spain, the United States, Mexico, France, Britain, Greece, Italy, Japan, Luxembourg, Montenegro, Holland, Persia, Portugal, Romania, Russia, Serbia, Siam, Sweden and Norway, Switzerland, Turkey and Bulgaria. Sir Julian Pauncefote represented Britain along with Sir Henry Howard, Sir John Fisher and Major General Sir John Ardagh.

A. The Impediment of the National Interest

On the 12th August 1899, the Tsar's invitation to the Conference appealed for the maintenance of universal peace and a possible reduction of the excessive armaments. Lord Salisbury supported these sentiments seeking 'a remedy for this evil'. But disarmament proved impossible. Germany would not reduce its army and Britain would not reduce its Navy. They discussed possible restraints of military budgets to keep armies at their current level for five years, but there was no real support for this from the Powers. In the words of David Stevenson, it was the 'self-reinforcing cycle of heightened military preparedness and more

[81] Translation of Rescript, J Brown Scott, *The Hague Peace Conferences II* (Oxford University Press, 1920–21) 1–7.
[82] *Ibid* 3–5.
[83] DeArmond Davis (n 28) 47.
[84] Langer (n 61) 584.
[85] *Ibid* 588.

acute political conflict' which proved to be 'an essential element in the conjuncture that led to war'.[86] It would therefore be incredible if the moral force of international law propounded by the world's leading jurists could stop such acute conflicts founded on national interests. All that was achieved excluded any reference to arbitrate matters of 'national honour': it could not stop an arms race. The diplomats and statesmen who supported arbitration also believed in national defence which they regarded as 'a defensive insurance premium' and again as Stevenson rightly observed that this period before 1914 saw a series of ever more serious tensions at shorter intervals building up to a far greater risk of conflict.[87] This was made far more dangerous by opposing alliances which would ensure a wider conflict without sustaining the balance of power they were designed to preserve. The warning of Vegetius, 'If you want peace prepare for war' was not ignored. It appears that society and diplomacy was militarised: it was difficult to legalise it. If armaments had converged sooner, then war might have come earlier: the key failure of The Hague sequence was the failure of the Powers to regulate arms and a failure to accept the rule of international law because it infringed national sovereignty and the national interest or honour. As against this serious problem international jurists, statesmen and diplomats were able to advance the cause of peace through international law by a Permanent Court of Arbitration, the dream of many.

B. Proceedings of the Conference

In opening the Conference its President, M de Staal,[88] spoke of some of the means of assuring peace. Idealistically Dean O'Foley of the English Church at The Hague intoned '… And your old men shall see visions and your young men dream dreams'.[89]

The Conference lasted from the 18th of May 1899 to the 29th July 1899. M de Staal represented Russia and its legal representative was M de Martens. Pauncefote took the leading part in the discussion for Britain on arbitration. Ambassador White represented the United States and was instructed to support the advancement of a system of international arbitration. The State Department approved the Tsar's idea for 'the employment of good offices, of mediation and facilitative arbitration in principle'. This became the subject of a third commission. Each state attending the Conference was given one vote. The delegates were instructed to prepare a plan for a tribunal of international arbitration, although the Americans had some reservations as to how this would work with the Monroe Doctrine.[90]

[86] D Stevenson, *Armaments and the Coming of War, Europe 1904–1914* (Clarendon Press, 1996) 412.
[87] *Ibid* 413–14.
[88] Russian diplomat and former ambassador to Britain.
[89] DeArmond Davis (n 28) 97.
[90] *Ibid* 107.

Part of the American plan called for the signatory states to agree to submit all questions of disagreement between them to an international tribunal, except matters of political independence or territorial integrity. This entailed a system of mandatory arbitration although dependent upon their contracting nations' acceptance. When the third Commission assembled, the Russian delegate presented proposals for mediation arbitration and international commissions of inquiry. M de Staal wanted the Russian proposal extended to cover international treaties and an international organisation to act as an intermediary. This would serve as a means of conciliation and act as an international tribunal. Whilst this was not quite what the Americans and the British envisaged, it was subject to much debate.[91] Sir Julian Pauncefote was convinced that it was absolutely necessary to constitute a permanent international tribunal. The Americans suggested a tribunal of nine to 12 arbitrators to be appointed by members of the Supreme Courts of the participating states.[92]

The Commission agreed to a *comité d'examen* to attempt a reconciliation of the British and Russian approaches, but surprisingly the Russians agreed with the British proposal.[93] This committee considered rules relating to good offices and mediation. Such ideas were by no means new and had been incorporated in the Declaration of Paris in 1856. Some progress was made in considering mediation. Whilst the American delegation abandoned its insistence on mandatory arbitration, Russia wanted to include disputes relating to interoceanic canals and international rivers as obligatory. This could be detrimental to the United States in terms of the St Lawrence River, a future Panama Canal, and an infringement of the Monroe Doctrine.[94] In the end it was Pauncefote's suggestion of a Permanent Court of Arbitration sitting *de diem* that was adopted whereby the signatories would select two jurists and they would be listed as members of the international tribunal.[95] The *comité d'examen* accepted the British approach and decided that the seat of the tribunal should be The Hague with judges listed for six years. The German delegation opposed this and thought it gave licence to interference from 'troublesome professors'.But the Americans undertook discussions with Prince Hohenlöhe[96] and Bülow and sought to convince them of the advantage Germany might gain as the 'arbiter of Europe'. Holls, the Secretary of that delegation and pro-German, hinted that it might strengthen ties between Germany and America to Britain's detriment and counter the influence of Irish Americans. That was not a view accepted in Washington but may have convinced the Kaiser.[97] He urged Hohenlöhe and Bülow to act as

[91] *Ibid* 137–39.

[92] *Ibid* 79–82. *Hill to Halls* (24 April 1899). Hall's Papers.

[93] J Brown Scott, *The Hague Peace Conferences 1899–1907* (Baltimore, 1909) 583–85.

[94] DeArmond Davis (n 28) 146.

[95] Brown Scott (n 93) 797–817 and 833–34 also DeArmond Davis (n 28) 142–48.

[96] Former German Ambassador to Paris (1874–1885) and Acting Secretary of State (1880–1881) made Chancellor by Wilhelm II in 1894.

[97] DeArmond Davis (n 28) 156–57.

'the train was going to start' and that such tribunal would not interfere with sovereignty.

One reason given in England for support of arbitration was the Duke of Devonshire's speech at the Central Association of Bankers' banquet who said that Britain's armaments had been instrumental in resolving difficulties between France, Russia and the United States. The Duke may have been right in the sense that the potential use of force may convince an adversary that the risk of war is not worth taking and it is better to settle the dispute through diplomatic or an arbitral process.

Arbitration was rejected by Germany because it could mobilise in 10 days and had an advantage. Arbitration would simply give rival powers time to get themselves ready, which would be a great disadvantage to Germany. Compulsory arbitration was therefore rejected by Germany, but it had to agree to the establishment of a Permanent Court of Arbitration upon which Holstein[98] resigned. This was a significant step as it might be said that it laid the foundation for a world organisation of international law.[99]

V. AN INTERNATIONAL COURT OF ARBITRATION

At the Conference there were three commissions: one as to the rules of warfare, another as to maritime warfare and a third on arbitration. The Third Commission was presided over by Mr Leon Bourgeois. Despite the impasse over armaments there was some advance in the proposal for arbitration with the formulation of a scheme of international arbitration by the creation of a Permanent Arbitral Tribunal at The Hague. This had been drafted by a committee of the Institute of International Law and adopted at a meeting of the Institute held at The Hague in 1875. The proposals included offers of mediation, the offer of a state to use its good officers in settling a dispute, and a Permanent Court of Arbitration. Such provisions assisted in the settlement of the Dogger Bank incident and facilitated relations between Russia, France and Britain influencing the *Triple Entente*.[100]

The idea of the Court emerged from a suggestion of Sir Julian Pauncefote.[101] Both the American and German delegates were opposed to this. Captain Mahon of the US Navy was quoted in *Armaments and Arbitration* (1912)[102] as stating that:

> Neither arbitration in a general sense nor arbitration in the more specific form of judicial decision based on a code of law, can always take place, either practically or beneficially, of the processes and results obtained by the free play of natural forces.

[98] An influential member of the German Foreign Office in Berlin from 1876. He never became Foreign Minister but had considerable influence in affecting policy.

[99] Langer (n 61) 589–91.

[100] AW Ward and GP Gooch, *Cambridge History of Foreign Policy 1783–1919* (Cambridge University Press, 2012) Vol 3 '1866–1919', 258–62, 439.

[101] ETS Dugdale, *German Diplomatic Documents 1871–1914* (Methuen & Co Ltd, 1930) Vol III, 76.

[102] AT Mahan, *Armaments and Arbitration* (Kessinger Publishing, republished in 2010).

Count Munster, the First German Delegate, told the Chancellor, Bernhard von Bülow on the 12th June 1899 that the US position was to protect private property at sea. His view was that this was all 'much ado about nothing'.[103] Von Bülow writing to Count Hatzfeldt on 14th June 1899 expressed serious objection to a Permanent Court which would be able to convene after hostilities had commenced. Von Bülow questioned such a court's independence and impartiality. Count Hatzfeldt informed Von Bülow that Salisbury said that the Court was for small claims of compensation not for political questions.[104] The Permanent Court would be optional and not obligatory. Salisbury said it would not deal with such questions as Egypt and Alsace. Von Bülow told the Kaiser that the idea of the court was 'utterly distasteful' but it might be useful to separate the United States from England.[105] Count Munster told Von Bülow on the 30th June 1899 that he had opposed the court which should be 'cut out' and any reference to the court should be strictly optional.[106]

In opening the Second Meeting of the Hague Conference 1899 on 20th May 1899, Mr Stall, the Chairman, said that:

> Following a general law diplomacy is no longer an art in which personal ability plays an exclusive part; its tendency is to become a science which shall have fixed rules for settling international disputes ... Accordingly we shall devote ourselves especially to the generalisation and codification of arbitral practice, and of mediation or good offices.[107]

He went on to proclaim that their general goal was: *the prevention of conflicts by peaceful means* and that 'it was not for us to enter into the domain of Utopia'.

During the two Hague Conferences of 1899 and 1907 three types of arbitration were suggested: universal, inclusive and exclusive obligatory arbitration. The first category, universal obligatory arbitration, was the most far-reaching process and considered impossible by the delegates at the First Hague Conference. It was later rejected by the Committee of Examination at the Second Hague Conference.[108] The second category of inclusive or obligatory arbitration for certain specified classes of international dispute was proposed by Russia at the First Conference and at the Second by Great Britain, Portugal, Sweden and Serbia. This form of arbitration was long debated as a means of international law which would remove the differences between states which might lead to war but would also allow states to argue their case and claim their rights without resorting to force. It appears that these arguments were accepted overall, but the problem was the scope given to such arbitral jurisdiction and the nature of cases referable to the arbitrators.

[103] Dugdale (n 101) 76–77.

[104] *Ibid* 77.

[105] *Ibid* 80.

[106] *Ibid* 81.

[107] J Brown Scott, *The Proceedings of the Hague Peace Conferences. Translation of the Official Texts* (Oxford University Press, 1920) 47.

[108] WI Hall, 'Arbitration and the Hague Conferences' (1908) 2 *American Journal of International Law* 732–42.

The Russian delegation to the First Conference proposed that the following matters would be referred to obligatory arbitration where national honour and vital interests were not concerned:[109] disputes or claims between citizens for pecuniary damages arising from tortious or illegal acts committed by a state or its citizens; claims relating to the interpretation and application of treaties regarding postal, telegraph and communication systems, prevention of collisions at sea, protection of copyright, commercial patents and trademarks; titles, sanitary and veterinary rules, inheritance, extradition, navigation of international waterways, judicial recognition and boundaries of a non-political or technical nature. Italy suggested a further category of reciprocal obligations to the sick and indigent. The German representative, Professor Zorn, opposed a proposal by the Netherlands to include treaties relating to sick and wounded soldiers in time of war. He opposed it because he felt it would impede the military operation as would any arbitration. German objections, however, went much further than Professor Zorn's rejection of the Netherlands proposal. The German Government rejected these suggestions on the basis that Germany had already accepted the jurisdiction of the Permanent Court of Arbitration. A compromise suggested by Professor Martens of Russia that the Conference accept the four categories of jurisdiction contained in the treaties already ratified by the Kaiserreich was also rejected by Germany. Thus, the Conference was unable to agree a universal treaty of obligatory arbitration and concluded that the Powers simply reserved the right to conclude:

> … either before the ratification of the present Convention more subsequent to that date, new agreements, general or particular, with the object of extending obligatory arbitration to all cases which they may consider possible to submit to it.[110]

Although the Convention did not secure a universal compulsory treaty of arbitration, it did succeed in encouraging the execution of 30 treaties where disputes were to be referred to arbitration. Elihu Root opined that this convention was defective in that it did not bind any state to arbitrate or to mediate or even to accept mediation.[111] In this sense he considered that there was too much diplomacy and not enough jurisprudence. What he cogitated was a Permanent Court of Arbitration Justice to resolve inter-state disputes. Like Charles Francis Adams,[112] the American Minister in London during the American Civil War and the American Arbitrator in the Geneva Arbitration, Elihu Root seems to have been like minded in believing that a general observance of international law norms would provide a means for resolving inert state disputes through arbitration, although Root was able to envisage a much wider application which the outbreak of war in 1914 reinforced. This establishment and that of a

[109] Bar-Yacoov (n 55) 21.
[110] Hall (n 108) 731, 734.
[111] Elihu Root, *Address on Opening the National Arbitration and Peace Congress*, New York, 15 April 1907.
[112] Jurist and Arbitrator.

complementary instrument for peacemaking, the inquiry process, were the two major advances of the First Hague Conference.

VI. THE INQUIRY PROCESS

International inquiries stemmed from the provisions of The Hague Conventions 1899 and 1907 which, excluding matters of national honour and vital interests, provided that nations could agree to resolve matters through an impartial and conscientious investigation on any matters arising from a difference of opinion on matters of fact. Brown Scott opined that states would be willing to submit differences to a tribunal even if it involved honour and national interests.[113]

The idea of an inquiry appears to have stemmed from boundary disputes and frontier incidents.[114] Inquiries had been known long before The Hague Conferences and have been classified by Nassim Bar-Yacoov[115] as:

1. Commissions composed of the nationals of the parties of an unequal number, eg the *Saint Croix River Dispute*, and Mixed Commissions under the Jay Treaty.
2. Commissions composed of an equal number of nationals of each party. If they disagreed the matter would be referred to a foreign head of state.
3. Commissions composed of an equal number of nationals. If Commissioners disagreed the matter could be referred to a foreign national appointed by and acting on behalf of a foreign sovereign, eg *United States v Mexico* (1839).
4. Commissions composed of an equal number of nationals where if they disagreed they would choose a foreign national as an umpire (*Italy v Switzerland* dispute over Alp of Cravairola).[116]
5. Commissions composed of an equal number of nationals and a foreign national chosen by the parties and participates in deliberations.[117]
6. Commissions composed of an equal number of nationals and an unequal number of foreign nationals who form a majority, eg the Treaty of Washington 1871 and constitution of the tribunal. This was categorised by Bar Yacoov as an inquiry but in fact it was an arbitration.
7. Commissions composed entirely of foreign nationals, eg the Anglo-Brazilian *Compromis* of 22 April 1873–the Dundonald case.

The benefit of the inquiry was that the disputed facts would be independently investigated and examined by an impartial and independent tribunal

[113] Brown Scott (n 58) 266.

[114] Bustamente y Sirvén, *La Seconde Conférence de la Paix réunie à la La Haye en 1907* (1909) 111–12.

[115] Bar-Yacoov (n 55) 41.

[116] J Bassett Moore, *History and Digest of International Arbitrations to which the United States has been a Party* (Forgotten Books, 2018) Vols 1–VI, 2027–50.

[117] *Ibid* 683–702.

with no interest in the outcome and politically neutral. The moral force of the pronouncement of an international tribunal of inquiry was often sufficient to facilitate a settlement or provide a basis for arbitration.

The Geneva Arbitration as has been considered encouraged international jurists to promote arbitration as a means by which states could settle their differences without resort to war. Certainly, that was the hope of Elihu Root[118] and M Martens.[119] The inquiry could facilitate a settlement based on the commissioner's report; if not it could lead to resolution through mediation or arbitration. Martens believed that an inquiry could find the cause of the dispute which in itself and the time it took in completing the investigation could lower tensions between disputants.[120] In an article published in 1899,[121] M Martens discussed the impasse between the United States and Spain over the sinking of the *USS Maine*. In his opinion this could have been resolved by a commission of inquiry.[122] The United States held its own inquiry which concluded that the Spanish authorities in Cuba were responsible, whilst a Spanish inquiry concluded that the sinking was due to internal causes. The American casualties were high, 260 officers and men. Spain declared war on the United States on 24th April 1898 resulting in the loss of her possessions in the Philippines, Guam and Puerto Rico.[123] Martens also considered the case of M Schnaebelé.[124] M Schnaebelé was the Commissioner of Police of Pagny-sur-Moselle who on the 20th April 1887 was invited to meet Herr Gautsch, Commissary of Police, in Lorraine. Both were arrested by German police and incarcerated in Metz. Schnaebelé was charged with treason (spying) on the German Empire.[125] Bismarck intervened and ordered Schnaebelé's release as he had been invited to meet Herr Gautsch on the border and should be protected by mutually assured safe conduct.[126]

Nassim Bar-Yacoov gives an example of an inquiry of the type later debated at The Hague. This was the French initiative regarding the British dispute with Greece over Don Pacifico, a British subject formerly in the consular service of the Portuguese Government.[127] In 1850 Don Pacifico's house and property were plundered by a mob including some Greek soldiers. He claimed that legal documents regarding his entitlement to certain property were destroyed

[118] Root was a corporate lawyer by profession, a US Attorney and a friend of Theodore Roosevelt. He was later a Secretary of War, and then Secretary of State. He was chief counsel for the United States in the North Atlantic Coast Fisheries Dispute with Great Britain at the Hague Tribunal.

[119] Permanent Member of the Council of the Russian Imperial Ministry for Foreign Affairs, Privy Councillor, delegate plenipotentiary to the Hague Conference.

[120] Bar-Yacoov (n 55) 23.

[121] M Martens, 'International Arbitration and the peace Conference at the Hague' (1899) 169 *North American Review* 604–13.

[122] Bar-Yacoov (n 55) 33.

[123] R Cavendish, 'The United States Battleship was Blown up in an Explosion during Cuba's Uprising against Spain. What Caused the Explosion and who was Responsible?' (1998) 48 *History Today*.

[124] Case reviewed in (1927) 16 *Recueil Des Cours* (Academie De Droit International De La Ha, Hague Academy of International Law).

[125] *The Spectator* (30 April 1887) 4.

[126] *Annual Register*, 1887, 247.

[127] Bar-Yacoov (n 55) 37–39.

in the rampage. The British Government reacted to this by sending a British battle squadron to blockade the Greek coast. France and Russia protested which, along with Britain, were protectors of Greece. An inquiry (two arbitrators and an umpire) was appointed and held that Pacifico was entitled to £150 for the loss of his papers, the originals of which were found in the Cortes at Lisbon. Whilst the episode is famous for British Prime Minister Palmerston's assertive interventionist policy and declaration liking British subjects to Roman Citizens: *Civis Romanus Sum*, it has perhaps a deeper lesson as to how a war could be averted.

At the 1899 Conference, the *comité d'examen* agreed proposals for non-mandatory Commissions of Inquiry which were enacted under Title III of the Convention for the Pacific Settlement of International Disputes whereby states that had agreed through diplomacy to institute an International Commission of inquiry to elucidate the facts by means of an impartial conscience investigation could do so. This process was chiefly concerned therefore with preliminary findings of fact or *actio prejudicialis* not matters of law. The rulings of such commissions would not necessarily be decisive and might result in either a reference to the Permanent Court of Arbitration or in the last resort to war. Their constitution was defined in Article X:

> The International Commissions of Enquiry are constituted by special agreement between the parties in conflict. The Convention for an enquiry defines the facts to be examined and the extent of the Commissioners' powers. It settles the procedure. On the enquiry both sides must be heard. The form and the periods to be observed, if not stated in the enquiry Convention, are decided by the Commission itself.

Article XIV provided for the appointment of Special Agents and Counsel following the prescription of the Geneva Arbitration. Article XV made provision for the use of the parties of facilities at the International Bureau of the Permanent Court of Arbitration in The Hague.

The Commission was empowered to set its own procedure under Article XVIII, but this was to follow the arbitration procedure. Investigations were made through agents and counsel as provided by Article XX. Such commissions took the same form as arbitrations under Article XXXII of the 1899 Convention and under Articles XLV and LVII of the 1907 Convention, the latter dealing with the powers of the Tribunal and the procedure. The procedure provided for site visits, examination of witnesses, disclosure of documentary evidence. Members of the Tribunal had diplomatic immunity. According to Bar-Yacoov, the process was likened to that of Official Referees in England under section 56 of the Judicature Act 1872 in terms of inquiry and report procedure. The Commissioners were to investigate the materiality of the facts without apportioning fault. Bar-Yacoov refers to Goodrich, Hambro and Simons who made a distinction between inquiry and other procedures in their study.[128] They considered that inquiry was not a method of settlement but a means of finding a basis for settlement.

[128] L Goodrich, E Hambro and A Simons, *Charter of the UN*, 3rd edn (Columbia University Press, 1969). N Bar-Yacoov (n 55) 16.

They described mediation and conciliation as procedures by which the parties seek to assist the disputants to reach a settlement in addition to diplomacy. They interpreted inquiry in a wider sense, whereas the definition in Article IX of both conventions has a narrower application confined to commissions of inquiry and report without any binding award on the parties.

The interventionist approach of Russia was resented by the Balkan states which considered that this would be a threat if it were compulsory. Serbia in particular had reservations, as did smaller states which felt threatened by the Great Powers.[129] M Descamps[130] took a different view. He thought that an international court was in the interest of smaller nations as he said: 'Every time that an international court is established in the world, there are more chances for it to serve as a defence for the weak than the strong.'[131] The Luxemburg delegate, Mr Eyschen,[132] thought the inquiry resembled arbitration, as indeed it did, whilst the German delegate said that the inquiry should be distinct from arbitration and each inquiry should set its own procedure. This German objection is interesting in the context of the July crisis of 1914 where Bethmann-Hollweg expressly rejected Grey's plan for a London Conference as a submission to arbitration by a sovereign state.

The key feature of the inquiry by commission was a common agreement by the disputing states to an investigation into the material causes of the dispute where they were unable to settle their differences or disputes through diplomatic channels. Mixed commissions were composed of representatives from the states in dispute to investigate the facts, unlike mixed preparatory diplomatic commissions which negotiated treaties, eg the Treaty of Washington 1871. A mixed arbitral commission rendered a binding award based on law and equity, whereas a mixed commission simply reported the facts as found in its investigation. The origin of such arbitral commissions is to be found in Article VII of the Jay Treaty between the United States and Great Britain which provided that a tribunal 'decide the claims in question acceding to the merits of several cases, and to justice, equity and the laws of nations'. A good example of the inquiry is the case of the Dogger Bank incident which is discussed in chapter 4.

VII. THE PERMANENT COURT OF ARBITRATION

The Permanent Court of Arbitration was established under Article XX of Chapter II of the Convention for the Pacific Settlement of International Disputes. This included a Bureau for administrative purposes and custody of its archives.

[129] N Bar-Yacoov (n 55) 23 and 26.

[130] Senator, delegate plenipotentiary to The Hague Conference.

[131] Bar-Yacoov (n 55) 28.

[132] Minister of State, President of the Grand Ducal Government of Luxemburg, delegate plenipotentiary.

Article XXIV provided:

> Each party appoints two Arbitrators, and these together choose an Umpire. If the votes are equal, the choice of the Umpire is intrusted to a third Power, selected by the parties by common accord. If an agreement is not arrived at on this subject, each party selects a different Power, and the choice of the Umpire is made in concert by the Powers thus selected. The Tribunal being thus composed, the parties notify to the Bureau their determination to have recourse to the Court and the names of the Arbitrators. The Tribunal of Arbitration assembles on the date fixed by the parties. The Members of the Court, in the discharge of their duties and out of their own country, enjoy diplomatic privileges and immunities.

It is important to appreciate the distinction between a Commission of Inquiry and the Permanent Court of Arbitration. In respect of arbitration there was an obligation to accept the award of the tribunal, whereas in an inquiry a state was at liberty to accept or reject the report of its findings. The Permanent Court of Arbitration could decide questions of law and fact; whereas an inquiry could only report on questions of fact. States going to arbitration agreed a special act (*compromis*), whereas an inquiry was preceded by a convention between the two parties. The procedural rules and form for a reference to the Permanent Court of Arbitration were settled under Articles XXIX to LVII of the Convention, whereas the process undertaken by a Commission of Inquiry was to be decided by the Commission itself under Article X. The Permanent Court of Arbitration sat in The Hague, whereas an inquiry could sit where appropriate. An award of the Permanent Court of Arbitration was capable of revision, but an inquiry decision was not. There were no rules of evidence relating to inquiries, nor to costs so that each state paid its own costs and expenses; in arbitration, under the Convention, each party paid their own costs and expenses as well as those of the tribunal in equal shares.

A code of arbitration procedure was adopted by the *comité d'examen* enacted under the 1899 Convention which would avoid as far as possible recourse to force.[133] A model form of arbitration agreement was drafted (*compromis*)[134] and delegates insisted on a right to appeal an Award. The title of the court was agreed as the Permanent Court of Arbitration. In such arbitration each side would pay its own costs and arbitrators' fees. Ominously the *comité d'examen* had reservations over the Balkan states which tended to place national honour before international law or court.[135]

In such cases of serious disagreement or conflict and before any resort to force, the Powers agreed to permit the good offices or mediation of one or more friendly Powers.[136] Third parties also had the right to offer their good offices

[133] Art 1 of The Hague Convention (29 July 1899).
[134] Proceedings, *ibid*, 730–44.
[135] DeArmond Davis (n 28) 172.
[136] Art 2 of the Hague Convention 1899.

during hostilities. The mediator's function was to reconcile the opposing claims and appease the feelings of resentment which may have arisen between the states at variance.[137] This function ceased when it was declared, either by one of the parties to the dispute, or by the mediator himself, that the means of reconciliation proposed by him were not accepted.[138] The good offices or mediation of another state was simply a matter of advice and was not binding.[139] In the context of the July crisis of 1914 it is worth considering that the acceptance of mediation would not have interrupted, delayed or hindered mobilisation or other measures in preparation for war unless the warring parties agreed. If mediation occurred after the commencement of hostilities it also would not have interrupted military operations in progress, unless otherwise agreed.[140] This point was forgotten in July 1914 when there was some discussion between London and Berlin as to the Austro-Hungarian armies halting in Belgrade. As will be noted, Grey's position became difficult when Austria-Hungary declared war on Serbia on 28 July 1914 and Russia mobilised as it could no longer act as mediator. No other country seems to have considered the possibility of a non-aligned country so acting.

The Signatory Powers to the Convention recommended when circumstances permitted a special form of mediation in cases of serious difference endangering the peace. The disputants could entrust a third Power(s) to enter into direct communication with its adversary 'with the object of preventing the rupture of pacific relations'. The third county's mandate was for 30 days unless otherwise agreed. The disputant states could not communicate with each other as the mediating third Power(s) was obliged to use its/their best efforts to settle it. In case of a definite rupture of pacific relations, these Powers were charged with the joint task of 'taking advantage of any opportunity to restore peace'.[141]

In addition to this, the Conference also agreed other conventions, namely, the Convention Regulating the Laws and Customs of Land Warfare 1899 (revised 1907) and adopted the principles of the Geneva Convention of 1864 relating to Maritime warfare. It denounced the use of projectiles from balloons, the diffusion of asphyxiating gases, the use of 'dum-dum' bullets, and later made declarations as to the rights and duties of neutrals, the inviolability of private (enemy) property, and the bombardment of ports, towns and villages by naval forces. The possibility of agreement with regards to arms limitation and defence budgets was mooted but not agreed.[142]

The General Act of the Conference was signed on the 19th of July 1899 by 26 Powers.

[137] Art 4 *ibid.*
[138] Art 5 *ibid.*
[139] Art 6 *ibid.*
[140] Art 7 *ibid.*
[141] Art 8 *ibid.*
[142] It is interesting that this was discussed and most unfortunately no action taken, the matter not being realised until after the Great War.

VIII. SECOND HAGUE PEACE CONFERENCE

A further attempt to gain acceptance for inclusive obligatory arbitration was made by Portugal at the Second Conference in 1907. Portugal's application was based on earlier treaties following the Russian proposal earlier in 1899 and the deliberations of the Inter-Parliamentary Union meeting in London in 1906. The Portuguese proposal included a list of 30 matters appropriate for arbitration, including: working men's protection, the gauging of ships, regulations for commerce and industry, customs duties, commercial procedure, repatriation, salvage and diplomatic and consular questions. These matters were debated in the context of legality, politics and economics, with concern being expressed as to national interests and national independence. The obvious problem was those cases where politics mixed with legality and national interest or sovereignty issues arose.

The attendance of Germany at the Conference had been in some doubt following Lord Haldane's visit to Berlin in early September 1904.[143] The Kaiser was reluctant to participate in any conference which discussed disarmament, but more than that Baron von Bieberstein representing Germany declared that the time was not right for such discussions as he said: 'in prematurely voting obligatory world arbitration we should only scatter seeds of discord among nations'.[144]

A Second Hague Peace Conference was held at the request of the Interparliamentary Union meeting at the St Louis Exposition in 1904. President Theodore Roosevelt suggested that the Conference consider the negotiation of arbitration treaties between the conference states and look at the possibility of establishing an International Congress to convene periodically to discuss international questions. In many respects this anticipated the formation of the League of Nations and the United Nations decades later following world conflagrations. The Conference was interrupted by the Russo-Japanese War and the Russian Revolution until June 1907. A total of 44 governments were represented, sending 256 delegates. Both Britain and the United States insisted on the prohibition of military force for the recovery of contract debts unless the state concerned refused arbitration or ignored the arbitral award. At the Conference the British Government tried to secure restrictions on limitations on armaments and military expenditure. This failed through German opposition. Perhaps like Germany's construction of a modern navy, it was an indication of intent.[145] On the other hand, this Peace Conference was successful in concluding 13 treaties, one declaration, several recommendations and in expressing three aspirations.

[143] FO 371/76 *Diary of Lord Haldane's Visit to Germany* (2 September 1904).

[144] Hall (n 108) 731, 736.

[145] It is further indicative of the subsequent course of events that both Germany and Austria-Hungary opposed a scheme of obligatory arbitration.

There were further discussions on exclusive obligatory arbitration which would exclude certain matters from arbitration tending towards a voluntary form of international dispute resolution. Indeed, the Brazilian delegation suggested that matters to be referred to arbitration should not include any questions which could be settled by diplomacy, good offices, or mediation except matters which affect independence, territorial integrity, essential interests, domestic laws and institutions, or the interests of third parties. But M de Martens[146] of the Russian delegation opposed the Brazilian proposal because it would, in his view, exclude many of the 55 arbitral awards made during the nineteenth century. Despite this there was a consensus as to how a tribunal would deal with questions of interpreting treaties which could not be settled by diplomatic means. A proposal was carefully drafted which excluded questions relating to national interests, independence, honour of states or the interests of third-party states. Understanding national honour was regarded as a sensitive issue, a combination possibly of state sovereignty and national interest, but one where the public were critically involved. After a long debate on these issues the United States and Great Britain favoured a general treaty, Austria-Hungary favoured a treaty 'in theory', whilst 13 small states were in favour of a general treaty of obligatory arbitration, but once again Germany opposed. It seems that the Kaiserreich preferred arbitration treaties between pairs of states. It appears that smaller states may have felt more secure with a form of obligatory arbitration, whereas Germany wanted freedom of movement with a view to *drang nacht osten* (push towards the East).

In the light of subsequent developments, it is interesting to note Germany's objections to compulsory arbitration. It had four main objections to the idea. First, reservations about the name 'obligatory arbitration'. Second that any such treaty would have to be ratified by the US Senate and, in the opinion of the German representative Dr Kriege, such ratification was unlikely. Third, the proposition exhibited little confidence in its objectives. Finally, Germany objected because such a global treaty would jeopardise bilateral arbitration treaties between states. In committee Dr Kriege was supported by the diplomatic skills of Baron von Bieberstein and M Mercy of Austria-Hungary. They questioned the enforceability and recognition awards in third-party states and whether it might be binding on them even though they were not parties. They also questioned the risk of legislatures failing to ratify the treaty especially in the United States and Great Britain, and whether there should be a separate treaty governing each dispute. Dr Scott of the United States and Professor Renault of France argued against Germany and Austria-Hungary and they were supported by Sir Edward Fry for England and Dr Drago and Professor de Martens of Russia. Their argument was that any general arbitration treaty would not impede any separate bilateral treaties, but would encourage arbitration globally. Sir Edward Fry

[146] Professor of International Law at the University of St Petersburg and Permanent member of the Ministry for Foreign Affairs of Russia, Member of the Russian Delegation at The Hague Peace Conference. President of the Venezuelan Arbitration Tribunal 1899.

argued that such a treaty would be: 'the expression of the conscience of the civilised world'.

When the vote was taken, 35 delegates were in favour of the treaty and nine were against wanting a postponement. The latter included Germany, Austria-Hungary, Greece, Romania, Turkey, Belgium, Bulgaria and Switzerland. Despite this a declaration was issued to the effect that the Second Peace Conference had recognised the principle of obligatory arbitration so that there was no impediment to arbitrating any matter of interpretation or application of international treaties.[147] The key outcomes of the Conference were the adoption of arbitration as a means of recovering debt and the establishment of the International Prize Court.[148] The International Prize Court, which was proposed by the British representative Sir Edward Fry, was a major achievement and the first truly organised court in history.[149]

What is interesting to note here in the light of the events of late July 1914 is the Kaiserreich's acceptance in principle of bilateral arbitration treaties, which in July 1914 Bethmann-Hollweg and Jagow rejected.[150] In that case they would not accept Austria-Hungary as a sovereign state submitting to the jurisdiction of an international tribunal. This raises many questions, which are addressed in chapter 7.

The conventions related to the pacific settlement of international disputes, the use of force, the laws and customs of land warfare, the rights and duties of neutrals in time of war, status of merchant ships, the conversion of merchant ships into warships, the laying of mines at sea, bombardments by naval forces, adoption of the principles of the Geneva Convention 1906 to Maritime warfare, the rights of capture of vessels, the establishment of an International Prize Court[151] and finally the rights and duties of neutral powers in naval warfare. So far as the Prize Court was concerned it was good to be staffed by 'jurists of known proficiency in questions of international maritime law and of the highest moral reputation'. It is interesting to note that the Convention for an International Prize Court provided inter alia Article VII:

> If a question of law to be decided is covered by a treaty in force between the belligerent captor and a Power which is itself or whose subject or citizen is a party to the

[147] Hall (n 108) 731, 741.

[148] *Ibid* 731, 742.

[149] *Ibid.*

[150] *Grey to Goschen Ambassador at Rome* (28 July 1914) BD (n 62) Vol 11, No 68. German Government accepted principle of mediation between Austria-Hungary and Russia by the four powers if necessary. This had earlier been confirmed by Prince Lichnowsky in his talks with Sir Edward Grey at the Foreign Office on 27 July 1940. BD (n 62) Vol 11, No 46.

Grey then confirmed to Goschen that he had asked the German Government to suggest any form of mediation between Austria-Hungary and Russia. As we shall see there was no dispute between Austria-Hungary and Russia but Austria-Hungary and Serbia. Germany interpreted Grey's initiative as arbitration and Jago seems to have raised some legal technicality which obstructed discussions between the Powers.

[151] Whilst agreed in principle as to constitution and function, it was impossible to reconcile the different approaches as between the civil law and common law rules of procedure.

> proceedings, the court is governed by the provisions of the said treaty. In the absence of such provisions the court shall apply the rules of international law. If no generally recognised rule exists, the court shall give judgement in accordance with the general principles of justice and equity.

This Convention was the product of experience in the resolution of numerous claims and counterclaims by belligerents and neutrals dating from the time of the Napoleonic Wars[152] to the American Civil War and the Russo-Japanese War. The American Civil War gave rise to claims by Great Britain against the United States in respect of English vessels being seized by the Federal Navy and United States' claims against Great Britain in respect of Confederate cruisers being constructed in England. In the Russo-Japanese War, Russia's Baltic Fleet sank two British trawlers and damaged others on its way to attack the Japanese fleet. This nearly caused a war between Russia and England, but fortunately the matter was settled, and war avoided. Thus, it was thought that these conventions enabling the enforcement of international law through a judicial system not only could contain the spread of war but contribute to its avoidance. However, all this was not to be because the Powers could not reach agreement at this Second Peace Conference because there were too many diverging views and practices. Sir Edward Grey thought that an International Prize Court was not acceptable because its jurisdiction would interfere with naval policy and practice. No agreement could be reached until the rules of law and principles of justice could be agreed at another conference.

The conference met in London on the 4 December 1908. The aim of this conference was to set out a code of international maritime law. The conference succeeded in agreeing a declaration, the Declaration of London[153] which was given on 26 February 1909 and included 71 articles concerning the law of blockade, contraband, continuous voyage, hostile aid or unneutral service, the destruction of natural prizes, the transfer of flag, enemy character and the right of convoy. Some of the rules that were applied originate from disputes that occurred during the American Civil War and British privateers' attempts to run the Federal blockade and such events as the Trent affair where Confederate agents Mason and Slidell were taken from a neutral British ship. Unfortunately for international law the Declaration of London was never ratified owing to opposition in the House of Lords.

[152] eg The Prussian Decree 28th March 1806, the Berlin Decree 14th October 1806 and the Milan Decree 17th December 1807 which were countered by the British Orders in Council dated respectively: 8th April 1806, 16th May 1806 and 7th January 1807.

[153] More importantly perhaps from the point of view of peaceful resolution of international disputes was the recommendation of the symmetry powers to adopt and enforce a convention of 35 articles for an organisation of a Court of Arbitral Justice. Unfortunately, this proposal was opposed by many smaller states. It provided for a permanent court of competent judges representing the various juridical systems of the world who would be appointed for a term of 12 years and capable of reappointment. The judges were to meet at The Hague once a year as necessary in the month of June to decide the allocation of cases and designate three judges to try them. Unfortunately, the Powers were unable to agree upon the constitution of the court or the selection of trial judges.

The real problem here seemed to be that nation states were unwilling to surrender sovereignty to an international court and what prevented progress towards the International Prize Court of the Judicial Arbitral Court at that time was a lack of adequate process to enforce the Court's decision.

Between 1872 and 1909, the Great Powers and many other states had attempted to bring about a framework of international order based on a form of arbitration overlaying the Congress system. Whilst arbitration proved successful between friendly powers which had fallen out, it was much more difficult to reconcile disputes between states where for reasons of aggrandisement such states disregarded diplomatic norms and sought political gain at others' expense. From the beginning of the twentieth century, we see evidence of this at Morocco, Agadir, Tangier, Casablanca, and in the Balkan crises of 1912–13 leading up to the Sarajevo assassination and its aftermath.

IX. CONCLUSIONS ON THE HAGUE CONFERENCES

The significant achievement of the 1899 Conference was the constitution of the Permanent Court of Arbitration, a scheme for inquiries and special form of mediation and a procedural code. It involved 26 governments representing seven-eighths of the world's population.[154] Whilst hopes were high of an understanding between nation states to secure world peace, such hopes were illusory. The imperial Powers Britain, France, Russia and Germany were soon involved in a competing naval and military arms race. Britain was involved in a colonial war in South Africa, the United States in an imperial war with Spain, and Russia was engaged in a war with Japan by 1905. Whilst some progress towards resolving inter-state conflicts was made, it was mainly in the area of matters which could be resolved by international law. The high-minded aspiration of the Secretary of the Peace Society, W Evans Darby, that it placed civilised mankind on 'a level of potential advantage' and was 'a great forward movement of humanity' whilst laudable was utopian. The dream of a 'Universal Parliament of Peace' or a 'Federation of the World' and that 'arbitration would replace the sword' was unrealised in terms of *realpolitik*.

In terms however of constructive progress towards peace there was some progress in arbitration with references to the Permanent Court of Arbitration. In the decade before the Conference there were 51 arbitrations involving the United States, Britain, France, Germany, Russia and Italy. After 1899 and ratification of the Convention, there were 63 cases involving those states with 10 referred to the Permanent Court of Arbitration.[155] *Wheaton's Elements of international Law*[156]

[154] Evans Darby (n 3).
[155] Cases cited in AM Stuyt, *Survey of International Arbitrations 1794–1938* (Martinus Nijhoff, 1939).
[156] *Wheaton's Elements of international Law* (edited by Coleman Phillipson) (Stevens & Sons, 1916).

states that there were 228 cases referred to arbitration under the Jay Treaty between 1794 and 1899; 137 held after the Geneva Arbitration of 1871, and 250 cases referred to Commissions or Boards. The Hague Convention of 1899 may be counted as a considerable advancement in that as between 1900 and 1908 there were 67 treaties which included arbitration provisions.

6

Diplomacy as an Instrument of Prevention

I. THE ANGLO-AMERICAN ARBITRATION TREATY

CHAPTER 3 CONSIDERED a background of increasing harmony between Britain and America culminating in the Anglo-Venezuelan Treaty of Arbitration of 1897 and in chapter four we saw how relations became more difficult for Britain to protect its interests under the Clayton-Bulwer Treaty 1850 and the Hay-Pauncefote Treaty of 1901 notwithstanding the Anglo-American Arbitration Treaty of 1908 and the support given to it by Presidents Roosevelt and Taft.

A. The American Approach

At the time the Treaty was signed, it appeared to be a landmark in Anglo-American relations because, in effect, both states were covenanting that they would not go to war with each other to settle any differences or disputes. President Taft's view was that:

> Questions of national honour and of vital interest include all those questions, the agitation of which is likely to lead to war, and, therefore, arbitration treaties which except such questions may be said to be treaties for the settlement of those questions that never would involve war in their settlement anyhow.[1]

In concept it gave expression to the peace movement and to those lawyers who perceived a world governed by an international rule of law. However, to pragmatic politicians in Britain and America it was welcomed with a degree of caution and even more so by some lawyer-politicians in the Senate. Whilst Elihu Root as Secretary of State had succeeded with the ratification of 24 bilateral arbitration treaties through the Senate, they had passed because they did not offend the vital interests, honour or independence of the United States and were all subject to a two-thirds majority vote in the Senate.[2]

[1] WH Taft, *Popular Government: Its Essence, Its Permanence, and Its Perils* (Yale University Press, 1913) 261.

[2] RW Leopold, *Elihu Root and the Conservative Tradition* (Little Brown and Company, 1954) 57.

Taft's proposed treaties with Britain and France included the all-embracing reference in the scope of the arbitration to include:

> All differences hereafter arising between the high contracting parties, which it has not been possible to adjust by diplomacy, relating to international matters in which the high contracting parties are concerned by virtue of a claim of right made by one against the other under treaty or otherwise, and which are justiciable in their nature by reason of being susceptible of decision by the application of the principles of law or equity …[3]

Whilst Root believed that international law and treaties were a guarantee against war and that diplomacy was its instrument, diplomacy in his view dealt with symptoms and ignored causes. Root supported the Treaty but he had reservations. He argued that the Treaty was too sweeping in its obligations and imposed wide commitments. He proposed to include a resolution on ratification as to how such obligations should be interpreted. As we shall note, in Sir Edward Grey's view it completely vitiated the Treaty.[4] Root and others preferred that the United States renewed the 1908 Treaty with Britain.

When the Senate Foreign Relations Committee submitted its reports on the treaties, they caused much debate. Attention focused on the meaning of the term 'justiciable' which greatly concerned the Senate and its powers to challenge any *compromis* or to check or amend such in defiance of a decision of the Joint High Commission.[5] Exception was taken to the fourth line of Article I of the General Arbitration Treaty 1911 as to claims of right that were justiciable between the parties without any reservation as to the national interest or national honour. The clause stated:

> All differences hereafter arising between the high contracting parties, which it has not been possible to adjust by diplomacy, relating to international matters in which the high contracting parties are concerned by virtue of a claim of right made by one against the other under treaty or otherwise, and which are justiciable in their nature by reason of being susceptible of decision by the application of the principles of law or equity …[6]

Under Article III of the Treaty the Joint High Commission was given power not only to examine and investigate the facts of the dispute to ascertain that such existed, but it was empowered to determine that the matter was within a tribunal's jurisdiction. In other words, the matter was taken out of Senate control.

[3] Art 1 of the General Arbitration Treaty Between Great Britain and The United States. Signed at Washington, 3 August 1911.

[4] Foreign Office Papers (FO) 800/83/2jj *Private Offices: Various Ministers' and Officials Papers Grey, Sir Edward (Viscount). United Sates of America. Folios 10–13: Letter from James Bryce to Sir Edward Grey* (3 January 1911).

[5] JP Campbell, 'Taft Roosevelt and the Arbitration Treaties of 1911' (1966) 53 *The Journal of American History* 279–98, 281.

[6] Article 1 of the General Arbitration Treaty 1911.

The offending clauses stated:

> Article III
>
> The Joint High Commission of Inquiry, instituted in each case as provided for in Article II, is authorized to examine into and report upon the particular questions or matters referred to it, for the purpose of facilitating the solution of disputes by elucidating the facts, and to define the issues presented by such questions, and also to include in its report such recommendations and conclusions as may be appropriate.
>
> ...
>
> It is further agreed, however, that in cases in which the parties disagree as to whether or not a difference is subject to arbitration under Article I of this treaty, that question shall be submitted to the Joint High Commission of Inquiry; and if all or all but one of the members of the commission agree and report that such difference is within the scope of Article I, it shall be referred to arbitration in accordance with the provisions of this treaty.

President Taft regarded Article III as the most important clause of the Treaty, but it was strongly rejected by Senator Henry Cabot Lodge as this would remove the Senate's power to decide what was justiciable.[7] The Senate could not delegate its responsibilities to an international commission.[8] The objection was to those 'traditional attitudes of the United States concerning American questions or other purely governmental policy'.[9] Theodore Roosevelt wrote to an editor that he did not state his opposition as strongly as he might: it made him 'indignant'.[10] John Bassett Moore argued that every *compromis*, whether submitted under Article I or as a result of a commission under Article III, would be subject to the advice of the Senate. In January 1912 Lodge proposed a compromise resolution where the Senate could reject any reference to arbitration and also confirm the appointment of any American commissioners.[11] Taft agreed this compromise. But when the Senate debated it, they excluded matters relating to the Monroe Doctrine, immigration, the admissibility of aliens to educational institutions and the territorial integrity or alleged indebtedness of any states.[12]

Taft found the amendments unacceptable and refused to ratify the Treaty. His enthusiasm for the Treaty was taken up in part by William Jennings Bryan, Secretary of State in Woodrow Wilson's administration. Bryan negotiated more

[7] Campbell (n 5) 282.

[8] JE Noyes, 'William Howard Taft and the Taft Arbitration Treaties' (2011) 56 *Villanova Law Review* 535, 546.

[9] Campbell (n 5) 282.

[10] T Roosevelt (1911) Theodore Roosevelt Papers: Series 3: Letters Sent, 1919; Subseries 3A: Carbon Copies of Letters Sent, 1894 to 1919; Vol 27, 1911, Sept 11–22. [Manuscript/Mixed Material] Retrieved from the Library of Congress, www.loc.gov/item/mss382990496/.

[11] Campbell (n 5) 284.

[12] Passed at Executive Session Senate of the United States. Legislative Day 5 March 1912.

than two dozen dispute settlement treaties in Latin America, Europe and Asia similar to the ones Knox had negotiated.[13] In Bryan's version the Joint High Commission was omitted in favour of a Conciliation Commission to investigate and give a non-binding recommendation.

B. The British Approach

At this time Anglo-American relations were focussed on three key issues: the Panama Canal Tolls, the Declaration of London[14] and the Arbitration Treaty. The adherence of the United States was considered crucial, especially considering the declared German intention regarding the treatment of food supplies as contraband of war. This still awaited approval by the Senate and Bryce was later told that the matter was postponed.[15]

In early January 1911, Sir Edward Grey wrote to Bryce hoping that the Arbitration Treaty would 'set a good public example'.[16] Bryce suggested that Grey encourage the idea that the United States Government should make a proposal to Britain.[17] Bryce took the view that Elihu Root's support was 'of the utmost consequence'.[18] This proved true later when Root took exception to the Treaty and promoted a Resolution in the Senate vitiating the Treaty. Grey met with Whitelaw Reid, the American Ambassador in London, on 8 April and stressed to him the importance of a preamble or provision in the Treaty of the desires of the two countries never to resort to war but to settle differences peaceably. This would show Europe a good example and reduce the need for the high expenditure on armaments. Reid said that the attachment to the Monroe Doctrine was still very strong in the United States.[19] This meant that matters of national policy should be excluded which caused Grey concern. Bryce could assure the President that Britain had no intention of acquiring any territory on the American continent.[20] Bryce reported that he had problems with the laziness of Knox and concerns about resolutions against the Treaty in the Senate, especially German American hostility.[21] The process was slow, and Bryce was anxious that it proceed to the Senate as quickly as possible.[22] Bryce asked Grey to confirm that Britain would not refer any question of the American fortification of the canal to arbitration under the Treaty. Grey appeared willing to accept this, although

[13] Noyes (n 8) 535, 550.
[14] FO 800/83/1 *Bryce to Grey* (1 April 1911).
[15] FO 800/83/1 *Bryce to Grey* (23 May 1911).
[16] FO 800/83/1 *Grey to Bryce* (6 January 1911).
[17] FO 800/83/1 *Bryce to Grey* (16 January 1911).
[18] FO 800/83/1 *Bryce to Grey* (17 March 1911).
[19] FO 800/83/1 *Grey to Bryce* (3 April 1911).
[20] FO 800/83/1 *Grey to Bryce* (11 May 1911).
[21] FO 800/83/1 *Bryce to Grey* (16 May 1911).
[22] FO 800/83/1 *Bryce to Grey* (19 May 1911).

such fortification was contrary to Article I of the Clayton-Bulwer Treaty, but not the Hay-Pauncefote Treaty.[23] On 5 June 1911, Bryce wrote to Grey urging the cabinet to complete the draft Treaty so it could go to the Senate. He was worried that the Senate might adjourn. Knox was raising questions as to what would be arbitrable and confirmation that this would exclude domestic matters. Bryce suggested some simple alterations to expedite the matter such as insertion of the word 'internationally' that would qualify the term 'justiciable'.[24] Whilst passage seemed elusive, Bryce had some success when the United States accepted the Declaration of London.[25] Bryce continued to press for the Treaty, but Knox wanted to use the Treaty as a precedent for treaties with France and Germany. Dealing with three countries at the same time in Bryce's view would make the process interminable. Knox was adamant as to the application of international law and references to arbitration that were 'internationally justiciable'. Knox wanted a legal determination rather than a compromise excluding domestic and policy matters.[26] As we have seen, by no means were the Geneva, or Behring Sea arbitration tribunals a compromise, but very much a legal impartial determination of great credit to the lawyers, diplomats and jurists involved.

On 3 August 1911, Bryce's objective was realised when the Treaty was signed, as he wrote to Grey: 'The definite renunciation of war as a means of settling disputes is an event of moment in the annals of the world …'[27] The signing of the Treaty probably marked the pinnacle of Bryce's career in Washington in so far as he had in a sense guided and engineered the epilogue to the family quarrel between the two great English-speaking nations. The signing was only a stage in the fight for the Treaty and neither Bryce nor Grey may have appreciated the legal and political challenges Taft and Knox faced in the Senate and the country.

Bryce felt that his job in Washington was complete, Grey said that he would find him very difficult to replace. He praised Bryce for his 'tremendous public service' in improving relations with both Canada and the United States.[28] Before Bryce left Washington, he reported that Taft was under political pressure from German and Irish émigré organisations in the United States that perceived the Treaty as one of alliance.[29] That was not the only pressure and was rather minor in comparison with the political, constitutional and legal issues.

Both Knox and Taft had to argue on those fronts. On the legal arguments Knox argued that some disputes were arbitrable, but others were not. The latter

[23] FO 800/83/1 *Bryce to Grey* (23 May 1911) and FO 800/83/2 *Bryce to Grey* (27 June 1911).
[24] FO 800/83/2 *Bryce to Grey* (5 June 1911).
[25] FO 800/83/2 *Bryce to Grey* (12 June 1911).
[26] FO 800/83/2 *Bryce to Grey* (27 June 1911).
[27] FO 800/83/2 *Bryce to Grey* (8 August 1911).
[28] FO 800/83/1 *Grey to Bryce* (11 March 1911).
[29] FO 800/83/3 *Bryce to Grey* (December 1911). Private Memorandum.

could be referred to an inquiry, investigation and advice.[30] Knox, despite Bryce's reservations about him, was an ardent advocate of the Treaty:

> The treaties rest upon the theory that arbitration is a judicial function and represents a principle, namely, the application of law and judicial methods to the determination of international disputes, and that I case to be one for arbitration must involve differences susceptible of being decided by the application of acknowledged principles of justice-that is to say, a justiciable difference.[31]

The Treaty, which was the same as that made between the United States and France, enabled any 'justiciable' controversy to be referred to arbitration and did not exclude matters of national honour or vital national interests unlike the 1908 treaties. Whatever the subsequent controversy raised by émigré communities in America, these fundamental matters would raise concern at domestic level in the United States because of adherence to the Monroe Doctrine and acknowledgement of President George Washington's Farewell Address warning about foreign alliances. But as many American international lawyers and academics argued, this was balanced by respect for a rule of law model embodied in the United States Constitution which gave the United States Supreme Court federal jurisdiction (as it did the federal courts) across all the states of the Union. Thus, as Noyes opined, such a movement for international arbitration and adjudication was not regarded by them as 'foreign'.[32]

In the Treaty the term 'difference' was qualified in that it had to arise in the future that could not be resolved by diplomacy, it had to be an international matter, and arise under a claim of right under a treaty or otherwise, and it had to be justiciable in its nature as determined by the Joint High Commission[33] applying the principles of law and equity. Such terms caused serious debates in the Senate. The word 'Equity' has a definite meaning in English Law but not in the French. The French jurisprudence offered a wider application of the English word in that it could be interpreted as 'equally right or just to all concerned' and 'the application of conscience'. This meant the Treaty had little limitation save what was considered 'justiciable'.[34] Whilst many in the Senate opposed the Treaty on these grounds, they seem to have ignored precedent, eg, Article XII of the Treaty of Washington 1871. Taft construed 'law and equity' to mean the terms as 'understood in law and international law'.[35] This was opposed, but Taft countered this by reference to the Federal court's jurisdiction over the states.[36]

Knox faced opposition from Root who argued that the Treaty should state what matters were not arbitrable. This was problematic because it might exclude

[30] Speech at Cincinnati, 8 November 1911.
[31] Senate Doc 298, 62nd Congress, 2nd Session, 4.
[32] Noyes (n 8) 535, 540.
[33] Article II of the Treaty Between Great Britain and the United States 1911.
[34] Senate Doc 98, 62nd Congress, 1st Session, 4–5.
[35] President Taft Address, Mountain Lake Park, 7 August 1911.
[36] Noyes (n 8) 535, 547.

matters in the same class which were sui generis under the principle *expressio unius est exclusio alterius*.[37]

As to constitutional issues, the crux of the argument concerned the power of the Senate. The Senate Committee objected to the Joint High Commission's membership under Article III confined and open to 'disinterested outsiders'. Furthermore, the terms of reference of the Joint High Commission were to be settled by exchange of Notes with no provision for submission to the Senate. The Joint High Commission could then refer matters to arbitration under Article III. It was the Joint High Commission that could decide whether the question was arbitrable under Article I, not the Senate. The Senate Committee regarded Article III as depriving it of 'its constitutional power to pass upon all questions involved in any treaty submitted to it in accordance with the constitution'.[38] This was despite the fact that three Commissioners would be approved by the Senate if a proposed Ratification Resolution to that effect were passed. Senator Burton argued that any special agreement to arbitrate would require Senate approval, but the Senate could refuse, in which case the United States would be in breach of the Treaty. Knox argued that if the governments agreed to arbitrate the agreement would be sent to the Senate and if the governments did not agree the matter would be determined by the Joint High Commission. The Commission would determine whether there was a dispute, if that was their finding then the parties Britain and the United States would still have to agree the terms of reference and that agreement would be sent to the Senate for approval.[39] Despite this riposte, further concern was raised by Root's amendment in January 1912[40] because Grey considered this would mean that nothing could be arbitrated if it were not in the United States' interest to arbitrate. Grey was anxious that any Senate Resolution would have marginal effect and that nothing would inhibit reference to the Joint Commission to determine whether the matter was referable to arbitration. Bryce felt that the 'Lodge Resolution' then before the Senate, which according to Taft would take weeks to debate, did not seriously affect the main purpose of the Treaty.[41] By 12 February 1912, Bryce was reporting better news in that the Root resolution was not being pressed and the Lodge resolution was not problematic,[42] but by the 30 April before Bryce's departure for New Zealand he reported further delay until November 1912.[43] It is arguable that the amendment presented by Senator Lodge clarified any ambiguity under Article III. Lodge might well have removed the constitutional objection, although it is difficult to understand why any submission seeking the interpretation of a treaty

[37] This would exclude other matters of the same class not expressly mentioned in the Treaty.
[38] Senate Doc 98, 62nd Congress, 1st Session, 5–6.
[39] Senate Doc 298, 62nd Congress, 2nd Session, 8.
[40] FO 800/83/3 *Grey to Bryce* (18 January 1912).
[41] FO 800/83/3 *Bryce to Grey* (23 January 1912).
[42] FO 800/83/3 *Bryce to Grey* (12 February 1912).
[43] FO 800/83/3 *Bryce to Grey* (30 April 1912).

to arbitrate could be unconstitutional. Knox did not find any non-conformity in the Lodge amendment.[44] The Senate rejected that argument and by a majority of two deleted Article III (3) of the Treaty so that the Joint High Commission could not determine justiciability. Although the Senate passed the Treaty with amendment and deletion of Article III (3) removing the Joint High Commission, Taft refused to ratify it. Even though Taft wanted to ratify it in its unamended form, he lost his re-election campaign and was replaced by Woodrow Wilson. It was left to Wilson's Secretary of State, William Jennings Bryan, to progress. It was another setback for Bryce when Roosevelt also opposed the Treaty, not because of Britain but because such Treaty could have been applied to other states other than those of the British Empire.[45]

In view of the problems Bryce wrote to tell Grey that he would stay in Washington until the new administration took over and the Panama Canal Tolls question was settled.[46] On 24 January 1912, Grey told Bryce that if the Panama Tolls question was not settled he would refuse to renew the Arbitration Treaty that was coming up for renewal.[47] But it was not so much that approach which killed the Treaty but the opposition of Senator Elihu Root whose amendment negated its purpose.[48]

On 23 June 1913, Spring Rice[49] sent a despatch to Grey reporting difficulty over German and Irish interests objecting to the Arbitration Treaty being ratified if it risked a possibility of the Panama Canal matter being referred to arbitration.[50] Whilst the Congress was willing to accept an arbitration treaty with France, they were not willing to renew the treaty with Britain because of Panama.[51] Some opposition in the Senate came from Senator O'Gorman of New York who was not only anti-British, but an agent of a coastwise shipping trust. Opposition also came from the trust's supporters in the German Hamburg-Amerika and Nord Deutsch Lloyd Line who had invested in O'Gorman's trust.[52] In his despatch to Grey it appears that Spring Rice had more constructive proposals rather than simply keeping silent as Bryce had suggested, but nothing like what the German Government had threatened – imprisoning American officials who conducted what they believed to be illegal inquisitions on German territory. If the German Government did this Spring Rice opined that the other

[44] Senator Root's Minority Report, Senate Doc 98, 62nd Congress, 1st Session, 9.

[45] HAL Fisher, *James Bryce* (Macmillan and Co Limited, 1927) 72.

[46] FO 800/83/3 *Bryce to Grey* (21 January 1913).

[47] FO 800/83/3 *Grey to Bryce* (24 January 1913).

[48] *Grey to Bryce* (17 September 1912) cited in Fisher (n 45) 71.

[49] Sir Cecil Spring Rice was of Anglo-Irish extraction and educated at Eton and Oxford and became a member of the Foreign Office who served with distinction in several British embassies. During his tenure he developed an expertise in Anglo-American relations through his visits to the United States and his close friendship with President and Mrs Roosevelt and other senior American officials. In 1912 he became British Ambassador to the United States.

[50] FO 800/83/4 *Spring Rice to Grey* (23 June 1913).

[51] *Ibid.*

[52] *Ibid.*

powers could retaliate with tariffs-*lex talionis*.[53] In a further despatch of 7 July 1913, Spring Rice suggested that it was not so much anti-British sentiment but dislike of the arrangement, in effect, their obligation under the Clayton-Bulwer Treaty that fuelled the opposition to an arbitration treaty.[54] He explained that the mood in the United States was then in favour of protectionism, so he was not as optimistic of settlement on the canal question as was the new American Ambassador, Hines Page, in London. In a more disturbing report, Spring Rice said that the United States seemed to be making a protectorate of the Caribbean and Central America and intending to exert its predominance over South America.[55] Mexico was causing problems and there was concern about war between the United States and Mexico in which Spring Rice advised a policy of 'friendly aloofness'.[56]

Apart from Spring Rice's perceptions, the Senate's opposition also stemmed from concern that the United States was delegating power to an international tribunal. Taft had rejected that argument because in *Geoffrey v Riggs*[57] the Court did not find any concern in that regard and in any event such objection had never been raised in any previous inter-state arbitration to which the United States had been a party.[58]

When Sir William Tyrell, Grey's Private Secretary, who had helped the embassy during Spring Rice's illness that year, returned to London from Washington on the 8 December 1913, he received a private letter from Bryan inviting Britain to make further suggestions on the Arbitration Treaty. Bryan sent a copy of the treaty they had made with Salvador for consideration.[59]

Considering all the tension in Europe, the Balkans and the diplomatic issues that arose with the United States and the resignation of Bryce, there must have been some added anxiety in the Foreign Office when Grey received a letter from Spring Rice dated 30 December 1913. The letter warned, if that were needed, that if civil war broke out in Ireland, America would be involved on both sides so that such a conflict would resemble the Civil War of the United States.[60] This was another reason why perhaps the Arbitration Treaty was regarded as a matter of some urgency because the Ulster-Home Rule crisis might foreseeably escalate not only into an Irish civil war between the Nationalist and Ulster Volunteers, but attract support in the United States. Such eventuality might have had very serious consequences in relations between Britain and America. It might well have resulted in a reversal of circumstances that led to the Geneva Arbitration in 1871.

[53] *Ibid*.
[54] FO 800/83/4 *Spring Rice to Grey* (7 July 1913).
[55] FO 800/83/4 *Spring Rice to Grey* (21 July 1913).
[56] FO 800/83/4 *Spring Rice to Grey* (19 August 1913).
[57] *Geoffrey v Riggs* 133 US 258 (1889).
[58] Noyes (n 8) 535, 547.
[59] FO 800/83/4 *Jennings Bryan to Tyrell* (13 December 1913).
[60] FO 800/83/4 *Spring Rice to Grey* (30 December 1913).

C. Conclusion: A Closer Relationship, but So Far and No Further

If the 1911 treaty envisaged by Taft, Knox, Grey and Bryce had been ratified by the Senate unamended it would have been epoch-making and cemented a relationship that had been fractured in 1776, partly restored by the Treaty of Ghent of 1814, narrowed by the resolution of the Geneva, Behring Sea and Anglo-Venezuelan arbitrations, and further reconciled in the Hay-Pauncefote Treaty only to be deflected by the Panama Canal Act and Root's opposition to the Treaty in 1911. Certainly, it appears that a closer relationship developed in the late 80s and 90s, but the Olney-Pauncefote negotiation failed through political reservations. It may also be concluded that the international jurists and lawyers were much ahead of the politicians in Britain and America, although Campbell has noted in *Anglo-American Understanding*[61] the 'exuberant affection' shown in America for Britain at that time. Certainly, Root and Knox as lawyer-politicians made considerable progress but there was a limit to which a sovereign state would go in surrendering to an international tribunal. The rescript of Nicholas II which was the catalyst for the Hague Conferences sparked a keen interest in international arbitration amongst jurists and statesmen, but the number of cases referred to the Permanent Court of Arbitration were few before 1914. Further, although Jennings Bryan and Elihu Root managed to arrange 22 bilateral treaties each during their tenures in office, even the United States would not accept universal arbitration.

Root's opposition to the 1911 treaties resembled his opposition to the Covenant of the League of Nations. He considered both far-fetched, and in terms of the 1911 Treaty the United States would not follow it when it was required. He opposed the Covenant of 1919 as he said: '… to accept sweeping obligations that might not be respected in the future was a hindrance, not a help, to World Peace.'[62]

Taft was a great advocate of the rule of international law and wanted a Permanent International Court after the Great War of 1914–18. He later supported the United States' membership of the League of Nations and the Statute of the Permanent Court of Arbitration at The Hague which his country rejected. In his article, Noyes speculates on what might have happened if the United States had become a member of the League and joined the Court.[63] Taft's argument was that such a court would provide more certainty than numerous tribunals appointed under various bilateral treaties, possibly he had in mind the way in which his court, the Supreme Court of the United States' federal jurisdiction,

[61] C Campbell, *Anglo-American Understanding* (John Hopkins Press, 1957) 49.

[62] Richard W Leopold, *Elihu Root and the Conservative Tradition* (Little Brown and Company, 1954) 128.

[63] Noyes (n 8) 535, 552.

gave certainty to the laws of the United States.[64] Otherwise he might well have seen the experiments in inter-state arbitration as a means to that end.

Lawyers such as Root, John Bassett Moore and James Brown Scott, whilst supporting arbitration as a means to resolve legal disputes, had reservations as to how far that could be extended when political matters came into play. The problem was that it was often difficult to distinguish what was a political and what was a legal matter. Thus, the 1897 Treaty was rejected, the Hay-Durand Treaty 1904 was withdrawn, but the Root-Bryce Treaty 1908 was accepted and renewed, and the Knox-Bryce Treaty 1911 was rejected by President Taft following the resolution on ratification. It was the wide scope of the 1897 and 1911 treaties that defeated them; in effect, 'all questions of difference incapable of being addressed by diplomacy were referred to arbitration':[65] this was a step too far. Article I of the Root-Bryce Treaty 1908 had purposely explicitly referred to 'differences of a legal nature' or 'relating to interpretation of treaties' and subject to the proviso that the reference to the Permanent Court of Arbitration did not affect 'the vital interests, the independence or the honour of the two contracting states, and do not concern the interests of third parties'.[66] In the final analysis the question of the national interest was a paramount consideration and when that clashed with a legal question it was the political consideration that was the overriding force. This is demonstrated in the cases where there was submission of claims as in the Geneva, Behring Sea and Anglo-Venezuelan arbitrations and in the Dogger Bank Inquiry, but when the critical moment came in 1914 the German Reich and the Austro-Hungarian Empire refused to submit to an international tribunal. What this line of treaties and disputes tended to demonstrate was that inter-state disputes could be resolved by willing parties especially where they had a common culture and heritage, a Common Law and spoke the same language. It was also possible to accommodate other parties in such a scheme provided that all the members accepted the same legal norms and the issues were legal. Beyond that where the national interest became involved it was far more difficult. To that extent arbitration could be an effective instrument, but where the issue was not legal *per se* then diplomacy was the means. Such was the means in the Moroccan crises.

II. *ENTENTE* DIPLOMACY AND THE MOROCCAN CRISES

Before considering the Moroccan crises, it is important to understand the improvement in relations between Britain and France in resolving differences. Just as relations between Britain and the United States had become closer

[64] Chief Justice of the United States 1921–30 presiding over the Supreme Court.
[65] Senate Doc 98, 62nd Congress, 1st Session, 47–50.
[66] *Ibid* 46.

towards the end of the nineteenth century culminating in the Haye-Pauncefote Treaty, Britain's emergence from its 'splendid isolation' in Europe inclined it towards resolving colonial issues with France. Thus, on the 16th July 1903, Delcassé instructed Paul Cambon, the French Ambassador in London, to discuss with Lansdowne an arbitration treaty dealing with 'differences of a juridical order'.[67] Barclay believed that this was a significant step in dispute resolution between states, the first being the Geneva Arbitration, the second The Hague Court and the third this treaty.

These discussions proved constructive and on the 14th October 1903 a Treaty of Arbitration was signed by Cambon and Lansdowne, the first between the Great Powers of Europe. Article 1 dealt with differences of a judicial order, and those relating to the interpretation of treaties existing between the two contracting parties, which could not be settled by diplomacy. These were to be submitted to the Permanent Court of Arbitration at The Hague under the Convention of 29 July 1899. Such references could not involve either vital interests or the independence or honour of the two contracting states, nor the interests of a third power. Article 2 provided that in each case the parties should sign 'a special arbitration bond setting forth clearly the subject under dispute, the extent of the powers of the arbitrators, and the details to be observed as regards the constitution of the arbitral tribunal and the procedure'. This marked another success for British and French diplomacy building on that of the Haye Pauncefote Treaty of 1901 between Britain and the United States.

A. The Anglo-French Declaration 1904 (*Entente Cordiale*)

The *Entente Cordiale* succeeded the Arbitration Treaty 1903 by providing a further process to resolve differences diplomatically and judicially. This consisted of several declarations, one concerning Egypt and Morocco, and other declarations regarding Siam, Madagascar and New Hebrides, including a Convention regarding Newfoundland and Africa. An Accord was signed on the 8th April 1904. Under Article 3 of the Accord, the signatory Powers could refer to an arbitral tribunal, not the Permanent Court of Arbitration at The Hague, but a specially constituted tribunal to deal with French indemnity claims for their citizens who had lost their fishing rights in Newfoundland, thus extending the scope of the process agreed in the Arbitration Treaty 1903. Nicolson[68] explained that

[67] T Barclay, *Thirty Years* (Constable and Company, 1914) 232.

[68] Harold Nicolson was a British diplomat and author and the son of Sir Arthur Nicolson, Lord Carnock. After leaving the Foreign Office, Harold became an MP and supported Churchill against his party's appeasement and isolationist policies. He was the author of numerous books including works on the H Nicolson *Congress of Vienna* (Methuen & Co Ltd, 1961) and *Peacemaking 1919* (Faber & Faber, 1933) exposing the problems of the Treaty of Versailles.

whereas Britain had earlier supported Moroccan independence, Britain could not support a corrupt regime as the Shereefian Empire.[69] Before the *Entente*, Joseph Chamberlain had given an invitation to Germany in 1899 of a 'natural alliance' but Germany had ignored it. Paul Cambon was the promoter of the *Entente*. He impressed Lansdowne with his arguments for such an arrangement to the extent that Lansdowne was given the royal seal of approval when King Edward VII declared that 'It is excellent. We must go on with it.'[70] Otte opines that the *Entente* was 'a sophisticated strategy of imperial consolidation'.[71] It was perceived as a foil to German expansionism and in practice Britain had to consider the French interest when dealing with Germany.[72] It secured British interests in Egypt.[73] But as Crowe pointed out, 'an entente is nothing more than a frame of mind, a view of general policy which is shared by the governments of two countries, but which may be, or become, so vague as to lose all content'.[74]

Two international legal obligations and two strategic considerations affected Britain's approach to the Moroccan crises. Legally, her obligation to France under Articles II and IV of the Anglo-French Declaration of 1904 (the *Entente)* giving France a free hand in Morocco and diplomatic support, and strategically ending her isolation policy. First, Britain was concerned about the prospect of losing naval supremacy protecting its trade routes and undermining its dominant strategic position in the Mediterranean: leading to the risk that the Russian Black Sea Fleet could threaten India.[75] Second, it was also concerned about the French encroachment in Morocco during the Boer War which had exposed the British naval base at Gibraltar.[76] The alarm was raised when it was reported that the French and Russian Fleets were mobilising.[77]

It was against this background and without Britain acquiescing in the French 'plundering of Morocco'[78] that on the 23rd July 1902 Paul Cambon proposed an Anglo-French arrangement in Morocco. This could be affected if Britain made concessions in the hinterland; the French would recognise the neutrality of Tangier and Spanish interest on the coast and in the hinterland. Such arrangement could also extend to British interests in Siam.[79] At a further meeting with Cambon on 6 August 1902, Lansdowne expressed his interest in maintaining

[69] H Nicolson, 'The Origins and Development of the Anglo-French Entente' (1954) 30 *International Affairs* 407–16.

[70] *Ibid*.

[71] T Otte, *The Foreign Office Mind* (Cambridge University Press, 2011) 286.

[72] *Ibid* 288.

[73] FO 800/162 *Mallet to Bertie* (13 April 1905) and see Otte (n 71) 301.

[74] Otte (n 71) 363.

[75] G Monger, *The End of Isolation* (Thomas Nelson and Sons Ltd, 1963) 1–2.

[76] *Ibid* 3.

[77] FO 27/3539 *Lansdowne to Monson* (11 June 1901).

[78] *Lansdowne to Chamberlain* (16 March 1901), Chamberlain MSS. Box JC 11/4.

[79] P Gooch and H Temperley (eds), *British Documents on the Origins of the War 1898–1914* Vols I–XI (Her Majesty's Stationery Office, 1927–38) (BD) Vol II, No 322.

the status quo and consolidation of their respective countries' colonial interests.[80] On 7 July 1902 Lansdowne discussed Morocco, New Hebrides, Egypt, Sokoto, Siam and the Kra Isthmus with M Delcassé.[81]

As to Morocco the Admiralty suggested that France take the eastern part, Britain the coastline from Tangier to Casablanca, and Germany the coast south of Casablanca. Lansdowne assured the Sultan that Britain would not acquiesce in any Power being given a free hand in Morocco.[82] Britain could separate her rival's interest through the construction of railways: Germany in a line from El Araih to Fez, France from Casablanca via Rabat to Fez and Britain from Casablanca via Mazagan to Marrakesh.[83]

The Director of Military Intelligence took the view that neither Power could take Tangiers.[84] If Germany had an interest in the Fez-Tangier section of the railway she would act as a counterpoise to France even if that meant Germany having Tangiers as a port. According to the Director of Naval Intelligence that would not be so serious because the British navy was between Germany's North Sea Fleet and Gibraltar.[85] In December 1903 there was a rebellion against the Sultan in Morocco. Britain sent five warships to the area to protect British residents. Lansdowne had to be cautious and not antagonise France as France would fight for Morocco.[86] Britain had supported Germany in Venezuela but was unable to support her in Morocco in the face of increasing opposition at home. Germany had increasingly sought means to divide France and Russia,[87] as it did France and Britain.

With the rise of Germany and the emergence of the United States, it became clear to the British Government that to maintain its extensive empire adjustments would have to be made to its foreign policy. The expansion of the German navy with new battleships which could match the Royal Navy was gradually perceived as a threat that could not be ignored.[88] At the same time there was a certain public fear of a German invasion and a 'spy scare'. Two books epitomised this public reaction: *Riddle of the Sands* by Erskine Childers,[89] and *Spies of the Kaiser* by William Le Queux. Both books were fictitious, Le Queux being a somewhat overenthusiastic former policeman who like Childers performed a public service in alerting Britain to the threat of a German invasion.

[80] *Ibid* Vol II, No 322.
[81] *Ibid* Vol II, No 357.
[82] FO 99/400 *Memo by Forestier-Walker* (9 September 1902).
[83] Monger (n 75) 81.
[84] FO 99/400 *Memoranda by Director of Military Intelligence (DMI)* (24th October and 22nd December 1902).
[85] *Ibid* (28th October 1902).
[86] Monger (n 75) 111.
[87] J Keiger, *France and the Origins of the First World War* (Macmillan Press, 1983) 18–21.
[88] The German ships were heavily armoured and well designed for combat in the North Sea.
[89] See also chapter 7 for his part in support for Irish Home Rule and independence.

Despite this it was not so much fear of Germany but Russia's encroachment in Manchuria that propelled discussions with France.[90] Britain supported France and Spain.[91]

To reach agreement Britain required three conditions to be met: the protection of British trade, neutralisation of the seaboard, and respect for Spanish interests. If Britain recognised France's dominant position in Morocco, France would recognise Britain's occupation of Egypt, abolition of the Caisse de la Dette, and capitulations.[92] Cambon suggested that as France advanced in Morocco, Britain would in Egypt *pari pasu*.[93] Although Britain occupied Egypt, Lansdowne was able to reach agreement which made provision for the Caisse de la Dette which was retained subject to limitations for service of the debt and consent by the other Powers to the arrangement.[94] If no consent was forthcoming Britain would act *recte si possumus, si non quocunque modo* and carry out the reform anyway.[95] Britain expected French consent in recognition of the *Entente*.[96]

B. The First Moroccan Crisis

The French mission to Fez in January 1905 may well have provoked the Kaiser's visit to Tangier. According to Radowitz, the Kaiser was 'always desirous of inspecting strange places' and visited Tangier on 1 April 1905.[97] It appears he did so as he said to 'cause the interests of German commerce to be respected'. This in effect was his response to the *Entente*,[98] also as the guarantor of Moroccan independence under the Madrid Convention of 1880. Whilst Lord Fisher interpreted the visit as notice that Germany might procure a naval base on the Moroccan coast threatening British interests,[99] France was not prepared for war. Her ally, Russia, had just suffered a naval defeat at the Battle of Tashima. The Kaiser's visit may have had a more subtle objective other than a warning not to ignore German commercial interests. Germany wanted a colonial empire: 'a place in the sun'.

[90] Monger (n 75) 81.
[91] *Ibid* 113.
[92] BD (n 79) Vol II, No 369.
[93] *Ibid* Vol II, No 370.
[94] *Ibid* Vol II, No 376.
[95] Monger (n 75) 144.
[96] This was the recognition by both parties of mutual diplomatic support which underpinned the *Entente*.
[97] BD (n 79) Vol III, No 70 *Nicolson to Lansdowne* (23 March 1905).
[98] *Ibid Mr White to Lansdowne* Tangier (6 April 1905).
[99] Monger (n 75) 186,189.

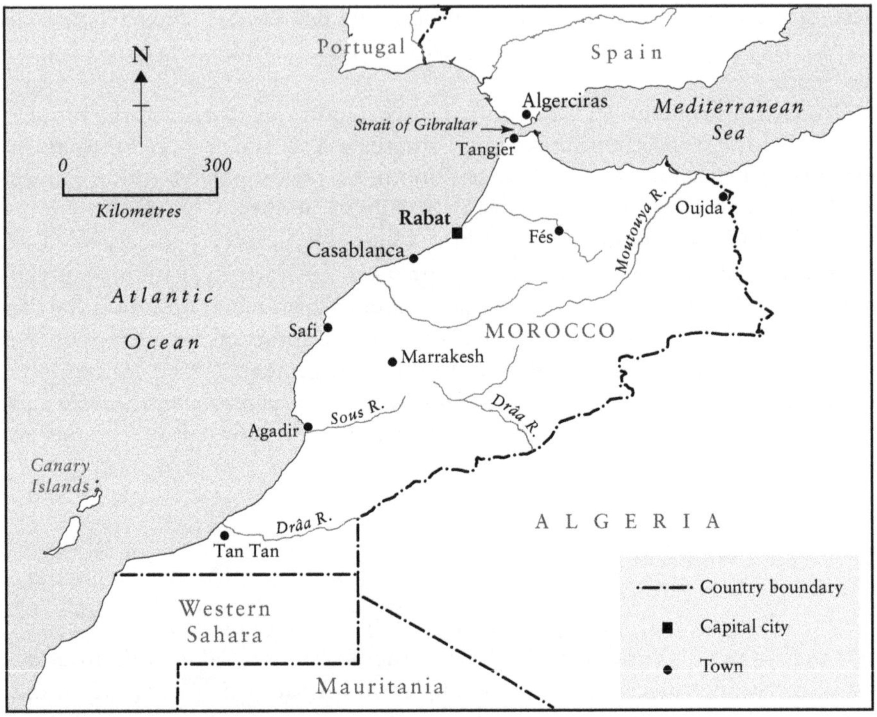

Figure 6.1 Map of Morocco during the Moroccan crises
Credit: Mina Moshkeri

i. Diplomatic Support

The Kaiser's visit to Tangier was perceived as a challenge to the *Entente* by Britain.[100] Britain was ready to support France against any German demands over Morocco.[101] Lansdowne saw the *Entente* as a valuable diplomatic arrangement although it was complicated by Britain's alliance with Japan during the Russo-Japanese war in 1905. As a matter of policy Lansdowne was concerned with imperial interests and naval supremacy and ignored continental military considerations.[102] Britain's support was also influenced by concerns over German designs or colonial acquisitions 'in other parts of the world' by way of exchanges with France.[103] Lansdowne intimated to Cambon that the *Entente* required 'the most absolute confidence'.[104] Diplomatically matters

[100] Nicolson (n 69) 412.
[101] *Mallett to Bertie* (24 April 1905). Minutes by Lansdowne and Balfour. Nicolson to Lansdowne (11 April 1905). K Hamilton, *Bertie of Thame* (Royal Historical Society Studies in History 60, 1990) 76.
[102] Monger (n 75) 194.
[103] BD (n 79) Vol III, No 94.
[104] *Ibid* Vol III, No 705, Encl 2 *Lansdowne to Cambon* (25 May 1905).

became more complicated when the new Premier, Rouvier, taking fright at German threats, ignored Delcassé's advice that Germany was bluffing and France had Britain's support forcing Rouvier to resign. On 22nd April 1905 Lansdowne instructed Sir Francis Bertie, the British Ambassador in Paris, to inform Delcassé that the British Government would give him 'all the support we can'.[105]

So far as naval supremacy was concerned, superiority in battleships was telling after the battle of Tsushima. Britain had superiority over the combined fleets of France, Germany and Russia at this time,[106] but the sudden resignation of Delcassé led to a loss of confidence in the *Entente*. This added to a fear of war between France and Germany over Morocco. Whilst the Royal Navy was in a dominant position at sea, Sir Arthur Wilson, the Commander in Chief of the Channel Fleet, considered that the military outcome would be determined on the French frontier.[107]

Tensions subsided when Cambon informed Lansdowne on the 1st July that France had reached agreement with Germany on an international conference.[108] This came at the price of Delcassé's dismissal by Rouvier, forced by Germany. Whilst this was an embarrassment for France the subterfuge of Bülow and Holstein resulted in their humiliation when their objectives suffered diplomatic defeat at the conference.[109]

On the 24th July the Tsar met the Kaiser at Björkö who warned the Tsar against any combination with France and Britain.[110] Although the Tsar signed the defence treaty it was rejected by the Tsar's advisers[111] and in April 1906 Grey opened negotiations and concluded an agreement on the 31st August 1907. Such an arrangement as the Björkö Treaty would have destroyed either the *Entente* or the Franco-Russian alliance.[112] It would also have made Britain's position in Asia more difficult.[113]

In December 1905 when the Unionist Government resigned, and Sir Edward Grey became Foreign Secretary he approached Germany in a different manner as he was not so tied to imperial interests as Lansdowne and whilst committed to diplomatic support was non-committal as to any military support. Britain would therefore fully support France at the forthcoming conference under Article IX

[105] *Ibid* Vol III, No 90 *Lansdowne to Bertie* (22 April 1905).

[106] Monger (n 75) 200.

[107] A Marder, *British Naval Policy*, 1880–1905 (Alfred A Knopf, 1940) 502–505. See also Committee of Imperial Defence Records Cab 4/1 Paper 65B.

[108] BD (n 79) Vol III, No 150 *Lansdowne to Bertie* (11 July 1905).

[109] J Keiger, *France and the Origins of the First World War* (Macmillan Press, 1983) 22.

[110] BD (n 79) Vol III, No 168 *Hardinge to Lansdowne* (3 August 1905).

[111] G Martel, *Origins of the First World War*, 4th edn (Routledge, 2007) 60–61.

[112] D Lieven, *Towards the Flame* (Penguin, 2015) 184.

[113] P Kennedy, *The Rise of Anglo-German Antagonism 1860–1914* (Humanity Books) 278.

of the Anglo-French Declaration 'nous serons bien sûrement avec vous'.[114] In *Twenty-Five Years*, Grey wrote:

> We should be isolated and discredited if we stood aside; hated by those whom we had refused to help and despised by others. I thought too, that when the time came, if it ever did come, when Germany attacked France public opinion here would be so moved that Britain would intervene on the side of France. But I was sure that much would depend upon how the war came about. If France appeared to be aggressive Britain would not help her-of that I felt sure-and also that the cabinet and Parliament would not bind themselves by a promise in advance.[115]

However, Grey went a little further in his discussions with Count Metternich on 3 January 1906 and told him '... if circumstances arose, public feeling in England would be so strong that it would be impossible to be neutral'.[116] This was Grey's personal opinion as he told Bertie that people in England would not be 'prepared to fight to put France in possession of Morocco'.[117] Grey tried to allay Metternich's fears about German economic interests by saying that Germany would participate in the Moroccan State Bank as part of the 'open door' policy.[118] On 10 January 1906, Cambon and Grey discussed the possibilities of British military support in the event of war between France and Germany. This was taken seriously at a meeting of the Committee of Imperial Defence which discussed dispositions of the army and the transport of 100,000 men to the continent within 14 days.[119] Grey's personal opinion was that 'public opinion in England would be strongly moved in favour of France'.[120] He told Bertie he pledged 'benevolent neutrality'.[121] Bertie advised that if Britain simply continued diplomatic support or neutrality, this would have serious consequences for British imperial interests because France might then be in a weaker position and make concessions to Germany 'outside Morocco'.[122] Bertie clearly favoured France as did Grey's advisers Nicolson, Crowe and Tyrrell.[123] Thus, Grey's foreign office beheld two schools of thought: the Grey-Tyrell model elusive and non-committal and the Crowe-Nicolson model which sought to define the

[114] BD (n 79) Vol III, No 197 *Grey to Bertie* (20 December 1905). Art IX: The two Governments agree to afford to one another their diplomatic support, in order to obtain the execution of the clauses of the present Declaration regarding Egypt and Morocco.

[115] E Grey, *Twenty-Five Years* (Hodder and Stoughton, 1928).

[116] BD (n 79) Vol III, No 229 *Grey to Lascelles* (9 January 1906).

[117] *Ibid* No 150 *Grey to Bertie* (31 January 1906).

[118] *Ibid* No 229 *Grey to Lascelles* (9 January 1906).

[119] *Ibid* No 221 *Written Statement of Lord Sydenham* (19 July 1927).

[120] *Ibid* No 210(a) *Grey to Bertie* (10 January 1906).

[121] *Ibid*.

[122] *Ibid* No 213 *Bertie to Grey* (13 January 1906).

[123] Tyrell was an interesting character with an Anglo-Irish Catholic background: his father was a lawyer and judge. He complemented Eyre Crowe with his Anglo-German background and continental education. Together they encompassed the essential intellectual qualities demanded in international relations, Tyrell adopting a more conciliatory approach and Crowe a more adversarial one.

situation.[124] These approaches emerged in this and the subsequent crises in 1911 and 1914.

C. The Algeciras Conference

To resolve the issues between France and Germany a conference was convened and met at Algeciras on 16th January 1906. Two questions were controversial: the Moroccan State Bank and the police. The French proposed joint control of the police by France and Spain, but Germany objected.[125] Britain was obliged to support France in accordance with Articles II and IX of the Anglo-French Declaration and give France a free hand in establishing Morocco. So far as the Bank was concerned there was an 'open door' for German interests.

By 7 February the German position had altered in that Germany did not accept or reject the principle of joint control but questioned the extent of the Sultan's control over it.[126] Nicolson reported that Tattenbach, the German representative at Algeciras, had suggested Morocco could be without police.[127] The police force was restricted to the coastal towns to protect foreigners and the French would simply provide officers instructors and non-commissioned officers for three years at Rabat, Tangier, Laraiche and at Casablanca.[128] France would respect the Sultan's sovereignty and independence in Morocco. Grey suggested that French and Spanish officers control the police at the ports and ensure the 'open door' for Britain's economic interests.[129] Whilst the Anglo-French position was clear from the Anglo-French Declaration, Germany's was not. As Sir Arthur Nicolson opined: 'Germany does not know what she wants'.[130]

Grey suggested that Germany could be accommodated by the concession of a port or coaling station at Mogador.[131] In a note Hardinge[132] suggested to Grey that Britain should stand 'solidaire' with France to deter Germany.[133] Austria-Hungary suggested that the ports be controlled by French and Spanish officers, except Casablanca which should be controlled by a Swiss or Dutch officer who was to have general inspection powers over all Morocco.[134] Grey told Cambon that Austria's proposal was a concession.[135] According to Monger, Bertie cautioned Grey that Britain must not be seen as the prime mover in this

[124] H Nicolson, *A Study in Old Diplomacy* (Constable & Co, 1930) 328–29.
[125] BD (n 79) Vol III, No 269. *A Nicolson to Grey* (6 February 1906).
[126] *Ibid* No 271 *A Nicolson to Grey* (7 February 1906).
[127] *Ibid* No 266 *A Nicolson to Grey* (4 February 1906).
[128] *Ibid* No 280 *Grey to Bertie* (13 February 1906).
[129] *Ibid* No 281 *Grey to Nicolson* (13 February 1906).
[130] H Nicolson, *Lord Carnock* (Constable & Co, 1930) 181.
[131] BD (n 79) Vol III, No 299 *Minute of Sir E Grey* (20 February 1906).
[132] Permanent Under Secretary of State 1906–10.
[133] BD (n 79) Vol III, No 299 *Minute of Sir E Grey*. Note by Sir C Hardinge (20 February 1906).
[134] Monger (n 75) 276.
[135] BD (n 79) Vol III, No 333 *Grey to Bertie* (9 March 1906).

as it could backfire.[136] Bertie had put the Austrian proposal to Rouvier, but he was not impressed.[137] Nicolson reported concern in the French delegation to Grey and Eyre Crowe, then a Senior Clerk, minuted his concerns that the French had to decide to accept the Austrian proposal or not. He thought that Britain should put the French case to President Roosevelt, and he could communicate with Berlin.[138]

Grey decided to give firm support to France after receiving a telegram from Nicolson confirming the French Government's position on the Austrian proposal.[139] Grey cabled Bertie having taken account of the warnings he had been wisely given to confirm British support for France's approach on policing.[140] Nevertheless some damage had been done as reflected in Bertie's cable to Grey on the 15th March stating that the Council of Ministers understood that Britain had made some arrangement 'behind the back of France'.[141] Grey countered this in his response to Bertie on the same day and Bertie confirmed the explanation had been accepted by Clemenceau the Minister for Foreign Affairs who first raised the matter with him,[142] Rouvier having resigned on the 14 March 1906.

The German attempt to gain some control in Morocco failed and France through British support was able to secure her interests. This was finally confirmed on the 26th March after a plenary sitting of the conference on the police question when Germany agreed to all eight ports being policed by French and Spanish inspectors.[143]

The General Act of Algeciras 1906 confirmed in its preamble: '… the triple principle of the sovereignty and independence of His Majesty the Sultan, the integrity of his domains, and economic liberty without any inequality.' It gave effect to establishing state sovereignty of Morocco subject to the Act's provisions as to the establishment of the police force, trading rights, the establishment of a State Bank, and provisions for regulating trade and customs, procurement of public works and penalties for fraud and smuggling. The police force was to be composed of Spanish officers and non-commissioned officers as instructors, with French officers and non-commissioned officers as instructors, by their respective Governments, to be approved by the Sultan. There were to be 20 Spanish and French officers and between 30 and 40 Spanish and French non-commissioned officers appointed in such positions. Under Article 7 these would be subject to a general inspection by a superior officer of the Swiss army, approved by the Swiss Federal Government. Under Article 13 the importation and sale of arms was prohibited including ammunition, powder, saltpetre, gun

[136] *Bertie to Grey* (12 March 1906) cited in Monger (n 75) 277 fn 7.
[137] BD (n 79) Vol III, No 340 *Bertie to Grey* (11 March 1906).
[138] *Ibid* No 342 *A Nicolson to Grey* (12 March 1906).
[139] *Ibid* No 349 *A Nicolson to Grey* (14 March 1906).
[140] *Ibid* No 350 *Grey to Bertie* (14 March 1906).
[141] *Ibid* No 356 *Bertie to Grey* (15 March 1906).
[142] *Ibid* No 357 *Grey to Bertie* (15 March 1906) and *ibid* No 213 *Bertie to Grey* (16 March 1906).
[143] *Ibid* No 382 *A Nicolson to Grey* (26 March 1906).

cotton, nitro-glycerine and all compositions destined exclusively for the manufacture of ammunition. Article 32 provided that the 'State Bank of Morocco' would have the exclusive privilege of issuing notes to the bearer, payable on presentation and receivable for public dues throughout the Moorish Empire. Any dispute between the Bank and the Moorish Government would be referred to the Federal Court of Lausanne.[144] The point Grey made to Germany about an open door policy regarding the Bank was preserved in Article 56 which provided that states wishing to avail themselves of their rights of subscription had to notify the Spanish Government within a period of four weeks from the signature of the Act. Foreigners were given the right to acquire property in Morocco.[145] There were provisions regulating trade and customs duties and importantly provisions regarding public procurement, eg building of railways which were an important consideration in the diplomatic considerations. In terms of foreign capital, investment in, or foreign industry engaged in the operation of public works, roads, railways, ports, telegraphs, and other public works, Article 106 provided that the Powers reserved the right to see to it that the authority of the state over these great enterprises of general interest remained.

As to disputes processes, there were provisions such as Article 116 for foreign owners whose property was expropriated for indemnity to be fixed by a special jury, or by arbitration. Interestingly under Article 117 the jury was composed of six expert appraisers, three to be selected by the owner and three by the administration desiring to expropriate. A majority vote would rule. If there was no majority, the owner and the administration would each appoint an arbitrator, and the two arbitrators would name an umpire. In case no agreement was reached in selecting an umpire he would be appointed by the Diplomatic Body at Tangier. It is interesting to note the use of the Diplomatic Body which also dealt with police complaints but effectively controlled key elements of the administration on behalf of the Powers. Under Article 118, the arbitrators were selected from a list drawn up at the beginning of each year by the Diplomatic Body, selected from experts not living within the district in which the work is to be carried out. The owner could appeal from the arbitrators' award to a competent jurisdiction, and in accordance with the rules set for arbitration cases by the law of the country to which he belongs.

Whilst there had undoubtedly been different approaches to the Moroccan settlement in 1906 between France and Britain, the *Entente* stood the test and the reciprocity of diplomatic support held. In that sense respective national interests gave way to the common interest of the *Entente*. Germany clearly miscalculated British intentions in 1906 and in 1911 and through Tattenbach's attempt to suborn Harold Nicolson during the conference it lost considerable credibility.[146] Holstein had misconceived the *Entente* and his 'demented hysteria'

[144] Article 46.
[145] Article 60.
[146] Nicolson (n 124) 178.

had destroyed all prospect of an Anglo-German alliance.[147] On the other hand, Grey was concerned to restrain France, not to commit Britain to a war.[148]

D. 1905 Crisis Conclusions

The crisis of 1905–1906 might well have resulted in another Franco-German war, but for diplomacy. Whilst Germany suffered a diplomatic setback, it rid France of Delcassé and Caillaux, and in doing so undermined the *Entente*. Personalities played some part in the crisis: the Kaiser by his interventions and meddling at Tangier and the French by their overzealous adventurist proclivities at Fez. According to Bertie, the German objective was to remove Delcassé and destroy the *Entente*.[149] Lord Fisher told Bertie 'it would not matter whether the Germans got Mogador or not. If they did Britain should have Tangier.'[150] From the naval point of view that might have been strategically acceptable, but from the diplomatic point of view and Britain's obligations to France that would constitute a breach of the Declaration and a breach of good faith.

Arthur Nicolson, Bertie, Crowe, Hardinge and Mallet effectively supported France and the French case. This was more effective because of the diplomatic skills of Paul and Jules Cambon. German diplomacy was discredited by its duplicity and underhandedness, although Caillaux and the fall of Delcassé caused serious concern in Britain. French suspicions of British intentions played into Germany's hands undermining the *Entente*. Britain could not be 'more French than the French' and there was a limit to its support over Morocco to the extent that it caused no detriment to British interests be they commercial in Morocco or imperial in Africa. Paul Cambon thought Germany was bluffing and should not be appeased.[151] Rouvier, frightened by the possibility of war, accepted Delcassé resignation against Cambon's advice.[152] Rouvier likely took exception to Lansdowne's offer of 'full and confidential discussions', as Paul Cambon exclaimed: 'la voie d'une entente générale qui constituerait en réalité une alliance'.[153] Both Holstein and Rouvier believed that Britain might gain from a Franco-German war.[154] Bertie believed that if there were such a war France would be defeated and Germany would dominate Europe.[155]

[147] Nicolson (n 69) 407–16.
[148] BD (n 79) Vol VII, No 219 *Grey to Bertie* (31 January 1906).
[149] FO 800/170 *Bertie to King Edward VII* (22 April 1905).
[150] FO 800/170 *Mallet to Bertie* (24th April 1905).
[151] K Eubank, *Paul Cambon Master Diplomat* (Norman, 1960) 98.
[152] BD (n 79) Vol II, Nos 72–75 *Lansdowne to Bertie* (22nd April 1905); *Bertie to Lansdowne* (25 April 1905).
[153] *Documents Diplomatiques Française, 3rd Service, 1911–1914, ed* Ministère des Affaires Ētrangères, 11 Vols (Paris, 1929–36) Vol VI, No 365.
[154] Hamilton (n 101) 96; Eubank (n 151) 102.
[155] Hamilton (n 101) 107.

E. The Agadir Crisis: '*A mon terrible ami, A mon aimable ennemi*'[156]

On 17th April 1911, Fez was occupied by French troops in order to suppress an uprising against the Sultan. Caillaux's[157] aim was to affect a de facto protectorate over Morocco. The force then proceeded to Meknés between Fez and Rabat in violation of the Act of Algeciras 1906 prohibiting such incursion. This played into Germany's hands alleging such action to be a breach of the Act of Algeria and it also encouraged Spain.[158] On 28 April, Kiderlen met Jules Cambon and informed him that Germany regarded that the Act of Algeciras was repudiated.[159] In a Memorandum on the 3rd May, Kiderlen noted that the Kaiser wanted warships sent to Mogador and Agadir to protect German firms.[160]

Grey counselled restraint and withdrawal of troops. The French did not withdraw from Fez and the Spanish occupied Laraiche and Alcazar on the 5th June.[161]

Grey had been prepared to suggest a conference if the negotiations between France and Germany broke down, if the offer was rejected then the matter might be referred to arbitration. This would have to be by agreement as there was no such provision in the Act of Algeciras. Discussions were carried out in Berlin to resolve the crisis, between Bethmann Hollweg and Jules Cambon.[162] Cambon tried to assuage German feelings by discussing compensation, but Germany demanded the whole of the French Congo. Ominously on the 31st June, Bethmann Hollweg instructed Metternich to notify the British Government that Germany would assume direct responsibility for the security of the lives and property of German nationals and protégés.[163]

It would appear that the British position at the outset of the crisis was: no German ports on the Mediterranean shore, no new fortified port in Morocco, and an open door for British trade.[164] Britain's view was that France should compromise, giving territory to Germany or abide by the Act of Algeciras 1906.[165] The German response was to send an obsolete gunboat, the *Panther*, to Agadir to protect their rights under agreements made in 1906 and 1909.[166]

[156] Words exchanged on the signing of the Franco-German Treaty, 4 November 1911 between Kiderlen and Jules Cambon. G Gooch, *Studies in Diplomacy and Statecraft* (Longmans Green and Co, 1942) 155.

[157] The new French Prime Minister.

[158] M Dockrill, 'British Policy During the Agadir Crisis of 1911' in F Hinsley (ed), *British Foreign Policy Under Sir Edward Grey* (Cambridge University Press, 2008) 271.

[159] German Diplomatic Documents (GDD) 1871–1914, IV (London, Methuen & Co Ltd, 1931) XXIX .97.

[160] *Ibid* XXIX .105.

[161] Dockrill (n 158) 272.

[162] GDD(n 159) XXIX .120.

[163] *Ibid* XXIX .155.

[164] S Williamson, *The Politics of Grand Strategy* (Harvard, 1969) 146.

[165] *Ibid* 149.

[166] J Keiger, *France and the Origins of the First World War* (Macmillan Press, 1983) 34–35.

The *Panther* was replaced four days later by the four-inch gun light cruiser *SMS Berlin*. Sending warships to Agadir was another example of German *faustpfand* as was the Kaiser's visit to Tangier.[167]

On 1st July 1911, Count Metternich told Nicolson that the *Panther* had been sent to Agadir. Nicolson considered this a breach of the Act of Algeciras 1906.[168] Metternich said the Act was invalid. It was violated in 1907 by the French occupation of Oujda, in July 1907, by the bombardment of Casablanca and in May 1911 by the occupation of Fez.[169] Kiderlen Waechter, the German Foreign Minister, told Jules Cambon that the *Panther* was sent because 'the French were monopolising everything and keeping Germans out of all undertakings in Morocco.'[170] It was suggested that 'Germany might squeeze France without raising any question with England'.[171] Britain requested consultation of 'any step involving serious consequences'.[172] Under the Franco-German Accord 1909, Germany agreed to 'disinterest herself politically' in consideration of economic concessions. The impression given by Kiderlen to Jules Cambon was that such concessions were not just some colonial concession but the whole French Congo.[173] Metternich was instructed to tell Grey that sending the *Panther* was 'a provisional measure of precaution' and that the French were acting outside the Act of Algeciras.[174] Grey told Metternich that the situation had changed by the arrival of the *Panther* and therefore this *demarche* could not be recognised. Britain was not consulted.[175] Two days later on the 6th July when Schoen met Jules Cambon in Paris, Schoen said resolution depended on guarantees for trade and compensation.[176] In a Memorandum to the Kaiser, Kiderlen advised that France be given *carte blanche* but the Kaiser wanted 'the lions share' in *échange de territoire*.[177]

By the 15th July the Kaiser was anxious that Kiderlen was steering Germany 'towards mobilisation' and the French offer seemed to be less than before.[178] On the 20th July, Bethmann Hollweg advised that some 'brusque' means of persuasion was required and suggested demanding that the French evacuate Morocco.[179] On the 21st July, the day of the Chancellor of the Exchequer's (Lloyd George) speech, Metternich reported that Grey was anxious about the situation. Grey gave the impression that Britain would oppose any German base in Morocco.[180]

[167] Nicolson (n 69) 414.
[168] Nicolson (n 124) 341.
[169] *Ibid* 342.
[170] BD (n 79) Vol VII, No 369 *Bertie to Grey* (11 July 1911).
[171] *Ibid.*
[172] *Ibid* VII, No 397 *Grey to Bertie* (19 July 1911).
[173] Nicolson (n 124) 343.
[174] GDD (n 159) XXIX .116, *Bethmann-Hollweg to Metternich* (4 July 1911).
[175] *Ibid* .117, *Metternich to German Foreign Office* (4 July 1911).
[176] *Ibid* .171, *Schoen to German Foreign Office* (6 July 1911).
[177] *Ibid* .174, *Memorandum by Kiderlen* (9 July1911).
[178] *Ibid* .184, *Bethmann-Hollweg to Kaiser* (15 July 1911).
[179] *Ibid.*
[180] *Ibid* .213, *Kiderlen to Metternich* (24 July 1911).

i. 'More French than the French'

The German and British documentary evidence suggest that by the 21st July, Grey had come to the view that a firmer stand was required in supporting France.[181] It was therefore no surprise that Lloyd George warned Germany in a speech at the Mansion House that night in the context of the Anglo-American Arbitration Treaty:

> ... I rejoice in my heart at the prospect of a happy issue to Sir Edward Grey's negotiations with the United States of America for the settlement of disputes which may occur in future between ourselves and our kinsmen across the Atlantic by some more merciful, more rational, and by a more just arbitrament than that of the sword.
>
> .... But if a situation were to be forced upon us in which peace could only be preserved by the surrender of the great and beneficent position Britain has won by centuries of heroism and achievement, by allowing Britain to be treated where her interests were vitally affected as if she were of no account in the Cabinet of nations, then I say emphatically that peace at that price would be a humiliation intolerable for a great country like ours to endure. National honour is no party question. The security of our great international trade is no party question; the peace of the world is much more likely to be secured if all nations realize fairly what the conditions of peace must be ....

Whilst Lloyd George's audience may not have understood what he meant, it certainly set alarms ringing in the chancelleries of Europe. Winston Churchill felt that 'we were drifting into war'.[182] After the speech, Grey met Metternich who gave Grey the impression that the fleet could be attacked at any moment.[183] Had Lloyd George not made his speech Grey would have had to warn Metternich that Britain would have to protect its interests by sending warships to Agadir.[184] Metternich told him that Germany intended not to ignore Britain's rights without consulting Britain.[185] Such an approach was clearly intended to separate French and British interests and up to the 21st July it was a possibility. Following the meeting with Metternich, Grey met Lloyd George and Churchill and told them that: 'We are dealing with people who recognise no law except that of force between nations.'[186] There was some speculation as to who Lloyd George was directing his remarks to; was it Caillaux or Metternich?[187] On balance it tends to Germany.[188]

During this crisis Nicolson believed that Germany would use her army and navy not as a means of defence but as a means of attack. Germany's aim was to

[181] BD (n 79) VII, No 409 *Minute by A Nicolson* (11 July 1911).
[182] W Churchill, *The World Crisis 1911–1918* (Penguin Books, 2007) 29.
[183] *Ibid* 30.
[184] BD (n 79) Vol VII, No 399 *Grey to Asquith* (19 July 1911).
[185] GDD (n 159) XXIX .213, *Metternich to Foreign Office* (4 July 1911).
[186] Gooch (n 156) 152.
[187] BD (n 79) Vol VII, No 461 *Grey to Mallet* (5 August 1911).
[188] See K Wilson, 'The Agadir Crisis, the Mansion House Speech and the Double Edgedness of Agreements' (1972) 15 *The Historical Journal* 513–32.

conquer and dominate Europe.[189] He considered that Britain was too indulgent in half measures. He continually urged Grey for greater clarity of the British position. According to Nicolson, Grey failed to reconcile his appeal to parliament with his approach to foreign statesmen, eg secretive military discussions.[190]

According to Goschen, the British Ambassador in Berlin, Kiderlen made a mistake – he wanted something but really wanted something else – compounded by the display of force from which it was 'difficult to retreat and dangerous to advance'.[191] The Kaiser misread British intentions, misinterpreting his welcome in England with Britain's obligations under the Franco-British Declaration 1904. He and his advisers were therefore abruptly disillusioned by Lloyd George' speech at Mansion House on the 21st July 1911. Kiderlen declared that 'the attitude of France made war almost inevitable'. This convinced Grey that Britain might be suddenly attacked and consequently warned the Admiralty to keep the fleet on alert.[192] That same day, however, Grey was informed by Bertie that discussions were progressing between France and Germany and that Germany was withdrawing many of its demands.[193]

Nicolson informed Hardinge on the 14th September 1911 that Churchill, Lloyd George and Haldane were prepared for eventualities and detailed preparations were completed for the transfer of four army divisions to the continent.[194] This action by the British Government produced a panic in the Berlin Stock Exchange so that Kiderlen was forced to retreat.[195]

France conceded part of the French Congo which was added to the German Cameroons and in consideration of that Germany recognised the French Protectorate of Morocco in a Convention signed on the 3rd November 1911, in effect ending the crisis.

The conduct of Caillaux, the President of the Council of Ministers, caused Arthur Nicolson some concern. Nicolson told Goschen on the 15th January 1912 that Caillaux had conducted secret negotiations with Germany and had rightly been removed from office.[196] Some evidence of this appeared in a Memorandum dated the 7th May 1911[197] from the German Ambassador to France, Schoen, who reported that a financier associate of Caillaux had been acting as an intermediary.

When Metternich met King Edward, the King expressed his regret that Europe had become divided into groups of Powers. Metternich's reaction was that the British had become 'more French than the French'.[198]

[189] Nicolson (n 124) 330.
[190] *Ibid* 330–31.
[191] *Sir E Goschen to A Nicolson* (17 September 1911). Nicolson (n 124) 344.
[192] *Grey to Nicolson* (17 September 1911). Nicolson (n 124) 346.
[193] BD (n 79) Vol VII, No 556 *Bertie to Grey* (19 September 1911).
[194] Nicolson (n 124) 347.
[195] *Ibid* 348. Also see Williamson (n 164) 162–63.
[196] Nicolson (n 124) 349.
[197] GDD (n 159) XXIX .115, *Schoen to Bethmann-Hollweg* (7 May 1911).
[198] *Ibid* .116, *Metternich to Bethmann-Hollweg* (25 September 1911).

ii. 1911 Reflections on the 'Coup d 'Agadir'

The aims of German diplomacy were not achieved. Her policy had been intended to break the *Entente*, gain colonies and exclude Britain from discussions. Lords Vansittart and Carnock (Arthur Nicolson), having experienced the extraordinary attitude of Germany and its proclivity 'to reach for the sword', considered that Germany should have anticipated the danger of its obduracy.[199] They also opined that the reason why the balance of power was ineffective was because no one knew that the *Entente* would go to war. It was not so much Bethmann-Hollweg's 'scrap of paper' but Paul Cambon's 'petit papier'.[200] Otte agrees that the crisis was an attempt by Germany to agree a colonial compromise excluding Britain.[201] The objectives of the 1904 Accords were achieved in 1911 and Britain's obligations discharged. Williamson suggests the *Entente* developed into a more extensive relationship through anxiety over German predilections.[202] Dockrill points to Germany's high-handed diplomacy in 1906 and 1911 which had the opposite effect of that intended. The French became more resistant and the British more committed to the *Entente*.[203] Dockrill also considers Grey's approach promoting discussion and concessions as against Crowe, and Bertie who advocated a more robust response.[204] Grey however changed his mind and was prepared to go to war to preserve the *Entente*,[205] although the Accords only required diplomatic support under Article 9 of the 1904 Declaration. The Kaiser, who was described by Kiderlen as 'a bull in a China shop',[206] told Kiderlen on the 30th April 1911 that he did not want war but an 'open door'.[207]

Reflecting on this episode Hardinge opined to Nicolson that foreign policy based on sentiment can only end in disaster[208] and in the same vein Nicolson wrote to Hardinge: 'If you wish to avoid war it is not always prudent to exclaim that you will not make it'.[209] In a letter to Fairfax Cartwright, Arthur Nicolson wrote that Paul Cambon concluded that despite the agreement a conflict was probable within two or three years. Nicolson concluded: 'The future therefore is not very bright'.[210] Nicolson, Hardinge and Cambon were to be proved right.

[199] Nicolson (n 69) 414.
[200] *Ibid* 415.
[201] Otte (n 71) 354–55.
[202] Williamson (n 164) 166.
[203] Dockrill (n 158) 273.
[204] *Ibid* 275.
[205] *Ibid* 285.
[206] L Cecil, *The German Diplomatic Service* (Princeton University Press, 1976) 311.
[207] GDD (n 159) XXIX .101.
[208] Otte (n 71) 323.
[209] *Ibid*. *Nicolson to Hardinge* Private (2 December 1908).
[210] *Nicolson to Fairfax Cartwright* (18th September 1911) *and to Sir Edward Goshen* (18th September 1911). Nicolson (n 12) 351.

III. THE BALKAN CRISIS 1912–13: AMBASSADORIAL CONSULTATIONS

Just nine days later Nicolson's words were to prove true in respect of the Italian action. Its Ambassador, the Marchase Imperialli, informed him that Italy would occupy Tripoli and Cyrenia. Nicolson said this would be an act of war and declined to give an assurance of British support. The next day Italy declared war on Turkey and landed troops at Tripoli and Benghazi and also occupied islands in the Dodecanese.[211] Britain remained neutral in this matter; France and Russia raised no objections. The war was not seriously fought, but according to Nicolson demonstrated the divide between the groupings of the Great Powers.

This episode set the backdrop for the Balkan Crises of 1912–13 and whilst this does not per se entail a legal question, it demonstrates a diplomatic dispute resolution process by means of ambassadorial consultations. These were effective to the extent of containing the Balkan crises without involving the Great Powers and culminating in the Treaty of London in 1913. It also shows how Austria-Hungary became more independent of Germany at this time and whilst Conrad and Archduke Franz Ferdinand considered a preventative war to stop Italy Aehrenthal, the Foreign Minister, did not and encouraged the Emperor Franz Joseph to dismiss Conrad which caused friction between the general staff and the Ballplatz.[212] The significant point was the tendency of Austria-Hungary and Italy to diverge from the Concert of Europe, and in 1914, Germany.

Whilst Russia encouraged Slav nationalism as the 'high protecting power' of the two Slav kingdoms[213] Sazanov, the Russian Foreign Minister, whilst doing so also proposed that Russia guarantee Constantinople and its adjacent territory to Turkey.[214] The Turks suggested an Anglo-Turkish alliance but Britain rejected it so Turkey turned to Germany which in turn had serious consequences in 1914.[215] When Aehrenthal died in February 1912 he was replaced by Count Berchtold who had been Ambassador at St Petersburg. In January 1912 Ironside, the British minister at Sofia in Bulgaria, informed Nicolson that a secret alliance was being formed between Serbia and Bulgaria promoted by Sazanov.[216] Nicolson advised that Britain should suggest a meeting between Austria-Hungary and Russia and that any diplomatic initiatives be taken jointly by the five Powers, not by France, Russia and Britain as proposed by President Poincaré.[217] Berchtold was unwilling to meet Sazanov in view of Sazanov's encouragement of Balkan alliances. Sazanov's meddling led to the Serbo-Bulgarian Treaty signed on the 13th March 1912 and another between Bulgaria and Greece on 29 May 1912 setting the scene for a Balkan War between the Balkan allies and Turkey.

[211] Nicolson (n 130) 357–58.
[212] *Ibid* 359–60.
[213] As described by O'Beirne, Chargé in St Petersburg.
[214] Nicolson (n 130) 360.
[215] *Ibid* 360.
[216] *Ibid* 377.
[217] *Ibid* 378. *Arthur Nicolson to Sir Fairfax Cartwright* (5 February 1912).

A. Setting the Balkans Ablaze

Bulgaria mobilised on the 29th September 1912. The Great Powers declared that no territory changes would be permitted, but nevertheless Bulgaria, Serbia, and Greece declared war on Turkey. The Eastern Question and the disintegration of the Ottoman Empire through the rise of Pan-Slavism and nationalism had been a time bomb awaiting explosion throughout the nineteenth century. Surprisingly, the Balkan states were quickly successful in defeating Turkey: the Bulgarians defeated Turkish forces at Kirk Kilisse on the 22nd October 1912, the Serbs routed another Turkish army at Koumanavo on the 26th October, and on the 8th of November the Greek forces entered Salonika.[218] Turkey was defeated in a month and lost all her European possessions save Tchataldja 12 miles from Constantinople. Whilst this resolved matters between the warring factions Austria-Hungary determined on military action to remove the Serbs from the Sanjak of Novibazar.[219] The Kaiser met Franz Ferdinand who along with Conrad supported this policy. Franz Ferdinand warned that Germany would not support Austria-Hungary, as the Kaiser remarked: 'You are rattling my Sabre a little too loudly'. Austria-Hungary appeared to be taking an independent stance.[220]

During this crisis Grey had an exchange of letters on the 22nd October 1912 with Paul Cambon, the French Ambassador, concerning military arrangements in time of war. Grey explained to his cabinet colleagues that Britain had no such commitments to France and Russia, but simply had 'conducted conversations'. Such commitments had not yet arisen or may not arise, but Grey had promised consultations in the event of an unprovoked attack by a third power. Britain was committed to having discussions and if they agreed as a result of such discussions to take defensive measures then Britain would so act if the Cabinet approved.[221]

According to Nicolson, overtures were made to Germany by Tyrell to Herr Von Kühlmann, the German Chargé d'Affaires, to seek accommodation of interests in China, Persia, Turkey and Africa. Arthur Nicolson reported that Germany agreed to cooperate if Britain abandoned the *Entente*.[222] Whilst Germany's latter requirement was impossible, the first was acknowledged in the Conference of Ambassadors convened in London on the 17th of December 1912. By the end of that month, Turkey had surrendered all its territories north of the Enos-Midia Line including Adrianople.[223] The Conference of Ambassadors was successful in facilitating a peace treaty between the warring factions on 30th May 1913. However, the Balkan allies then arrayed against Bulgaria when it attacked its former allies. Greece, Serbia and Montenegro were joined by Rumania in a Second Balkan War at the expense of Bulgaria which lost territory to those allies and to Turkey which won back Adrianople.

[218] Nicolson (n 130) 381.
[219] *Ibid* 382.
[220] BD (n 79) Vol IX (ii), No 13 *Buchanan to Grey* (10 October 1912).
[221] Nicolson (n 130) 374.
[222] *Ibid* 384. Erik Brandenburg, *Von Bismarck zum Weltkreig* (Insel-Verlag, 1939) 389.
[223] Nicolson (n 130) 387.

Figure 6.2 Carnegie Maps illustrating territorial modifications regarding the treaties of London and Bucharest 1913

Reprinted with permission from the publisher, from George Kennan, *Other Balkan Wars: A 1913 Carnegie Endowment Inquiry in Retrospect* (Washington, DC, Carnegie Endowment for International Peace, 1993).

B. The Conference of Ambassadors: The Concert of Europe's Last Hurrah

In 1912 the statesmen of the Great Powers realised the stakes were very high if any conflict broke out in the Balkans. It may be considered that in averting war this was Grey's finest hour. The story of his courage and persistence at a highly dangerous time is in some ways a model of diplomacy in resolving crises by peaceful means. Arthur Nicolson considered rightly that it was important to keep Austria-Hungary and Russia in touch so the war in the Balkans could be contained and localised. There was concern about Britain as a Christian state intervening in the Ottoman Empire considering the effect such intervention might have on the Muslim population of India. The secret alliance between Greece, Bulgaria, Serbia and Macedonia was encouraged by Sazanov without full consideration of the risks and consequences were Serbia and Bulgaria to take parts of Macedonia, or what Austria-Hungary might do or what atrocities might follow in revenge in that volatile region.[224] On the 10th October 1912 Buchanan reported to Grey from St Petersburg that a warning should be given to Serbia with regard to the Sanjak and later the same day Grey reported to Paget that the Serbian minister had told him that if Austria-Hungary moved on the Sanjak there would be war with Serbia.[225] Grey wrote to Bertie on the 12th October stating that Paul Gambon had told him that the French Foreign Minister said that if Turkey would accept the invitation to discuss reforms then a conference of powers should be announced.[226] This was the first intimation of a Balkan conference.

On the 18th October, Granville reported a meeting with Bethmann Hollweg in Berlin. Bethmann Hollweg said there was no need for the Powers to interfere yet, but they should wait for the outcome when both sides were weakened by the war which would give mediation a better chance.[227] On the 25th October, Grey reported to Buchanan in St Petersburg that Benckendorff, the Russian Ambassador in London, had told Arthur Nicolson of his conversation with the Greek Chargé warning that any Greek hostile action might close the Straits and hinder Russian Commerce.[228] A day later in Berlin Jules Cambon reported a discussion with Von Kiderlen suggesting that France, Britain and Germany propose a settlement. Grey considered it preferable that discussions took place between Austria-Hungary and Russia directly.[229] On the 28th October, Grey informed Bertie that if the Balkan League went to war then Russia and Austria-Hungary could propose a settlement as a basis for mediation.[230] The Powers wanted territorial boundaries maintained,

[224] BD (n 79) Vol IX (ii) 6, No 10 *Nicolson to Hardinge* (9 October 1912).
[225] *Ibid* Vol IX (ii) 10, No 13 *Buchanan to Grey* (10 October 1912).
[226] *Ibid* 15, No 20 *Grey to Bertie* (9 October 1912).
[227] *Ibid* 36–38, No 47 *Granville to Nicolson (Privste)* (18 October 1912).
[228] *Ibid* 51, No 63 *Grey to Buchanan* (25 October 1912).
[229] *Ibid* 53, No 66 (26 October 1912).
[230] *Ibid* 54, No 69 *Grey to Bertie* (28 October 1912).

but the problem was that Russia did not trust Austria-Hungary or Germany. Germany might suggest a scheme to France and Britain with Russia but if the *Entente* Powers did not agree then they could not restrain Austria-Hungary. Poincaré thought the Turks would accept mediation but there was some uncertainty about Bulgaria.[231] Once the war had started Sazanov began to regret his encouragement and suggested direct talks between the Balkan League and Turkey. Russia was counselling mediation.[232] There was strong support in the Russian press for the Slavs in the Balkans. Sazanov wanted France to take the lead in the Concert of Europe, not Austria-Hungary and Russia. On the 30th October Paget wrote to Grey saying that the Turks were in retreat. Most of the fighting was carried out by the Albanians but the Turkish regular army was not heavily engaged.[233] The same day President Poincaré proposed a settlement conference to discuss four key points.[234] Grey was in favour of the proposal for mediation when the time was right. But Bertie's reply on the 1st November was somewhat sceptical and he believed that Austria-Hungary would deal with Serbia with Germany's support and the outcome would be similar to the acquisition of Bosnia-Herzegovina.[235] On the 2nd November 1912, Russia prepared to join the other powers in sending warships to prevent the Bulgarians taking Constantinople.[236] Significant confirmation was received from Berlin that Germany was encouraging Vienna to bring about peaceful settlement and Germany was ready for a conference with Balkan representatives.[237] On 26 November 1912, Nicolson learned that Germany and Austria were encouraging Turkey and advised that 'some kind of a conference should assemble before too long'.[238] It appears from a Memorandum written by Mr Fitzmaurice of the Foreign Office that he was instrumental in causing direct negotiations to come about between the Porte and the Balkan League.[239]

On the 27th of November 1912, the Austrian army groups started to mobilise 150,000 men and up to 300,000 men against Serbia. Austria-Hungary became alarmed at the rapid advances of the Bulgarian armies which were halted by the Turkish defences at the Tchataldja Lines, and Adrianople which was holding out but later fell.[240] Grey's aim then was to hold the Concert together and to limit the scope of the territorial claims to the status of Albania and the claim of Serbia to an Adriatic port. The danger was that Italy and Austria-Hungary had competing interests in Albania, as did the Greeks and Serbs. Serbian claims

[231] *Ibid* 56–57, No 71 *Bertie to Grey* (28 October 1912).
[232] *Ibid* 62–63, No 77 *Cartwright to Grey* (30 October 1912).
[233] *Ibid* 66–67, No 79 *Paget to Grey* (30 October 1912).
[234] *Ibid* 68, No 81 *Grey to Bertie* (30 October 1912).
[235] *Ibid* 70, No 84 *Bertie to Grey* (1 November 1912).
[236] *Ibid* 79, No 98 *Buchanan to Grey* (2 November 1912).
[237] *Ibid* 80–81, No 100 *Buchanan to Grey* (2 November 1912).
[238] *Ibid* 209, No 286 *Nicolson to Bax-Ironside* (26 November 1912).
[239] AT Park, 'International Commission, The Birth of Albania and Sir Edward Grey's Prevention Diplomacy During the Balkan Wars' (2020) 31 *Diplomacy and Statecraft* 22–43.
[240] BD (n 79) Vol IX (ii) 213–14, No 289 *Cartwright to Grey* (27 November 1912).

to an Adriatic port were opposed by Austria-Hungary and Italy.[241] Montenegrin claims to Scutari were opposed by Austria-Hungary. Grey did not want a war over a Serbian port. Grey appreciated the gravity of the situation and the possibility that Austria-Hungary and Germany would take military action. Benckendorff told Grey that Russian public opinion would not acquiesce in any Austro-Hungarian-German reduction of the Balkan League's gains.[242]

With so much at stake, Grey was anxious that the conference was not frustrated by the Powers setting out preconditions, especially Italy and Austria-Hungary which might deter Russia.[243] He was anxious for the conference to begin as soon as possible.[244] Benckendorff was anxious to resolve the issue of Serbian access to the Adriatic, stating inter alia: 'Nous plaçons en première ligne la question de l'Albanie et celle de l' accès de la Serbie à la mer Adriatique' and ensure that Serbia was politically and economically independent.[245]

i. The Meetings of Ambassadors

The first meeting took place on the 17th December 1912 and it was agreed that all meetings would be confidential and that the Albanian question would be discussed first on the agenda. Austria-Hungary considered Albania as an autonomous state with a separate existence. Russia said that Albania should be guaranteed and controlled by the six Great Powers under the suzerainty of the Sultan, Italy preferred that it be 'exclusively' controlled by the six Powers.[246] It was generally agreed that Albania could be neutralised with agreed frontiers bordering Montenegro in the north and Greece to the south. Austria-Hungary did not favour an Albanian-Montenegrin border. No Albanians should be detached, but Russia disagreed its implied 'une ingérence' interference in the negotiations between Montenegro and Turkey. It was clear that there would be no Adriatic access for Serbia if the boundary between Montenegro and Serbia remained limitrophe. Austria-Hungary objected to allowing Scutari to be occupied. The Turks were then in occupation of Scutari, but it was besieged by Montenegrin forces which subsequently took occupation.[247]

A second meeting of ambassadors convened on the 18th December 1912 at the Foreign Office in London. Count Mensdorff, the Austro-Hungarian Ambassador, considered that if the littoral matters were agreed then Austria-Hungary proposed that Lake Ochrida should be given to Albania. The Aegean islands of Lemnos, Tenedos, Imbros and Samothrace should be under Turkish control with autonomous institutions for the guarantee of the local populations.

[241] FO 50589/42842/12/44 *Grey to Cartwright* (25 November 1912).
[242] FO 50769/42842/12/44 *Grey to Bertie* (28 November 1912).
[243] FO 52635/42842/12/44 *Grey to Rodd* (5 December 1912).
[244] FO 52335/42842/12/44 *Grey to Buchanan* (9 December 1912).
[245] FO 53444/42842/12/44 *Grey to Buchanan* (11 December 1912).
[246] FO 54360/42842/12/44 *Grey to Cartwright* (17 December 1912).
[247] *Ibid.*

Grey questioned this if the islands declared for Greece. Benckendorff suggested Turkish troops would be on the islands 'to maintain the Turkish flag'. Grey thought the Turks might fight the Greeks. Grey suggested that the islands be neutralised under guarantee of the Powers. Cambon said France would have no objection if the islands went to Greece. Crete would go to Greece. Mensdorff raised concern about Salonika and freedom of commercial access. France believed it should remain in the Ottoman possession. Benckendorf agreed. The communique said that the principle of autonomy for Albania was recognised as well as commercial access for Serbia to the Adriatic.[248]

A third meeting of the conference was held on the 20th December 1912 at which Grey was authorised to make a communique to the Palace and to the Serbian Government. Russia made certain stipulations regarding Serbia. They concluded a preliminary agreement as to Serbian access to the Adriatic and Albanian autonomy. Considerable progress had been made and the conference was adjourned to the 2nd of January 1913.[249]

At a meeting on the 30th December, Grey gave assurances to Benckendorf regarding support over Scutari and the possible need for a Frontier Commission to deal with Prizrend, Ipek and Djakova, as well as Serbia's control of a railway line and port which would be 'equal to that of any Great Power'.[250] On the 31st December, Grey informed Rodd that Bulgaria would demand Adrianople. The Italian Ambassador thought Bulgaria would accept Scutari instead of Adrianople. Austria-Hungary would object to Serbia receiving munitions through a port in the Adriatic in time of war. Grey thought that Austria-Hungary's fleet would seize such contraband of war.[251]

Paget warned Grey that Serbia would never accept Austria-Hungary's proposals. Serbia had given way on Durazzo and the coast.[252] Grey reported to Rodd that he had met the Italian Ambassador on the 27th December, emphasising the importance of Scutari as Albanian – 'l'ame de l' Albanie'.[253]

The ambassadors' meeting reconvened on the 2nd January 1913 but there was no discussion on Albania; they discussed sovereignty of the islands. Grey proposed giving Crete to Greece. France and Russia supported this. Austria-Hungary and Germany had to consider. Peace talks were progressing well between Bulgaria and Turkey but if no agreement was reached within 48 hours, ie by the 4th January, the ambassadors would consider appropriate representations.[254] That day Benckendorf met Arthur Nicolson and said he understood that Austria-Hungary would demobilise if negotiations with Serbia were concluded. Russia saw no need for Austria-Hungary's military

[248] FO 54513/42842/12/44 *Grey to Cartwright* (18 December 1912).
[249] FO 54893/42842/12/44 *Grey to Cartwright* (20 December 1912).
[250] FO 172/1/13/44 *Grey to Buchanan* (30 December 1912).
[251] FO 252/1/13/44 *Grey to Rodd* (31 December 1912).
[252] FO 448/135/13/44 *Paget to Grey* (31 December 1912).
[253] FO 36/1/13/44 *Grey to Rodd* (1 January 1913).
[254] *Grey to Cartwright* (2 January 1913).

preparedness. Russia had 350,000 men in Europe and Asiatic Russia. If Austria-Hungary demobilised Russia would send her reserves home. Grey summarised the position as:

> Count Berchtold said that he would put away his revolver when all questions as to Albania etc., had been solved and Mr Sazanov said that he did not want to discuss Albania till the revolver had been put away. Benckendorff said that this was shortly the position.[255]

After the meeting Cambon suggested to Grey that Austria-Hungary and Italy had to agree how to satisfy Montenegro and proceed to forgo discussions on Albania until Austria-Hungary withdrew its forces. 'Russia would not be more Montenegrin than Montenegro'. If satisfied Russia would not care. Once that was settled the conference could consider Albania. Austria-Hungary might yield on Prizrend, Ipek and Djakova.[256]

Benckendorf told Grey that Serbian troops would withdraw from Durazzo after the peace treaty with Turkey.[257] Austria-Hungary wanted Scutari as the capital of Albania but Russia wanted it to go to Montenegro. Russia required some compensation for Serbia as its protector, although Sazanov said it had 'no direct interest'.[258]

Grey informed Rodd in Rome that he might be able to compromise Scutari with railway commercial access to the Adriatic for Serbia, but Russia would not give way and therefore he would support Benckendorf in discussions.[259] Rodd told Grey that Italy had made wider representations at Vienna regarding the importance of Scutari which was regarded as Albanian irredentism. Austria-Hungary wanted Scutari settled straight away.[260]

Grey told Cartwright on 7th January that there was an impasse with Austria-Hungary over Scutari, it already having conceded the Sanjak. Russia could not give way over Scutari having given way on the Serbian port on the Adriatic. Possibility that Ipek could be attractive with its fertile lands. If this could be agreed the eastern border of Albania could be settled. Grey thought Italy would influence Montenegro towards settlement. Mensdorfff feared the Italians were 'more Montenegrin than the Montenegrins themselves'.[261] Grey told Buchanan that he was receiving British consular reports of atrocities committed along the Albanian border by the Serb forces. The Powers would agree to exclude Ipek, Prizrend and Dibra from Albania. Scutari would go to Albania, bar Djakova.[262] Grey told Buchanan on the 14th January that having had discussions with Benckendorff

[255] FO 250/1/13/44 *Grey to Buchanan* (2 January 1913).
[256] FO 639/1/13/44 *Grey to Bertie* (3 January 1913).
[257] FO 757/1/13/44 *Grey to Buchanan* (3 January 1913).
[258] FO 546/1/13/44 *Buchanan to Grey* (4 January 1913).
[259] FO 973/1/13/44 *Grey to Rodd* (4 January 1912).
[260] FO 666/1/13/44 *Rodd to Grey* (5 January 1912).
[261] FO 1209/1/13/44 *Grey to Cartwright* (7 January 1913).
[262] FO 11186/185/13/44 *Grey to Buchanan* (8 January 1913).

and Cambon there would still be difficulties over Scutari. Grey considered the futility of a general war just because Serbia was getting 'so many square kilometres more or less'. Cambon thought Germany and Italy did not want war and would intimate this to Austria-Hungary. Grey suggested an International Commission to examine the ethnographical and geographical conditions. Austria-Hungary's policy was defeated in Grey's view because Austria-Hungary no longer had any territorial access to Salonika.[263] Grey informed Goschen on the 17th January that he consulted the German Ambassador, Prince Lichnowsky, who said that Austria-Hungary would fight over Scutari. Austria-Hungary he said was prepared to surrender Ipek and Prizrend to Serbia.[264] On the 21st January, Grey told Paget that Serbia was anxious to secure territorial acquisition rather than as a result of a great war when the issue would be determined by the result which was uncertain.[265] Grey warned the British Ambassador to Montenegro, Count de Salis, that the Montenegrin delegates were obstinate and would not surrender Scutari. If they refused Austria-Hungary would march and Russia would move against Austria-Hungary, and if that happened France would defend Russia – all because of Scutari.[266] An expectation was that Montenegro might accept Ipek and Djakova as compensation, considering the Sanjak was valueless in their view.

On the 6th February Grey wrote to Buchanan reporting on the meeting of ambassadors that day. Germany was exerting considerable pressure on Austria-Hungary to make concessions, but Benckendorff did not consider that sufficient compensation for the loss of Scutari. Grey viewed Scutari and Djakova as Albanian, but the matter was muddled by the ethnographical and geographical circumstances. It was difficult for Russia to give way on Scutari, Djakova and Dibra, but Lichnowsky pointed out that Austria-Hungary had given way on the Sanjak and territorial access to Salonika.[267] What emerges here is that whilst ethnographical and geographical factors were considered in the final analysis it appears that the Great Powers acted in their own national interest using these factors to support strategic interests.[268]

Grey reported to Bertie on the 10th February that he had proposed an international boundary commission to settle the boundaries of Albania.[269] On the 15th February he informed Buchanan that the German, Italian and Austria-Hungarian ambassadors had private conversations with Benckendorff. Mensdorff was disappointed but Grey said Russia could not give way on Scutari, Djakova and Dibra. They discussed giving Montenegro Tarabosch which dominated

[263] FO 2265/1/18/44 *Grey to Buchanan* (14 January 1913).

[264] FO 639/1/13/44 *Grey to Goschen* (17 January 1913).

[265] FO 3522/135/18/44 *Grey to Paget* (21 January 1913).

[266] FO 250/1/13/44 *Grey to de Salis* (28 January 1913).

[267] FO 6128/135/13/44 *Grey to Buchanan* (6 February 1913).

[268] NC Guy, 'Fixing the Frontiers? Ethnography, Power Politics and The Delimitation of Albania, 1912 to 1914' (2005) 1 *Studies in Ethnicity and Nationalism* 27.

[269] FO 6120/135/13/44 *Grey to Bertie* (10 March 1913).

Scutari and for excluding the plain of Luma from Albania. Grey had to find some compromise between the Russian line and the Austria-Hungarian line with a possible concession on Djakova or Dibra or if not, prepare an *International Commission d'Enquiete*.[270] Austria-Hungary was to consider Russia's proposals and to state grounds for objection. On 15th March 1913 Mensdorff gave a negative response but suggested the Commission be free to decide Djakova free of the Balkan States.[271] A few days later Grey informed Buchannan that Austria-Hungary would agree to the exclusion of Dibra and the valley of Roca from Albania. Grey suggested they give up both and he would support a settlement but Berchtold would not agree. Austria-Hungary would not give way on more than three of the five towns Djakova, Dibra, Ipek, Prizrend and Scutari. Grey saw Prince Lichnowsky who confirmed Austria-Hungary would not give way on Djakova and Dibra. The Italian and German governments made representations to Austria-Hungary to secure a concession on Dibra. Russia warned that holding out for Djakova and Dibra could collapse the conference. Russia insisted on the exclusion of Prizrend, Ipek and Dibra from Albania.[272]

In an aide memoir Mensdorff expressed concern that a Commission would cause delay. The conference was near breakdown.[273] Buchanan informed Grey that Sazanov had told him that whilst Russia yielded on Tarabosch, Lumar and Radomir, Russia could not agree to the exclusion of Dibra and Djakova from Serbian territory.[274] Grey informed Goschen in Berlin on the 23rd February that Serbia would not withdraw its troops from Dibra or Djakova. Grey could not press the matter further just for 6,000 people at Djakova but refer it to a Commission. Austria-Hungary was not willing to give up Djakova: Serbia wanted it for strategic reasons.[275] On the 6th March, Cartwright informed Grey that he had a meeting with Berchtold regarding northern Albania but there was concern over Scutari. Berchtold suggested that Austria-Hungary might give way on Djakova if there were 'suitable compensations'.[276] Another ambassadors' meeting took place on that day and most questions were settled save Djakova. There was discussion about the withdrawal of Serb forces from Albania and reports of atrocities. Britain was to make representations to the Greek Government as to the plight of Vallona as there was considerable anxiety as to the plight of civilians in the war.[277] The meeting then discussed the north and north-eastern boundaries of Albania but Djakova was adjourned subject to determining the south and south-eastern boundaries of Albania. If there was agreement about Djakova then the Powers could draw the northern boundary

[270] FO 7688/135/13/44 *Grey to Buchanan* (15 February 1913).
[271] FO 12737/135/13/44 *Grey to Bertie* (15 February 1913).
[272] FO 8627/135/13/44 *Grey to Buchanan* (20 February 1913).
[273] FO 54360/42842/12/44 *Grey to Cartwright* (20 February 1913).
[274] FO 8229/135/13/44 *Buchanan to Grey* (20 February 1913).
[275] FO 8905/135/13/44 *Grey to Goschen* (23 February 1913).
[276] FO 10595/135/13/44 *Cartwright to Grey* (6 March 1913).
[277] FO 11179/135/13/44 *Ambassadors Meeting* (6 March 1913).

with Scutari settled.[278] If Djakova was settled then Russia could prevent Macedonia taking Scutari and seek the withdrawal of Serbian troops from Albania. If commercial advantages were given to Albania, Austria-Hungary would agree to an International Commission on Djakova. Austria-Hungary raised concern over the Catholic and Muslim population of Djakova.[279]

By the 10th March 1913 matters became critical with news of a Serbian Expeditionary force heading for Scutari. Austria-Hungary was not prepared to give up Djakova because of reported atrocities by Serbs against the population, but did not object to a reference to an international Commission.[280] Berchtold was as concerned about Djakova as about Scutari, anxious that the siege be lifted and Macedonian and Serb forces withdraw from Albania. The Powers were anxious that Turkey must concede. The frontier should be the Enos-Media line, the islands should be decided by the Powers and territory west of the new frontier should be ceded save for Albania which would be decided by the Powers. The Balkan allies would have no claim for indemnity but could discuss the allocation of debt in Paris.[281]

Grey told Cartwright that if Russia convinced Macedonia to vacate Scutari it would be conditional on Serbia obtaining Djakova and Dibra.[282] On the 14th March Grey confirmed that he was prepared to inform Belgrade and Cettinje (Montenegro) that the Powers démarche was that Scutari go to Albania. Grey told Cambon that he could do no more with Austria-Hungary after the settlement of Scutari and the Adriatic littoral. It would be difficult to get Austria-Hungary to concede Dibra and Djakova.[283]

On 15th March 1913 Mensdorff saw Grey. Berchtold considered Russian proposals as 'indiscrutable'(*sic*) in the light of Serb atrocities against Muslims and Catholics continuing. Grey said it was difficult for Russia to press Serbia to evacuate Djakova as well as Scutari.[284] Nevertheless on the 18th March Grey confirmed that he proposed a collective démarche at Belgrade and Cettinje warning them against any territorial changes in the boundaries of Albania without assent of the Powers. It followed that neither Montenegro nor Serbia could acquire rights in Albania and if Montenegro took Scutari its destiny would be decided by the Powers.[285]

Arthur Nicolson wrote a Memorandum on the 18th March after reading a cable from Sazanov to the Russian Ambassador in Vienna to the effect that if the Commission adopted the guiding principle based on the geographical and

[278] FO 100595/135/13/44 *Grey to Cartwright* (6 March 1913).
[279] FO 11424/135/13/44 *Grey to Buchanan* (10 March 1913).
[280] FO 11609/135/13/44 *Grey to Cartwright* (10 March 1913).
[281] Private. *Grey to Buchanan* (11 March 1913).
[282] FO 12370/135/13/44 *Grey to Cartwright* (13 March 1913).
[283] FO 12440/135/13/44 *Grey to Cartwright* (14 March 1913).
[284] FO 12736/135/13/44 *Grey to Cartwright* (15 March 1913).
[285] FO 13002/135/13/44 *Grey to Cartwright* (18 March 1913).

economic connection between Djakova and Serbia, Russia would accept the Commission.[286]

On the 19th of March after meeting with Mensdorff, Grey confirmed to Cartwright that if the Commission were instructed as to guarantees over the protection of refugees, their religious and national rights and liberties, of urban and rural non Serbian populations of Djakova, Berchtold would be willing to meet Sazanov and leave the composition of the Commission to Grey.[287] Sazanov insisted on the exchange of Djakova for Scutari, but on the 20th March Grey learned that Scutari had been bombarded and the Austro-Hungarian consulate and a monastery damaged. Austria-Hungary threatened to send warships to this south dalmatian coast, but Grey was anxious for a Great Power demonstration instead.[288] The following day Grey told Buchanan that it was important that Sazanov agreed to protection for Catholics and Muslims and that hostilities should immediately cease. Serbia was assured of Dibra and Djakova and should withdraw from Scutari.[289]

On the 28th March there was a meeting of the ambassadors to discuss admission of a Greek delegation. There was a precedent in that the Romanian minister had been admitted earlier. A Résumé of the Romanian ambassador's views was to be put to the Greeks. Austria-Hungary was not opposed to any proposal for the evacuation of territories occupied by Serbia in Albania. It was resolved to employ coercive measures if the Montenegrins did not comply with the démarche. This took the form of a naval demonstration at Antivari against Montenegrin forces at Scutari.[290]

On the 1st April Arthur Nicolson made it clear to the Montenegrin representative M Popovitch that the Powers were all agreed that Scutari was to be in Albania and that unless the siege of Scutari was raised the Powers would make the naval demonstration.[291] On the 10th of April Grey told Bertie that they were close to a cessation of hostilities provided the Scutari question was settled.[292] On the 11 April the Serbian army started its withdrawal from Albania.

At the meeting of the ambassadors on 21st April, consideration was given to seeking the Ottoman Government's assistance in facilitating the handover of Scutari which might make it easier for the Montenegrin King Nicholas to accept the Powers taking control of the city.[293] Following this, on the 1st May, a draft peace treaty between Turkey and the Balkan allies was presented for consideration. A question as to financial support for the Montenegrin economy was raised

[286] FO 12894/135/13/44 *Memorandum by Sir A Nicolson* (18 March 1913).
[287] FO 13283/135/13/44 *Grey to Cartwright* (6 March 1913).
[288] FO 12847/135/13/44 *Grey to Buchanan* (20 March 1913).
[289] FO 13787/135/13/44 *Grey to Buchanan* (21 March 1913).
[290] FO 14813/18799/13/44 *Grey to Cartwright* (28 March 1913).
[291] FO 15167/135/13/44 *Grey to de Salis* (1 April 1913).
[292] FO 17253/18799/13/44 *Grey to Bertie* (10 April 1913).
[293] FO 18031/14538/18/44 *Grey to Bertie* (21 April 1913).

subject to the evacuation of Scutari.[294] It surrendered to the Montenegrins on the 23rd April but on the 4th May the Montenegrin forces evacuated the city. That day Grey was warned by Goshen in Berlin that he had reports of Italy's designs on Vallona and Santi Quaranta which would inflame Greek opinion.[295] Grey informed Goschen the next day that King Nicholas had conceded Scutari and this would prevent any division of Albania by Austria-Hungary or Italy. The assumption underpinning the conferences had been 'that no Power was going to ask for any territory for itself as a result of the Balkan troubles'.[296]

At a further meeting of ambassadors on the 5th May, Scutari was placed under the protection of the Powers with instructions to the naval blockade's commanders to open communications with the Montenegrins for the evacuation of their forces.[297] On 7th May Grey told Rodd that 'the Great Powers must not play with fire' and that every action by Italy and Austria-Hungary should be avoided. Possible financial assistance to Montenegro might be possible but not any territorial compensation which would alienate Austria-Hungary. There was a problem over the Aegean islands. Italy occupied Rhodes. It would not surrender it to Greece, but to Turkey. Grey said it was a decision for the Powers. Imperiali, the Italian Ambassador, assured Grey that Italy had no intentions of keeping it. Mytilene and Chios could go to Greece as Austria-Hungary agreed but there was some reservation in Berlin.[298]

There was a further ambassadors' meeting on the 8th May. Mensdorff and Imperiali submitted a plan for Albania under Turkish suzerainty. Grey was anxious that a peace treaty between Turkey and the Balkans be concluded as soon as possible. Scutari's incorporation in Albania was conditional on Serbia getting Djakova.[299] Italy was prepared to give up the Greek islands to facilitate settlement of the southern Albanian border subject to various conditions.[300] Grey also addressed the issue of a Serbian request for a guarantee in the treaty as to rights to the Adriatic. Grey said the conference would consider such provision a statute for the organisation of Albania.[301]

On the 30th May the Treaty of London was signed ending the First Balkan War. Grey had to consider settlement of the Aegean islands and the south-eastern frontier of Albania. Imperiali wanted the islands to go to Turkey, but the Powers decided they should go to Greece. Lichnowsky agreed to Greece having all the islands except for Tenedos and Imbros, and Thasos which would go to Bulgaria as agreed earlier. The Montenegrin troops and the remaining military

[294] FO 20463/185/13/44 *Grey to Bertie* (10 April 1913).
[295] FO 20486/20477/13/41 *Goschen to Grey* (4 May 1913).
[296] FO 20974/135/18/44 *Grey to Goschen* (5 May 1913).
[297] FO 21208/20810/13/44 *Grey to Cartwright (*5 May 1913).
[298] FO 21566/20477/13/44 *Grey to Rodd* (7 May 1913).
[299] FO 22131/9564/13/44 *Grey to Cartwright* (8 May 1913).
[300] FO 23425/13799/13/44 *Grey to Rodd* (19 May 1913).
[301] FO 23424/9564/13/44 *Grey to Paget* (19 May 1913).

infrastructure and war material should be taken from Scutari. The Powers would consider a loan guarantee after complete evacuation of all Albanian territory.[302]

Grey had succeeded to a remarkable degree in containing the Balkan War and also in steering the Great Powers through a very serious crisis which otherwise may have led to a general war. By the 25th June, Grey confided in Mr Carnegie that the Reunions, as the meetings were called, had been going on for months without any break and he proposed to adjourn the conference after the following week. Following the outbreak of a Second Balkan War on the 29 June when Bulgaria launched a pre-emptive attack on Serbia and Greece, there was nothing that could be done effectively by conference. There were tedious problems over a multiplicity of conditions of detail and points of form rather than substance which impeded discussion of Albania and its southern frontier. The final Reunion should enable a Swedish Gendarmerie to be part of the Commission of Control of Albania. Grey suggested after the following week that matters be dealt with through diplomatic channels and not by the ambassador's conference. On the 29th July 1913 at the 54th session of the conference Albania was declared an independent sovereign state. So ended the conference of ambassadors.

C. Great Powers Must Not Play with Fire

The Balkan Crisis of 1912–13 exposes the fault lines in Europe as between the Triple *Entente* and the Triple Alliance through what Christopher Clark described as 'continental geopolitical ecosystems'.[303] There were competing interests between the Austro-Hungarian Empire, the German Empire, the decaying Ottoman Empire and the Balkan states, as well as the rivalry between the Great Powers and their particular interests in the Balkans and Mediterranean. David Lieven opined that the Great Powers intervened in order to preserve the status quo. However, he states that the Balkans epitomised irreconcilable interests between Austria-Hungary and Russia and that it was Austria-Hungary and not Russia that wanted war.[304] Zara Steiner and Kenneth Neilson opine that Germany was not prepared for war over the Balkans. Bethmann Hollweg was against war at that stage and so Germany co-operated with Britain in reaching a settlement but at the same time increased its military strength.[305]

Keith Robbins suggests that Grey and Arthur Nicolson may have underestimated the 'infinite capacity of the Balkan states in creating difficulties'.

[302] FO 25582/9564/13/44 *Grey to Cartwright* (30 May 1913).

[303] C Clark, *The Sleepwalkers* (Penguin, 2013) 289.

[304] D Lieven, *Towards the Flame* (Penguin, 2015) 250–51.

[305] Z Steiner and K Neilson, *Britain and the Origins of the First World War* (Palgrave, 2003) 118 and BD (n 79) Vol X (II), No 456 *Captain H Watson to Sir E Goschen Confidential. A Review of the Policy and Position of the German Naval Expansionist Party* (20 January 1913).

Nicolson wanted more support for Russia whilst Tyrell favoured a firmer line.[306] It may be that the success of the Reunions or conferences of ambassadors was due also to the rapport between the ambassadors and Grey and in no mean measure to the cordial and professional relationship between Grey and Lichnowsky, and Grey and Cambon.[307]

Perhaps it may also be said that the Balkan War of 1912–13 marked a turning point in the cohesion of the Concert of Europe. The conferences were successful generally in preventing and delaying a European war, but the national interests of Italy and Austria-Hungary, not to mention Serbia, Bulgaria, Greece, Montenegro and Turkey led to independent action. Whilst Grey demonstrated initiative and independence as well as considerable patience, there was a limit to how much could be achieved when it came to micro-management. The international concert gave way to the national interest for Italy and Austria-Hungary so that when the crisis came in July 1914 it took priority. Grey's success was attributable to his ability to co-ordinate and manage a collective response from the ambassadors, taking pains to keep in touch with the parties to the conflict through his own ambassadors. Grey could not control the Balkan League but he could influence the Great Powers' ambassadors. In July 1914 national interests outweighed the collective will and undermined any influence Grey might otherwise have achieved. After April 1913, Crompton opines 'both Germany and Britain sacrificed cooperation in the Near East to the well-being of the respective power groups'.[308] That might be the obituary of the Reunions.

[306] K Robbins, *Sir Edward Grey* (Cassell, 1971) 265, 267.

[307] Suggested also in H Young, *Prince Lichnowsky and the Great War* (University of Georgia Press, 1977) 68–69.

[308] RJ Crampton, 'The Decline of the Concert of Europe in the Balkans 1913–14' (1974) 52 *The Slavonic and East European Review* 393, 415.

7

When 'National Honour' Led to War

I. THE UTILITY OF INTERNATIONAL ARBITRATION IN THE CONTEXT OF THE WORLD CRISIS OF 1914

IN THE CONTEXT of the crises which arose in the late nineteenth and early twentieth centuries, it is important to understand what was meant by arbitration and mediation. This is especially so in the light of the German rejection of Sir Edward Grey's mediation proposal of July 1914 which was opposed by German Chancellor Bethmann-Hollweg on the basis that it was arbitration to which no sovereign power could accede. Herr Bethmann-Hollweg was right in terms of legal principle that no state need surrender its sovereignty to an international tribunal, the parties must consent to the tribunal's jurisdiction. Consent is the key point. As in the Geneva Tribunal what gave credibility to the Tribunal was the agreement to set it up within the Treaty of Washington 1871 and the composition with representation for the disputants and neutral states. The circumstances in 1914 however were very different from those in 1871.

According to John Westlake,[1] writing in 1896, there was no power to enforce an international award between states, nor any power that could compel states to arbitrate. Each Great Power was sovereign and independent. Thus, according to Westlake, an award would merely create a new right between them.[2] As between states the arbitrators' jurisdiction was dependent upon the terms of the Treaty of Arbitration or the treaty under which the parties referred the dispute to that process. The Treaty of Washington 1871 discussed earlier is an exemplar in that respect.

As to mediation, Westlake opined that it was akin to taking the advice of a common friend. In his view this was a matter of statesmen giving advice to each other, but unlike in arbitration it did not give rise to the creation of a new right. A state as mediator it seems

> ... commits itself to an opinion about what two other powers had best do, the hope arises on one side and the fear on the other, or perhaps the fear on both sides, that it may interfere actively in support of its opinion.[3]

[1] Professor of International Law at Cambridge 1888 to 1908. He was a member of the International Court of Arbitration at The Hague. See J Westlake, 'International Arbitration' (1896) 7 *International Journal of Ethics* 5.

[2] *Ibid* 1–20.

[3] *Ibid* 5–6.

This worked at times for fear of some interference if there was no agreement, but the other factor recognised by Westlake was the 'moral weight' that it gave to a state whose case was vindicated which succeeded in facilitating an agreement between the disputant states.[4] In the context of July 1914 mediation has to be seen, not in the modern legal context of a neutral facilitating a resolution between disputants, but as diplomats or ambassadors engaging with their counterparts and encouraging a certain course of action. Thus, when Sir Edward Grey suggested Four Power mediation through a conference of ambassadors in London, this essentially would have followed the pattern adopted in the earlier Balkans' crises of a conference between ambassadors. In 1912 the ambassadors worked in concert but by 1913 there was some divergence which became more significant as we shall see in 1914.

It seems that both mediation and arbitration in Grey's time depended upon the *bone fides* of the states concerned and trust in the good offices of the arbitrator or mediator. The essential point was that those exercising such offices were independent, impartial and neutral in that their respective states had no vested interest in the outcome. Although the London Conference of Ambassadors achieved a result in 1913, by late July 1914 Grey found it difficult to treat as between Austria-Hungary and Serbia. Many may attribute the failure of diplomacy in 1914 to the intransigence of Germany or the impetuosity of Austria-Hungary and Russia. Others may consider as M Dreyfus that 'there are controversies to which there can be no obligation to apply it. When the independence or the integrity of the nation is at stake, all the treaties in the world could not force that nation to accept it'.[5]

But another explanation may simply be that there can be no reconciliation because the national honour will not permit it.[6]

II. SIR EDWARD GREY

Sir Edward Grey was perhaps first officially directed to the Austro-Hungarian problem by a confidential dispatch dated the 13th December 1905[7] from Goschen, then British Ambassador in Vienna, congratulating Grey on his appointment as Foreign Secretary. He reported that so far as Austria-Hungary was concerned in relation to Macedonia: 'the eyes of Austria-Hungary are turned, not outwards, but inwards'. Austria-Hungary was focussed on the question of universal suffrage and the dual monarchy had 'set machines to work which have taken

[4] *Ibid* 6.

[5] F Dreyfus, *L'Arbitrage International* (d'Institut, 1892) 355.

[6] An example being the Washington Conference in March 1861 between US Congressmen that failed to reconcile the differences between the northern and southern states.

[7] Foreign Office Papers (FO) 800–40 (1) Austria-Hungary-Hungary. *Goschen to Grey* (13 December 1905).

charge and are now beyond control'. Goschen reported that the Hungarians were apprehensive over Austria-Hungary, asking them to increase the recruits to the imperial army. Hungary contended that it was an independent Kingdom, but Austro-Hungarians treated Hungary as a Province. More significantly Goschen informed Grey that as regards its foreign policy, Austria-Hungary was 'well under the thumb of Germany'.[8] Whatever Grey's impression at that time, he was well versed in Balkan matters by the time of the July crisis, and just as Britain had upheld the Ottoman Empire, Germany, the rising Power on the continent, now protected the declining Austro-Hungarian Empire.

A. An Obligation of Honour

Sir Edward Grey's approach to the European crisis was strange. On the one hand, he valued close relations with friendly states and on the other shied away from any formal or legal obligation to such states restrained by the domestic political complications of foreign entanglements. He leaned however towards Britain's *Entente* partners so that he was perceived by Germany and Austria-Hungary as having a conflict of interest when it came to him acting as a mediator.

The July crisis happened to coincide with a major domestic crisis over Home Rule for Ireland and as late as the 25th July it was uncertain as to whether Britain would have to deal with a civil war in Ireland with the clash of leading Tory and Unionist politicians such as Arthur Balfour, Bonar Law, FE Smith and Sir Edward Carson as against the Liberal Government of Herbert Asquith[9] and the Irish Nationalist Party led by John Redmond. The British position was also more complex because of Britain's geographical position. It was not attached to the continent as an integral part of the land mass, but an island off its coast. It looked to the sea and its colonies rather than to Europe for expansion. It therefore had a large navy, but small army. It had not fought a major continental war since the Battle of Waterloo apart from the Crimea campaign and the Boer war. Despite Haldane's army reforms it was not ready to fight a major European war against Germany. It could help the French army and with luck might hold the German juggernaut in check, but there was little prospect of beating Germany on land at least until British resources in her Empire could be fully mobilised.

Sir Eyre Crowe wrote: 'The general character of England's foreign policy is determined by the immutable condition of her geographical situation on the ocean flank of Europe as an island state with vast oversees colonies and dependencies.'[10]

[8] *Ibid.*

[9] Asquith had a very good knowledge of the Irish Question having been Sir Charles Russell's junior counsel at the Special Commission in 1888.

[10] FO 371/237 *Memorandum by Mr Eyre Crowe* (1 January 1907). GP Gooch and H Temperley (eds), *British Documents on the Origins of the War 1898–1914* Vols I–XI (Her Majesty's Stationery Office, 1927–38) (BD) Vol III, Appendix A, 397.

But Crowe also believed that appeasement was no safeguard for democracy.[11] Neither he nor Sir Arthur Nicolson believed that Britain could just stand by and let France be defeated by Germany.

In a parliamentary debate on the 3 August 1914, Grey stated that England had no 'obligation of honour' to France. That however is questionable when military exchanges between Britain and France are considered as well as naval arrangements between Britain and Russia. He was focused on the British interest. He also placed considerable emphasis on the legal requirements of such relations. According to Trevelyan,[12] respecting legality was the only way by which war in the end could be avoided. According to Parry, Grey and his colleagues had quite a different perception of law and policy from the approach today.[13] In those years international law was confined to treaties and the law of that treaty. International law, in that context, was what today we might regard as international customary law,[14] essentially a matter of practice or choice of the nation state which has legal effects for all states that recognise it.[15] But in the July crisis, although suggested by the Tsar, there was no recourse to the Permanent Court of Arbitration or to arbitration which was dismissed out of hand by Bethmann-Hollweg. As noted in chapter 4 there had been a successful reference to an *ad hoc* international commission of inquiry in the *Dogger Bank* case.[16]

B. Grey and International Law

Sir Edward Grey functioned within the framework of the Concert System which provided some semblance of a public law system for Europe.[17]

In those days, as Parry reminds us, war was an instrument of international law as it condoned war.[18] Grey would have been familiar with Westlake's notion that international law was a regulation of warfare and recognising this he would have expected states to offer mediation or arbitration before they commenced hostilities. Lawrence considered that war altered the relationship between states and that the causes of war were not the concern of international law. On the

[11] R Vansittart, *The Mist Procession* (Hutchinson & Co Ltd, 1958) 63.

[12] GM Trevelyan, *Grey of Falloden* (Longmans, Green and Co, 1937) 225.

[13] C Parry, 'Foreign Policy and International Law' in FH Hinsley (ed), *British Foreign Policy under Sir Edward Grey* (Cambridge University Press, 2008) 91.

[14] *Ibid.*

[15] A Abass, *International Law, Text, Cases and Materials* (Oxford University Press, 2012).

[16] It was the first case referred to under Arts 9–14 of the Hague Convention of 1899.

[17] Reference in Treaty of Paris to Turkey's admission to the Concert would participate in 'the advantages of the Public Law and System of Europe'. Also, referred to as part of the 'public law of Europe' regarding Switzerland's joinder of the Concert under the Treaty of Vienna 1815. See discussion in Parry (n 13) 91.

[18] Parry (n 13) 92. Grey may have been familiar with such works on international law such as those by J Westlake (1904 and 1907), TJ Lawrence's *Principles of International Law* and LFL Oppenheim's *Treatise on International Law* (1905 and 1912).

other hand, Hall considered that international law ought to determine when war could be justly or unjustly undertaken:

> As international law is destitute of any judicial or administrative machinery, it leaves states, which think themselves aggrieved, and which have exhausted all peaceful methods of obtaining satisfaction, to exact redress for themselves by force. It thus recognises war as a permitted mode of giving effect to its decisions. Theoretically therefore, as it professes to cover the whole field of the relations of states which can be brought within the scope of law, it ought to determine the causes for which war can be justly undertaken; in other words, it ought to mark out as plainly as municipal law what constitutes a wrong which a remedy maybe sought at law.[19]

International law in Grey's time could not stop war and mechanisms such as arbitration and mediation were only effective by mutual consent and a willingness to submit the sovereign jurisdiction of a nation state to an international forum. But at that time, international law did not have the international legal mechanisms or institutional structures, eg the League of Nations or United Nations, to do so. The law was not codified save for The Hague Conventions and treatises on the subject. Grey's view therefore according to Parry was that treaties were binding in 'honour' only; they were not legally binding.[20] Grey may have considered that international law was irrelevant to his conduct of international relations. Any application of *pacta sunt savanda* that such agreements are intended to be binding was not applicable in that context. A treaty is not a contract as in domestic law and is not so accepted by statesmen although in international law they are regarded as binding on a state but because states are sovereign they may choose to follow them or not. Often it appears that domestic political considerations override the treaty obligation when it comes down to a matter of party policy and what the government of the day determines to be party/government policy. But sometimes the 'will of Parliament' may influence that. No wonder then with a very divided Cabinet in early August 1914 Grey was of the view that the naval and military conversations between British and French and British and Russian forces were not binding and Britain had no obligation. That may, as Lloyd George pointed out, have been the English view, but not the French or the Russian and certainly not that of France's Ambassador to London Paul Cambon. Grey was undoubtedly placed in something of a dilemma on 28 July 1914 when Austria-Hungary declared war on Serbia. When Grey saw Prince Lichnowsky on 29 July, he would not make a statement of British intentions. Neither would he make a statement to M Cambon. He distinguished this problem from the Moroccan crises of 1905 and 1911. The 1914 crisis was a question of Russian and Austro-Hungarian rivalry in the Balkans. To Grey and his colleagues, the British interest was not involved since any conflict would be limited to that between

[19] WE Hall, *International Law* (Clarendon Press, 1880) 51.
[20] See Parry (n 13) 96–97.

Austria-Hungary, Serbia or Russia. However, if Germany assisted Austria-Hungary and France became involved with Russia, the question of the balance of power would arise and England would have to consider whether to intervene.[21]

The obvious difficulty here was that Grey could not commit England to any action because the Cabinet and public opinion was divided. But there was also his perception of the understanding that had been reached over military and naval conversations. The disposition of the French fleet to protect the Mediterranean, whilst the Grand Fleet and other British naval squadrons protected the Channel and Atlantic ports placed France in an awkward position if Germany attacked. Similarly, any uncertainty as to the deployment of the British Expeditionary Force would obviously affect the French armies' plans. Worse, delay by Britain in the face of German mobilisation, which according to reports had commenced on 25 July 1914, would place France at considerable military disadvantage. In this context, the British Government's tendency to remain neutral was causing Cambon serious anxiety. Grey's dilemma was not only a divided country and Cabinet, but also how he could use the instruments of diplomacy to restrain Austria-Hungary and Russia. What frustrated that role was the Russian preparations for war but even then, Grey tried to avoid war between Germany and France. In that he came unstuck because he had no authority to promise French neutrality in the event of war between Germany and Russia, France being the ally of Russia.

It is not the task here to second guess Grey's approach, but to consider if the instruments of international law and diplomacy could resolve such a delicate and implacable problem. According to his contemporaries, Grey was a fair-minded statesman.[22] Trevelyan states that he listened to advice whether from Arthur Nicolson, Eyre Crowe, Lord Hardinge or Sir William Tyrrell, but took his own view. To what extent they influenced him is difficult to assess but undoubtedly he could not ignore them, and as a politician he could neither afford to ignore his Cabinet colleagues, Parliament nor public opinion. Of all Cabinet members his role, as that of any Foreign Secretary, must balance a plethora of interests, surely one of the most interesting but also most difficult of all Cabinet posts. Grey it seems navigated his way through this diaspora of competing and conflicting interests saying, 'I did not regard anything except my own letters and official papers as deciding policy'.[23] The contrast between his advisers Sir Eyre Crowe and Sir William Tyrrell is interesting. Tyrrell favouring a rapprochement with Germany which he considered much in Britain's interest and

[21] K Eubanks, *Paul Cambon Master Diplomatist* (University of Oklahoma Press, 1960) 172. BD (n 10) Vol XI *Grey to Bertie* (29 July 1914) 180; *Cambon to Viviani* (29 July 1914), *Documents Diplomatiques Française, 3rd Service, 1911–1914, ed.* Ministère des Affaires Étrangères, 11 Vols (Paris, 1929–36) Vol XI, 228–29.

[22] Sir Algernon Law wrote to Professor Trevelyan that his was: 'the fairest of minds'. Trevelyan (n 12) 168.

[23] *Ibid* 169.

Crowe, who well understood the militaristic tendency of the *Kaiserreich* and the Prussian Junker, warning of the menace of a dominant Germany. Despite all this advice it seems that Grey's policy was reactive to German armament. England had no forward military planning regime; it had no sizeable army with sufficient resource to fight a continental war. When it came to war England's strategy seemed dislocated with risky diversions in Turkey and the Middle East weakening the western front.

So, in the challenging situation that arose in June to August 1914, how far did Grey succeed in his quest for peace and mediation between the rival alliances of the Dual Alliance (the Central Powers of Germany and Austria-Hungary Hungary) and the Triple *Entente* of England, France and Russia and the Franco-Russian Alliance given also the understandings reached between members of the Triple *Entente* in 1904, 1907 and 1911?

An answer to this lies to some extent in an analysis of the diplomatic documents as recorded in the *Collected Diplomatic Documents Relating to the Outbreak of the European War*[24] and *British Documents on the Origins of the War 1898–1914*.[25] Both these sources require close analysis especially because they contain quite different selections. Such analysis must also consider post war scholarship especially that of later twentieth century historians.

The following analysis considers the key efforts and difficulties that Grey faced in trying to save the peace of Europe. Whilst peace was an overriding factor in the Asquith Cabinet, the dominant influence was the British interest. Since 1815 British foreign policy had adhered to notions of a balance of power, the hegemony of Europe and that no single country should dominate the continent. Much of this was the design of Lord Castlereagh who was instrumental with M Talleyrand in establishing the Concert System whereby all the great European Powers would meet through their representatives in conference to discuss and resolve inter-state disputes. In the Balkan crisis Grey, Cambon, Lichnowsky, Mensdorff and Benckendorff had managed to contain the Balkan conflict preventing a collision between Russia and Austria-Hungary, under Grey's chairmanship. The challenge in 1914 was to repeat the success of that process. Why was it that the Great Powers were unwilling to assert the Concert System and participate in a conference as they did in 1912, and why did Grey abandon that approach? These are questions that cannot be fully answered here but simply follow the unfolding of events and efforts of the diplomats to try and reconcile competing interests in a search to preserve the peace. The essential difference in 1914 was that Germany and Austria-Hungary were not prepared to co-operate with Grey as they had previously. Grey should have been aware of Germany's

[24] *Collected Diplomatic Documents Relating to the Outbreak of the European War* (Her Majesty's Stationery Office, 1915).

[25] BD (n 10).

changed policy following the difficulties that arose during the Algeciras crisis in 1906, the annexation of Bosnia in 1909, followed by the two Balkan Wars and the London Conference in 1912–1913. It was obvious that as Austria-Hungary was Germany's ally Germany would support Austria-Hungary in any war with Russia. Germany also had interests in Turkey with Von Sanders' military mission and the construction of a Berlin to Bagdad railway.

It appears that neither Grey nor M Viviani, the French Foreign Minister, nor Paul Cambon, the highly experienced French Ambassador to London, thought war was imminent in July 1914,[26] although Britain's relations with Germany had been improving as demonstrated by a British naval squadron's visit to Kiel in July 1914. However, as events unfolded the threat of war loomed large.

In the *Collected Diplomatic Documents* published in 1915 there are 161 documents; telegrams passing between diplomatic channels: the chancelleries of Europe and their respective embassies. This narrative as to efforts to resolve the crisis commenced on the 22nd July 1914, 24 days after the murder of the Austro-Hungarian heir Archduke Franz Ferdinand. On that day Sir Horace Rumbold,[27] the British Chargé in Berlin, had a meeting with the German Chancellor Theobald von Bethmann-Hollweg.[28] The Chancellor told Rumbold that the question was a matter between Austria-Hungary and Serbia; it was not for others to interfere. Bethmann-Hollweg apparently considered that any dispute should be localised and was anxious for it not to spread. So long as it was confined, then other Powers would not be interested, but if any of the allied powers became involved then there was a risk of a general European war.

i. Grey's Approach

Whilst Grey is a central figure in this analysis, his influence on the Powers drifting to war was limited first by the ambiguity of his policy and the Cabinet's indecisiveness, second by a very divided public opinion, and third restrained by the threat of a civil war in Ireland.[29] His task was not easy by any means, but it lacked his more effective approach in 1912 and 1913. In 1914 he had a tendency to be indirect in his warnings to Germany and Austria-Hungary through Britain's allies. Thus, in Berlin there was some misapprehension regarding British neutrality in a continental war. In Grey's defence it has to be said that he had mixed signals from his Cabinet colleagues and could not be very forthright.

[26] However, some like the Comte Albert du Mann quoted in the *Echo de Paris* in 1913 as saying 'All Europe, uncertain and troubled prepares for an inevitable war, the immediate cause of which remains still unknown to her'.

[27] *Collected Diplomatic Documents* (n 24) *Rumbold to Grey* No 2.

[28] Theobald von Bethmann-Hollweg served as Chancellor of Germany from 1909–17.

[29] E Grey, *Twenty-Five Years* (London, Hodder and Stoughton, 1928) 72–74; BD (n 10) Vol III, No 210(a) *Grey to Bertie* (10 January 1906) 170–71.

In 1914 after the Ulster threat from 'Carson's insurrection', Grey's first serious problem was the Austria-Hungary ultimatum to Serbia. If Russia became involved France would as well. Therefore, he first counselled direct talks between Russia and Austria-Hungary. This was scuppered by France and Poincaré's advice to Sazanov.[30] When this did not work, he warned Lichnowsky that Russia would support Serbia. He suggested a Four Power mediation without Austria-Hungary and Russia. Just why he did not propose a convening of the Concert of Europe at this point is not clear, but it could be that Germany would have been reluctant to act contrary to the interest of its ally. Diplomatically, as Ferguson argues,[31] Grey found himself in a quandary. He could pressure the Triple Alliance by threat of a quasi-Triple *Entente* but that would encourage Russia, and France was already doing that. Grey's mediation proposal was dismissed outright by Bethmann-Hollweg and Jagow, as surrendering their ally to a court of arbitration.[32] In their view to permit their ally to agree to arbitration was to surrender the sovereignty of Austria-Hungary to an international court. The only solution then seemed bilateral discussions between Austria-Hungary and Russia. The offer of talks was accepted on the 30th July, but Russian mobilisation operations frustrated the process. Grey was not able to control these events. Germany had suspicions of Russia's re-emerging power after 1907 following the Anglo-Russian rapprochement and her recovery after the Russo-Japanese War. That shift in the balance of influence in south-east Europe and the Balkans could only buttress Serbia even more so after her success in the Balkan Wars.

III. THE DIPLOMATIC COUNTERPOISE

Before Austria-Hungary issued its ultimatum to Serbia Raymond Poincaré, the French President, then visiting St Petersburg, told the British Ambassador Sir George Buchanan that he opposed bilateral talks between Austria-Hungary and Russia. He favoured the 'moderating counsels' of England and France at Vienna. In London Sir Eyre Crowe[33] felt that Germany should be putting pressure on Austria-Hungary not Britain and Sir Arthur Nicolson[34] felt that it would be resented.[35]

On 23 July 1914 Austria-Hungary issued its ultimatum to Serbia making demands that removed any vestige of state sovereignty and humiliated Serbia in response to the murder of Archduke Franz Joseph in Sarajevo on 28 June 1914.

[30] N Ferguson, *1914: Why the World Went to War* (Penguin Books, 2005) 23–24, and see N Ferguson, *The Pity of War* (Penguin Books, 1999) 154–58.

[31] Ferguson, *1914: Why the World Went to War, ibid* 24.

[32] *Ibid* 27.

[33] Assistant Under Secretary of State, Foreign Office, London.

[34] Permanent Under Secretary, Foreign Office, London.

[35] T Otte, *July Crisis* (Cambridge University Press, 2014) 205.

Whilst Serbia may have disclaimed involvement in the outrage, much to the condemnation of the Austro-Hungarian Government and the European press, it was implicated through the activities of its military intelligence and members of its Government.[36] The Bosnian assassins of the Archduke Franz Ferdinand had connections to the Serbian secret organisation known as 'the Black Hand'.[37] One of the Serbian army officers, Tankošić, recruited the three conspirators[38] to the organisation whilst his colleague trained them in the use of weapons. But the connection went deeper linking the head of the Serbian Military Intelligence section of the Serbian General Staff, Colonel Dragutin T Dimitrijević[39] and also a member of the Serbian Government.

That Sunday, 23 July 1914, Sir Edward Grey[40] had a meeting with the Austro-Hungarian Ambassador Count Albert von Mensdorff-Pouilly-Dietrichstein. Fearing an escalation through possible Russian intervention, Grey warned Mensdorff that Austria-Hungary should not make unreasonable demands without justification. He also warned him before publication of the ultimatum that it might inflame and excite Russian opinion. Grey went further in that discussion and he warned Mensdorff of the possibility of war between the Four Great Powers; Austria, Germany, France and Russia 'which would be equal to the bankruptcy of Europe'. This implied that Britain would stay out. He added that 'many a standing institution would be swept away'.[41] Mensdorff described Grey as being as 'cool and unprejudiced as ever, friendly and not without sympathy for our side. But he was undoubtedly very anxious as to the possible consequences'.[42] In Vienna, Foreign Minister Count Berchtold advised his diplomatic colleagues in Madrid, Rome, Washington and Tokyo that: 'It is possible that the following development of things will lead to warlike conflict with Serbia eventually with Russia'.[43] This was Austria-Hungary's intention. It was also the very danger that Grey foresaw and warned against as soon as the terms of the Austrian ultimatum were known in London.

In Paris, Vosnic, the Serbian Ambassador, met M Berthelot[44] the Assistant Political Director at the French Ministry for Foreign Affairs, and was

[36] L Albertini, *The Origins of the War of 1914: The Crisis of July 1914 Volume II* (Enigma Books, 2014) 107–108.

[37] Described by Otte (n 35) as a nationalist-revolutionary avant-garde designed to foment revolutionary activities outside Serbia proper.

[38] Prinčip, Čabrinović and Grabež.

[39] Otte (n 35) 16.

[40] *Collected Diplomatic Documents* (n 24) *Grey to Bunsen* (Vienna) No 3.

[41] Austrian Red Book in *Collected Diplomatic Documents Relating to the Outbreak of The European War* (London, 1915) No 59 *Count Mensdorff to Count Berchtold* (23 July 1914).

[42] *Ibid.*

[43] *Ibid* No 70 *Count Berchtold to Imperial and Royal Ambassadors* (23 July 1914).

[44] A Mombauer, *The Origins of the First World War Diplomatic and Military Documents* (Manchester University Press, 2013) xvii. Berthelot regarded himself as 'the person' on French Foreign Affairs, not Bienvenue Martin as he told Granville, Francis Bertie's counsellor in Paris. FO 800-55 *Bertie to Tyrrell* (27 July 1914) 800–55.

advised that Serbia should play for time and appeal for mediation by the other Powers.[45]

The next day, contrary to Grey's understanding, Mensdorff received a copy of the Austro-Hungarian ultimatum to Serbia. This made demands that no sovereign state could reasonably accept and was clearly intended to provoke Serbia or provide a *casus belli* for war.[46] Austria-Hungary demanded that Serbia reply by 6pm on Saturday 25 July 1914. Grey warned Mensdorff of the danger of a European war if Austria-Hungary invaded Serbia. Grey said that it was absolutely essential to reach a solution by negotiation. Indeed, Lichnowsky's opinion was that Grey was doing everything to 'avoid European complications'.[47] Grey suggested mediation by the four disinterested Powers – Britain, Germany, France and Italy – in case the conflict should lead to 'dangerous tension' between Austria-Hungary and Russia.[48] The problem there was a lack of common interest as these states increasingly pursued their own interest. Again, Grey was aware of the possible consequences and attentive to the foreseeable dangers. Sir Eyre Crowe noted on Lichnowsky's communication[49] that owing to the extreme nature of the Austro-Hungarian demands and the time limit imposed, the localisation of the conflict had been made exceedingly difficult. He added: 'Because the Austrian terms bear on their face the character of a design to provoke a war'. The whole ultimatum of Austria-Hungary was designed to provoke war. The demands made by Austria-Hungary were not based on evidence available to the mediating Powers. Time would be required but was not given. Grey noted significantly that in his conversations with Lichnowsky he had assumed such a war between Austria-Hungary and Serbia could not be localised. Grey warned specifically of a wider conflict as between Russia, Austria-Hungary, Germany and France without indicating the British position which may have suggested non-involvement to Lichnowsky and the Wilhelmstrasse. Lichnowsky duly reported the warning to the Wilhelmstrasse and suggested a longer time limit, which the Kaiser considered 'useless'.[50] In Berlin, Bethmann-Hollweg noted that: 'Paris and London are working closely to localise the conflict'.[51] If Germany's objective was to restore the honour of Austria-Hungary then localisation surely met that object. If there was a danger of escalation then surely Grey's initiative through the intervention of the Powers not directly involved made sense. Germany understandably supported Austria-Hungary, but given its interests it is

[45] P Renouvin, *The Immediate Origins of the War* (Howard Fertig, Inc, Ed, 1969) 93.

[46] *Collected Diplomatic Documents* (n 24) No 4 *Berchtold to Mensdorff* (24 July 1914). On this Grey remarked to Bunsen at Vienna that he had 'never seen such a formidable document addressed by one state to another'.

[47] Renouvin (n 45) 86–87.

[48] BD (n 10) Vol XI, No 99 *Grey to Rumbold* (24 July 1914).

[49] *Ibid* 79. No 100 (25 July 1914).

[50] *Lichnowsky to Foreign Office Berlin* (24 July 1914) in Prince Lichnowsky, *Heading for the Abyss Reminisces* (Payson and Clarke Ltd, 1928) 387.

[51] Renouvin (n 45) 86–87.

difficult to understand its opposition to localisation unless Germany had some undisclosed wider objective.

IV. COULD A DISPUTE PROCESS HAVE STOPPED THE DESCENT INTO WAR?

In this context it is important to consider the prospect of what, if any, dispute process might at this stage have facilitated any accommodation between the Great Powers' competing interests. James Headlam-Morley[52] opined in relation to the Austria-Hungary/Serbia dispute that it turned on great national ambitions which were inconsistent with the maintenance and therefore the vital interest of another state. Headlam-Morley went further to suggest that if a court of inquiry had been convened it might have been able to make a decision with regard to Serbia's responsibility and any question of the complicity of the Serbian Government in the murders of the Archduke and Archduchess. It may also have given a judgment on whether Serbia had complied with her obligations to the Great Powers given in 1909 as to good relations with Austria-Hungary. Were it a legal matter, a question of treaty obligations or an international inquiry, determination may have been possible, but in this case the national interests of both Serbia and Austria-Hungary subsumed all else. The clash of nationalism, Pan-Slavism, unification of Slav states of Serbia, Bosnia Herzegovina and Croatia against the imperial aspiration of the Hapsburg monarchy impeded any such resolution. Headlam-Morley considered that sometimes submission to arbitration might cause postponement of war but not avoidance. As he noted arbitration clauses are often found in treaties, but these do not operate where the national interest or national honour is concerned.[53] National honour was a term he found changed in meaning, but Sir Stafford Northcote[54] is said to have defined it as:

> National honour does not consist in never admitting that one is in the wrong, but rather in seeking in all justice to recognise the rights of others as against one's own, and even to go further than strict justice, and in case of doubt to pronounce against oneself rather than for oneself.

Thus, arbitration had its limits where the national honour was concerned. Headlam-Morley's answer seems to have been that: '... in International affairs, war can only be permanently avoided when a political system has been established under which each nation, feeling that its reasonable demands are met, respects the reasonable demands of others'.[55]

[52] J Headlam-Morley, *Studies in Diplomatic History* (Methuen & Co Ltd, 1930) 39.

[53] *Ibid* 39.

[54] Headlam-Morley cites the source for this as Lapradelle and Politis, *Recueil des Arbitrages Internationaux* (Forgotten Books, 2017) Vol II, 905. But Lapradelle and Politis cite at 905 reference to E de Laveley, *Des causes actuelles en Europe et de l'arbitrage* (Paris, 1873) 191.

[55] Headlam-Morley (n 52) 49.

The reaction to the Austro-Hungarian ultimatum in St Petersburg was alarming and Buchanan, the British Ambassador, had to inform Sergei Sazonov, the Russian Minister for Foreign Affairs, that the British interest was not involved directly and, in any event, public opinion in Britain would not support any intervention. Both Sergei Sazonov and Maurice Paléologue, the French Ambassador to Russia, urged Buchanan to present a united front as the 'only chance of averting war'.[56] As a result Buchanan telegraphed Grey, warning that:

> I said I thought you might be prepared to represent strongly at Vienna and Berlin danger to European peace of an Austrian attack on Serbia. You might perhaps point out that it would in all probability force Russia to intervene, that this would bring Germany and (France) into the field and that if war became general, it would be difficult for England to remain neutral.

Both Crowe and Nicolson advised that Buchanan's report should be taken seriously by the Cabinet, Crowe going so far as to advise that the fleet should be mobilised as soon as any other Power mobilised.[57] The Russian Chargé at Vienna told Bunsen that he had protested to Berchtold, the Austro-Hungarian Foreign Minister,[58] about the note to Serbia. Berchtold told him that the Austro-Hungarian Ambassador to Belgrade had instructions to leave Belgrade by 4pm on the 25th July.[59] This was two hours before the ultimatum expired and such a move was usually followed by hostilities.[60] This was causing the Russian Government 'the greatest anxiety' as it could not remain indifferent in the dispute between Austria-Hungary and Serbia.[61] The German Ambassador in Paris, Baron von Schoen, saw Bienvenu-Martin, the Acting Minister of Foreign Affairs in the absence of Viviani. Viviani was then returning to Paris with President Poincare after discussions in St Petersburg.[62] Von Schoen encouraged Bienvenu-Martin to use France's good offices to urge Russia to mediation, but when von Schoen was requested to reciprocate at Vienna he refused. Bienvenu-Martin decided then not to take any action in the absence of his chief.[63] Von Schoen advised Berlin that if the French placated Russia then Germany should do the same with Austria-Hungary at Vienna since Serbia had already accepted most of

[56] JW Young, 'Ambassador Buchanan and the July Crisis' (2018) 40 *The International History Review* 211.

[57] BD (n 10) Vol XI, No 101 *Buchanan to Grey* (24 July 1914) and Minutes (see in particular note by EAC 25 July 80–82.

[58] Berchtold von und zu Ungarschitz, Leopold Graf, Austro-Hungarian diplomat and Foreign Minister 1863–1942.

[59] *Collected Diplomatic Documents* (n 24) No 7 *Bunsen to Grey* (24 July 1914).

[60] Whilst such a measure was prescribed by The Hague Convention as a prelude to war, the justification for it is highly questionable.

[61] Russian Orange Book in *Collected Diplomatic Documents Relating to the Outbreak of The European War* (Foreign Office, 1915) No 10 Announcement of the Russian Government (25 July 1914).

[62] They left St Petersburg on the day Austria-Hungary gave its ultimatum to Serbia. This was not an accident.

[63] Renouvin (n 45) 102–103.

the demands. This would seem entirely logical if the Central Powers' objective was in keeping the war local. But this is debatable. Germany seemed reluctant to do so at that stage and it was only later that Bethmann-Hollweg attempted some lukewarm *démarche* at Vienna in favour of Grey's proposal of halting the Austro-Hungarian army in Belgrade.[64] At this time, 25th July, a possible German aim was to divide the *Entente* Powers, especially France and Russia. Such a possibility may be inferred from instructions Bethmann-Hollweg gave to Roedern, the Secretary of State for Alsace-Lorraine. 'If we are successful not only in keeping France quiet, but in having St Petersburg admonished to keep the peace, it would have what would be for us a most favourable effect on the Franco-Russian alliance'.[65]

Bethmann-Hollweg's warning of the 22nd July to Rumbold was repeated to Prince Lichnowsky in London in a Note issued by the Wilhelmstrasse on the 24 July making it clear that Germany saw the conflict as one between Austria-Hungary and Serbia to the exclusion of all other Powers.[66] Grey met Paul Cambon on the 24th July and told him he would be meeting Lichnowsky and caution Lichnowsky that if the ultimatum to Serbia led to any conflict between Austria-Hungary and Russia then it would be difficult for Grey to restrain Russia. Grey told Cambon that he would tell Lichnowsky that the better view was that the Four Great Powers: France, Germany, Italy and Britain should act together. Cambon's view was that mediation would be difficult given the time limit of 48 hours after which Austria-Hungary would march on Serbia. Grey hoped the Powers' intervention would stop the Austro-Hungarian advance and halt the Russian mobilisation pending mediation. Cambon did not think Grey's plan feasible and said that Germany should be involved and urge Austria-Hungary to mediate with Serbia.[67] At the meeting with Lichnowsky, Grey told him that he could not see how mediation at St Petersburg could be effective in the light of the Austro-Hungarian ultimatum. The only possibility he saw was for the Four Powers to work simultaneously at Vienna and St Petersburg. Lichnowsky thought that a positive reply must be sent from Serbia which might forestall an Austro-Hungarian attack.[68] Grey then sent instructions to Crackanthorpe, the British Chargé at Belgrade. His view was that Serbia ought to give a satisfactory reply concerning the assassination enquiry into the murder of the Archduke and reply as favourably as possible to other demands.[69]

To undertake productive diplomatic discussions between the Four Powers within 48 hours was a practical impossibility given the threat of an

[64] Grey may well have been misled by German intentions and Bethmann-Hollweg's lukewarm enthusiasm for his proposal.

[65] Renouvin (n 45) 86–87.

[66] *Collected Diplomatic Documents* (n 24) No 9. Note communicated by the German Ambassador, 24 July 1914.

[67] *Ibid* No 10 *Grey to Bertie* (24 July 1914).

[68] *Ibid* No 11 *Grey to Rumbold* (24 July 1914).

[69] *Ibid* No12 *Grey to Crackanthorpe* (24 July 1914).

Austro-Hungarian invasion of Serbia. If Austria-Hungary and Serbia would not engage in discussions could their proxies do so? This was unlikely within the restricted timeframe. Nevertheless, on 25th July Sazonov sent the Russian Chargé at Vienna a Note requesting an extension of time to the Austro-Hungarian ultimatum.[70] That day Grey saw Mensdorff and Mensdorff explained that the Austro-Hungarian note to Serbia was not an ultimatum but a démarche. If Serbia rejected it then Austria-Hungary would break off diplomatic relations. But it was unlikely that hostilities would begin; military operations would not begin, only preparations.[71] In Paris Bertie was told that mediation should be attempted in Belgrade and Vienna and that the Serbian reply would be sufficient. But Serbia could not be expected to accept all Austria-Hungary's demands because that would cause a revolution in Serbia.[72] The Russian view communicated by Buchanan the same day was that Belgrade would be abandoned and Serbia would appeal to the Great Powers. However, he warned Grey that Britain should stand by France and Russia so there would be no war. Buchanan told Sazonov that Britain needed to mediate and therefore could not be an ally. Sazonov thought that Germany considered Britain neutral.[73]

Here we notice how complicated matters were becoming and how despite Grey's efforts the time restraints and the questions of mediating or having a conference and acting in concert were becoming confused by continental allegiances. Also, significantly we can see the different approaches emerging; France and Russia coordinating their response, but subject to communication problems because of Viviani's visit to St Petersburg and being at sea at a critical time, a fact known presumably to those orchestrating events in Berlin. The reactive policy of France and Russia contrasts with the pro-active stance of Austria-Hungary and Germany which was focussed on a local war, not a general one at that time overlooking Serbia's recent military successes in 1913.

That same day, 25th July 1914, Rumbold reported another meeting with Bethmann-Hollweg at which the Chancellor had confirmed sending Grey's suggestion of an extension of time to Vienna. Whilst saying this he also intimated that Austria-Hungary would teach Serbia a lesson although he acknowledged that Austria-Hungary had invited Russian delegates to Vienna for discussions and that Austria-Hungary would not seize Serbian territory. The last thing he said Germany wanted was a general war and thus he would support Grey's suggestion of the Four Powers working in favour of moderation at Vienna and St Petersburg.[74] The Chancellor agreed to the Four Powers acting in concert for moderation, a change from his position on the 23 July when he did not favour

[70] *Ibid* No 13 *Sazonov to Prince Kudachef* (25 July 1914).

[71] *Ibid* No 14 *Grey to Bertie* (Paris) and *to Buchanan* (St Petersburg) *Grey to Crackanthorpe* (24 July 1914).

[72] *Ibid* No 16 *Bertie to Grey* (25 July 1914).

[73] *Ibid* No 17 *Buchanan to Grey* (25 July 1914).

[74] *Ibid* No 18 *Rumbold (Berlin) to Grey* (25 July 1914).

it. On the face of it this response seems positive, but Bethmann-Hollweg was simply forwarding Grey's proposal he was not supporting it. Also, the idea that Austria-Hungary would not seize Serbian territory was misleading.

Meanwhile in Belgrade, Crackanthorpe had learned that Serbia was accepting most of Austria-Hungary's demands and that 'unless the Austro-Hungarian Government want war at any cost, they cannot but be content with the full satisfaction offered by the Serbian reply'.[75] He also understood that Russia was urging the utmost moderation on Serbia.[76] Grey then cabled Buchanan accepting Buchanan's report of the 24th July. Grey was of the view that the way to preserve peace was for the Great Powers to act in concert to restrain Austria-Hungary and Russia from crossing borders. In such effort, the co-operation of Germany was essential. Any such intervention would not be accepted by the belligerents unless impartial and included its allies and friends of both.[77] In hindsight this is difficult to see where the national interest of Austria-Hungary and the national honour of Russia came into play.

Despite the discussion as to Four Power intervention, Grey and Lichnowsky discussed mediation between Austria-Hungary and Russia which the latter thought possible. Grey said he had 'no title' to intervene between Austria-Hungary and Serbia having previously explained the British position. But here the problem of French participation became an issue because the French Government were then travelling back from its conference at St Petersburg and communications were unreliable.[78] Grey informed Rumbold that there might be more time after the expiry of the ultimatum as Austria-Hungary would take time to mobilise. It seems that if Austria-Hungary and Russia were involved then according to Grey all the Four Powers would need to be involved. It is therefore not clear whether Grey could effectively mediate or not. It seems doubtful and proved so. His only chances of resolving the matter would appear to rest on concerted action by the Four Powers. Here there were two emerging problems. First, the involvement of the French, and second, the willingness of Germany to participate in good faith. For both Germany and France which were allied to the potential belligerents, the difficulty is obvious. Britain also had some difficulty regarding her obligations to France, but at this stage that had not become an issue. That same day Grey cabled Crackanthorpe to confirm Serbia's reply which was acceptable so far as *terrain juridique* went, but Serbia would not accept the political demands. The point was made that the assassins of the Archduke Franz Ferdinand and his wife were Austro-Hungarian subjects from Bosnia.[79] Bunsen reported that the Austro-Hungarian Government rejected the

[75] *Ibid* No 21 *Crackanthorpe (Belgrade) to Grey* (25 July 1914).

[76] *Ibid* No 22 *Crackanthorpe to Grey* (25 July 1914).

[77] *Ibid* No 24 *Grey to Buchanan* (St Petersburg) (25 July 1914), originally omitted from the White Paper published in 1914. Grey (n 29) Vol II, 164.

[78] *Ibid* No 25 *Grey to Rumbold* (Berlin) (25 July 1914).

[79] *Ibid* No 30 *Grey to Crackanthorpe* (25 July 1914).

Serb reply which meant that war was inevitable. Grey received this report on the 26th July.[80] Bunsen also reported more disturbing news having spoken with the German Ambassador Tschirschky in Vienna. Tschirschky told him that: 'Serbia was about to receive a lesson which she required …'. The German view was that Serbia was already preparing for war and its reply was a sham.[81] The view from the Wilhelmstrasse in Berlin, according to Rumbold, was that if Austria-Hungary did not occupy Serbian territory Russia would not intervene.[82]

V. DANGER OF CIVIL WAR IN IRELAND

Just as the crisis in the Balkans was deepening, a more immediate constitutional crisis faced Asquith's Government. The Home Rule Bill offended Ulster and Irish Unionists like Sir James Craig from Belfast and Sir Edward Carson from Dublin who wanted Ireland to remain within the United Kingdom. These leaders were strongly supported in Parliament by the Tory party. Bearing in mind the great crisis now deepening on the continent with the entanglement of alliances, coupled with the eccentricity of the Kaiser and the disintegrating Austro-Hungarian Empire as well as the rise of nationalism in the Balkans, the question of Home Rule made it even more difficult for Britain to focus on the European crisis with a divided cabinet, Parliament and country.

Britain's position could easily have become untenable if her attention was diverted to averting civil war in Ireland. Sir Edward Carson had over 100,000 well equipped Ulster volunteers opposed to the Nationalist volunteers of a similar number, but far less armed. Britain's army of six fully equipped divisions might well have had their hands full when needed for some emergency in France. For Grey and his colleagues, it is hard to think of a more difficult situation: maintaining peace in Ireland and preventing a civil war and fighting a continental war at the same time.

Thus, in June–July 1914 Grey and his colleagues were faced with the more immediate threat of rebellion from the Ulster Volunteers if their demands for exclusion from the provisions of the Home Rule Bill were not met. The problem was that a majority of the population living in Ireland were Irish, but the population of the north east of Ulster were descended from English Protestant settlers and Scots Presbyterians who came to Ireland in the Plantation of Ulster. The majority of people in Ireland as a whole wanted Home Rule and self-government, while the Unionists supported by the Tory party wanted to keep Ireland as part of the United Kingdom. Both, the Belfast and Dublin Bar as well as the Irish and Ulster Volunteers did not want Ulster separated from the rest of Ireland. The Liberal Party supported by the Irish Nationalist Party wanted to pass Home Rule. The country, Ireland, Parliament and the Cabinet were split.

[80] *Ibid* No 31 *Bunsen to Grey* (25 July 1914).
[81] *Ibid* No 32 *Bunsen to Grey* (26 July 1914).
[82] *Ibid* No 33 *Rumbold (Berlin) to Grey* (26 July 1914).

By January 1914 matters were coming to a head when Sir Edward Carson's Ulster Volunteers received 20,000 rifles and ammunition from the Steyr factory in Austria, as well as Mauser rifles from Germany. These were landed at Larne ignored by the British forces. In an advice to the Cabinet in February 1914, the Cabinet was informed of a customs seizure of 240 rifles destined for the Ulster Volunteers.[83] Legal proceedings were started by the consignee Hunter & Son, an arms dealer in Belfast, and the Government needed to agree the defence to an action in detinue for alleged unlawful seizure of the arms by the Customs. The arms were sent in breach of a Proclamation against the importing of illegal weapons which the Government rightly suspected of being used as part of a seditious conspiracy against Home Rule. The Cabinet was asked to consider whether counsel should raise the defence that these arms were intended as part of a treasonable conspiracy in Ulster. If that were the submission then they had to consider prosecuting the leaders of the conspiracy which was undoubtedly Carson, who later became Attorney General, Sir James Craig and possibly FE Smith who later became Lord Chancellor. This would undoubtedly have caused bitter opposition from the Conservative Party. In March 1914 Asquith considered proposals to use the army to crush 'Carson's rebellion' but later that month many officers at the Irish base of the army said they would not take part in any such action. In June 1914, a consignment of guns was landed at Howth by Erskine Childers, a former Clerk at the House of Commons, who sympathised with the cause of Irish independence.[84] Feelings in Ireland ran high when the army opened fire on people covering the landing of the weapons. Home Rule was unlikely to pass with fierce opposition from Ulster and English Tory Unionists, the House of Lords as well as elements in the army including the Chief of the General Staff himself. This played into the hands of the German High Command who perhaps wrongly calculated that Britain was too busy with Ireland to make any difference in Europe. It also weakened Grey's bargaining position and his ability to give a serious warning when half the British army might be tied up in an Irish civil war. The cabinet's preoccupation with Ireland is evident from Grey's telegram to Buchanan on 19 July when Grey confirmed his immersion in the Irish situation by telling Buchanan that he would consider the suggestion of an Anglo-Russian-Japanese guarantee when 'the Parliamentary and Irish situation gave time to do so'.[85]

[83] FO 6/26 Confidential. *Threatened Legal Proceedings over Seizure of Arms at Belfast* (17 February 1914).

[84] See J de Wiel, '1914: What will the British Do? The Irish Home Rule Crisis in the July Crisis' (2015) *The International History Review*. Incredibly, Childers sailed his yacht the *Askard* through the British fleet off Plymouth where it was concentrated in case of an emergency to deliver arms to the Irish Volunteers in Dublin. Once war was declared however Childers re-joined the services as a naval intelligence officer and distinguished himself in the Great War. He returned later to Ireland and was part of the Irish delegation that took part in the Anglo-Irish treaty talks. He fought on the side of the IRA in the civil war, was captured by the Free State Forces, and shot for possessing a pistol which Michael Collins the Commander of the Free State forces had given him.

[85] BD (n 10) Vol XI, I *Grey to Buchanan* (19 July 1914).

Between the 31st July and 3rd August, it was not clear what would happen in Ireland and only when John Redmond, leader of the Irish Nationalist Party, pledged support to defend Ireland with the Irish and Ulster Volunteers could Grey be confident of a united front.[86] The Ulster dilemma was certainly a factor occupying the Cabinet during the July crisis and may well have played a part in diminishing the effect of Grey's warnings to Lichnowsky. On the other hand, it also brought into focus the importance of the Conservative opposition which despite being against Home Rule was alarmed at the Austria-Hungary ultimatum to Serbia and the threat to Belgium neutrality. This became more serious after Austria-Hungary declared war on Serbia and Russia fully mobilised on 30th July. Some discussion took place between Churchill, FE Smith, Carson and others and included Grey and Asquith as there was a risk that certain Cabinet members would resign and there might have to be a coalition government.[87] At the same time there was pressure from an ardent Unionist supporter, the Director of Military Operations, Sir Henry Wilson, to support the French as his military strategy called for the British Expeditionary Force's[88] immediate support of the French armies. The effect of such discussions and indications of Conservative intentions strengthened the hand of Asquith and Grey in convincing their colleagues to support the *Entente* or face a coalition of Liberal Imperialists and Conservative Unionists. As evidence of that Asquith was assured by Bonar Law's letter to him dated 2 August 1914:

> Private
>
> Dear Mr Asquith,
>
> Lord Lansdowne and I feel it our duty to inform you that in our opinion as well as in that of all the colleagues with whom we have been able to consult it would be fatal to the honour and security of the United Kingdom to hesitate in supporting France and Russia at the present juncture; and we offer our unhesitating support to the Government in any measures they may consider necessary for that object.
>
> Yours very truly,
>
> A Bonar Law.[89]

Having considered the domestic difficulties confronting the British Cabinet at this critical time from Ulster and the threat from Austria-Hungary towards Serbia we turn to consider the volatile nature of Russian diplomacy as the threat of war occurring by accident or mistake or misunderstanding was a more likely possibility from this quarter than others.

[86] Hansard, HC Deb 3 August 1914, vol 65, col 1829.

[87] JW Young, 'Conservative Leaders, Coalition and the British Decision for War in 1914' (2014) 25 *Diplomacy and Statecraft* 214–39.

[88] Four infantry divisions and a cavalry division were sent to France to support the French armies resisting the German invasion of Belgium and France in August 1914.

[89] *Bonar Law to Asquith*, 2 August 1914. Parliamentary Archives, House of Lords Research Office, London. C/G/11/10.

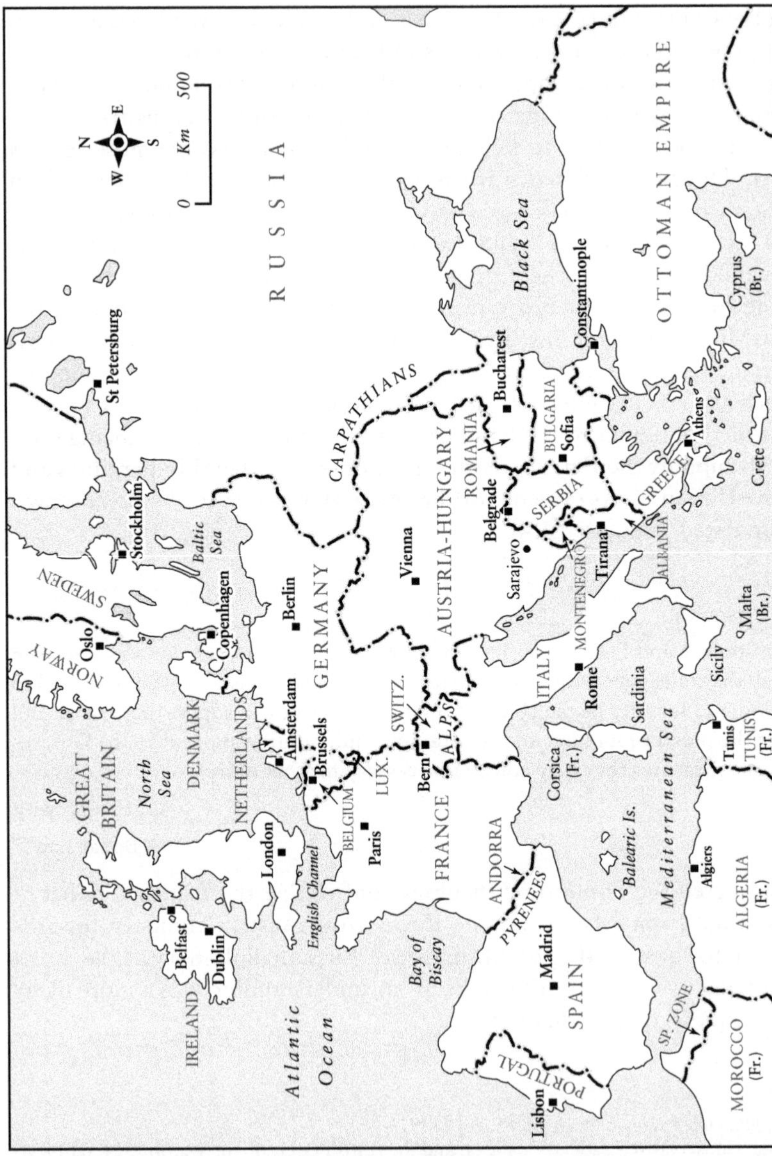

Figure 7.1 Map of Europe in 1914
Credit: Mina Moshkeri

VI. THE PREDICAMENT OF RUSSIA

By the 26th July the risks of a war between the Great Powers had become greater. Grey had not been so concerned about a war between Austria-Hungary and Serbia per se, as its implication would trigger war between Austria-Hungary and Russia which in turn would automatically involve France and Germany. Then there was a possibility of Britain being involved (as Grey had warned Lichnowsky at his morning meeting on the 25th July) that Britain would not stand aside if there was a war.[90] It appears that in response to Lichnowsky's report Jagow telephoned Rumbold to confirm that Germany would support Grey's initiative at Vienna.[91] This would seem to be at variance with the German Ambassador's view that Serbia should be taught a lesson. Grey wanted to lower the tension between the Powers, giving time for mediation. He could only gain this time if Austria-Hungary did not mobilise or possibly if Russia mobilised, but Germany did not. This was unlikely. His thinking was that Germany could mobilise in hours and Russia in days.[92] The view in the Wilhelmstrasse was that Russia was not a threat and could be beaten off before the full might of the German armies turned on France.[93] Italy supported Grey's initiative for a conference[94] and Grey then cabled the British ambassadors in Paris, Rome and Berlin instructing them to invite the respective states' Ministers of Foreign Affairs to send their ambassadors to a meeting in London 'for the purpose of discussing an issue which would prevent complications'.[95] The offer was conditional upon Austria-Hungary, Serbia and Russia suspending all active military operations. This new initiative was the idea of Arthur Nicolson. Approaches were to be made at Vienna, Belgrade and St Petersburg and it was essential that Austria-Hungary be restrained so the conference could proceed.[96] Lichnowsky's report to Berlin on the 26th July is telling. He clearly understood the gravity of the position which those in Berlin could not, namely the unlikelihood of the war being confined to two Powers. He emphatically told Berlin that: 'it is absolutely indispensable for the success of the conference and for the maintenance of peace that there shall be a cessation of military movements'.[97] So long as Serbia was not attacked a conference was possible. The problem here however was greater than any

[90] *Collected Diplomatic Documents* (n 24) No 24 *Grey to Buchanan* (St Petersburg) (25 July 1914).

[91] *Ibid* No 34 *Rumbold (Berlin) to Grey* (26 July 1914) *cf* No 32 regarding Tschirschky's view.

[92] *Ibid* No 24 *Grey to Buchanan* (St Petersburg) (25 July 1914) and see Grey (n 29) Vol II, 165.

[93] View of the High Command which believed in the Schlieffen Plan. This was a battle plan designed by Count von Schlieffen in 1905 for Germany to fight a war on two fronts simultaneously. It required a stict timetable without allowing for unforeseeable delays and, despite adjustments by the Chief of the General Staff von Moltke, the plan of attack and offence became one of defence and stalemate on the Western Front.

[94] *Collected Diplomatic Documents* (n 24) No 35 *Rodd (Rome) to Grey* (26 July 1914).

[95] *Ibid* No 36 *Grey to Bertie (Paris) Rumbold (Berlin) Rodd (Rome)* (26 July 1914).

[96] Renouvin (n 45) 107

[97] *Lichnowsky to Foreign Office Berlin* (26 July 1914) in Lichnowsky (n 50) 397–98.

question of intervention in a dispute between Russia and Austria-Hungary. Here Grey was suggesting intervention between Austria-Hungary and Serbia. This was against Germany's policy of restoring its ally's credibility as a Great Power. But from a British point of view a war that might spread along the Danube would be a threat. On the other hand, intervention between Austria-Hungary and Russia did not please Count Benckendorff, the Russian Ambassador in London, as it might give the impression of driving a wedge between the *Entente* Powers. Grey's suggestion of intervention in the Austria-Hungary/Serbia dispute seems to contradict an earlier remark he made to Lichnowsky that he did not feel Britain should intervene in that dispute, but as soon as such a matter involved Russia, the peace of Europe was challenged.[98] Sir George Buchanan, the British Ambassador in St Petersburg, reported that whilst Benckendorff had misgivings about Grey's approach Sazonov, the Russian Foreign Minister, agreed to it.[99] In his telegram Buchanan referred to the Serb suggestion in the context of an appeal to the Powers in the event of invasion and reference to arbitration. Whether that would be to the Permanent Court of Arbitration, or a reference to the Hague Tribunal (as Russia later proposed under threat from Germany) is not clear. Opinions of Buchanan amongst historians are divided, but it does seem that he had a tendency to advocate the Russian approach without the emotional detachment required to impartially report the position. John Young[100] opined that Buchanan was committed to the notion of the Triple *Entente* and that he attempted to maintain the peace, although he appeared to be more interested in defending Russian action than giving an accurate report of events.[101] Sidney Fay took the view that Buchanan sought to restrain Russia but was undermined by his government. It appears that whilst Buchanan was initially quite cautious as the crisis deepened, it appears he became more personally involved with Russian reactions. The Russians feared a German attack but were determined not to be humiliated by Austria-Hungary again. In the event Austria-Hungary and Germany refused Grey's offer and following the Tsar's review of his troops on the 24th July, the Tsar ordered a period preparatory to war to take effect on the 26th July.[102]

If Austria-Hungary had attacked Serbia and Russia did not intervene then it is possible the Powers – Britain, France, Italy and Germany – might have constituted some international tribunal, but this is hard to imagine in the light of events. As Bertie warned Grey on 27 July 1914, Austria-Hungary would resent Grey calling it a conference between France, Germany and Italy because it would demean

[98] BD (n 10) Vol XI, No 132 *Grey to Buchanan* (25 July 1914).

[99] *Ibid* Vol XI, No 125 *Buchanan to Grey* (25 July 1914).

[100] Young (n 56) 206–24.

[101] *Ibid* 207.

[102] From this point on, it appears that *control* of events was moving from the political to the military forces. These were 'not lions led by donkeys' but of a military generation that was acutely aware of the challenges and risks of warfare on an industrial scale. See D Lieven, *Towards the Flame* (Alton Lane, 2015) 325–26.

Austria-Hungary to the status of a minor Balkan state.[103] Thus, it is understandable that Germany would not have agreed to it and as Bethmann-Hollweg later immoderately declared, Austria-Hungary would not surrender sovereignty to an international arbitration court.[104] Sazonov pointed out to Buchanan the obligations that Serbia had assumed after the Bosnian crisis of 1908–1909. These had been delegated to all the Powers as a group and not to Austria-Hungary alone so that Serbia would be quite justified in appealing to the Powers. Sazonov also told him that if Britain took its stand firmly with France and Russia there would be no war.[105] But the problem for Grey in taking such a stance would mean that Britain could no longer play the role of the mediator as between Austria and Russia. Grey's view was that it was better for Britain to act as a mediator and counsel moderation rather than to declare itself Russia's ally, which would militate against its role as a mediator and raise questions of conflict of interest.[106] The comments made by Sazonov were echoed by Lloyd George and others against Grey later, but Grey's explanation is quite sound weighing the potential for settlement and the alternative of taking sides at that critical time. His approach then was to dissuade Russia from warlike acts in the hope that if Russia adopted a more conciliatory stance Germany would have less difficulty in persuading Austria-Hungary to do the same. Unfortunately, although Germany made an appearance of efforts at Vienna to encourage Austria-Hungary, Austria-Hungary had other plans behind the scenes where it played a double game encouraging the Austrians to resist mediation, until the 27th July. Berchtold reported his discussion with the German Ambassador Tschirschky on the 26th July.[107] Berchtold wrote that it was his opinion that since Austria-Hungary had no intention of occupying Serbian territory temporarily or otherwise 'transitory operations could not be counted on as temporary occupation – this was not the time to take the question into serious consideration'. Berchtold was undoubtedly being disingenuous here such that Germany might have had reservations about its ally's intentions. This might have led Germany to believe that the Austro-Hungarian armies might have halted in Belgrade and then retired. But it seems the Austro-Hungarian government had other ideas which were hidden from Germany at that time. It also seems that the Germans were not interested in 'Halt in Belgrade' at this stage. The die seems to have been cast.

That same day Nicholson sent an urgent telegram to Grey at Itchen Abbas suggesting that he call a conference of ambassadors as suggested by Sazonov.[108]

[103] FO 800-49 *Bertie to Grey* (27 July 1914).

[104] Since that was the case the question arises as to why Grey did not adopt the Concert System approach.

[105] BD (n 10) Vol XI, No 125 *Buchanan to Grey* (25 July 1914).

[106] *Ibid.*

[107] Austrian Red Book (n 41) No 63 *Count Berchtold, Report of Meeting with German Ambassador* (26 July 1914).

[108] This suggestion caused Sir Francis Bertie, the British Ambassador in Paris, some concern. He wrote to Grey on 27th July warning that: 'If you get together meetings between yourself and the

This was all the more urgent in view of Austria-Hungary's rejection of Serbia's general acceptance of the Austro-Hungarian ultimatum of the 23rd July. In response to Nicolson's suggestion and Grey's initiative, France and Italy accepted; Russia accepted conditionally, and Germany refused. Russia's condition was that she wanted to explore discussions with Austria-Hungary further and if these failed Russia would accept the Four Power proposal.[109] Bethmann-Hollweg explained that Germany's refusal to Lichnowsky was because ... 'we could not take part in such a conference, as we should not be able to summon Austria-Hungary before a European Court of Justice in a case with Serbia'.[110] This seems a rather curious reason, not least as to what European Court would have jurisdiction. The Permanent Court of Arbitration was an administrative body with a panel of arbitrators who were qualified to deal with boundary disputes of a legal nature, but political questions of this magnitude were beyond its reach.[111] Nicholson's idea was undoubtedly a good one. This scheme worked in the earlier Balkan crisis but, as suggested earlier, Germany was minded to take its own course despite Prince Lichnowsky's best intentions.

Bethmann-Hollweg went further in his advice to Lichnowsky that Germany would not be able to act as a mediator in any conflict between Austria-Hungary and Serbia, but she might later be able to act as a mediator between Austria-Hungary and Russia. This is curious in the light of Grey's objection to supporting Russia when in doing so there would have been a conflict of interest in Grey's acting as mediator and being an ally of Russia. This is the very mischief that Bethmann-Hollweg was suggesting Germany could undertake, albeit as an ally of Austria-Hungary. But as late as the 30th July, Bethmann-Hollweg was suggesting just that. In the meantime, he refused to discuss the question with Britain and France because he felt, according to Renouvin, that it would give Russia more time to mobilise against Austria-Hungary and presumably at Germany's expense.[112] Moltke had warned of such a danger on 28th July. Again, it appears that Germany was reluctant to stop its ally attacking Serbia even if it risked a general war.

On 28th July 1914,[113] Grey confirmed to Goschen, Ambassador at Rome, that the German Government appeared to accept the idea of discussions between Austria-Hungary and Russia by the Four Powers, if necessary. On the following

French German and Italian ambassadors call them consultations for the Austrians would resent a sort of repetition of the London reunions which ended in being dubbed the London Conference. They would consider they were being treated as a Balkan minor state' FO 800-49 *Bertie to Grey* (27 July 1914).

[109] *British Diplomatic Correspondence* No 53 M *Sazonov to Benckendorff*, 27 July 1914. Communicated by Benckendorff to Grey.

[110] Renouvin (n 45) 86–87.

[111] Neither the Permanent Court of International Justice nor the International Court of Justice were established at this time.

[112] Renouvin (n 45) 111.

[113] BD (n 10) Vol11, No 218 *Grey to Goschen* (28 July 1914).

day, 29th July 1914, Grey informed Goschen that he had asked the German Government to suggest any form of procedure under which the idea of mediation between Austria-Hungary and Russia, already accepted by the German Government in principle, could be applied. Although as noted earlier there was no direct dispute between Austria-Hungary and Russia at that moment, the Russian interest would be involved in respect of its Pan-Slav policy towards Serbia. Any hope of mediating between Austria-Hungary and Serbia was destroyed on that day by Austria-Hungary's declaration of war on Serbia. Grey's options became very limited, and events now seemed out of the control of diplomats and statesmen, the norms of diplomacy and international law, increasingly inclining towards war to protect national interests and national honour. As the crisis mounted the room for manoeuvre became less and complexity greater even between allies. There was divergence between Germany and Austria-Hungary over halting in Belgrade and rejecting mediation, and between Britain, France and Russia as to the free hand adopted by Britain generally.

France especially had some reservations about Britain and a possible Anglo-German rapprochement[114] and they were not, as of March 1914, entirely happy with the *Entente*. An impression may have been given by the affability of Prince Lichnowsky, the German Ambassador in London, who was more successful in promoting Anglo-German relations than his predecessor on the basis that according to Bertie '... an Anglo-German understanding would be much more advantageous to England than the Entente to France'.[115] Bertie told Wickham Steed of *The Times* that the possibility of British support removed French anxiety regarding a German attack and this influenced their approach in confronting the German Government.[116] Bertie's view was that: 'England would be bound in her own interest to support France lest she be crushed'. In the final analysis this was the critical point – Britain could not easily survive if Germany dominated the continent. Britain was fortunate in having Bertie as its Ambassador in Paris as was France in having Paul Cambon in London and his brother Jules Cambon in Berlin: diplomats who fully understood their brief and their country's interests.

Russia gave contradictory signals as Buchanan noted to Grey on the 27th July. Sazonov had made one suggestion and two proposals, all different, over three consecutive days. Sir Arthur Nicolson commented: 'One really does not know where one is with M Sazonov and I told Count Benckendorff so this afternoon'.[117] First he suggested that if Serbia made an appeal to the Powers

[114] This was a suggestion made by Editor of *The Times*, W Steed, in conversation with Francis Bertie in Paris as recorded by Bertie in his *Memorandum* of 8 March 1914 (FO 800/55).

[115] *Bertie Memorandum*, *ibid*. Lichnowsky played on the British fear of a German seaborne invasion which had grown since the publication of Erskine Childers' *Riddle of the Sands*, in March 1903 and by William Le Queux's *Spies of the Kaiser* published in 1909.

[116] *Bertie Memorandum* (n 114).

[117] BD (n 10) Vol XI, No 179 *Buchanan to Grey* (27 July 1914). Note by A Nicolson.

Russia would stand aside. Then on the 26th July he proposed to the Austria-Hungarian Ambassador at St Petersburg, Count Szápáry, that Britain and Italy should co-operate with Austria-Hungary to resolve the matter. On the 27th July, Szápáry proposed that Russia would discuss matters directly with Austria-Hungary. This final proposal had some prospect for hope, although Russia took steps 'preparatory to war' on the 26th July as a 'premobilisation' which, according to Sazonov, would entail Russian armies halting at the frontier.[118] Renouvin suggests that Austria-Hungary and Russia could have agreed mediation by the King of England and the King of Italy.[119] Szápáry would not however discuss the terms of the Austro-Hungarian ultimatum to Serbia without reference to Berchtold.[120] Sazonov then conferred with Count Pourtalès, the German Ambassador at St Petersburg, but Germany was refusing to mediate in terms of counselling moderation and seeking accommodation of common interests.[121] Schebeko, the Russian Ambassador at Vienna, was instructed by Sazonov to make representations, but these were similarly rebuffed, although according to Buchanan this is precisely what Portales the German Ambassador at St Petersburg had suggested to Sazonov. The Tsar explained his mobilisation to King George because of complete Austria mobilisation, the bombardment of Belgrade, the concentration of Austrian troops in Galicia and of secret military preparations being made by Germany. He did not think this would lead to war but hoped that Britain would support France and Russia in preserving the balance of power in Europe.[122] This leaves open the question as to whether Russia had some good reason to mobilise in the face of German *male fides*.

All this demonstrates that whatever efforts the *Entente* Powers made; the Central Powers rejected them. Grey had offered mediation, Four Power talks and supported Russia's parley with Austria-Hungary. Serbia had largely accepted the terms of the ultimatum and although Russia had not until the 31st July, Russia was still open to negotiation to avoid war. Two days later however Austria-Hungary declared war on Serbia.

Both in the tone, tenor and unreasonable demands of her ultimatum and in her rush to declare war on Serbia, Austria-Hungary made it even more difficult to conciliate or mediate the impasse that she had caused through her rash actions. Count Szögyény, the Austria-Hungarian Ambassador in Berlin, reported to Berchtold that the 'general belief here is that if Serbia gives an unsatisfactory answer our declaration of war and war operations will follow immediately'.[123]

[118] This was triggered by the proclamation the previous evening as a 'period preparatory to war' and was readily detected by the N.D. (German Army Intelligence). Russian frontier guards were on alert on the Prussian border and railway transport was being readied. Ulrich Trumpener, 'War Premeditated? German Intelligence Operations in July 1914' (Cambridge University Press, 1976) 69.

[119] Renouvin (n 45) 116.

[120] *Ibid.*

[121] Renouvin (n 45) 86–87.

[122] Young (n 56) 218. The reply of the Tsar to the King may have been drafted with Buchanan's assistance. See also BD (n 10) Vol XI, No 384 *Grey to Buchanan* (1 August 1914).

[123] Austrian Red Book (n 41) No 32 *Szögyény to Berchtold* (Berlin, 25 July 1914).

The rest of the telegram is much more revealing and goes to the point of collusion between Austria-Hungary and Germany. It stated:

> Here every delay in the beginning of war operations is regarded as signifying the danger that foreign powers might interfere. We are urgently advised to proceed without delay and to place the world before a fait accompli.
>
> I am completely of the same mind as the German Foreign Office.

In other words, neither of the Central Powers were serious about mediation, and both considered resolving the matter by resort to military means even when Serbia largely acceded to their demands. Although this is quite sufficient to demonstrate the Central Powers' *male fides*, further direct evidence of their approach is contained in Berchtold's telegram to Count Szögyény which bluntly stated: 'Declaration of war within a few days'.[124] Count Szögyény was to inform the German Foreign Minister Gottlieb von Jagow accordingly.[125] Following this, on the 27th July, Mensdorff reported to Berchtold that Grey had told him that Serbia was humiliated and had agreed to all Austria-Hungary's demands save for one point which was capable of agreement. Grey concluded that this was just a pretext to extinguish Serbian and Russian influence in the Balkans.[126] In a subsequent telegram, Mensdorff reported to Berchtold that Grey had mentioned a conference between the Four Powers that would isolate the conflict, but if Russia mobilised and Germany decided to act there could be no conference.[127] Crampton opines that what was present in 1912 was absent in 1914, whereas Germany had restrained Austria-Hungary's ambitions in 1912 it would not do so in 1914, as did Britain's interest in restraining Russian ambitions which had diminished by March 1914.[128]

VII. THE BRITISH INTEREST

It seems that as the crisis became more serious, the Wilhelmstrasse began to reconsider the issues, especially when the British interest came into question. The German approach had been predicated upon a local Balkan War with Austria-Hungary, rapidly defeating Serbia without regard to Russia's interest as Protector

[124] This demonstrates quite bluntly the lack of respect for the Concert System whereby the Great Powers' representatives would meet to discuss solutions. Grey adjourned the Conference of Ambassadors on the Balkans on 11 August 1913, Austria-Hungary and Italy and later Germany having decided to take unilateral action instead of collective action which proved ominous for what was to happen a year later. See: FO 371/1804 *Goschen to Grey*, Telegram 213, Confidential (14 December 1913) as to the point that Germany would not restrain her allies.

[125] Austrian Red Book (n 41) No 69 *Berchtold to Szögyény* (24 July to 28 July 1914).

[126] *Ibid* No 71 *Mensdorff to Berchtold* (27 July 1914).

[127] *Ibid* No 72 *Mensdorff to Berchtold* (27 July 1914).

[128] RJ Crampton, 'The Decline of the Concert of Europe in the Balkans 1913–1914'. (1974) 52 *Slavonic and Eastern European Review* 128.

of the Pan-Slav race. If Russia became involved as Grey warned, then the British interest would also come into play. Thus, on the evening of the 27th July having received two telegrams from Prince Lichnowsky, Bethmann-Hollweg instructed Tschirschky in Vienna to submit Grey's proposal. But Tschirschky was not given any immediate reply until the 28th July by which time Austria-Hungary had declared war on Serbia and was 'overtaken by events'. The Kaiser having been on vacation in Norway had expected matters between Austria-Hungary and Serbia to have been resolved by a military victory for Austria-Hungary, but instead Austria-Hungary had given an inexplicable ultimatum to Serbia. Wilhelm wrote that: 'every reason for war drops away' and that the outstanding matters 'could be settled by negotiation'.[129] He went so far as to suggest that Austria-Hungary take Belgrade as hostage ensuring full compliance with the ultimatum, and he would mediate without other Powers' interference. Whilst the Kaiser was right to conclude that the causes for war had vanished, he was wrong to suggest he could mediate when Germany was allied to Austria-Hungary and by no means had Germany's conduct been neutral or impartial. He also differed from Grey in that at this time Grey was suggesting mediation between the Powers on the condition there was no military action.

Further difficulties arose on the 28th July when Bethmann-Hollweg learned of Austria-Hungary's secret plans to dismember Serbia and give the spoils to Bulgaria and Albania. He did little to encourage Austria-Hungary to accept Grey's proposal. When the British interest became involved, Germany sought to fix the blame for any war on Russia which was taking preparatory steps for war and then mobilised on the 31st July after Austria-Hungary's declaration of war on Serbia.[130] But before the Tsar took the irrevocable step, he requested that the matter be referred to The Hague Tribunal for resolution. The Tsar had been the instigator of the First Hague Conference in 1899 as noted in chapter 5.[131] The Kaiser refused, and Bethmann-Hollweg excluded such possibility.[132] Thus, another opportunity for settlement was lost. Yet despite all this negativity from the Central Powers, the Austrian declaration of war and Russian mobilisation, Grey persisted in his efforts to mediate.[133] Grey admitted that Russia and Austria-Hungary could not have further discussions, but there could still be mediation *à quatre* because Germany had accepted the idea in principle. Grey believed this could be effected even after the occupation of Belgrade. The Kaiser's response to that was that Britain should declare she would not support Russia and France. Lichnowsky was forthright in putting his view that Germany

[129] Renouvin (n 45) 86–87.

[130] *Ibid* 456, 328. Renouvin (n 45) 116.

[131] The Hague Conference had concluded that references could be made by states, but not in matters of national honour or national interest which in this case Austria-Hungary could make.

[132] Renouvin (n 45) 86–87.

[133] Lichnowsky (n 50) 495.

should direct Berchtold to suspend all military operations, as should Russia so that the matter could be mediated.[134]

It seems that Lichnowsky's remonstrance had some effect in Berlin because Bethmann-Hollweg informed Lichnowsky that he was 'continuing to mediate to Vienna' but no serious effort was made. What he meant by that is open to interpretation, but it does appear that the approach to Russia was tempered by urging restraint in not taking any action against Austria-Hungary.[135] The Kaiser was in no mood for this as the Tsar admitted that he had ordered mobilisation preparations five days earlier. But the Kaiser was persuaded to make further *démarches* at St Petersburg and Vienna.[136] This was thwarted however because Russia went to full mobilisation and would never accept Austria-Hungary taking Belgrade. That suggestion was one apparently discussed between the King of England and Prince Henry of Prussia.[137]

A. A Pause for Thought

On the 30th July Grey rejected the German suggestion of British neutrality in his cable to Goschen in Berlin.[138] Grey's counter-proposal was that he would be willing to promote some arrangement in the future if this crisis were resolved which would lead to a rapprochement between the Powers.[139]

On the 30th July, Bethmann-Hollweg had confirmed to his ambassadors that Germany was still mediating, but after a meeting with von Moltke he was persuaded as to the danger of a failure to mobilise in view of the Russian threat. Thus, at 11pm that evening he issued a counter-instruction to his ambassadors to the effect that 'all mediation attempts should be stopped'. He cancelled his instruction No 300 and simply instructed Vienna to confirm receipt of the British proposal. The Council of Ministers in Vienna rejected Grey's proposal, sounding conciliatory, but making it clear that Austria-Hungary would continue military preparations and Russia should cease mobilisation. Russia nonetheless started to mobilise although the Tsar told the Kaiser that his troops would not take any provocative action whilst 'negotiations with Austria on Serbia's account

[134] *Ibid* 409 *Prince Lichnowsky to Wilhelmstrasse* (30 July 1914).
[135] Renouvin (n 45) 180.
[136] *Ibid* 181.
[137] Renouvin (n 45) 86–87.
[138] *Collected Diplomatic Documents* (n 24) No 101 *Grey to Goschen* (30 July 1914).
[139] This idea was later considered by Lord Bryce in his *Proposals for the Avoidance of War*, 24 February 1915. House of Lords Record Office, Parliamentary Archives. Papers of David Lloyd George. LG/C/1/2/8. Bryce followed Grey's idea of a rapprochement with Germany into a wider union or association of Sovereign states in Europe and America. Under this scheme, disputes which were not resolved through diplomatic channels would be referred to arbitration or to a council of conciliation. Union members could not declare war until the reference had been decided and any member that did so would be sanctioned economically, diplomatically or forcibly.

were taking place'.[140] Although Austria could not come to full mobilisation until the 12th August, Berchtold was persuaded by General Conrad von Hôtzendorff, the Chief of the General Staff, that Austria must mobilise in response to Russia 'as soon as Berlin has agreed to it'.[141] Conrad had been advised by Moltke not to declare war on Russia but to await the attack.[142] It seems that the crisis became a conflict when Germany refused to counsel Austria-Hungary to moderation, and when Russia mobilised Germany refused mediation or any peaceful determination.

Russian mobilisation was very slow because of the distances involved, but its general mobilisation provoked reaction from Germany and France.

On the 30th July Count Szápáry was instructed to renew his discussions with Russia despite the fact that both countries were mobilising.[143] The discussions in St Petersburg were cordial but general. In Vienna Berchtold met Schebeko, the Russian Ambassador, and discussed vaguely the question of Austria-Hungary's intentions subject to Serbia complying with the conditions of the ultimatum.[144] It seems however that Berchtold agreed to further discussions despite mobilisation but would not alter the terms of the ultimatum. This is what Schebeko told Dumaine, the French Ambassador at Vienna.[145] It therefore seems odd that Germany would not counsel moderation at Vienna if Berchtold was still authorising discussions. As long as some discussions were taking place and no armies were crossing frontiers negotiation was surely possible. Thus, in Paris, the French sought assurances that 'Serbia would not be destroyed'. Berchtold instructed Count Szécsen, his Ambassador in Paris, to tell the French that Austria-Hungary did not seek any territorial acquisition or 'attack the sovereignty' of Serbia. This was quite misleading as Austria-Hungary had already decided to dismember Serbia.[146] This was hardly 'territorial disinterestedness'. The Russian Government at Grey's request proposed that if the Austro-Hungarian advance halted, Russia's forces would act as 'onlookers'. Even on the 31st July Grey still hoped for a resolution so that Serbian territory would not be made hostage, but the Powers would ensure that Austria-Hungary's grievances would be satisfied. At 5pm Asquith informed the House of Commons that Russia had mobilised. At midnight Lichnowsky informed the Foreign Office that if Russia did not cease mobilisation in 12 hours Germany would declare war. At 12.35am on the 1st August Belgium mobilised, the French Government confirmed their respect for Belgium neutrality, but Germany did not. At 8am Grey was informed by

[140] Renouvin (n 45) 86–87.

[141] B Schmidt, *The Coming of the War, 1914* (Charles Scribner's Sons, 1930) 182. See Tschirschky's note on G 385 30 July 1914. *Zur Vorgeschichte des Weltkrieges* I, 98.

[142] Schmidt, *ibid* 182.

[143] Renouvin (n 45) 225.

[144] Schmidt (n141) 178.

[145] *Collected Diplomatic Documents* (n 24) No 104 *Dumaine to Viviani* (30 July 1914) 212.

[146] Renouvin (n 45) 56–57.

Crackanthorpe, the British First Secretary, that Belgrade was being shelled.[147] But despite all this Grey persisted in his efforts.[148]

VIII. RUSSIAN MOBILISATION

Austria-Hungary proposed that she would suspend mobilisation of her army corps in Galicia if the Russians would suspend their mobilisation but would still operate against Serbia localising the war. Grey persisted in his efforts to stop the war by instructing Buchanan to ask Sazonov to suspend mobilisation. Buchanan saw the Tsar who regretfully told him the mobilisation could not be stopped because Germany had that day declared war on Russia despite his assurances to the Kaiser that his troops would not move 'so long as mediation negotiations continued'.[149] Renouvin says that Grey was misled by Bethmann-Hollweg who said that news of the Russian general mobilisation reached the Austro-Hungarian Council of Ministers during their discussions before they had reached any decision.[150] These discussions concluded that the direct talks between Austria-Hungary and Russia would replace FourPower mediation. Sir M de Bunsen told Schebeko that Britain would agree to this course of action. Schebeko told him that his government would approach the discussions on a much broader view and that Russia desired an agreement acceptable to both empires.[151] Russian mobilisation undoubtedly complicated matters and made it easier for Germany to excuse the conduct of its ally. It also made it possible for Germany to put more pressure on Britain, not just to play the mediator but to be the neutral. A war between Austria-Hungary and Russia was of no direct interest to Britain, save for the *Entente* with France and Russia, and if France could be kept out Germany's *Drang nach osten* design would be possible. Thus, after Germany had declared war on Russia, diplomacy turned to the attitude of Britain.

IX. BRITISH NEUTRALITY

The extraordinary circumstances that presented themselves to Grey on the morning of the 1st August were unprecedented. The Cabinet was against any intervention on the continent and frustrated by the prospect of a civil war in Ireland. Grey's freedom of manoeuvre was limited, and he was forced to make desperate efforts to meet the Cabinet's demands. Having no definite decision

[147] BD (n 10) Vol XI 11, No 388 *Crackanthorpe to Grey* (31 July 1914) 237; *ibid* No 382 *Bertie to Grey* (31 July 1914) 234; and *ibid* No 383 *Goschen to Grey* (31 July 1914) 234–35.
[148] *Ibid* Vol XI, No 411 *Grey to Goschen* (1 August 1914) 246.
[149] *Ibid* Vol XI, No 490 *Buchanan to Grey* (2 August 1914) 490, 276.
[150] Renouvin (n 45) 86–87.
[151] *Collected Diplomatic Documents* (n 24) No 104 *Dumaine to Viviani* (30 July 1914) 212, 213.

from the Cabinet, Grey was constrained in his dealings with the German and French ambassadors. He invited Lichnowsky through his private secretary Sir William Tyrrell to see him that afternoon to discuss neutrality. At that meeting Grey read Lichnowsky a note from the Cabinet. Following the meeting with Grey, Lichnowsky sent a cable to the Wilhelmstrasse confirming that Britain would remain neutral if Germany did not attack France. Britain, he said, would guarantee French neutrality. But Lichnowsky went further and said that Britain would remain neutral: 'even in the event of our being at war with France and Russia'.[152] This was denied later that day by Grey. The King was advised to disillusion the Kaiser as to the 'misunderstanding'.[153] In a second meeting at 3.30pm, Grey suggested that if the armies of Germany and France were opposing each other they could halt on the frontier and not fight.[154] This was confirmed by Grey in his despatch to Bertie.[155] Grey then sent another telegram to Bertie that day[156] excusing Britain from supporting France in the event that Germany agreed not to attack France and France remained neutral in a war between Russia and Germany. This contradicts Grey's explanation of his telephone conversation with Lichnowsky where he recalled that he was referring to Austria-Hungary not Germany at war with Russia. It is very difficult to imagine how one sovereign state (Britain) could guarantee the neutrality of another without agreement and when the terms of that state's (France) alliance with the victim of an attack (Russia) were unknown or how Germany could have abstained in any Austro-Hungarian-Russian war.

Valone considered that Grey did not actually propose Anglo-French neutrality in a Russian-German war in conversation with Lichnowsky.[157] In his autobiographical account, Grey[158] refers to Goshen's telegram to him on the 29th July which referred to the 'strong bid by Bethmann-Hollweg for British neutrality'. Grey explains such a dishonourable offer could not be accepted. On the 30th July, Grey told Goschen 'it would be a disgrace for us to make this bargain with Germany at the expense of France'. It would also breach Britain's treaty obligations to Belgium. Grey's account[159] refers to Lichnowsky's telegram to Berlin of the 1st August, published after the outbreak of the war in which Lichnowsky referred to Grey telephoning him on that same day asking that if France remained neutral in a Russo-German war Germany would not attack France. Lichnowsky was happy to 'assume responsibility for this'. Grey suggests that Lichnowsky misunderstood the conversation and that Grey was actually

[152] *Lichnowsky to Jagow* (1 August 1914). Lichnowsky, (n 50) 413–14.
[153] See BD (n 10) *Grey to Bertie* Vol XI, No 419: 450, and Lichnowsky (n 50) 75–76.
[154] Lichnowsky (n 50) 415–16.
[155] BD (n 10) Vol XI 11, No 419 *Grey to Bertie* (1 August 1914) 250.
[156] *Ibid* No 426 *Grey to Bertie* (1 August 1914) 253.
[157] S Valone, 'There Must be a Misunderstanding: Sir Edward Grey's Diplomacy of 1 August 1914' (1988) 27 *Journal of British Studies*. 412.
[158] Grey (n 29) Vol 2, 175–80.
[159] *Ibid* Vol 3, 323.

referring to a war between Austria-Hungary and Russia, and not one between Germany and Russia where Germany was neutral and 'engaged not to attack France'. Grey later told Lichnowsky at his 3.30pm meeting that he could not say whether France would remain neutral if Germany attacked Russia. This was contrary to the impression Lichnowsky had received at the earlier 11am meeting with Grey.

Lichnowsky sent for Tyrrell and confirmed that he had further telegraphed Berlin as to the misunderstanding.[160] According to KM Wilson, it appears that Tyrrell understood the offer of British neutrality referred to Germany being at war with France and Russia. This does not make sense because Grey's policy was clearly expressed over the years following 1904 and in his telegram of the 27th July.[161] Wilson opines that it is unlikely Grey would have authorised Tyrrell to make such a statement. Grey wrote that it was also rectified by his cable to Bertie in Paris.[162] He told Bertie that he had refused all overtures from Germany and would not entertain suggestions of neutrality unless it was of benefit to France.[163] However, Bertie rightly questioned Grey's instructions.[164]

In Grey's reply he said no action was required. Belgium neutrality was now the focus of concern.

The question of Belgium neutrality was different from that of the position of Luxembourg. According to Wheaton, liability may be joint or collective, or it may be separate, several or individual.[165] In the Treaties of 1831 and 1839, Britain, France, Prussia, Russia and Austria guaranteed the neutrality and independence of Belgium. That guarantee, according to Wheaton,[166] was always regarded as one of individual liability whereas the guarantee to Luxembourg of 1867 was simply a collective guarantee. Thus, in the event of a German invasion Britain would not be under any legal obligation to Luxembourg as it was a collective guarantee but would be under an obligation by way of its individual guarantee to uphold the neutrality and independence of Belgium.[167]

Whilst Grey had been in a very difficult dilemma, as was the Cabinet, the position became clearer that afternoon when the British Military Attaché in Berlin confirmed that German units would advance through Belgium.[168] In addition the King's reply to the Kaiser explaining the 'misunderstanding' relieved

[160] *Lichnowsky to Foreign Office (Berlin)* 1 August 1914. Lichnowsky (n 50) 416.

[161] BD (n 10) Vol XI, No 176 *Grey to Goschen* (27 July 1914).

[162] *Bertie to Grey*, 1 August 1914. Mombauer (n 44) 509 and BD (n 10) Vol XI, No 419 *Grey to Bertie* (1 August 1914).

[163] Mombauer (n 44) *War* 509 and BD ibid. Bertie's reply is published in Grey's *Twenty-Five Years* (n 29) but not in the British Documents. Compare Lichnowsky's telegram to Berlin as discussed in Albertini (n 36) Vol 3, 380.

[164] BD (n 10) Vol XI 11, No 453 *Bertie to Grey* (2 August 1914) 1, 15.

[165] C Phillipson, *Wheaton's Elements of International Law*, 5th edn (Stevens and Sons Ltd, 1916) 380.

[166] *Ibid*.

[167] *Ibid*.

[168] BD (n 10) Vol XI, No 404 *Goschen to Grey* (1 August 1914) 243.

Grey of the need to restrain France any further.[169] Soon after, Germany declared war on Russia and Asquith authorised Winston Churchill, the First Sea Lord, to mobilise the British fleet. Grey was then permitted to tell Cambon that 'we shall not allow the German fleet to come into the Channel'.[170] During the day Bonar Law, the Conservative Leader, wrote to Asquith giving his and his colleagues 'unhesitating support'.[171]

This episode, at a critical stage of the European crisis, has been the subject of much controversy over the decades since 1918. Historians differ in their views. Some suggest Lichnowsky misunderstood Grey, eg Franz Fischer and Imanuel Geiss, but others such as Herman Lutz consider there was no misunderstanding. Lutz points out a number of inaccuracies in Grey's explanation given to the House of Commons on the 28th August and the documentary evidence. Grey said it was Lichnowsky's suggestion. That is not corroborated by Lichnowsky's reports to Berlin. Grey said he meant German neutrality against Russia as well as against France so that the war was between Austria-Hungary and Russia as well as Serbia.[172] But this contradicts what he told Cambon on the afternoon of the 1st August when he referred to France remaining neutral if Germany was at war with Russia.[173] He also said, as Lutz points out, that French neutrality in the event of Germany entering a Austro-Russian war would be 'in all probability incompatible with the Franco-Russian alliance. This, Lutz says, conflicts with Grey's telegram to Bertie.[174] According to Valone what Grey was trying to do was to dissuade France and Germany from war. He argues that Grey indicated that Britain could not support France, whilst on the 31st July he had suggested to Lichnowsky that if France became involved Britain could be drawn in.[175]

It may be argued that by suggesting that Britain would remain neutral this simply gave the High Command in Berlin encouragement. Grey felt that France may have been drawn into a dispute that was not hers but a dispute between Austria-Hungary and Serbia.[176] Be that as it may, the reality was that Russia was mobilising and Germany was threatening to follow suit.

What is hard to reconcile is Grey's *volte face* on the morning of the 1st August which goes against the fundamental basis of the policy the Foreign Office pursued since 1904, the *Entente Cordiale*. Harold Nicolson gives a dramatic account of Grey's meeting with Paul Cambon, the French Ambassador, that day.[177] He tells how Grey told Cambon that he could not confirm British support

[169] King George to Kaiser Wilhelm, 1 August 1914 in *Documents Diplomatiques* (n 21) No 612, 103–104.

[170] Valone (n 157) 423.

[171] *Bonar Law to Asquith*, 2 August 1914. Parliamentary Archives. Papers of David Lloyd George. LG/C/6/11.

[172] H Lutz, *Lord Grey and the World War* (Alfred A Knopf, 1928) 465.

[173] *Ibid* 461.

[174] *Ibid* 296.

[175] *Ibid* 294 and BD (n 10) Vol XI, No 340 *Grey to Goschen* (31 July 1914) 215–16.

[176] BD (10) Vol XI, No 352 *Grey to Bertie* (31 July 1914) 220.

[177] H Nicolson, *Lord Carnock* (Constable & Co Ltd, 1930) 419.

and France would have to make its own decision. Arthur Nicolson was alarmed when Cambon came to his room after the meeting with Grey and exclaimed: 'Ils vont nous lâcher, Ils vont nous lâcher!' ('They're going to let us go!'). Nicolson then went down to see his chief and exclaimed to Grey: 'You will render us a by-word among nations'. In Paris, Bertie could only reflect on the effect that such a declaration of intent by Britain would have on France and the French people – 'Perfide Albion'.[178] Not only did Paul Cambon have such a conversation with Sir Arthur Nicolson but in conversation with Wickham Steed, the Editor of *The Times*, he is reported to have suggested that the word 'honour' be deleted from the English dictionary. When this was put to Grey at an interview with GP Gooch on the 14th February 1929, Grey said 'We always made it clear that the conversations (as to military plans and dispositions) left the governments free, and we stated it in the letters of 1912 …'.[179] The arrangement as to the disposition of the respective fleets was one which Grey had described to Churchill in May 1912 as that 'in time of war the French should look after the Mediterranean and we should look after the North Sea'.[180]

Grey came under some criticism for this 'misunderstanding' but in the extraordinary unprecedented circumstances that presented themselves with Cabinet colleagues so divided and the Irish Question dominating all Cabinet meetings from 24 June until 31 July,[181] the confusion is understandable. Lord Haldane, the Lord Chancellor and former Secretary of State for War, counselled delay in sending the British Expeditionary Force to the continent. In that event Grey had to buy time and Haldane's advice may have influenced Grey in finding a way to postpone any Franco-German conflict.[182]

It was a bold bid for peace at the eleventh hour but on a questionable basis, first because he had no authority from either the Cabinet or the French Government, and second, he did not know the terms of the Franco-Russian alliance. If Valone's analysis is right then it seems that Grey had everything to gain for quarantining the war to the east between Austria-Hungary and Serbia or Austria-Hungary, Serbia and Russia. But as Valone points out, this would have disrupted the *Entente Cordiale* and the Franco-Russia alliance, but there might not have been a general war in Europe. That possibility is hard to imagine given the alliance and cultural ties between Austria-Hungary and Germany[183] and those natural ties between Russia and Serbia. More than that Russia had suffered a

[178] Lady Algernon Lomax, *The Diary of Lord Bertie*. 1914–1918. (Hodder and Stoughton, 1924) 8.
[179] GP Gooch, *Studies in Diplomacy and Statecraft* (Longmans, Green and Co, 1942) 105.
[180] BD (10) Vol X Pt II, No 389 *Grey to Churchill* (11 May 1912). See also text of Grey's letter to Cambon on the 22nd November 1912 as to the contingency of co-operation in the event of an unprovoked attack by a third power. Trevelyan (n 12) 139–40.
[181] The Earl of Oxford and Asquith, *Memories and Reflections* (Cassell and Company Limited, 1928) 3–7.
[182] KM Wilson, 'Understanding the Misunderstanding of 1 August 1914' (1994) 57 *The History Journal* 887.
[183] Valone (n 157) 413–14.

diplomatic setback in the Balkan Wars and did not want to lose more prestige. As for France, it would find it difficult to stand aside if Germany attacked Russia in the light of the Poincare/Sazanov meeting in St Petersburg and their alliance. As to Grey's other initiative that opposing armies should halt on the frontier it is difficult to see how militarily or politically speaking two great armies could have just faced each other without confrontation given the war fever in Berlin and Paris at the time.[184]

X. DECISION FOR WAR

The decision for war regarding the Treaty of London 1839 was not regarded by the Cabinet as a legal obligation but as a matter of policy.[185] On the 2nd August, the Cabinet decided to permit Grey to assure the French Government that the British fleet would give 'all the protection in its power' to protect the French coast, the North Sea and the Channel.[186] The Cabinet was in crisis and the following day Burnes, Morley and Simon resigned, although the latter withdrew his resignation. David Lloyd George for all his critique of Grey later did not resign. The Cabinet was against intervention simply to uphold the balance of power. Despite all the criticism of Grey from General Wilson, Nicolson, Crowe, Law, and others for intervention and those in Cabinet opposed to intervention, Grey eventually succeeded in convincing his Cabinet colleagues and the House of Commons to support the *Entente*. The difficulty he had was one of timing and course of events; political factors which were out of his control most of the time because the framework upholding international diplomatic norms – the Concert System – was broken, the country was deeply divided and there was a crisis over Ulster. Despite the efforts of Grey and his *Entente* colleagues, Germany declared war on France on the 3rd August and Asquith, after much soul searching with his colleagues and some Cabinet resignations, sent an ultimatum to Berlin.

XI. NATIONAL HONOUR: THE DIPLOMATIC COUNTERFACTUAL

In the final analysis it may be that Russia preferred war to a further humiliation and Germany pursued national honour over the humiliation of its ally

[184] There was however a standoff in the 'Phony War' 1939–1940 when allied armies faced the German army on the Rhine. But it is difficult to accurately assess the public mood in those capitals in 1914. Given the German enthusiasm for *Deutschland Uber Ales* the same might not be said for Paris albeit the *New York Times* was reporting that hundreds of thousands of people lined the streets from the Gare du Nord to the Élysée Palace shouting 'Vive Poincaré', 'Vive l'armée', 'Vive France', 'Vive l'Alliance'. Cited in Erik Ringmar, 'The Spirit of 1914: A Redefinition and a defence' (2018) 25 *War in History* 26–47.

[185] KM Wilson, 'The British Cabinet's Decision for War, 2 August 1914' (1975) 1 *British Journal International Studies* 148–59.

[186] BD (n 10) Vol XI, No 487 *Grey to Bertie* (2 August 1914) 274–75 and Wilson, *ibid* 150.

Austria-Hungary. Essentially, the collision of the alliances was brought about by the fragmentation of the Ottoman Empire and the rise of nationalism on the one hand, and the disintegration of the Austro-Hungarian Empire on the other hand. In essence, as Lieven suggests, this was an Eastern European war.[187]

In critical conflicts it seems that it is the national interest that determines policy but more than that we learn from 1914 that it was also a question of national honour. International law buttressed by the Hague Conferences of 1899 and 1907 proclaimed a framework and guidelines for civilised warfare. But in war the rules of law are often forgotten. International law is more effective during peacetime, but enforcement in 1914 was impossible given the attitudes of Germany, Italy and Austria-Hungary which in 1913 signalled their aversion to the concert approach to diplomacy.

Germany feared encirclement and the possibility of Russian military parity in a few years. Germany had a 'place in the sun' but to a lesser extent than her rivals. The acquisition of a fleet and expansion to the east became her approach which inevitably caused the clash with the *Entente*. The Kaiser had dreams of rivalling Britain at sea, but had reservations about war with Britain, his mother's country. Bethmann-Hollweg supported Austria-Hungary and also had reservations about Britain. He and others in Germany misread British intentions whilst at the same time performing a wondrous feat of prestidigitation of theirs.

Grey made various proposals to resolve the crisis as it unfolded. First, discussions with and between ambassadors, then suggested mediation by Britain and a conference of ambassadors in London, and then a suggested 'halt in Belgrade', followed by proposals of British/French neutrality and finally an ultimatum to Germany regarding its obligations under the Treaty of London. For their part France and Russia had discussed the matter with their heads of state in St Petersburg before the crisis became acute. Subsequently, discussions between ambassadors in Berlin, Paris and Vienna took place but to no avail. Once Austria-Hungary's ultimatum had been given and once Russia mobilised, the die was cast.

Strenuous diplomatic efforts were made by the *Entente* Powers to prevent the war especially by Grey, the Cambon brothers, Bertie and Goschen. It must also be said in fairness to Prince Lichnowsky that he never deserved to be made the scapegoat for the war. Margot Asquith described him as: 'the most true and honourable of men'.[188] So far therefore as the statesmen in London were concerned it may be said that they used the norms of diplomacy, the instruments of peacemaking, but in the end, whatever skills they possessed, it was the national will and national honour that stirred the masses in the capitals of Europe.

[187] Lieven (n 102) 2.
[188] H Young, *Prince Lichnowsky and the Greta War* (University of Georgia Press, 1977) 127.

Bibliography

Monographs and Works of Reference

Abass, A, *International Law, Text, Cases and Materials* (Oxford University Press, 2012).

Albertini, L, *The Origins of the War of 1914: The Crisis of July 1914* Vols I, II and III (Enigma Books, 2014).

Albrecht-Carrie, R, A Diplomatic History of Europe Since the Congress of Vienna (Methuen, 1965).

Angell, N, *The Great Illusion* (GP Pitman's Sons, 2010).

Ayliffe, J, *New Pandects of Roman Civil Law* (Thomas Osborne, 1734).

Barclay, T, *Thirty Years* (Constable and Company, 1914).

Bar-Yaacov, N, *The Handling of International Disputes by Means of Enquiry* (Oxford University Press, 1974).

Bassett Moore, J, *History and Digest of International Arbitrations to which the United States has been a Party* Vols 1–VI (Forgotten Books, 2018).

Bernard, M, *A Historical Account of the Neutrality of Britain During the American Civil War* (Longmans, Green Reader and Dyer, 1870).

Bigelow, J, *Breaches of Anglo-American Treaties* (Sturgis & Walton Company, 1917).

Bindschedler RL, and others, *Encyclopaedia of Public International Law*, Max Planck Institute Vol 2 *Decisions of International Courts and Tribunals and International Arbitrations* (North-Holland Publishing Company, 1981).

Brandenburg, E, *Von Bismarck zum Weltkreig* (Insel-Verlag, 1939).

Brown Scott, J, *The Hague Peace Conferences 1899–1907* (Baltimore, 1909).

—— (ed), Texts of the Peace Conferences at the Hague,1899 and 1907 (Boston and London, 1908) 1–2.

—— (ed), *The Hague Reports* (Oxford University Press American Branch, 1916).

—— *The Proceedings of the Hague Peace Conferences. Translation of the Official Texts* (Oxford University Press 1920).

Bullock, JD, *The Secret Service of the Confederate States in Europe* Vol 1 (GP Putnam's and Sons, 1884).

Campbell, Jr CS, *Anglo-American Understanding.* 1898–1903 (The John Hopkins Press, 1957).

Cecil, L, *The German Diplomatic Service* (Princeton University Press, 1976).

Churchill, W, *The World Crisis 1911–1918* (Penguin Books, 2007).

Clark, C, *The Sleepwalkers* (Penguin, 2013) 289.

Coleman Phillipson edn, *Wheaton's Elements of International Law* (Stevens & Sons, 1916).

Cook, A, *The Alabama Claims* (Cornell University Press, 1975).

Cornwall Lewis, G, *On Foreign Jurisdiction and the Extradition of Criminals* (JW Parker and Son, 1859).

Cushing, C, *The Treaty of Washington: Its Negotiation, Execution and the Discussions Relating Thereto* (Harper & Brothers Publishers, 1873).

DeArmond Davis, C, *The United States and the First Hague Conference* (Cornell University Press, 1962).

Dudley Field, D, *Draft Outlines of An International Code* (Diossy & Company, 1872).

Dugdale, ETS, *German Diplomatic Documents 1871–1914* (Methuen & Co, 1930) Vols 1–IV.

Eubank, K, *Paul Cambon Master Diplomat* (Norman, 1960).

Evans Derby, W, *International Tribunals* (Forgotten Books, 2015) Reprint.

Ferguson, N, *The Pity of War* (Penguin Books, 1999).

—— *1914: Why the World Went to War* (Penguin Books, 2005).

Fisher, HAL, *James Bryce* (Macmillan and Co Ltd, 1927).

German Diplomatic Documents 1871–1914 (Methuen & Co Ltd, 1930) XXIX.

Gessner, L, *The Law of Neutrality at Sea* (Berlin, 1865).

Gooch, G, *Studies in Diplomacy and Statecraft* (Longmans Green and Co, 1942).

Gooch, P and Temperley, H (eds), *British Documents on the Origins of the War 1898–1914* Vols I–XI (Her Majesty's Stationery Office, 1927–38).

Goodrich, L, Hambro, E and Simons, A, *Charter of the UN*, 3rd edn (Columbia University Press, 1969).

Grenville, JAS, *Lord Salisbury and Foreign Policy at the Close of the Nineteenth Century* (University of London, The Athlone Press, 1964).

Grey, E, *Twenty-Five Years* (Hodder and Stoughton, 1928).

Grotius, H, *On the Law of War and Peace* (Book II) (edited by SC Neff) (Cambridge University Press, 2012) Ch xxiii (xlvii).

Hall, W, *International Law* (Clarendon Press, 1880).

—— *A Treatise of International Law*, 8th edn (Oxford University Press, 1924).

Hamilton, K, *Bertie of Thame* (Royal Historical Society Studies in History 60, 1990).

Headlam-Morley, J, *Studies in Diplomatic History* (Methuen & Co, 1930).

Hershey, A, *The International Law and Diplomacy of The Russian Japanese War* (The Macmillan Company, 1906).

Historia Corographica de la Nueva Andalucia, Provincias de Cumaná, Guyana y Vertientes del Orinoco, por el R.P. Antonio Caulin, Provincial de los R.R.P.P. Observantes en el Reino de la Nueva Granada (Published 1779).

Hopkirk, P, *The Great Game* (John Murray, 1990).

Jackson, R and Sørensen, G, *Introduction to International Relations Theories and Approaches*, 5th edn (Oxford University Press, 2013).

Kant, *Rechtslehre Part II*.

Keenan, GF (ed), Carnegie Endowment for International Peace, *The Other Balkan Wars* (Carnegie Endowment, 1993).

Keiger, J, *France and the Origins of the First World War* (Macmillan Press, 1983).

Kennedy, P, *Strategy and Diplomacy (1870–1945)* (George Allen and Unwin, 1983).

—— *The Rise of Anglo-German Antagonism 1860–1914* (Humanity Books, 1988) 278.

Kissinger, H, *World Order* (Penguin Books, 2015).

Langer, W, *The Diplomacy of Imperialism 1890–1902* (Alfred A Knopf, 1956).

Lapradelle and Politis, *Recueil des Arbitrages Internationaux* (Forgotten Books, 2017) Vol II, 905.

Lemnitzer, J, *Power Law and the End of Privateering* (Palgrave Macmillan, 2014).

Leopold, RW, *Elihu Root and the Conservative Tradition* (Little Brown and Company, 1954).

Lichnowsky, M, *Heading for the Abyss Reminisces* (Payson and Clarke Ltd, 1928).

Lieven, D, *Towards the Flame* (Penguin, 2015).

Locke, J and Laslett, P (ed), *Treatise of Government* (Cambridge University Press, 1988).

Lomax, A, *The Diary of Lord Bertie*. 1914–1918 (Hodder and Stoughton, 1924).

Lutz, H, *Lord Grey and the World War* (Alfred A Knopf, 1928) 465.

Maine, H, *International Law* (John Murray, 1888).

Mahan, AT, *Armaments and Arbitration* (Kessinger Publishing, 2010).

Marder, A, *British Naval Policy*, 1880–1905 (Alfred A Knopf, 1940).

Mead, E, *The Literature of the New Peace Movement* (World Peace Foundation Pamphlets, 1912).

Merli, F, *The Alabama, British Neutrality and the American Civil War* (Indiana University Press, 2004).

Miller, H, *Treaties and Other International Acts of the United States of America* (Department of State, 1937) V.

Mombauer, A, *The Origins of the First World War Diplomatic and Military Documents* (Manchester University Press, 2013).

Monger, G, *The End of Isolation* (Thomas Nelson and Sons Ltd, 1963).

Morgenthau, HJ, *Scientific Man versus Power Politics* (Il Phoenix Books, 1965) 180.
Nicolson, H, *A Study in Old Diplomacy* (Constable & Co, 1930) 328–29.
—— *Lord Carnock* (Constable & Co, 1930) 181.
—— *The Congress of Vienna* (Methuen, 1961).
Nijhoff, M, Conventions and Declarations between the Powers Concerning War, Arbitration and Neutrality, 1915th edn (Springer, 1915).
Oppenheim, L, *The Panama Canal Conflict*, 2nd edn (Cambridge University Press, 1913).
—— *International Law A Treatise* (Longmans, 1948) Vol I.
Otte, T, *The Foreign Office Mind* (Cambridge University Press, 2011).
—— *July Crisis* (Cambridge University Press, 2014).
Palmer, R, Speech in the House of Commons 4 August 1871 (Macmillan & Co, 1871).
Parry, C, 'Foreign Policy and International Law' in FH Hinsley (ed), *British Foreign Policy under Sir Edward Grey* (Cambridge University Press, 2008) 91.
Renouvin, P, *The Immediate Origins of the War* (Howard Fertig, Inc, Ed, 1969).
Robbins, K, *Sir Edward Grey* (Cassell, 1971).
Root, E, Addresses *by Elihu Root on International Subjects* (Holmes Beach, James Brown and Robert Bacon, Gaunt, 1997).
Schmidt, B, *The Coming of the War, 1914* (Charles Scribner's Sons, 1930).
Sirvén, B, La Seconde Conférence de la Paix réunie à la La Haye en 1907 (1909).
Smith, FE, *International Law* (Georgen Morang Co Ltd, 1903).
Smith, FE and Sibley, NW, *International Law as Interpreted During the Russo-Japanese War* (T Fisher Unwin, 1905).
Sontag, RJ, *European Diplomatic History 1871–1932* (Appleton-Century-Crofts, 1933).
Steiner, Z and Neilson, K, *Britain and the Origins of the First World War* (Palgrave, 2003).
Stevenson, D, *Armaments and the Coming of War, Europe 1904–1914* (Clarendon Press, 1996).
Stuyt, AM, *Survey of International Arbitrations 1794–1938* (Martinus Nijhoff, 1939).
Taft, WH, *Popular Government: Its Essence, Its Permanence, and Its Perils* (Yale University Press, 1913).
The Hague Court Reports, Carnegie Endowment for International Peace (Pranara Books, 2020).
Thucydides, *The Peloponnesian War* (EP Dutton, 1910).
Tooley, M, *The Peace That Almost Was.* (Nashville, Nelson Books, 2015).
Trevelyan, GM, *Grey of Falloden* (Longman's Green and Co, 1937).
Tucker, RW, *The Law of War and Neutrality at Sea* (Naval War College, 1955).
Twiss, T, *The Law of Nations* (Clarendon Press, 1884).
Van Alstyne, RW, *The American Empire* (Historical Association, 1960).
Vansittart, R, *The Mist Procession* (Hutchinson & Co Ltd, 1958).
Vattel, E, *The Law of Nations, Or, Principles of the Law of Nature, Applied to the Conduct and Affairs of Nations and Sovereigns, with Three Early Essays on the Origin and Nature of Natural Law and on Luxury* (edited by B Kapossy and R Whatmore) (Liberty Fund, 2008).
Walker, TA, *The Science of International Law* (CJ Clay and Sons, Cambridge University Press, 1893).
Ward, AW and Gooch, GP, *Cambridge History of Foreign Policy 1783–1919* (Cambridge University Press, 2012) Vol 3: 1866–1919.
Watts, J, *The Facts of the Cotton Famine* (Simpkin Marshall & Co, 1866).
Weston Janis, M, *America and the Law of Nations.* 1776–1939 (Oxford University Press, 2010).
Wheaton's Elements of international Law (edited by Coleman Phillipson) (Stevens & Sons, 1916).
Williamson, S, *The Politics of Grand Strategy* (Harvard, 1969) 146.
Woolsey, T, *Introduction to the Study of International Law* (University of Michigan, 2006).
Young, H, *Prince Lichnowsky and the Great War* (University of Georgia Press, 1977).

Articles and Contributions

Bingham, T, 'The Alabama Claims Arbitration' (2005) 54 *ICLQ* 1, 8.
Bourne, K, 'The Clayton Bulwer Treaty and The Decline of British Opposition to The Territorial Expansion of The United States, 1857– 60' (1961) *The Journal of Modern History* 287.

Brown Scott, J, 'The Nature and Form of the Agreement for the Submission of Justiciable Disputes to an International Court' (1907–17) *Proceedings of the American Society of International Law at its Annual Meeting.*

Burton, T, 'The Claims of the Candidates: William Howard Taft' (1908) 187 *The North American Review* 641.

Campbell, J, 'Taft Roosevelt and the Arbitration Treaties of 1911' (1966) 53 *The Journal of American History* 279.

Carroll, F, 'Belfast and the American Civil War' (2011) 19(3) *Irish Studies Review.*

Cavendish, R, 'The United States Battleship was Blown up in an Explosion during Cuba's Uprising against Spain. What Caused the Explosion and who was Responsible?' (1998) 48 *History Today.*

Coker, WS, 'The Panama Canals Controversy: A Different Perspective' (1968) *The Journal of American History* 555.

Crampton, RJ, 'The Decline of the Concert of Europe in the Balkans 1913–14' (1974) 52 *The Slavonic and East European Review* 128, 393, 415.

Dockrill, M, 'British Policy During the Agadir Crisis of 1911' in F Hinsley (ed), *British Foreign Policy Under Sir Edward Grey* (Cambridge University Press, 2008).

Dreyfus, F, *L'Arbitrage International* (d'Institut, Paris, 1892) 355.

Foster, K, 'The Diplomats Who Sank A Fleet: The Confederacy's Undelivered European Fleet and the Union Consular Service' (2001) 33 Prologue, Washington 3.

Hall, WI, 'Arbitration and the Hague Conferences' (1908) 2 *American Journal of International Law* 732.

Hershey, AS, 'History of International Law Since the Peace of Westphalia' (1912) 6 *American Journal of International Law* 30.

Hickson, GF, 'Palmerston and the Clayton Bulwer Treaty' (1931) 3 *The Cambridge Historical Journal.*

Hinsley, FH, *Power and the Pursuit of Peace* (Cambridge University Press, 1963) 2667.

Howe, GF, 'The Clayton-Bulwer Treaty: An Unofficial Interpretation of Article VIII in 1869' 42 (1937) *American Historical Review.*

Joseph, CL, 'The Venezuelan Boundary Arbitration 1899: Part 1' (1970) 10 *Caribbean Studies* 56–61.

Keasbey, LM, 'The Terms and Tone of the Clayton-Bulwer Treaty' (1899) 161 *The Annals of the American Academy of Political and Social Science* 8.

Marder, A, *British Naval Policy*, 1880–1905 (Alfred A Knopf, 1940).

Matzen, Fry, Martens, Asser, and Savorin Lohman, 'Note From the Members of The Arbitral Tribunal In The Pious Fund Case To The Netherlands Minister For Foreign Affairs, Making Some Suggestions As To The Conduct Of Future Arbitrations' (1911) 5 *American Journal of International Law* 73–78.

Neary, PF, 'The Panama Canal Tolls Dispute' (1966) *The Journal of Transport History* 173.

Nicolson, H, 'The Origins and Development of the Anglo-French Entente' (1954) 30 *International Affairs* 407–16.

Noyes, JE, 'William Howard Taft and the Taft Arbitration Treaties' (2011) 56 *Villanova Law Review* 535.

Park, AT, 'International Commission: The Birth of Albania and Sir Edward Grey's Prevention Diplomacy During the Balkan Wars' (2020) 31 *Diplomacy and Statecraft.*

Politis, 'Les Commissions Internationales d'enquette' (1912) 19 *Revue Générale de Droit International Public* 152.

Reynolds, MP, 'Indictment of a Nation' (1982) 33 *Northern Ireland Law Quarterly Review* 277–85.

Ringer, E, 'The Spirit of 1914.' A Redefinition and a Defence (2018) 25 *War in History* 26–27.

Russell, C, 'Address before the American Bar Association at Saratoga 20 August 1896' (1896) 2 *Virginia Law Register* 399.

Valone, S, 'There Must be a Misunderstanding: Sir Edward Grey's Diplomacy of 1 August 1914' (1988) 27 *Journal of British Studies* 412.

Van Alstyne, RW, 'Anglo-American Relations, 1953 1957: British Statesman on The Clayton-Bulwer Treaty and American Expansion' (1937) 42 *American Historical Review.*

—— 'British Diplomacy and the Clayton-Bulwer Treaty 1850–60' (1939) 11 *The Journal of Modern History*.
Waddell, D, 'British Honduras and Anglo-American Relations' (1957) 5 *Caribbean Quarterly* 50.
Westlake, J, 'International Arbitration' (1896) 7 *International Journal of Ethics* 1.
de Wiel, J, '1914: What will the British Do? The Irish Home Rule Crisis in the July Crisis' (2015) *The International History Review*.
Wilson, K, 'The Agadir Crisis, the Mansion House Speech and the Double Edgedness of Agreements' (1972) 15 *The Historical Journal* 513–32.
—— 'The British Cabinet's Decision for War' 2 August 1914 (1975) 1 *British Journal International Studies* 148–59.
—— 'Understanding the Misunderstanding of 1 August 1914' (1994) 57 *The History Journal* 887.
Young, JW, 'Conservative Leaders, Coalition and the British Decision for War in 1914' (2014) 25 *Diplomacy and Statecraft* 214–39.
—— 'Ambassador Buchanan and the July Crisis' (2018) 40 *The International History Review* 211.

Other Articles

'Anglo-American Relations, 1853–1857: British Statesman on the Clayton Bulwer Treaty and American Expansion' (1937) 42 *The American Historical Review* 496 *Bulwer to Clarendon* March 1854.
'Letters of Bancroft and Buchanan on the Clayton-Bulwer Treaty 1849,' 1850 (1899) 5 *The American Historical Review* 95.
'The Anglo-Venezuelan Arbitration Commission: British Case, Counter Case, and Argument' (1900) *The Edinburgh Review* 191.
'The Casablanca Incident and Its Reference to Arbitration at The Hague' (1909) 3 *American Journal of International Law* 176.
'The Geneva Arbitration and its Results' (1872–73) 7 *American Law Review* 193, 194.
'The Repeal of the Provision of the Panama Canal Act Exempting American Coastwise Traffic Vessels from the Payment of Tolls' (1914) 8 *American Journal of International Law* 592–97.
Reference submitted to them for Enquiry under the terms of the Declaration of St. Petersburg 12th November 1904 (1931) 2 *American Journal of International Law* 931.

Permanent Court of Arbitration

Permanent Court of Arbitration under the Hague Convention 1899. *United States v Republic of Mexico*. Statement and Brief on behalf of the United States of America (1902).
The Hague Court Reports Comprising the Awards, Accompanied by Syllabi, the Agreements for Arbitration, and Other Documents in Each Case Submitted to the Permanent Court of Arbitration and to the Commissions of Inquiry Under the Provisions of the Conventions of 1899 and 1907 for the Pacific Settlement of International Disputes, Carnegie Endowment for International Peace Division of International Law (Pranara Books, Reprint, 2020).
France v Germany: The Casablanca Arbitration Award, 22 May 1909 The Hague Court Reports 112–13.

Theses

Murray, C, *Salus Populi: Suprema lex The Developing National Security Jurisprudence Prior to the First World War* (Durham University, 2006).
Reynolds, MP, 'Caseflow Management: A Rudimentary Official Referee Process 1870–1970' (PhD Thesis, London School of Economics, 2008).

Journals

The Spectator (30 April 1887).

Newspapers

London Gazette (17 December 1895).
New York Herald (1, 24 November, 19 December 1849).
New York Herald (22 December 1895).
New York Times (5 October 1899).
The Times (9 October 1862).
The Times (28 March 1863).
The Times (16 March 1898).
The Times (1 March 1905).
The Times (11 November 1904).
The Times (14 November 1904).
The Times (17 December 1904).
The Times (21 December 1904).
The Times (16 January 1909).

Index

Lightning Source UK Ltd.
Milton Keynes UK
UKHW021359280721
387870UK00002B/119

9 781509 938308